3-

THE NATION AND ITS FRAGMENTS

E D I T O R S

Sherry B. Ortner, Nicholas B. Dirks, Geoff Eley

T I T L E S   I N   S E R I E S

High Religion:
A Cultural and Political History of Sherpa Buddhism
by Sherry B. Ortner

A Place in History:
Social and Monumental Times in a Cretan Town
by Michael Herzfeld

The Textual Condition
by Jerome J. McGann

Regulating the Social:
The Welfare State and Local Politics in Imperial Germany
by George Steinmetz

Hanging without a Rope:
Narrative Experience in Colonial and Postcolonial Karoland
by Mary Margaret Steedly

Modern Greek Lessons:
A Primer in Historical Constructivism
by James Faubion

The Nation and Its Fragments:
Colonial and Postcolonial Histories
by Partha Chatterjee

PRINCETON STUDIES IN
CULTURE / POWER / HISTORY

THE NATION AND ITS FRAGMENTS

COLONIAL AND POSTCOLONIAL HISTORIES

Partha Chatterjee

PRINCETON UNIVERSITY PRESS
PRINCETON, NEW JERSEY

Published by Princeton University Press, 41 William Street,
Princeton, New Jersey 08540
In the United Kingdom: Princeton University Press,
West Chichester, West Sussex

Library of Congress Cataloging-in-Publication Data

Chatterjee, Partha, 1947–
The nation and its fragments : Colonial and
postcolonial histories / Partha Chatterjee.
p. cm. — (Princeton studies in culture/power/history)
Includes bibliographical references and index.
ISBN 0-691-03305-6 (cloth : alk. paper) —
ISBN 0-691-01943-6 (pbk : alk. paper)
1. India—History—British occupation, 1765–1947.
2. India—History—20th century. 3. Nationalism—India—History.
4. Nationalism—India—Bengal—History. I. Title. II. Series.
DS468.C47 1993
954.03—dc20 93-15536 CIP

This book has been composed in Adobe Sabon

Princeton University Press books are printed
on acid-free paper and meet the guidelines for
permanence and durability of the Committee on
Production Guidelines for Book Longevity
of the Council on Library Resources

Printed in the United States of America

1 3 5 7 9 10 8 6 4 2

(Pbk.)
1 3 5 7 9 10 8 6 4 2

TODAY I WISH TO SAY TO YOU ONCE MORE

WHAT I'VE TOLD YOU MANY, MANY TIMES BEFORE.

Part of the importance of the "fragmentary" point of view lies in this, that it resists the drive for a shallow homogenisation and struggles for other, potentially richer definitions of the "nation" and the future political community.

—Gyanendra Pandey, "In Defence of the Fragment"

Contents

Preface and Acknowledgments

By now knowledgeable people all over the world have become familiar with the charges leveled against the subject-centered rationality characteristic of post-Enlightenment modernity. This subject-centered reason, we have now been told, claims for itself a singular universality by asserting its epistemic privilege over all other local, plural, and often incommensurable knowledges; it proclaims its own unity and homogeneity by declaring all other subjectivities as inadequate, fragmentary, and subordinate; it declares for the rational subject an epistemic as well as moral sovereignty that is meant to be self-determined, unconditioned, and self-transparent. Against this arrogant, intolerant, self-aggrandizing rational subject of modernity, critics in recent years have been trying to resurrect the virtues of the fragmentary, the local, and the subjugated in order to unmask the will to power that lies at the very heart of modern rationality and to decenter its epistemological and moral subject. In this effort at criticism, materials from colonial and postcolonial situations have figured quite prominently.

However, a persistent difficulty has been that by asserting an inseparable complicity between knowledge and power, this critique has been unable adequately to vindicate its own normative preferences and thus to provide valid grounds for claiming agency on behalf of persons, groups, or movements. I do not propose to offer in this book a general solution to this problem. What I attempt instead is a series of interventions in different disciplinary fields, localized and bound by their own historically produced rules of formation, but thematically connected to one another by their convergence upon the one most untheorized concept of the modern world—the nation.

In this project, the present work carries forward an argument begun in my *Nationalist Thought and the Colonial World* (1986). All my illustrations come from colonial and postcolonial India, and even more particularly from Bengal. But it must also be remembered that the very form of imagining nations is such that even as one talks about a particular historically formed nation, one is left free to implicate in one's discourse others that have not been so formed or whose forms remain suppressed, and perhaps even some whose forms have still not been imagined.

I thought about and wrote various parts of this book over the past four years but put it together in its present form in an inspired two-week spell in April 1992. Not surprisingly, I have a long list of acknowledgments.

My colleagues at the Centre for Studies in Social Sciences, Calcutta—Pradip Bose, Amitav Ghosh, Anjan Ghosh, Tapati Guha-Thakurta, Debes Roy, Tapti Roy, Ranabir Samaddar and Asok Sen, in particular—have been a constant source of ideas, criticisms, and encouragement. My colleagues in the Editorial Group of *Subaltern Studies*—Shahid Amin, David Arnold, Gautam Bhadra, Dipesh Chakrabarty, Ranajit Guha, David Hardiman, Gyan Pandey, and Sumit Sarkar—have been the most active and faithful partners in my intellectual life for more than a decade; they have a share in the production of most of the ideas that have gone into this book. I am also deeply indebted to Raghab Chattopadhyay, Ajit Chaudhuri, Sushil Khanna, Rudrangshu Mukherjee, Bhaskar Mukhopadhyay, Kalyan Sanyal, and Anup Sinha (besides, of course, the shadowy presence of Arup Mallik), with whom I participated in that remarkable reading circle which went by the name of the Kankurgachhi Hegel Club and which met every week for three years to make the texts of Hegel the pretext for intense debates on many of the subjects discussed here. Two semesters of teaching at the New School for Social Research, New York, in 1990 and 1991 gave me the respite from my routine obligations to allow me to get on with my writing; I thank Talal Asad, Debbie Poole, Rayna Rapp, Bill Roseberry, and Kamala Visweswaran for reading and commenting on several parts of this book.

I have presented much of the material discussed here in conferences or talks at Calcutta, Shimla, Istanbul, Moscow, Berlin, Tübingen, London, and Sussex, and at universities in the following places in the United States: New York, New Haven, Princeton, Rochester, Philadelphia, Charlottesville, Pittsburgh, Chicago, Madison, Minneapolis, Berkeley, Stanford, Santa Cruz, and Los Angeles. These discussions have all contributed to the present form of this text. I must also express my thanks to the participants of those invigorating meetings in Chicago in 1990 and 1991 of the Forum on Social Theory organized by Benjamin Lee and the Center for Psychosocial Studies.

I am particularly grateful to Craig Calhoun, Nicholas Dirks, Prabhakara Jha, and Gyan Prakash for their generous and detailed comments, appreciative as well as critical, on the entire manuscript.

I take this opportunity to thank my students in the last few years in Calcutta and New York who were forced to tackle many of the themes dealt with here in their early, half-formed stages.

The research on this book was carried out in Calcutta at the Centre for Studies in Social Sciences and at the National Library. Four or five short spells of work at the India Office Library, London, allowed me to find from its Vernacular Tracts collection much material from little-known nineteenth-century Bengali sources. When I was in New York, the School of International and Public Affairs at Columbia University was kind enough to grant me the status of a Visiting Scholar, which allowed me to use the Butler Library at Columbia. The first draft manuscript of this book was produced during my short stay in April 1992 as Visiting Fellow at the A. E. Havens Center in the Department of Sociology at the University of Wisconsin at Madison: I thank Allen Hunter and Polly Ericksen for their generous help.

In the matter of finding books, I have to express my deep indebtedness to Nirmalya Acharya, whose native knowledge of the labyrinthine world of College Street publishing continues to be of invaluable help to me. And to Susanta Ghosh I remain indebted for his encouragement as well as criticism, well meant if not always well deserved.

I am grateful to the publishers of the following journals for allowing me to use in this book sections from my previously published articles: "Whose Imagined Community?" *Millennium: Journal of International Studies* 20, no. 3 (Winter 1991): 521–26; "History and the Nationalization of Hinduism," *Social Research* 59, no. 1 (Spring 1992): 111–49; "Colonialism, Nationalism, and Colonialized Women: The Contest in India," *American Ethnologist* 16, no. 4 (November 1989): 622–33; "For an Indian History of Peasant Struggle," *Social Scientist* 16, no. 11 (November 1988): 3–17; "A Response to Taylor's Modes of Civil Society," *Public Culture* 3, no. 1 (Fall 1990): 119–32. I am also grateful to Blackwell Publishers for permission to use parts of my article "Their Own Words? An Essay for Edward Said," in Michael Sprinker, ed., *Edward Said: A Critical Reader* (Oxford: Blackwell, 1992), pp. 194–220; and to the School for American Research for permission to use my article "Alternative Histories/Alternative Nations," to be published in the forthcoming conference volume "Making Alternative History," edited by Peter A. Schmidt and Tom Patterson.

Except when otherwise stated, all translations in this book from Bengali sources are my own.

My thanks to Mary Murrell, Beth Gianfagna, and Cindy Crumrine of Princeton University Press for their enthusiasm about this book and the care they have taken over its production.

And finally, as always, my thanks to Gouri.

Calcutta
10 November 1992

THE NATION AND ITS FRAGMENTS

CHAPTER ONE

Whose Imagined Community?

NATIONALISM has once more appeared on the agenda of world affairs. Almost every day, state leaders and political analysts in Western countries declare that with "the collapse of communism" (that is the term they use; what they mean is presumably the collapse of Soviet socialism), the principal danger to world peace is now posed by the resurgence of nationalism in different parts of the world. Since in this day and age a phenomenon has first to be recognized as a "problem" before it can claim the attention of people whose business it is to decide what should concern the public, nationalism seems to have regained sufficient notoriety for it to be liberated from the arcane practices of "area specialists" and been made once more a subject of general debate.

However, this very mode of its return to the agenda of world politics has, it seems to me, hopelessly prejudiced the discussion on the subject. In the 1950s and 1960s, nationalism was still regarded as a feature of the victorious anticolonial struggles in Asia and Africa. But simultaneously, as the new institutional practices of economy and polity in the postcolonial states were disciplined and normalized under the conceptual rubrics of "development" and "modernization," nationalism was already being relegated to the domain of the particular histories of this or that colonial empire. And in those specialized histories defined by the unprepossessing contents of colonial archives, the emancipatory aspects of nationalism were undermined by countless revelations of secret deals, manipulations, and the cynical pursuit of private interests. By the 1970s, nationalism had become a matter of ethnic politics, the reason why people in the Third World killed each other—sometimes in wars between regular armies, sometimes, more distressingly, in cruel and often protracted civil wars, and increasingly, it seemed, by technologically sophisticated and virtually unstoppable acts of terrorism. The leaders of the African struggles against colonialism and racism had spoiled their records by becoming heads of corrupt, fractious, and often brutal regimes; Gandhi had been appropriated by such marginal cults as pacifism and vegetarianism; and even Ho Chi Minh in his moment of glory was caught in the unyielding polarities of the Cold War. Nothing, it would seem, was left in the legacy of nationalism to make people in the Western world feel good about it.

This recent genealogy of the idea explains why nationalism is now viewed as a dark, elemental, unpredictable force of primordial nature threatening the orderly calm of civilized life. What had once been successfully relegated to the outer peripheries of the earth is now seen picking its way back toward Europe, through the long-forgotten provinces of the Habsburg, the czarist, and the Ottoman empires. Like drugs, terrorism, and illegal immigration, it is one more product of the Third World that the West dislikes but is powerless to prohibit.

In light of the current discussions on the subject in the media, it is surprising to recall that not many years ago nationalism was generally considered one of Europe's most magnificent gifts to the rest of the world. It is also not often remembered today that the two greatest wars of the twentieth century, engulfing as they did virtually every part of the globe, were brought about by Europe's failure to manage its own ethnic nationalisms. Whether of the "good" variety or the "bad," nationalism was entirely a product of the political history of Europe. Notwithstanding the celebration of the various unifying tendencies in Europe today and of the political consensus in the West as a whole, there may be in the recent amnesia on the origins of nationalism more than a hint of anxiety about whether it has quite been tamed in the land of its birth.

In all this time, the "area specialists," the historians of the colonial world, working their way cheerlessly through musty files of administrative reports and official correspondence in colonial archives in London or Paris or Amsterdam, had of course never forgotten how nationalism arrived in the colonies. Everyone agreed that it was a European import; the debates in the 1960s and 1970s in the historiographies of Africa or India or Indonesia were about what had become of the idea and who was responsible for it. These debates between a new generation of nationalist historians and those whom they dubbed "colonialists" were vigorous and often acrimonious, but they were largely confined to the specialized territories of "area studies"; no one else took much notice of them.

Ten years ago, it was one such area specialist who managed to raise once more the question of the origin and spread of nationalism in the framework of a universal history. Benedict Anderson demonstrated with much subtlety and originality that nations were not the determinate products of given sociological conditions such as language or race or religion; they had been, in Europe and everywhere else in the world, imagined into existence.[1] He also described some of the major institutional forms through which this imagined community came to acquire concrete shape, especially the institutions of what he so ingeniously called "print-capitalism." He then argued that the historical experience of nationalism in Western Europe, in the Americas, and in Russia had supplied for all subsequent nationalisms a set of modular forms from which nationalist elites in Asia and Africa had chosen the ones they liked.

Anderson's book has been, I think, the most influential in the last few years in generating new theoretical ideas on nationalism, an influence that of course, it is needless to add, is confined almost exclusively to academic writings. Contrary to the largely uninformed exoticization of nationalism in the popular media in the West, the theoretical tendency represented by Anderson certainly attempts to treat the phenomenon as part of the universal history of the modern world.

I have one central objection to Anderson's argument. If nationalisms in the rest of the world have to choose their imagined community from certain "modular" forms already made available to them by Europe and the Americas, what do they have left to imagine? History, it would seem, has decreed that we in the postcolonial world shall only be perpetual consumers of modernity. Europe and the Americas, the only true subjects of history, have thought out on our behalf not only the script of colonial enlightenment and exploitation, but also that of our anticolonial resistance and postcolonial misery. Even our imaginations must remain forever colonized.

I object to this argument not for any sentimental reason. I object because I cannot reconcile it with the evidence on anticolonial nationalism. The most powerful as well as the most creative results of the nationalist imagination in Asia and Africa are posited not on an identity but rather on a *difference* with the "modular" forms of the national society propagated by the modern West. How can we ignore this without reducing the experience of anticolonial nationalism to a caricature of itself?

To be fair to Anderson, it must be said that he is not alone to blame. The difficulty, I am now convinced, arises because we have all taken the claims of nationalism to be a *political* movement much too literally and much too seriously.

In India, for instance, any standard nationalist history will tell us that nationalism proper began in 1885 with the formation of the Indian National Congress. It might also tell us that the decade preceding this was a period of preparation, when several provincial political associations were formed. Prior to that, from the 1820s to the 1870s, was the period of "social reform," when colonial enlightenment was beginning to "modernize" the customs and institutions of a traditional society and the political spirit was still very much that of collaboration with the colonial regime: nationalism had still not emerged.

This history, when submitted to a sophisticated sociological analysis, cannot but converge with Anderson's formulations. In fact, since it seeks to replicate in its own history the history of the modern state in Europe, nationalism's self-representation will inevitably corroborate Anderson's decoding of the nationalist myth. I think, however, that as history, nationalism's autobiography is fundamentally flawed.

By my reading, anticolonial nationalism creates its own domain of sovereignty within colonial society well before it begins its political battle with the imperial power. It does this by dividing the world of social institutions and practices into two domains—the material and the spiritual. The material is the domain of the "outside," of the economy and of statecraft, of science and technology, a domain where the West had proved its superiority and the East had succumbed. In this domain, then, Western superiority had to be acknowledged and its accomplishments carefully studied and replicated. The spiritual, on the other hand, is an "inner" domain bearing the "essential" marks of cultural identity. The greater one's success in imitating Western skills in the material domain, therefore, the greater the need to preserve the distinctness of one's spiritual culture. This formula is, I think, a fundamental feature of anticolonial nationalisms in Asia and Africa.[2]

There are several implications. First, nationalism declares the domain of the spiritual its sovereign territory and refuses to allow the colonial power to intervene in that domain. If I may return to the Indian example, the period of "social reform" was actually made up of two distinct phases. In the earlier phase, Indian reformers looked to the colonial authorities to bring about by state action the reform of traditional institutions and customs. In the latter phase, although the need for change was not disputed, there was a strong resistance to allowing the colonial state to intervene in matters affecting "national culture." The second phase, in my argument, was already the period of nationalism.

The colonial state, in other words, is kept out of the "inner" domain of national culture; but it is not as though this so-called spiritual domain is left unchanged. In fact, here nationalism launches its most powerful, creative, and historically significant project: to fashion a "modern" national culture that is nevertheless not Western. If the nation is an imagined community, then this is where it is brought into being. In this, its true and essential domain, the nation is already sovereign, even when the state is in the hands of the colonial power. The dynamics of this historical project is completely missed in conventional histories in which the story of nationalism begins with the contest for political power.

In order to define the main argument of this book, let me anticipate a few points that will be discussed more elaborately later. I wish to highlight here several areas within the so-called spiritual domain that nationalism transforms in the course of its journey. I will confine my illustrations to Bengal, with whose history I am most familiar.

The first such area is that of language. Anderson is entirely correct in his suggestion that it is "print-capitalism" which provides the new institutional space for the development of the modern "national" language.[3] However, the specificities of the colonial situation do not allow a simple transposition of European patterns of development. In Bengal, for instance, it is at the initiative of the East India Company and the European missionaries that the first printed books are produced in Bengali at the end of the eighteenth century and the first narrative prose compositions commissioned at the beginning of the nineteenth. At the same time, the first half of the nineteenth century is when English completely displaces Persian as the language of bureaucracy and emerges as the most powerful vehicle of intellectual influence on a new Bengali elite. The crucial moment in the development of the modern Bengali language comes, however, in midcentury, when this bilingual elite makes it a cultural project to provide its mother tongue with the necessary linguistic equipment to enable it to become an adequate language for "modern" culture. An entire institutional network of printing presses, publishing houses, newspapers, magazines, and literary societies is created around this time, *outside* the purview of the state and the European missionaries, through which the new language, modern and standardized, is given shape. The bilingual intelligentsia came to think of its own language as belonging to that inner domain of cultural identity, from which the colonial intruder had to be kept out; language therefore became a zone over which the nation first had to declare its sovereignty and then had to transform in order to make it adequate for the modern world.

Here the modular influences of modern European languages and literatures did not necessarily produce similar consequences. In the case of the new literary genres and aesthetic conventions, for instance, whereas European influences undoubtedly shaped explicit critical discourse, it was also widely believed that European conventions were inappropriate and misleading in judging literary productions in modern Bengali. To this day there is a clear hiatus in this area between the terms of academic criticism and those of literary practice. To give an example, let me briefly discuss Bengali drama.

Drama is the one modern literary genre that is the least commended on aesthetic grounds by critics of Bengali literature. Yet it is the form in which the bilingual elite has found its largest audience. When it appeared in its modern form in the middle of the nineteenth century, the new Bengali drama had two models available to it: one, the modern European drama as it had developed since Shakespeare and Molière, and two, the virtually forgotten corpus of Sanskrit drama, now restored to a reputation of classical excellence because of the praises showered on it by Orientalist scholars from Europe. The literary criteria that would presumably direct the new drama into the privileged domain of a modern national culture were therefore clearly set by modular forms provided by Europe. But the performative practices of the new institution of the public theater made it impossible for those criteria to be applied to plays written for the theater. The conventions that would enable a play to succeed on the Calcutta stage were very different from the conventions approved by critics schooled in the traditions of European drama. The tensions have not been resolved to this day. What thrives as mainstream public theater in West Bengal or Bangladesh today is modern urban theater, national and clearly distinguishable from "folk theater." It is produced and largely patronized by the literate urban middle classes. Yet their aesthetic conventions fail to meet the standards set by the modular literary forms adopted from Europe.

Even in the case of the novel, that celebrated artifice of the nationalist imagination in which the community is made to live and love in "homogeneous time,"[4] the modular forms do not necessarily have an easy passage. The novel was a principal form through which the bilingual elite in Bengal fashioned a new narrative prose. In the devising of this prose, the influence of the two available models—modern English and classical Sanskrit—was obvious. And yet, as the practice of the form gained greater popularity, it was remarkable how frequently in the course of their narrative Bengali novelists shifted from the disciplined forms of authorial prose to the direct recording of living speech. Looking at the pages of some of the most popular novels in Bengali, it is often difficult to tell whether one is reading a novel or a play. Having created a modern prose language in the fashion of the approved modular forms, the literati, in its search for artistic truthfulness, apparently found it necessary to escape as often as possible the rigidities of that prose.

The desire to construct an aesthetic form that was modern and national, and yet recognizably different from the Western, was shown in perhaps its most exaggerated shape in the efforts in the early twentieth century of the so-called Bengal school of art. It was through these efforts that, on the one hand, an institutional space was created for the modern professional artist in India, as distinct from the traditional craftsman, for the dissemination through exhibition and print of the products of art and for the creation of a public schooled in the new aesthetic norms. Yet this agenda for the construction of a modernized artistic space was accompanied, on the other hand, by a fervent ideological program for an art that was distinctly "Indian," that is, different from the "Western."[5] Although the specific style developed by the Bengal school for a new Indian art failed to hold its ground for very long, the fundamental agenda posed by its efforts continues to be pursued to this day, namely, to develop an art that would be modern and at the same time recognizably Indian.

Alongside the institutions of print-capitalism was created a new network of secondary schools. Once again, nationalism sought to bring this area under its jurisdiction long before the domain of the state had become a matter of contention. In Bengal, from the second half of the nineteenth century, it was the new elite that took the lead in mobilizing a "national" effort to start schools in every part of the province and then to produce a suitable educational literature. Coupled with print-capitalism, the institutions of secondary education provided the space where the new language and literature were both generalized and normalized—outside the domain of the state. It was only when this space was opened up, outside the influence of both the colonial state and the European missionaries, that it became legitimate for women, for instance, to be sent to school. It was also in this period, from around the turn of the century, that the University of Calcutta was turned from an institution of colonial education to a distinctly national institution, in its curriculum, its faculty, and its sources of funding.[6]

Another area in that inner domain of national culture was the family. The assertion here of autonomy and difference was perhaps the most dramatic. The European criticism of Indian "tradition" as barbaric had focused to a large extent on religious beliefs and practices, especially those relating to the treatment of women. The early phase of "social reform" through the agency of the colonial power had also concentrated on the same issues. In that early phase, therefore, this area had been identified as essential to "Indian tradition." The nationalist move began by disputing the choice of agency. Unlike the early reformers, nationalists were not prepared to allow the colonial state to legislate the reform of "traditional" society. They asserted that only the nation itself could have the right to intervene in such an essential aspect of its cultural identity.

As it happened, the domain of the family and the position of women underwent considerable change in the world of the nationalist middle class. It was undoubtedly a new patriarchy that was brought into existence, different from the "traditional" order but also explicitly claiming to be different from the "Western" family. The "new woman" was to be modern, but she would also have to display the signs of national tradition and therefore would be essentially different from the "Western" woman.

The history of nationalism as a political movement tends to focus primarily on its contest with the colonial power in the domain of the outside, that is, the material domain of the state. This is a different history from the one I have outlined. It is also a history in which nationalism has no option but to choose its forms from the gallery of "models" offered by European and American nation-states: "difference" is not a viable criterion in the domain of the material.

In this outer domain, nationalism begins its journey (after, let us remember, it has already proclaimed its sovereignty in the inner domain) by inserting itself into a new public sphere constituted by the processes and forms of the modern (in this case, colonial) state. In the beginning, nationalism's task is to overcome the subordination of the colonized middle class, that is, to challenge the "rule of colonial difference" in the domain of the state. The colonial state, we must remember, was not just the agency that brought the modular forms of the modern state to the colonies; it was also an agency that was destined never to fulfill the normalizing mission of the modern state because the premise of its power was a rule of colonial difference, namely, the preservation of the alienness of the ruling group.

As the institutions of the modern state were elaborated in the colony, especially in the second half of the nineteenth century, the ruling European groups found it necessary to lay down—in lawmaking, in the bureaucracy, in the administration of justice, and in the recognition by the state of a legitimate domain of public opinion—the precise difference between the rulers and the ruled. If Indians had to be admitted into the judiciary, could they be allowed to try Europeans? Was it right that Indians should enter the civil service by taking the same examinations as British graduates? If European newspapers in India were given the right of free speech, could the same apply to native newspapers? Ironically, it became the historical task of nationalism, which insisted on its own marks of cultural difference with the West, to demand that there be no rule of difference in the domain of the state.

In time, with the growing strength of nationalist politics, this domain became more extensive and internally differentiated and finally took on the form of the national, that is, postcolonial, state. The dominant elements of its self-definition, at least in postcolonial India, were drawn from the ideology of the modern liberal-democratic state.

In accordance with liberal ideology, the public was now distinguished from the domain of the private. The state was required to protect the inviolability of the private self in relation to other private selves. The legitimacy of the state in carrying out this function was to be guaranteed by its indifference to concrete differences between private selves—differences, that is, of race, language, religion, class, caste, and so forth.

The trouble was that the moral-intellectual leadership of the nationalist elite operated in a field constituted by a very different set of distinctions—those between the spiritual and the material, the inner and the outer, the essential and the inessential. That contested field over which nationalism had proclaimed its sovereignty and where it had imagined its true community was neither coextensive with nor coincidental to the field constituted by the public/private distinction. In the former field, the hegemonic project of nationalism could hardly make the distinctions of language, religion, caste, or class a matter of indifference to itself. The project was that of cultural "normalization," like, as Anderson suggests, bourgeois hegemonic projects everywhere, but with the all-important difference that it had to choose its site of autonomy from a position of subordination to a colonial regime that had on its side the most universalist justificatory resources produced by post-Enlightenment social thought.

The result is that autonomous forms of imagination of the community were, and continue to be, overwhelmed and swamped by the history of the postcolonial state. Here lies the root of our postcolonial misery: not in our inability to think out new forms of the modern community but in our surrender to the old forms of the modern state. If the nation is an imagined community and if nations must also take the form of states, then our theoretical language must allow us to talk about community and state at the same time. I do not think our present theoretical language allows us to do this.

Writing just before his death, Bipinchandra Pal (1858–1932), the fiery leader of the Swadeshi movement in Bengal and a principal figure in the pre-Gandhian Congress, described the boardinghouses in which students lived in the Calcutta of his youth:

> Students' messes in Calcutta, in my college days, fifty-six years ago, were like small republics and were managed on strictly democratic lines. Everything was decided by the voice of the majority of the members of the mess. At the end of every month a manager was elected by the whole "House," so to say, and he was charged with the collection of the dues of the members, and the general supervision of the food and establishment of the mess. . . . A successful manager was frequently begged to accept re-election; while the more careless and lazy members, who had often to pay out of their own pockets for their mismanagement, tried to avoid this honour.
>
> . . . Disputes between one member and another were settled by a "Court" of the whole "House"; and we sat night after night, I remember, in examining these cases; and never was the decision of this "Court" questioned or disobeyed by any member. Nor were the members of the mess at all helpless in the matter of duly enforcing their verdict upon an offending colleague. For they could always threaten the recalcitrant member either with expulsion from the mess, or if he refused to go, with the entire responsibility of the rent being thrown on him. . . . And such was the force of public opinion in these small republics that I have known of cases of this punishment on offending members, which so worked upon him that after a week of their expulsion from a mess, they looked as if they had just come out of some prolonged or serious spell of sickness. . . .

> The composition of our mess called for some sort of a compromise between the so-called orthodox and the Brahmo and other heterodox members of our republic. So a rule was passed by the unanimous vote of the whole "House," that no member should bring any food to the house . . . which outraged the feelings of Hindu orthodoxy. It was however clearly understood that the members of the mess, as a body and even individually, would not interfere with what any one took outside the house. So we were free to go and have all sorts of forbidden food either at the Great Eastern Hotel, which some of us commenced to occasionally patronise later on, or anywhere else.[7]

The interesting point in this description is not so much the exaggerated and obviously romanticized portrayal in miniature of the imagined political form of the self-governing nation, but rather the repeated use of the institutional terms of modern European civic and political life (republic, democracy, majority, unanimity, election, House, Court, and so on) to describe a set of activities that had to be performed on material utterly incongruous with that civil society. The question of a "compromise" on the food habits of members is really settled not on a principle of demarcating the "private" from the "public" but of separating the domains of the "inside" and the "outside," the inside being a space where "unanimity" had to prevail, while the outside was a realm of individual freedom. Notwithstanding the "unanimous vote of the whole House," the force that determined the unanimity in the inner domain was not the voting procedure decided upon by individual members coming together in a body but rather the consensus of a community—institutionally novel (because, after all, the Calcutta boardinghouse was unprecedented in "tradition"), internally differentiated, but nevertheless a community whose claims preceded those of its individual members.

But Bipinchandra's use of the terms of parliamentary procedure to describe the "communitarian" activities of a boardinghouse standing in place of the nation must not be dismissed as a mere anomaly. His language is indicative of the very real imbrication of two discourses, and correspondingly of two domains, of politics. The attempt has been made in recent Indian historiography to talk of these as the domains of "elite" and "subaltern" politics.[8] But one of the important results of this historiographical approach has been precisely the demonstration that each domain has not only acted in opposition to and as a limit upon the other but, through this process of struggle, has also shaped the emergent form of the other. Thus, the presence of populist or communitarian elements in the liberal constitutional order of the postcolonial state ought not to be read as a sign of the inauthenticity or disingenuousness of elite politics; it is rather a recognition in the elite domain of the very real presence of an arena of subaltern politics over which it must dominate and yet which also had to be negotiated on its own terms for the purposes of producing consent. On the other hand, the domain of subaltern politics has increasingly become familiar with, and even adapted itself to, the institutional forms characteristic of the elite domain. The point, therefore, is no longer one of simply demarcating and identifying the two domains in their separateness, which is what was required in order first to break down the totalizing claims of a nationalist historiography. Now the task is to trace in their mutually conditioned historicities the specific forms that have appeared, on the one hand, in the domain defined by the hegemonic project of nationalist modernity, and on the other, in the numerous fragmented resistances to that normalizing project.

This is the exercise I wish to carry out in this book. Since the problem will be directly posed of the limits to the supposed universality of the modern regime of power and with it of the post-Enlightenment disciplines of knowledge, it might appear as though the exercise is meant to emphasize once more an "Indian" (or an "Oriental") exceptionalism. In fact, however, the objective of my exercise is rather more complicated, and considerably more ambitious. It includes not only an identification of the discursive conditions that make such theories of Indian exceptionalism possible, but also a demonstration that the alleged exceptions actually inhere as forcibly suppressed elements even in the supposedly universal forms of the modern regime of power.

The latter demonstration enables us to make the argument that the universalist claims of modern Western social philosophy are themselves limited by the contingencies of global power. In other words, "Western universalism" no less than "Oriental exceptionalism" can be shown to be only a particular form of a richer, more diverse, and differentiated conceptualization of a new universal idea. This might allow us the possibility not only to think of new forms of the modern community, which, as I argue, the nationalist experience in Asia and Africa has done from its birth, but, much more decisively, to think of new forms of the modern state.

The project then is to claim for us, the once-colonized, our freedom of imagination. Claims, we know only too well, can be made only as contestations in a field of power. The studies in this book will necessarily bear, for each specific disciplinary field, the imprint of an unresolved contest. To make a claim on behalf of the fragment is also, not surprisingly, to produce a discourse that is itself fragmentary. It is redundant to make apologies for this.

CHAPTER TWO

The Colonial State

THE COLONIAL STATE AS A MODERN REGIME OF POWER

I will begin by asking the following question: Does it serve any useful analytical purpose to make a distinction between the colonial state and the forms of the modern state? Or should we regard the colonial state as simply another specific form in which the modern state has generalized itself across the globe? If the latter is the case, then of course the specifically colonial form of the emergence of the institutions of the modern state would be of only incidental, or at best episodic, interest; it would not be a necessary part of the larger, and more important, historical narrative of modernity.

The idea that colonialism was only incidental to the history of the development of the modern institutions and technologies of power in the countries of Asia and Africa is now very much with us. In some ways, this is not surprising, because we now tend to think of the period of colonialism as something we have managed to put behind us, whereas the progress of modernity is a project in which we are all, albeit with varying degrees of enthusiasm, still deeply implicated.

Curiously though, the notion that colonial rule was not really about colonial rule but something else was a persistent theme in the rhetoric of colonial rule itself. As late as ten years before Indian independence, a British historian of the development of state institutions in colonial India began his book with the following words: "It was the aim of the greatest among the early British administrators in India to train the people of India to govern and protect themselves . . . rather than to establish the rule of a British bureaucracy."[1] And at about the same time, Edward Thompson and G. T. Garratt, two liberal British historians sympathetic toward the aspirations of Indian nationalism, closed their book with the following assessment:

> Whatever the future may hold, the direct influence of the West upon India is likely to decrease. But it would be absurd to imagine that the British connection will not leave a permanent mark upon Indian life. On the merely material side the new Federal Government [the Government of India reorganized under the 1935 constitutional arrangements] will take over the largest irrigation system in the world, with thousands of miles of canals and water-cuts

> fertilising between thirty and forty million acres; some 60,000 miles of metalled roads; over 42,000 miles of railway, of which three-quarters are State-owned; 230,000 scholastic institutions with over twelve million scholars; and a great number of buildings, including government offices, inspection bungalows, provincial and central legislatures. The vast area of India has been completely surveyed, most of its lands assessed, and a regular census taken of its population and its productivity. An effective defensive system has been built up on its vulnerable North-East frontier, it has an Indian army with century-old traditions, and a police force which compares favourably with any outside a few Western countries. The postal department handles nearly 1500 million articles yearly, the Forestry Department not only prevents the denudation of immense areas, but makes a net profit of between two and three crores. These great State activities are managed by a trained bureaucracy, which is to-day almost entirely Indian.[2]

Having read our Michel Foucault, we can now recognize in this account a fairly accurate description of the advance of the modern regime of power, a regime in which power is meant not to prohibit but to facilitate, to produce. It is not without significance, therefore, that Thompson and Garratt should mention this as the "permanent mark" left by the colonial presence in India. It is also significant that they entitle their history the *Rise and Fulfilment of British Rule in India.*

Indian nationalists are not, of course, quite so generous in attributing benevolent intentions to the colonial mission. But their judgment on the historical value of the state institutions created under British rule is not fundamentally different. The postcolonial state in India has after all only expanded and not transformed the basic institutional arrangements of colonial law and administration, of the courts, the bureaucracy, the police, the army, and the various technical services of government. M. V. Pylee, the constitutional historian, describes the discursive constraints with disarming simplicity. "India," he says, "inherited the British system of government and administration in its original form. The framers of the new Constitution *could not think* of an altogether new system."[3]

As a matter of fact, the criticism Indian nationalists have made in the postcolonial period is that the colonial institutions of power were not modern enough, that the conditions of colonial rule necessarily limited and corrupted the application of the true principles of a modern administration. B. B. Misra, the nationalist historian of colonial bureaucracy, identified these limits as proceeding

> from two premises. The first was the Indian social system which was governed by irrational and prescriptive customs rather than a well-regulated rational system of law and a common code of morality. The second . . . was

> the British Imperial interest, which bred discrimination in the Services on racial grounds as well as differentiation in respect of social status and conditions of service.

Yet, despite these limits, "the degree of administrative rationalization during this period of bureaucratic despotism was far ahead of the country's Brahmanic social order, which knew of no rule of law in the contractual sense."[4]

Whether imperialist or colonialist, all seem to share a belief in the self-evident legitimacy of the principles that are supposed universally to govern the modern regime of power. It is something of a surprise, therefore, to discover that a persistent theme in colonial discourse until the earlier half of this century was the steadfast refusal to admit the universality of those principles.

THE RULE OF COLONIAL DIFFERENCE

Although Vincent Smith was not the most distinguished imperial historian of India, he was probably the most widely known in India because of the success of his textbooks on Indian history. In 1919, Smith published a rejoinder to the Montagu-Chelmsford constitutional proposals seeking to placate nationalist demands by conceding a certain measure of "responsible government" to Indians. The proposals, Smith said, were based on two propositions: "(1) that a policy, assumed to have been successful in Western communities, *can* be applied to India; and (2) that such a policy *ought* to be applied to India, even at the request of an admittedly small body of Indians, because Englishmen believe it to be intrinsically the best."[5] His argument was that both propositions were false.

The policy of responsible and democratic government, "supposed to be of universal application," could not be applied to India because it went against "a deep stream of Indian tradition which has been flowing for thousands of years. . . . The ordinary men and women of India do not understand impersonal government. . . . They crave for government by a person to whom they can render loyal homage." The reason for the legitimacy of British rule in India lay in the fact that the King-Emperor was regarded by the Indian people as "the successor of Rama, Asoka and Akbar. Their heartfelt loyalty should not be quenched by the cold water of democratic theory."[6] In terms of social divisions, "India has been the battle-ground of races and religions from time immemorial," and the anticipation of a common political identity was "not justified either by the facts of history or by observation of present conditions." The fundamental principle of social organization in India was caste, which was incompatible with any form of democratic government. More importantly, the spread of modern institutions or technologies had not weakened the hold of caste in any way.

> The necessities of cheap railway travelling compel people to crowd into carriages and touch one another closely for many hours. . . . The immense practical advantages of a copious supply of good water from stand-pipes in the larger towns are permitted to outweigh the ceremonial pollution which undoubtedly takes place. . . . But such merely superficial modifications of caste regulations . . . do not touch the essence of the institution. . . . The Brahman who rides in a third-class carriage or drinks pipe-water does not think any better of his low-caste neighbour than when he travelled on foot and drank from a dirty well. . . . So long as Hindus continue to be Hindus, caste cannot be destroyed or even materially modified.[7]

Smith then went on to argue that contrary to the plea of the reformers, the policy of promoting responsible government in India was bad even as a practical strategy of power. It would produce not consent for authority but its very opposite.

> Contentment, so far as it exists, is to be deliberately disturbed by the rulers of India in order to promote the ideal of Indian nationhood, the formation of a genuine electorate, and the development of the faculty of self-help. Do the high officials charged with the government of India, who propose deliberately to disturb the contentment of three hundred millions of Asiatic people, mostly ignorant, superstitious, fanatical, and intensely suspicious, realize what they are doing? Have they counted the cost? Once the disturbance of content has been fairly started among the untutored masses, no man can tell how far the fire may spread. Discontent will not be directed to the political objects so dear to Mr. Montagu and Mr. Curtis. It will be turned fiercely upon the casteless, impure foreigner, and, inflamed by the cry of "religion in danger," will attract every disorderly element and renew the horrors of 1857 or the great anarchy of the eighteenth century. The lesson of history cannot be mistaken.[8]

Our reaction today would be to dismiss these arguments as coming from a diehard conservative imperialist putting up what was even then a quixotic defense of old-style paternalistic colonialism. Yet Smith's rejection of the claims to universality of the modern institutions of self-government raises, I think, an important question.

Let me put this plainly, even at the risk of oversimplification. If the principal justification for the modern regime of power is that by making social regulations an aspect of the self-disciplining of normalized individuals, power is made more productive, effective, and humane, then there are three possible positions with regard to the universality of this argument. One is that this must apply in principle to all societies irrespective of historical or cultural specificities. The second is that the principle is inescapably tied to the specific history and culture of Western societies and cannot be exported elsewhere; this implies a rejection of the universality of the principle. The third is that the historical and cultural differences, although an impediment in the beginning, can be eventually overcome by a suitable process of training and education. The third position, therefore, while admitting the objection raised by the second, nevertheless seeks to restore the universality of the principle.

While these three positions have been associated with distinct ideological formations, they are produced, however, in the same discursive field. My argument is, first, that all three remain available today; second, that it is possible easily to slide from one to the other, because, third, all three adopt the same tactic of employing what I will call the rule of colonial difference. The implication of this argument is that if a rule of colonial difference is part of a common strategy for the deployment of the modern forms of disciplinary power, then the history of the colonial state, far from being incidental, is of crucial interest to the study of the past, present, and future of the modern state.

I will first demonstrate the application of this rule in two well-known colonial debates over bureaucratic rationality, rule of law, and freedom of speech. I will then show that the same rule is effective in contemporary debates over colonial history.

RACE AND RATIONAL BUREAUCRACY

It is in the fitness of things that it took an event such as the suppression of a rebellion of the scale and intensity of the Great Revolt of 1857 for the various pieces of the colonial order properly to fall into place. The rebels ripped the veil off the face of the colonial power and, for the first time, it was visible in its true form: a modern regime of power destined never to fulfill its normalizing mission because the premise of its power was the preservation of the alienness of the ruling group.

The debates over colonial policy in the decades following the revolt are instructive. Historians generally characterize this period as an era of conservatism. Metcalf's well-known study traces this shift to a decline in the enthusiasm for Benthamism and evangelism in Britain. Strengthening this reluctance to embark upon any further reform in India was the suspicion that the earlier attack upon "immoral" native customs might have had something to do with the rebellion. Official opinion was now virtually unanimous in thinking that local customs were best left to themselves. "Radical reform," says Metcalf, "was not just dangerous, it had ceased to be fashionable."[9]

In keeping with this move away from liberal reform was the hardening of a certain intellectual opinion in Britain that was particularly influential in the making of colonial policy. Distressed by the extension of suffrage and of the politics of Gladstonian liberalism at home, this school of opinion sought to reestablish the precepts of property and order upon unashamedly authoritarian foundations and increasingly turned to British India as the ground where these theories could be demonstrated. James Fitzjames Stephen and Henry Maine were two leading figures in this campaign to unmask the "sentimentality" of all reformist postures in matters of colonial policy. The Indian people, Stephen reminded his countrymen, were "ignorant to the last degree" and "steeped in idolatrous superstition." The British were under no obligation to fit such people for representative institutions. All they were expected to do was administer the country and look after the welfare of the people. The empire, he said,

> is essentially an absolute Government, founded, not on consent, but on conquest. It does not represent the native principles of life or of government, and it can never do so until it represents heathenism and barbarism. It represents a belligerent civilization, and no anomaly can be so striking or so dangerous as its administration by men who, being at the head of a Government . . . having no justification for its existence except [the] superiority [of the conquering race], shrink from the open, uncompromising, straightforward assertion of it, seek to apologize for their own position, and refuse, from whatever cause, to uphold and support it.[10]

The merit of hard-nosed arguments such as this was to point unambiguously to the one factor that united the ruling bloc and separated it from those over whom it ruled. Marking this difference was race. As officials in India attempted, under directions from London, to install the processes of an orderly government, the question of race gave rise to the most acerbic debates. Indeed, the more the logic of a modern regime of power pushed the processes of government in the direction of a rationalization of administration and the normalization of the objects of its rule, the more insistently did the issue of race come up to emphasize the specifically colonial character of British dominance in India.

It seems something of a paradox that the racial difference between ruler and ruled should become most prominent precisely in that period in the last quarter of the nineteenth century when the technologies of disciplinary power were being put in place by the colonial state. Recent historians have shown that during this period there was a concerted attempt to create the institutional procedures for systematically objectifying and normalizing the colonized terrain, that is, the land and the people of India. Not only was the law codified and the bureaucracy rationalized, but a whole apparatus of specialized technical services was instituted in order to scientifically survey, classify, and enumerate the geographical, geological, botanical, zoological, and meteorological properties of the natural environment and the archaeological, historical, anthropological, linguistic, economic, demographic, and epidemiological characteristics of the people. Yet, a social historian of the period notes that "racial feeling among the British became more explicit and more aggressive in the course of the nineteenth century and reached its peak during Lord Curzon's viceroyalty, between 1899 and 1905."[11]

There is, however, no paradox in this development if we remember that to the extent this complex of power and knowledge was colonial, the forms of objectification and normalization of the colonized had to reproduce, within the framework of a universal knowledge, the truth of the colonial difference. The difference could be marked by many signs, and varying with the context, one could displace another as the most practicable application of the rule. But of all these signs, race was perhaps the most obvious mark of colonial difference.

In the case of bureaucratic rationalization, for instance, which had proceeded through the middle decades of the century, the most difficult political problem arose when it became apparent that the system of nonarbitrary recruitment through competitive academic examinations would mean the entry of Indians into the civil service. Several attempts were made in the 1870s to tamper with recruitment and service regulations in order first to keep out Indians, and then to split the bureaucracy into an elite corps primarily reserved for the British and a subordinate service for Indians.[12]

But it was the so-called Ilbert Bill Affair that brought up most dramatically the question of whether a central claim of the modern state could be allowed to transgress the line of racial division. The claim was that of administering an impersonal, nonarbitrary system of rule of law. In 1882 Behari Lal Gupta, an Indian member of the civil service, pointed out the anomaly that under the existing regulations, Indian judicial officers did not have the same right as their British counterparts to try cases in which Europeans were involved. Gupta's note was forwarded to the Government of India with a comment from the Bengal government that there was "no sufficient reason why Covenanted Native Civilians, with the position and training of District Magistrate or Sessions Judge, should not exercise the same jurisdiction over Europeans as is exercised by other members of the service."[13] The viceroy at this time was Ripon, a liberal, appointed by Gladstone's Liberal government. But it did not require much liberalism to see that the anomaly was indeed an anomaly, and after more or less routine consultations, Ilbert, the law member, introduced in 1883 a bill to straighten out the regulations.

Some historians have suggested that if Ripon had had even an inkling of the storm that was to break out, he would not have allowed such a minor issue to jeopardize the entire liberal project in India.[14] As it happened, it was the force of public opinion of the dominant race that organized itself to remind the government what colonial rule was all about. The nonofficial Europeans—planters, traders, and lawyers in particular, and in Bengal more than anywhere else—rose in "almost mutinous opposition."[15] The agitation reached a fever pitch in Calcutta. Meetings were held to denounce the bill that sought to take away "a much-valued and prized and time-honoured privilege of European British subjects" and aroused "a feeling of insecurity as to the liberties and safety of the European British subjects employed in the *mufassal* and also of their wives and daughters."[16] The British Indian press, with the *Englishman* of Calcutta at its head, declared a call to arms by claiming that the Europeans were "fighting against their own ruin and the destruction of British rule in India."[17] A European and Anglo-Indian Defence Association was formed, functions at Government House were boycotted, and there was even a conspiracy "to overpower the sentries at Government House, put the Viceroy on board a steamer at Chandpal *ghat*, and send him to England *vîa* the Cape."[18]

Gladstone, surveying the fracas from the vantage point of the metropolitan capital, was in a better position than most to see how this episode fitted into a longer story. "There is a question," he said,

> to be answered: where, in a country like India, lies the ultimate power, and if it lies for the present on one side but for the future on the other, a problem has to be solved as to preparation for that future, and it may become right and needful to chasten the saucy pride so apt to grow in the English mind toward foreigners, and especially toward foreigners whose position has been subordinate.[19]

Ripon, on the other hand, chose to see his move as "an error in tactics" and decided to beat a retreat. The provisions of the bill were so watered down that the earlier anomalies were not only reinstated but made even more cumbrous.

The question was not, as some historians have supposed, whether Ripon was "too weak a man" to carry out the liberal mission of making Indians fit for modern government. What his "failure" signaled was the inherent impossibility of completing the project of the modern state without superseding the conditions of colonial rule. When George Couper, lieutenant governor of the Northwestern Provinces, said in 1878 that the time had come to stop "shouting that black is white," he was not being metaphorical. "We all know that in point of fact black is *not* white. . . . That there should be one law alike for the European and Native is an excellent thing in theory, but if it could really be introduced in practice we should have no business in the country."[20]

The argument, in other words, was not that the "theory" of responsible government was false, nor that its truth was merely relative and contingent. Rather, the point was to lay down in "practice" a rule of colonial difference, to mark the points and the instances where the colony had to become an exception precisely to vindicate the universal truth of the theory.

RACE AND PUBLIC OPINION

Another question on which the Ilbert Bill Affair threw light was the relation between the state and those relatively autonomous institutions of public life that are supposed to constitute the domain of civil society. The interesting feature of this relation as it developed in colonial Calcutta, for instance, in the nineteenth century was that the "public" which was seen to deserve the recognition due from a properly constituted state was formed exclusively by the European residents of the country. Their opinion counted as public opinion, and the question of the appropriate relationship between government and the public came to be defined primarily around the freedoms of the British Indian press.

English-language newspapers began to be published in Calcutta from the 1780s. In those early days of empire, when power was restrained by little more than brute force and intrigue and commerce was driven by the lust for a quick fortune, the press not unexpectedly provided yet another means for carrying out personal and factional feuds within the small European community in Bengal. Governors-general were quick to use legal means to "tranquilize" newspaper editors and even deport those who refused to be subdued. By the 1820s a more stable relation had been established and the censorship laws were lifted. But the events of 1857, when the very future of British rule seemed to be at stake, forced the issue once more into the open. "Public opinion" was now defined explicitly as the opinion of the "nonofficial" European community, and the English-language press of Calcutta, crazed by panic, directed its wrath at a government that, in its eyes, seemed too soft and indecisive in punishing the "d——d niggers." Canning, the governor-general, was a special target of vituperation, and in June 1857 he imposed the censorship laws once again, for a period of one year.[21]

The contours of state-civil society relations in the new context of the Raj were revealed in interesting ways in the so-called Nil Durpan Affair. The origin of the case lay, curiously enough, in an effort by officials in Bengal to find out a little more about "native" public opinion. In 1861, when the agitations in the Bengal countryside over the cultivation of indigo had begun to subside, John Peter Grant, the governor, came to hear about Dinabandhu Mitra's (1830–73) play. Thinking this would be a good way "of knowing how natives spoke of the indigo question among themselves when they had no European to please or to displease by opening their minds," he asked for a translation to be prepared of *Nīldarpaṇ*. Grant's intentions were laudable.

> I have always been of opinion that, considering our state of more than semi-isolation from all classes of native society, public functionaries in India have been habitually too regardless of those depths of native feeling which do not show upon the surface, and too habitually careless of all means of information which are available to us for ascertaining them. Popular songs everywhere, and, in Bengal, popular native plays, are amongst the most potent, and most neglected, of those means.[22]

Seton-Karr, the secretary to the Government of Bengal, arranged for James Long, an Irish missionary later to become a pioneering historian of Calcutta, to supervise the translation "by a native" of the play. He then had it printed and circulated, along with a preface by Dinabandhu and an introduction by Long, to several persons "to whom copies of official documents about the indigo crisis had been sent."[23]

The planters were immediately up in arms. They charged the government with having circulated "a foul and malicious libel on indigo planters." When it was clarified that circulation of the play did not mean the government's approval of its contents and that in any case the circulation had not been expressly authorized by the governor, the planters' association went to court. An "extraordinary" summing up by the judge, which is said "not to have erred on the side of impartiality," influenced the jury at the Supreme Court into pronouncing James Long guilty of libel. He was sentenced to a fine and a month's imprisonment. Long became a cause célèbre among the Indian literati of Calcutta: his fine, for instance, was paid by Kaliprasanna Sinha (1840–70), and a public meeting presided over by Radhakanta Deb (1783–1867) demanded the recall of the judge for his "frequent and indiscriminate attacks on the characters of the natives of the country with an intemperance . . . not compatible with the impartial administration of justice." But, more interestingly, Long also attracted a good deal of sympathy from Europeans, particularly officials and missionaries. They felt he had been punished for no offense at all. The bishop of Calcutta remarked that the passages "which the Judge described as foul and disgusting, are in no way more gross than many an English story or play turning on the ruin of a simple hunted rustic which people read and talk about without scruple."[24] At the same time, Canning, the viceroy, rebuked Grant for having allowed things to go this far and Seton-Karr, despite an apology, was removed from his posts both in the Bengal government and in the legislative council. The planters, it would seem, won an unqualified victory.

Nevertheless, it is worth considering what really was on trial in this curious case. It was to all intents and purposes a conflict between government and the public, the "public" being constituted by "nonofficial"

Europeans. The charge against the government was that by circulating the play, it had libeled an important section of this public. Long was a scapegoat; in fact, neither he nor the play was on trial. Or rather, to put it more precisely, although Long was an ostensible culprit in the circulation of a libelous tract, the play itself and the body of opinion it represented were not recognized elements in this discourse about free speech. Such in fact was the confusion about where this principle of freedom of expression was supposed to apply that when one of Long's supporters remarked that his punishment was "exactly as if the French clergy had prosecuted Molière,"[25] it did not strike him that Dinabandhu Mitra, the author of the play, had not even been deemed worthy of being named in a suit of libel and that Long was neither the author nor even the translator of the impugned material. Within these assumptions, of course, there really was no confusion. The real target of attack was clearly the government itself, and Canning, in trying to appease "public opinion," recognized this when he moved against Grant and Seton-Karr.

The original intent of the Bengal officials, however, had been to familiarize themselves and members of the European community with the state of "native" public opinion—a perfectly reasonable tactic for a modern administrative apparatus to adopt. What incensed the planters was the implicit suggestion that the government could treat "native" public opinion on the same footing as European opinion. A native play, circulated under a government imprint, seemed to give it the same status of "information" as other official papers. This the planters were not prepared to countenance. The only civil society that the government could recognize was theirs; colonized subjects could never be its equal members. Freedom of opinion, which even they accepted as an essential element of responsible government, could apply only to the organs of this civil society; Indians, needless to add, were not fit subjects of responsible government.

LANGUAGE AND FREEDOM OF SPEECH

The question of native public opinion came up once again in the 1870s. In 1878, when the government felt it necessary to devise legal means to curb "seditious" writings in the native press, the law made an explicit distinction between the English-language and the vernacular press. An official pointed out that this would be "class legislation of the most striking and invidious description, at variance with the whole tenour of our policy,"[26] but the objection was overruled on the ground that in this instance the exception to the general rule was palpable. The presumed difficulty, said Ashley Eden, the Bengal governor, was "imaginary rather than real." That is to say, the notion of an undifferentiated body of public opinion that the government was supposed to treat impartially was only a theoretical idea; in practice, it was the duty of a colonial government to differentiate, and language was a simple and practical sign of difference.

> The papers published in this country in the English language are written by a class of writers for a class of readers whose education and interests would make them naturally intolerant of sedition; they are written under a sense of responsibility and under a restraint of public opinion which do not and cannot exist in the case of the ordinary Native newspapers. It is quite easy and practicable to draw a distinction between papers published in English and papers published in the vernacular, and it is a distinction which really meets all the requirements of the case, and should not be disregarded merely because some evil-disposed persons may choose to say that the Government has desired to show undue favour to papers written in the language of the ruling power.
>
> . . . On the whole the English Press of India, whether conducted by Europeans or Natives, bears evidence of being influenced by a proper sense of responsibility and by a general desire to discuss public events in a moderate and reasonable spirit. There is no occasion to subject that Press to restraint, and therefore, naturally enough, it is exempted. It would be a sign of great weakness on the part of Government to bring it within the scope of this measure merely to meet a possible charge of partiality.[27]

The Vernacular Press Act of 1878 was enacted in great haste so as to forestall long debates over principles, especially in Britain. Lytton, the viceroy, himself described it as "a sort of coup d'état to pass a very stringent gagging Bill."[28] The provisions were indeed stringent, since local officers were given the power to demand bonds and deposits of money from printers and publishers, and the printing of objectionable material could lead to confiscation of the deposit as well as the machinery of the press, with no right of appeal in the courts. Four years later, Ripon in his liberalism repealed the act, and "a bitter feeling obtained among officials that they were denied proper and reasonable protection against immoderate Press criticism."[29] In the 1890s, when the question of "sedition" acquired a new gravity, provisions were included in the regular penal law to allow the government to move against statements "conducing to public mischief" and "promoting enmity between classes." The distinction by language had by then ceased to be a practical index of difference because native publications in English could no longer be said to be confined in their influence to a class "naturally intolerant of sedition." Other, more practical, means emerged to distinguish between proper members of civil society and those whom the state could recognize only as subjects, not citizens. And in any case, a contrary movement of nationalism was then well on its way to constituting its own domain of sovereignty, rejecting the dubious promise of being granted membership of a second-rate "civil society of subjects."

NATIONALISM AND COLONIAL DIFFERENCE

This domain of sovereignty, which nationalism thought of as the "spiritual" or "inner" aspects of culture, such as language or religion or the elements of personal and family life, was of course premised upon a difference between the cultures of the colonizer and the colonized. The more nationalism engaged in its contest with the colonial power in the outer domain of politics, the more it insisted on displaying the marks of "essential" cultural difference so as to keep out the colonizer from that inner domain of national life and to proclaim its sovereignty over it.

But in the outer domain of the state, the supposedly "material" domain of law, administration, economy, and statecraft, nationalism fought relentlessly to erase the marks of colonial difference. Difference could not be justified in that domain. In this, it seemed to be reasserting precisely the claims to universality of the modern regime of power. And in the end, by successfully terminating the life of the colonial state, nationalism demonstrated that the project of that modern regime could be carried forward only by superseding the conditions of colonial rule.

Nevertheless, the insistence on difference, begun in the so-called spiritual domain of culture, has continued, especially in the matter of claiming agency in history.[30] Rival conceptions of collective identity have become implicated in rival claims to autonomous subjectivity. Many of these are a part of contemporary postcolonial politics and have to do with the fact that the consolidation of the power of the national state has meant the marking of a new set of differences within postcolonial society. But the origin of the project of modernity in the workings of the colonial state has meant that every such historical claim has had to negotiate its relationship with the history of colonialism. The writing of the history of British India continues to this day to be a matter of political struggle.

In this contemporary battle, the case for a history of subordinated groups has often been stated by pointing out the continuities between the colonial and the postcolonial phases of the imposition of the institutions of the modern state and by asserting the autonomous subjectivity of the oppressed.[31] But since the modern discourse of power always has available a position for the colonizer, the case on behalf of the colonizing mission can now also be stated in these new terms. To show the continued relevance of the question of the universality of the modern regime of power and of the rule of colonial difference, I will end this chapter by reviewing a recent attempt to revise the history of colonialism in India.

"IT NEVER HAPPENED!"

This revisionist history begins by challenging the assumption, shared by both colonialist and nationalist historiographies, that colonial rule represented a fundamental break in Indian history. There are two parts to this argument.

The first part of the argument has been advanced by Burton Stein.[32] He disputes the assumption in both imperialist and nationalist historiographies that the British regime in India was "completely different from all prior states." The recent work of Christopher Bayly, David Washbrook, and Frank Perlin shows, he says, that "early colonial regimes" were "continuations of prior indigenous regimes," that the eighteenth century was a time of "economic vigour, even development," and not of chaos and decline and that the period from 1750 to 1850 was a "period of transition" from extant old regimes to the colonial regimes. The continuations were marked in two ways.

One "structural contradiction" in pre-British state formations was between "centralizing, militaristic regimes" and numerous local lordships. The British inserted themselves into these formations, "not as outsiders with new procedural principles and purposes (as yet), but, contingently, as part of the political system of the subcontinent, but possessed of substantially more resources to deploy for conquest than others." The colonial state resolved the contradiction in favor of the centralizing tendency of "military-fiscalism" inherited from previous regimes. Here lay the continuity of the colonial state with its predecessors.

The other contradiction was between "sultanism" (Max Weber's term), which implied a patrimonial order based on personal loyalty of subordination to the ruler, and the existence of ideological discontinuities between ruler and local lordships, which made such patrimonial loyalties hard to sustain. Patrimonial sultanism was incompatible with the economic tendencies inherent in military-fiscalism. After initial hesitations, the colonial state in the second half of the nineteenth century broke entirely with the sultanist forms and founded a regime based not on patrimonial loyalties but on modern European principles, different both from the old regimes and the early colonial regimes. Here lay the discontinuity of the later colonial state with its predecessors.

Although Stein appeals, inter alia, to the work of Perlin,[33] the latter actually makes a much more qualified argument,[34] a qualification important for the revisionist position as well as for our judgment on it. Perlin argues that the process of centralization that characterized colonial rule "possessed roots in the earlier period." But in accelerating this process, colonial rule gave it "a new, more powerful form deriving from its location in the agency of a conquest regime possessing sources of fiat external to the subcontinent, from its radical concentration of decision making, and from the surplus of new knowledge in the instruments of rule." This produced "a substantial break" between the early colonial polity and its predecessors, despite the colonial use of "old-order institutions and its social underpinnings." Moreover, whereas in the indigenous regimes of the eighteenth century the attempt to centralize produced large areas of "quasi-autonomy," where contrary forces and contrary principles of rights and social organization could emerge to resist the larger order, colonial rule up to the early nineteenth century was marked by a substantial loss of this "intermediary ground." "Beneath the carapace of old terms and institutional shells, there has occurred a fundamental alteration of both State and state. This is bound up with the European origins and international character of the new colonial polity."

Notwithstanding Perlin's qualification, the idea of continuity from the precolonial to the early colonial period dominates this part of the revisionist argument. Since the later phase of colonialism is specifically distinguished from its early phase, one is justified in wondering if the revision is merely a matter of dates. Is the question one of identifying *when* the decisive break of colonialism took place? Earlier historians, whether imperialist or nationalist, with their simple faith in the proclamations of political rulers, had assumed that this occurred in the middle of the eighteenth century; are the revisionist historians, more skeptical of legal fictions and more sensitive to underlying social processes, now telling us that the date must be pushed forward by a hundred years?

If this is all there is to the debate, the matter is easily settled. For if the period from the middle of the eighteenth century to the middle of the nineteenth is to be seen as a period of "transition," then it must reveal not only the traces of continuity from the earlier period, as claimed by our recent historians, but surely also the signs of emergence of all of those elements that would make the late colonial period structurally different from the precolonial. In terms of periodization, then, the hundred years of transition must be seen as constituting the "moment" of break, the "event" that marks the separation of the precolonial from the colonial. The apparent conundrum of continuity and discontinuity then becomes one more example of the familiar historiographical problem of combining, and at the same time separating, structure and process. One might then react to the revisionist argument in the manner of the student radical in a Calcutta university in the early 1970s who, when asked in a history test whether Rammohan Roy was born in 1772 or 1774, replied, "I don't know. But I do know that he grew up to be a comprador."

But it would be unfair to our revisionist historians to judge them on what is only one part of their argument. In its stronger version, the revisionist argument contains another part in which the continuity from the precolonial to the early colonial period is given a new construction. Not only was it the case, the argument runs, that the Europeans in the late eighteenth and early nineteenth centuries achieved "on a larger and more ominous scale what Indian local rulers had been doing for the last century," but in responding to this conquering thrust Indians too "became active agents and not simply passive bystanders and victims in the creation of colonial India." This, says Chris Bayly in a recent book-length survey of the early colonial period, gives us a "more enduring perspective" on modern Indian history than do the earlier debates about the success or failure of the "progressive" impact of colonialism.[35]

This perspective reveals, first of all, the economic history of India from the eighteenth century to the present as a history of "Indian capitalism," born prior to the colonial incursion and growing to its present form by responding to the forces generated by the European world economy. Most of the economic institutions of capitalism in India today, such as commodity production, trading and banking capital, methods of accounting, a stock of educated expertise and of mercantile groups that would ultimately become industrial entrepreneurs, emerged in the precolonial period. So did many of the political and cultural movements, including the rise of intermediary groups between townsmen and the countryside, the formation of regional cultures, movements for cultural reform and self-respect among disprivileged groups, and even the politics of "communalism."[36]

Second, such a perspective on Indian history also shows the resilience of both townspeople and country people in resisting the onslaughts on their means of survival and ways of life, especially in the period of colonialism. Indigenous propertied groups frustrated the "more grandiose economic plans" of both the colonial state and European businessmen to extract Indian wealth, while peasants overcame the pressures of war, taxation, and repression "to adapt in a creative way to their environment." By recovering these connections, Bayly says, the new perspective enables one to construct a narrative running from the precolonial past to the postcolonial present in which the Indian people are the subjects of history.

What, then, of colonialism? Surprisingly, there is no clear answer to this question. Nevertheless, it is not difficult to read the implication of the argument. At the time of their entry, the European trading companies were merely so many indigenous players in the struggle for economic and political power in eighteenth-century India, striving for the same goals and playing by the same rules. In the latter half of the nineteenth century, when the British appear to have achieved complete dominance at the apex of the formal structure of power, their ability to reach into the depths of

Indian social life was still severely restricted. By the early twentieth century, even this hold at the top was seriously challenged, and of course by the middle of the century the colonial power was forced to leave. Looked at from the "more enduring" perspective of Indian history, then, colonialism appears as a rather brief interlude, merging with the longer narrative only when its protagonists manage to disguise themselves as Indian characters but falling hopelessly out of place and dooming itself to failure when it aspires to carry out projects that have not already taken root in the native soil.

We have a more detailed presentation of this stronger version of the revisionist argument in Washbrook. Once again, the claim is made that by tracing the continuities from precolonial to early colonial processes, one can restore the "Indianness" of this historical narrative and "recover the subject from European history." Further, and this is Washbrook's contribution to the argument, "historical theory" "is put on a rather more objective, or at least less ethnocentric, footing." It is on this high ground of "historical theory," then, that the revisionist flag is finally hoisted.[37]

What is this theory? It is the familiar theme of capitalist development, which in one form or another has framed all discussions of modern history. The new twist on this theme has as its vortex the claim that not all forms of development of capital necessarily lead to modern industrialism. The development of industrial capital in England, or in Western Europe and North America, was the result of a very specific history. It is the perversity of Eurocentric historical theories that has led to the search for similar developments everywhere else in the world; whenever that search has proved fruitless, the society has been declared incapable of producing a true historical dynamic. Instead of tracing the particular course of the indigenous history, therefore, the practice has been to see the history of "backward" countries as a history of "lack," a history that always falls short of true history.

The perspective can be reversed, says Washbrook, by taking more seriously the similarities rather than the differences between the development of capitalism in Europe and, in this case, in India. We will then see that the similarities are indeed striking. Contrary to the earlier judgment of imperialist, nationalist, and even Marxist historians, recent researches show that the economic and social institutions of precolonial India, far from impeding the growth of capitalism, actually accommodated and encouraged most of the forms associated with early modern capital. Not only did trading and banking capital grow as a result of long-distance trade, but large-scale exchange took place even in the subsistence sector. The legal-political institutions too acquired the characteristic early modern forms of military fiscalism, centralization of state authority, destruction of community practices, and the conversion of privileged entitlements into personal rights over property. Despite the cultural differences with Europe in the early capitalist era, India too produced institutions that were "capable of supplying broadly similar economic functions." The East India Company entered the scene as one more player capable of pursuing the same functions: "rather than representing a set of governing principles imported from a foreign and 'more advanced' culture, the early East India Company state might be seen as a logical extension of processes with distinctively 'indigenous' origins." And if one is not to disregard the "preponderant evidence" of early capitalist groups in India subverting indigenous regimes in order to seek support from the Company, one must accept the conclusion that "colonialism was the logical outcome of South Asia's own history of capitalist development."[38]

The tables have been turned! Once colonialism as an economic and political formation is shown to have been produced by an indigenous history of capitalist development, everything that followed from colonial rule becomes, by the ineluctable logic of "historical theory," an integral part of that same indigenous history. Thus, the restructuring of the Indian economy in the period between 1820 and 1850, when all of the principal features of colonial underdevelopment emerged to preclude once and for all the possibilities of transition to modern industrialization, must be seen not as a process carried out by an external extractive force but as one integral to the peculiar history of Indian capitalism. The colonial state, responding as it did to the historical demands of Indian capital, offered the necessary legal and political protection to the propertied classes and their attempts to enrich themselves: "rarely in history," says Washbrook, "can capital and property have secured such rewards and such prestige for so little risk and so little responsibility as in the society crystallizing in South Asia in the Victorian Age." The result was a process in which not only the British but all owners of property—"capital in general"—secured the benefits of colonial rule. The specific conditions of capitalism in India had, of course, already defined a path in which the forms of extractive relations between capital and labor did not favor a transition to industrialism. The late colonial regime, by upholding the privileges of capital, destroying the viability of petty manufacturers, pulling down the remnants of already decrepit community institutions, and consolidating the formation of a mass of overexploited peasants constantly reduced to lower and lower levels of subsistence, made the transition more or less impossible. On the cultural side, the colonial regime instituted a "traditionalization" of Indian society by its rigid codification of "custom" and "tradition," its freezing of the categories of social classification such as caste, and its privileging of "scriptural" interpretations of social law at the expense of the fluidity of local community practices. The result was the creation by colonial rule of a social order that bore a striking resemblance to its own caricature of "traditional India": late colonial society was "nearer to the ideal-type of Asiatic Despotism than anything South Asia had seen before." All this can now be seen as India's own history, a history made by Indian peoples, Indian classes, and Indian powers.

COLONIAL DIFFERENCE AS POSTCOLONIAL DIFFERENCE

There is something magical about a "historical theory" that can with such ease spirit away the violent intrusion of colonialism and make all of its features the innate property of an indigenous history. Indeed, the argument seems to run in a direction so utterly contrary to all received ideas that one might be tempted to grant that the revisionist historians have turned the tables on both imperialist and nationalist histories and struck out on a radically new path.

Like all feats of magic, however, this achievement of "historical theory" is also an illusion. If the revisionist account of Indian history makes one suspicious that this is one more attempt to take the sting out of anticolonial politics, this time by appropriating the nationalist argument about colonialism's role in producing underdevelopment in India and then turning the argument around to situate the origins of colonialism in India's own precolonial history, then one's suspicion would not be unjustified. There is much in this new historiographic strategy that is reminiscent of the debates I cited at the beginning of this chapter between conservative and liberal imperialists and their nationalist opponents. Like those earlier debates, this account shows a continued effort to produce a rule of colonial difference within a universal theory of the modern regime of power.

Washbrook argues, for instance, that Eurocentrism and the denial of subjectivity to Indians were the result of the emphasis on difference; emphasizing similarity restores to Indian history its authenticity. It is obvious, of course, though not always noticed, that the difference which produces India (or the Orient) as the "other" of Europe also requires as its condition an identity of Europe and India; otherwise they would be mutually unintelligible. By "emphasizing" either identity or difference, however, it is possible to produce varied meanings; in this case, the effects noticed by Washbrook are those of Indian authenticity on the one hand and Eurocentrism on the other. What he does not recognize is that the two histories are produced within the same discursive conditions. All that Washbrook is doing by emphasizing "similarity" is restating the condition of discursive unity.

This condition is nothing other than the assumption that the history of Europe and the history of India are united within the same framework of universal history, the assumption that made possible the incorporation of the history of India into the history of Britain in the nineteenth century: Europe became the active subject of Indian history because Indian history was now a part of "world history." The same assumption has characterized the "modern" historiography of India for at least the last hundred years, although the principal task of this nationalist historiography has been to claim for Indians the privilege of making their own history.

There have been many ways of conceptualizing this universal history. Washbrook chooses the one most favored in the rational, scientific discussions of academic social theory, namely, the universality of the analytical categories of the modern disciplines of the social sciences. In his version, this takes the form of assuming the universality of the categories of political economy. Thus, although the history of Indian capitalism, in his argument, is different from that of European capitalism, it is nonetheless a history of "capitalism." The distinctness, and hence the authenticity, of Indian capitalism is produced at the level of Indian history by first asserting the universality of capitalism at the level of world history. Instead of saying, as do his predecessors in the discipline of political economy, that India was so different that it was incapable of capitalism and therefore required British colonialism to bring it into the orbit of world history, Washbrook has simply inverted the order of similarity and difference within the same discursive framework. In the process, he has also managed to erase colonialism out of existence.

What he has produced instead is a way of talking about postcolonial backwardness as the consequence entirely of an indigenous history. Indian capitalism today, his argument seems to say, looks so backward because it has been, from its birth, *different* from Western capitalism. It was ridiculous for anyone to have believed that it could be made to look like Western capitalism; if it ever did, it would stop being itself. Fitzjames Stephen or Vincent Smith would have understood the argument perfectly.

It is possible to give many instances of how the rule of colonial difference—of representing the "other" as inferior and radically different, and hence incorrigibly inferior—can be employed in situations that are not, in the strict terms of political history, colonial.[39] These instances come up not only in relations between countries or nations, but even within populations that the modern institutions of power presume to have normalized into a body of citizens endowed with equal and nonarbitrary rights. Indeed, invoking such differences are, we might say, commonplaces in the politics of discrimination, and hence also in the many contemporary struggles for identity. This reason makes it necessary to study the specific history of the colonial state, because it reveals what is only hidden in the universal history of the modern regime of power.

Having said this, we need to move on to the next, and more substantial, part of our agenda, which is to look at the ways in which nationalism responded to the colonial intervention. That will be my task in the rest of this book. This, then, will be the last time that we will talk about Gladstone and Curzon, Lytton and Ripon, and pretend that the history of India can be written as a footnote to the history of Britain. Leaving such exiguous projects behind us, let us move on to a consideration of the history of India as a nation.

CHAPTER THREE

The Nationalist Elite

THE TERMS *middle class, literati,* and *intelligentsia* all have been used to describe it. Marxists have called it a petty bourgeoisie, the English rendering of *petit* marking its character with the unmistakable taint of historical insufficiency. A favorite target of the colonizer's ridicule, it was once famously described as "an oligarchy of caste tempered by matriculation." More recently, historians inspired by the well-meaning dogmas of American cultural anthropology called it by the name the class had given to itself—the *bhadralok,* "respectable folk"; the latter interpreted the attempt as a sinister plot to malign its character. Whichever the name, the object of description has, however, rarely been misunderstood: in the curious context of colonial Bengal, all of these terms meant more or less the same thing.

Needless to say, much has been written about the sociological characteristics of the new middle class in colonial Bengal.[1] I do not wish to intervene in that discussion. My concern in this book is with social agency. In this particular chapter, my problem is that of mediation, in the sense of the action of a subject who stands "in the middle," working upon and transforming one term of a relation into the other. It is more than simply a problem of "leadership," for I will be talking about social agents who are preoccupied not only with leading their followers but who are also conscious of doing so as a "middle term" in a social relationship. In fact, it is this "middleness" and the consciousness of middleness that I wish to problematize. Of all its appellations, therefore, I will mostly use the term *middle class* to describe the principal agents of nationalism in colonial Bengal.

THE "MIDDLENESS" OF THE CALCUTTA MIDDLE CLASS

Like middle classes elsewhere in their relation to the rise of nationalist ideologies and politics, the Calcutta middle class too has been generally acknowledged as having played a pre-eminent role in the last century and a half in creating the dominant forms of nationalist culture and social institutions in Bengal. It was this class that constructed through a modern vernacular the new forms of public discourse, laid down new criteria of social respectability, set new aesthetic and moral standards of judgment, and, suffused with its spirit of nationalism, fashioned the new forms of political mobilization that were to have such a decisive impact on the political history of the province in the twentieth century.

All this has also been written about at length. But this literature adopts, albeit necessarily, a standpoint external to the object of its inquiry. It does not let us into that vital zone of belief and practice that straddles the domains of the individual and the collective, the private and the public, the home and the world, where the new disciplinary culture of a modernizing elite has to turn itself into an exercise in self-discipline. This, however, is the investigation we need to make.

I propose to do this by taking up the question of middle-class religion.[2] As a point of entry, I will consider the phenomenon of Sri Ramakrishna (1836–86), which will afford us an access into a discursive domain where "middleness" can be talked about, explored, problematized, lived out, and, in keeping with the role of cultural leadership that the middle class gave to itself, normalized.

The colonial middle class, in Calcutta no less than in other centers of colonial power, was simultaneously placed in a position of subordination in one relation and a position of dominance in another. The construction of hegemonic ideologies typically involves the cultural efforts of classes placed precisely in such situations. To identify the possibilities and limits of nationalism as a hegemonic movement, therefore, we need to look into this specific process of ideological construction and disentangle the web in which the experiences of simultaneous subordination and domination are apparently reconciled.

For the Calcutta middle class of the late nineteenth century, political and economic domination by a British colonial elite was a fact. The class was created in a relation of subordination. But its contestation of this relation was to be premised upon its cultural leadership of the indigenous colonized people. The nationalist project was in principle a hegemonic project. Our task is to probe into the history of this project, to assess its historical possibility or impossibility, to identify its origins, extent, and limits. The method, in other words, is the method of critique.

I will concentrate on a single text, the *Rāmkṛṣṇa kathāmṛta*,[3] and look specifically at the construction there of a new religion for urban domestic life. The biographical question of Ramakrishna in relation to the middle class of Bengal has been studied from new historiographical premises by Sumit Sarkar:[4] I will not address this question. Rather, I will read the *Kathāmṛta* not so much as a text that tells us about Ramakrishna as one that tells us a great deal about the Bengali middle class. The *Kathāmṛta*, it seems to me, is a document of the fears and anxieties of a class aspiring to hegemony. It is, if I may put this in a somewhat paradoxical form, a text that reveals to us the subalternity of an elite.

But before we turn to the *Kathāmṛta*, it will be useful to recount the story of how Ramakrishna quite suddenly entered the spiritual life of the Calcutta middle class. It is an interesting episode in the secret history of nationalism and modernity.

DOUBTS

At the time, Belgharia was little more than a village five miles north of Calcutta. Today it is an indistinguishable part of the northern industrial belt of the city, gloomy and dilapidated, its days of vigor well behind it. But in 1875, it was beginning to enter the industrial age as British entrepreneurs, many of them from the Scottish town of Dundee, set up jute factories along the banks of the Hooghly.[5] Nevertheless, Belgharia, like the other townships of northern 24-Parganas, still retained a largely rural character. However, since it was close to Calcutta and not far from the riverside, it contained, besides the large houses of the local landed families, several garden houses owned by wealthy residents of Calcutta who used them as holiday retreats and pleasure spots.

It was one such house that Keshabchandra Sen (1838–84), the Brahmo leader, had converted into his *sādhan kānan*, a place where he often retired with his followers to engage in spiritual exercises. Sibnath Sastri (1847–1919), once a close associate of Keshab but now becoming increasingly critical of the new turn in his leader's spiritual views, later described the place as one given to asceticism, where everyone cooked his own food, sat under trees on tiger hides in imitation of Hindu mendicants, and spent long hours in meditation.[6] Keshab had begun to come here only a few months before, and the move marked both his own inner turmoil regarding the course of the religious reformation in which he had engaged since his youth and the trouble he was having with his critics within the Brahmo movement in Calcutta.

Keshab had, however, made up his mind about the general direction in which he and his movement needed to go. In his youth he had been a fiery reformer, working tirelessly within the Brahmo Samaj as the younger associate of Debendranath Tagore (1817–1905) and becoming perhaps the most charismatic figure among the college-going young men of Calcutta in the 1860s. Grandson of Ramkamal Sen (1783–1844), who was a senior official of the Calcutta Mint and treasurer of the Bank of Bengal, Keshab had been born into one of the leading families of the new Bengali elite of Calcutta. Ramkamal had not only become wealthy; he was also a leading figure in the Asiatic Society, one of the founders of Hindu College,

Sanskrit College, and the Horticultural Society, and the author of a Bengali-English dictionary. But he belonged to what later historians would call the "conservative" faction among the Bengali notables of the city, and his home was run according to the canons of Vaishnav orthodoxy.

The grandson, however, went to Hindu College, took to Western learning, joined the followers of Rammohan Roy, and wrote and lectured exclusively in English. In 1865 he led the campaign in the Brahmo Samaj against Debendranath Tagore, accusing the old guard of compromising with Hindu ritualism and custom. He traveled extensively through India, organizing the Brahmo Samaj principally among the middle-class Bengali diaspora that had fanned out into the cities and towns of British India and performed its role as loyal underlings of the colonial power. In 1870 he made a trip to England that his followers regarded as triumphant. He addressed numerous meetings, had breakfast with Prime Minister Gladstone and an audience with Queen Victoria, and was noticed in all the major newspapers. His visit even elicited the following doggerel in *Punch*:

> Who on earth of living men,
> Is Baboo Keshub Chunder Sen?
> I doubt if even one in ten
> Knows Baboo Keshub Chunder Sen?
>
> Let's beard this "lion" in his den—
> This Baboo Keshub Chunder Sen.
> So come to tea and muffins, then,
> With Baboo Keshub Chunder Sen.[7]

Keshab was a man of too keen an intelligence to look at everything he saw in England with starry-eyed admiration; he was also sufficiently self-assured not to hide his feelings. In his farewell address in London he expressed his surprise at the "vast amount of poverty and pauperism" in the streets of the city and at "so much moral and spiritual dissolution and physical suffering, caused by intemperance." He had been astonished to discover in England an institution he "certainly did not expect to find in this country—I mean caste. Your rich people are really Brahmins, and your poor people are Sudras."[8]

He also realized that he had taken too literally the claims made on behalf of modern Christian civilization. Of course, the representatives of colonial power in India did not usually measure up to the models of Christian humility. Four years ago, in an electrifying lecture in Calcutta, he had said:

> I regard every European settler in India as a missionary of Christ, and I have a right to demand that he should always remember and act up to his high responsibilities. (*Applause*) But alas! owing to the reckless conduct of a num-

> ber of pseudo-Christians, Christianity has failed to produce any wholesome moral influence on my countrymen. ("*Hear! hear!*" "*They are only nominal Christians!*") Yes, their muscular Christianity has led many a Native to identify the religion of Jesus with the power and privilege of inflicting blows and kicks with impunity. (*Deafening cheers*) And thus has Jesus been dishonoured in India.[9]

But now in England he saw that the defect lay in European Christianity itself. "English Christianity appears too muscular and hard," he told his English audience.

> It is not soft enough for the purposes of the human heart. . . . Christian life in England is more materialistic and outward than spiritual and inward. . . . In England there is hardly anything like meditation and solitary contemplation. Englishmen seek their God in society; why do they not, now and then, go up to the heights of the mountains in order to realize the sweetness of solitary communion with God?[10]

Returning to India, Keshab began to introduce changes in the organizational practices of the Brahmo Samaj. Many of his Brahmo followers were puzzled and dismayed, some outraged. On the one hand, he opened a communal boarding house called the Bharat Asram, "a modern apostolic organization," as Keshab himself described it, in which "a number of Brahmo families were invited to live together, boarding together in the fashion of a joint family, each bearing its portion of the expenses and sharing in common the spiritual and educational advantages of the institution."[11] The idea was to train a group of Brahmo families who were most active in the organization "to ideas of neatness, order, punctuality and domestic devotions, which form such striking features in a well-regulated middle-class English home." On the other hand, Keshab experimented with new, or rather newly revived, methods of popular communication. He introduced into Brahmo worship the Vaishnav forms of collective singing and processions through the streets, accompanied by instruments such as the *khol* and the *kartāl*, typical symbols of popular *boṣṭam* religion regarded with much scorn by urban people of enlightened sensibilities. Even in his personal life, Keshab began to cultivate a certain asceticism: he replaced the metal drinking cups he used with earthen cups and cooked his own food in a little thatched room on the terrace of his house. More significantly, as Sibnath Sastri notes, "Mr Sen no longer spoke in English, except once a year on the occasion of the anniversary festival."[12]

Keshab was certain that a new direction was needed, and he was keen to find it. Half a century after Rammohan Roy's campaigns to change a tradition steeped in what he saw as superstition, degeneracy, and unthinking allegiance to religious ritual, Keshab had come face-to-face with the limits of rationalist reform. The Brahmo religion, influential as it had been in the social life of urban Bengal, was undoubtedly restricted in its appeal to a very small section of the new middle class. In the 1870s there were scarcely more than a hundred Brahmo families in Calcutta; fewer than a thousand persons in the city declared themselves as Brahmos in the 1881 census.[13] Keshab was beginning to feel that there was something inherently limiting in the strict rationalism of the new faith. In his writings and speeches of the mid-1870s, Keshab talked frequently of the importance of a faith that was not shackled by the debilitating doubts of cold reason. Indeed, he was pleading for a little madness.

> By madness I mean heavenly enthusiasm, the highest and most intense spirituality of character, in which faith rules supreme over all sentiments and faculties of the mind. . . . The difference between philosophy and madness is the difference between science and faith, between cold dialectics and fiery earnestness, between the logical deductions of the human understanding and the living force of inspiration, such as that which cometh direct from heaven. . . . Philosophy is divine, and madness too is divine. . . . The question naturally suggests itself—why should not men be equally mad for God?[14]

Of course, Keshab was too much of a modernist not to anticipate the obvious objection to his plea and was quick to make the necessary qualification.

> I admit that both Hinduism and Buddhism, whose chief principle was meditation, have done incalculable mischief by teaching their votaries to forsake the world and become dreamy devotees and hermits. But there is no reason why if the mischief has been once perpetrated it must be wrought again. In these days of scientific thought, and within the citadel of true philosophy, there is no possibility of the reign of quietism being revived. Gentlemen, we are going to combine meditation and science, madness and philosophy, and there is no fear of India relapsing into ancient mysticism.[15]

There was something else in Keshab's search for a new path. He was deeply concerned that the rationalist ideal which he and his predecessors had pursued was alien to the traditions of his country and its people. When in England, he had remarked: "Truth is not European, and it would be a mistake to force European institutions upon the Hindus, who would resist any attempt to denationalize them."[16] He seemed to suggest that the ideals of reason and rational religion that may have been suitable for Europe were not so for India. Something else, something different, was needed for an authentic Indian religion of modernity. Indeed, far more than the strength of British arms, it was this alien moral force which British rule had brought with it which was holding India in subjection.

> Who rules India? . . . You are mistaken if you think that it is the ability of Lord Lytton in the Cabinet, or the military genius of Sir Frederick Haines in the field that rules India. It is not politics, it is not diplomacy that has laid a firm hold of the Indian heart. It is not the glittering bayonet, nor the fiery cannon of the British army that can make our people loyal. No, none of these can hold India in subjection. . . . That power—need I tell you?—is Christ. It is Christ who rules British India, and not the British Government. England has sent out a tremendous moral force, in the life and character of that mighty prophet, to conquer and hold this vast empire.

And it was the very alienness of this moral power, its lack of conformity with the beliefs and practices of the people of India, that made it inadequate for its purpose.

> It is true that the people of India have been satisfied in some measure with what they have read and heard of Jesus, but they have been disappointed in a far greater measure. For England has sent unto us, after all, a Western Christ. This is indeed to be regretted. Our countrymen find that in this Christ, sent by England, there is something that is not quite congenial to the native mind, not quite acceptable to the genius of the nation. It seems that the Christ that has come to us is an Englishman, with English manners and customs about him. Hence is it that the Hindu people shrink back and say—who is this revolutionary reformer who is trying to sap the very foundations of native society, and establish here an outlandish faith and civilization quite incompatible with oriental instincts and ideas? Why must we submit to one who is of a different nationality? Why must we bow before a foreign product? . . . Hundreds upon hundreds, thousands upon thousands, even among the most intelligent in the land, stand back in moral recoil from this picture of a foreign Christianity trying to invade and subvert Hindu society; and this repugnance unquestionably hinders the progress of the true spirit of Christianity in this country.

But there was no reason why this "true spirit of Christianity" should remain hidden under an English, or even a European, mask. After all, was not Christianity itself born in the East? "Why should you Hindus go to England to learn Jesus Christ? Is not his native land nearer to India than to England? Is he not, and are not his apostles and immediate followers, more akin to Indian nationality than Englishmen?" Why could not one, then, recover Christ for India? To Europeans, he had this to say: "if you wish to regenerate us Hindus, present Christ to us in his Hindu character. When you bring Christ to us, bring him to us, not as a civilized European, but as an Asiatic ascetic, whose wealth is communion, and whose riches prayers."[17]

It is also significant that in his search for a path of reform in consonance with Eastern spirituality, Keshab was looking for an inspired messenger through whom God makes his appearance in human history. The idea was repugnant to many enlightened Brahmos, for it smacked of the age-old Hindu belief in the *avatāra* (divine incarnation); Debendranath Tagore is said to have remarked that in a country where even fish and turtles were regarded as incarnations of God, he found it strange that Keshab should aspire to be one.[18] But Keshab's doubts were of a different sort: he had become skeptical about the powers of the human intellect and will. The soul, he said,

> wants godly life, and this can never be had by the most rigid tension of mental discipline, or the highest effort of human will. . . . It is God's free gift, not man's acquisition. It comes not through our calculation or reasoning, not through industry or struggle, but through prayerful reliance upon God's mercy. . . . It keeps man in a state of holy excitement. . . . He is then seized with the frenzy of devotion, and is not only above sin, but also above temptation; for nothing is then attractive to him except holiness.[19]

This was roughly Keshab Sen's frame of mind when, one day in the middle of March 1875, he retired as usual to the quiet of the garden house in Belgharia and had a visitor.

THE MEETING

Ramakrishna, it is said, had seen Keshabchandra once, in 1864.[20] Led by his insatiable curiosity about every variety of religious experience, the saint of Dakshineswar, then a relatively young man of twenty-eight, had gone to watch a prayer meeting in the Brahmo Samaj in Calcutta. Keshab and Ramakrishna did not speak to each other on that occasion, although Ramakrishna later said that of all the people assembled on the stage, he thought Keshab was the one most advanced in spiritual qualities. But Ramakrishna maintained his interest in the activities of the Brahmos. Once he had been to see Debendranath Tagore, in the company of Mathuranath Biswas, son-in-law of his patron Rani Rasmani (1793–1861). The social distance between Debendranath and Ramakrishna was virtually unbridgeable, but Mathuranath had been to Hindu College with Debendranath and, seeing Ramakrishna's eagerness to visit the eminent religious leader, had agreed to take him to the Tagore house in Jorasanko. The meeting apparently passed unremarkably and ended with Debendranath inviting Ramakrishna to the anniversary ceremony at the Brahmo Samaj. Ramakrishna pointed to his clothes and expressed doubts about whether he would be entirely presentable at such a gentlemanly gathering. Debendranath laughed off the objection, but the next morning wrote to Mathuranath withdrawing the invitation.

Ramakrishna was at this time entirely unknown among the Calcutta middle class. True, he had been patronized by Rani Rasmani of Janbazar, and she along with several members of her family regarded Ramakrishna with much veneration. But Rasmani's family, largely because of its lower-caste background, was not a part of the culturally dominant elite of Calcutta, although she herself was well known as a spirited and philanthropic woman. The only other prominent person close to Ramakrishna before 1875 was Sambhucharan Mallik, a wealthy and generous landlord and trader—and he died in 1876. And there was also Captain Viswanath Upadhyay, a businessman from Nepal who did not belong to Calcutta.

On this particular day in the middle of March 1875, Ramakrishna was in Calcutta when he had a great urge to meet Keshabchandra. Accompanied by his nephew Hriday and Captain Viswanath, he went to Keshab's house in Kolutola only to be told that Keshab was in Belgharia. Ramakrishna declared that he had to go there straightaway. There was, of course, the small matter of finding the fare for the long carriage ride, but Captain Viswanath agreed to pay it.

Thus it was that in order to meet Keshab, Ramakrishna had to take a carriage all the way from Calcutta past Dakshineswar to a garden house in Belgharia. For it is a fact of history that when Ramakrishna went looking for him in Calcutta, Keshab Sen had already made his way to his spiritual retreat somewhere in the vicinity of Dakshineswar.

Hriday got off the carriage and went looking for Keshabchandra. He found the leader sitting with his companions on the steps of a pool in front of the house. Hriday walked up to him and said that his uncle, who was sitting outside in the carriage, would like to see him. When asked who his uncle was, he explained that he was the Paramahamsa of Dakshineswar. Keshabchandra immediately asked Hriday to bring him in.

Pratap Mozoomdar (1840–1905), a childhood friend and close associate of Keshab who was present on the occasion, later described the scene:

> There came one morning in a ricketty *ticca gari*, a disorderly-looking young man, insufficiently clad, and with manners less than insufficient. . . . His appearance was so unpretending and simple, and he spoke so little at his introduction, that we did not take much notice of him at first.[21]

Mozoomdar, of course, gives the date of this meeting as March 1876, although all later historians agree that it took place in March 1875. It is also curious that twelve years after the incident he remembered Ramakrishna as a "young man," although the latter was then thirty-nine years old, two years older than Keshab Sen and four years older than Mozoomdar himself.

What might be called the official biography of Ramakrishna, the *Rāmkṛṣṇa līlāprasaṅga*, describes Ramakrishna on this day as clothed in "a dhoti with a red border, one end thrown across the left shoulder." On being introduced, he said, "Babu, I am told that you people have seen God. I have come to hear what you have seen." This is how the conversation began. After some time, Ramakrishna began to sing one of his favorite songs—a composition by Ramprasad Sen—"Who Knows What Kālī Is Like?" As he sang, he swooned and went into a trance. Hriday began to whisper in his ears, "Hari Om! Hari Om!" Slowly, Ramakrishna recovered consciousness.[22]

The same incident is described by Pratap Mozoomdar from the point of view of Keshab's followers. "Soon he began to discourse in a sort of half-delirious state, becoming now and then quite unconscious. What he said, however, was so profound and beautiful that we soon perceived he was no ordinary man."[23]

Ramakrishna was talking about the nature of God, telling his half-skeptical audience some of the stories that two decades later would be familiar to all of literate Bengal.

> A man who had seen a chameleon under a tree returned and said, "I have seen a beautiful red chameleon under the tree." Another said, "I was there before you. The chameleon is not red, but green. I have seen it with my own eyes." A third said, "I too know it well. I saw it before either of you, and it was neither red nor green, but—and I saw with my own eyes—it was blue." Others declared it was yellow, or grey, and so on. Soon they began to quarrel among themselves as to who was correct. A man passing by asked what the trouble was. When he was told he said, "I live under that very tree, and I know the chameleon well. All of you are right, every one. The chameleon is sometimes green, sometimes blue, it is all colours by turn, and sometimes it is absolutely colourless."[24]

Ramakrishna was beginning to enjoy himself. "When a strange animal comes into a herd of cattle," he said, "the cows go after it with their horns. But when they see another cow, they lick its hide. That's what has happened to me here." Suddenly, he turned to Keshab and said, "Yes, your tail has dropped off." Undoubtedly Keshab and his followers were taken aback by this remark. Ramakrishna quickly explained himself, however. "You must have seen tadpoles. As long as they have tails, they must live in water; but when the tail falls away they can live on land as well as in water. . . . Your mind, Keshab, is in such a state now. You can live in the world, and enjoy divine bliss as well."[25]

THE DISCOVERY

Keshab Sen ran two newspapers. The English paper, the *Indian Mirror*, began as a weekly and in 1871 became a daily. The Bengali weekly, *Sulabh samācār*, was started in November 1870 and in three months reached a peak circulation of twenty-seven thousand. Even in 1877 when its circulation had dropped somewhat because of competition from other publications it was still the most widely circulated paper in Bengali.[26]

Two weeks after the meeting between Keshab Sen and Ramakrishna, the *Indian Mirror* published an article entitled "A Hindu Saint." After describing the great Hindu devotees talked about in the religious literature of India and still revered in popular memory, it continued:

> We met one not long ago, and were charmed by the depth, penetration and simplicity of his spirit. The never-ceasing metaphors and analogies in which he indulged are, most of them, as apt as they are beautiful. The characteristics of the mind are the very opposite of those of Pandit Dayanand Saraswati, the former being gentle, tender and contemplative as the latter is sturdy, masculine and polemical. Hinduism must have in it a deep source of beauty, truth and goodness to inspire such men as these.[27]

It is more than likely that the article was written by Keshab himself and a few weeks later something along the same lines appeared in *Sulabh samācār*, the first of several articles on Ramakrishna published in that paper.

Suddenly Ramakrishna became an object of great curiosity among the educated young men of Calcutta. Ramchandra Datta, a doctor at the Calcutta Medical College, and his cousin Manomohan Mitra, a businessman, read about Ramakrishna in *Sulabh samācār* and came to Dakshineswar in 1879 to see him.[28] Surendranath Mitra, a friend of Ramchandra and a fairly wealthy man with a job in a British firm, was troubled by his incurable weakness for liquor and women and began visiting Dakshineswar. Ramakrishna told him, "But, Suren, when you drink, why do you think of it as ordinary wine? Offer it first to the Mother and drink it as her *prasād* [sanctified food]. Then you will never get drunk." Henceforth, before Surendranath drank, he offered some wine to Kālī. This action filled him with devotion, and he began to cry like a child. He never became intoxicated again.[29]

Balaram Bose, who came from a wealthy family of landlords and was one of Ramakrishna's principal patrons in the last years of his life, first read about him in Keshab Sen's newspapers.[30] So did Girishchandra Ghosh, the foremost personality in the Calcutta theater at this time.[31] By the early years of the 1880s, when most of the men who would form the closest circle of disciples around Ramakrishna had gathered in Dakshineswar,[32] he was a frequently discussed personality in the schools, colleges, and newspapers of Calcutta.

Remarkably, the enormous legend that would be built around Ramakrishna's name in the words and thoughts of the Calcutta middle class was the result of a fairly short acquaintance, beginning only eleven years before his death. Only in those last years of his life did he cast his spell over so many distinguished men, who would make his name a household word among educated Bengalis.

The followers of Keshabchandra and Ramakrishna have, of course, never managed to agree on which of the two great leaders influenced the other. The hagiographers of Ramakrishna write as though Keshab, a determined seeker after truth who roamed aimlessly for the greater part of his life, finally found salvation at the feet of the Master. Saradananda, for instance, writes of Keshab's break with the Brahmo Samaj and his founding of a new order: "As this faith came into existence shortly after Kesav's acquaintance with the Master, it is probable that it was a partial acceptance and propagation of the Master's final conclusion." Saradananda nevertheless remains skeptical about Keshab's ability to accept Ramakrishna in the true spirit of the devotee: "Although he was dearly loved by the Master and had many opportunities to see and hear him, it is doubtful whether Kesav, inspired with Western ideas and ideals as he was, understood him perfectly" (*GM*, p. 314). A biographer of Keshab, on the other hand, complains: "It is sad to contemplate that such friendship should be misunderstood, misinterpreted. It has even been suggested that Keshub borrowed his religion of Harmony, the New Dispensation, from Ramakrishna."[33]

With the advantage of a hundred years of hindsight, we have no need to take sides in this quarrel. But for precisely that reason—the fact that we are prisoners of an incorrigibly historical vision of our selves and the world—we had to begin our story with the meeting in Belgharia on a spring afternoon in 1875.

DIVINE PLAY

This, however, is not how the story is supposed to begin. Those who tell the story of Ramakrishna remind us that the Master's life was not the life of any ordinary man, not even that of an extraordinary man. The Absolute Being, in one of his inscrutable, playful decisions, appears on earth from time to time in the guise of a human being to act out an exemplary life for the edification of the world. According to the authorized version, therefore, the story of Ramakrishna's life must be told as one more episode in an eternal *līlā*.

The story, in fact, is supposed to begin with a dream. In the winter of 1835, Kshudiram Chattopadhyay of Kamarpukur in Hugli, then already a man of sixty, went to Gaya to offer worship to his forefathers. There he dreamed of himself in the temple, surrounded by his forefathers, who appeared before him "in luminous celestial bodies," accepting the *piṇḍa* he offered to them. He then saw the temple fill "with divine light," and there in front of him was "a wonderful divine being"—Viṣṇu himself in the form of Gadādhar—"seated happily on a beautiful throne." Then the divine being spoke to him. "I bless you and will be born as your son and will receive your loving care" (*GM*, pp. 31–32).

Soon after this, Kshudiram's wife, Chandra, then forty-five years old, conceived. Saradananda, Ramakrishna's biographer, tells us that "one peculiar characteristic of divine and subtle origin was shared by every one of Kshudiram's pious household": they all had a predilection for unusual spiritual experiences (*GM*, p. 29). Chandra's visions became more numerous after she had conceived (*GM*, p. 37). The birth of the son was again followed by something of a miracle, because the child disappeared from the place where Dhani, the midwife, had kept it. Looking around in panic, she found it lying in a hollow fireplace "with its body adorned with ashes, and still not crying." Everyone marveled at the beauty and size of the child, for it was as large as a six-month-old infant. The astrologers agreed that Kshudiram's son had been born at an especially auspicious moment (*GM*, p. 40).

In the *Līlāprasaṅga*, Saradananda takes great pains to explain to what he presumes will be a skeptical readership the significance of these extraordinary and miraculous happenings surrounding Ramakrishna's birth.[34] He argues, for instance, that such events are common to the life stories of all great souls "who sanctify the earth by their birth," stories that "are recorded in the religious books of all races." Similar events portray "the unique spiritual experiences and visions" of the parents of Rama, Krishna, the Buddha, Jesus, Śaṅkara and Caitanya (*GM*, p. 33). Again, he suggests that there must be some significance to the fact that with the exceptions of Rama and the Buddha, "all the great souls who are to this day worshipped as the incarnations of the Divine," such as Krishna, Jesus, Śaṅkara, Caitanya or Muhammad, were born "in poverty and hardship" (*L* 1:24; *GM*, p. 17). Miraculousness, it would seem, is the aura that surrounds the life histories of those who are the incarnations of God and marks out their lives as different from history itself.

But Saradananda also has other arguments to offer. India, he thinks, has been particularly blessed by the Almighty Being in the matter of incarnations. This explains the spirituality of Indian culture.

> When we make a comparative study of the spiritual beliefs and ideals of India and of other countries, we notice a vast difference between them. From very ancient times India has taken entities beyond the senses, namely, God, the self, the next world, etc., to be real, and has employed all its efforts towards their direct realization. . . . All its activities have accordingly been coloured by intense spirituality throughout the ages. . . . The source of this

> absorbing interest in things beyond the senses is due to the frequent birth in India of men possessing a direct knowledge of these things and endowed with divine qualities. (*GM*, p. 5)

Knowledge of a similar kind, Saradananda is sure, is denied to the West, for the procedures of Western knowledge are "attracted only by external objects."

> Although capable of achieving great progress in physical science, the [Western] procedure . . . could not lead men to the knowledge of the Atman. For the only way to attain that knowledge is through self-control, selflessness and introspection, and the only instrument for attaining it is the mind, with all its functions brought under absolute control.

Western knowledge could not accomplish this. Consequently, Western people "missed the path to Self-knowledge and became materialists, identifying themselves with the body" (*GM*, p. 13).

We have here the familiar nationalist problematic of the material and the spiritual, the identification of an incompleteness in the claims of the modern West to a superior culture and asserting the sovereignty of the nation over the domain of spirituality. In itself, this is not surprising because Saradananda himself was very much a part of the middle-class culture of Bengal that had, by the turn of the century, come to accept these criteria as fundamental in the framing of questions of cultural choice. What is curious is that instead of "cleaning up" the layers of myth and legend from the life story of someone like Ramakrishna and presenting it as the rational history of human exemplariness, as in Bankim's *Kṛṣṇacaritra*, for instance, Saradananda seeks to do the very opposite: he authenticates the myth by declaring that the life of Ramakrishna is not to be read as human history but as divine play.[35]

Indeed, Saradananda is forthright in stating his purpose. Why does he feel called upon to write the story of Ramakrishna's life for his educated readership? The reason has to do with "the occupation of India by the West."

> Coming more and more under the spell of the West, India rejected the ideal of renunciation and self-control and began to run after worldly pleasures. This attitude brought with it the decay of the ancient system of education and training, and there arose atheism, love of imitation and lack of self-confidence. Thus the nation lost its backbone. People came to believe that their long-cherished beliefs and practices were erroneous, and they felt that perhaps their traditions were crude and semi-civilized, as the West with its wonderful knowledge of science said them to be. . . . Finding that, even for worldly enjoyment, she had to depend upon others, India was overcome with a sense of frustration. Having thus lost the way both to enjoyment and

> to liberation, and yet being bent on imitating others, the nation was now buffeted by waves of desires, like a boat drifting without a helmsman. . . . Prostrate India was made to listen to lectures—delivered at public meetings held in the Western manner—on politics, sociology, the freedom of women and widow-marriage. But the feeling of frustration and despair, instead of lessening, grew stronger. . . . The influence of the West had brought about its fall. Would it not be futile, then, to look to the atheistic West for its resurrection? Being itself imperfect, how could the West make another part of the world perfect? (*GM*, p. 15)

The conditions of the problem were clear. The assertion of spirituality would have to rest on an essential difference between East and West, and the domain of autonomy thus defined would have to be ordered on one's own terms, not on those set by the conqueror in the material world. If myth is the form in which the truth is miraculously revealed in the domain of Eastern spirituality, then it is myth that must be affirmed and the quibbles of a skeptical rationalism declared out of bounds.

Saradananda thus goes on to talk about many extraordinary events from Ramakrishna's childhood, all of which showed him, even at an early age, as a person with a touch of divinity in him. Thus, there are stories about his "remarkable memory and intelligence" and about his "remarkable courage" (*GM*, pp. 44, 47). There is also the story about how young Gadadhar, at the age of nine, resolved a scriptural dispute at a scholarly gathering (*GM*, p. 55). Of course, there were spiritual experiences too—meditation, ecstasy, and visions.

Ramakrishna's marriage at the age of twenty-two puts Saradananda into something of a quandary. Ramakrishna never consummated the marriage, and although he had his wife Sarada come and live in Dakshineswar, it could never have been his intention to lead the life of a family man. Why then did Ramakrishna agree to marry? Saradananda finds an answer.

> At the present time we have almost forgotten that, besides the satisfaction of the senses, there is a very sacred and high purpose of marriage and this is why we are reducing ourselves to being worse than beasts. It is only in order to destroy this beastliness of men and women of modern India that the Master, the teacher of his people, was married. Like all the other acts of his life the act of marriage also was performed for the good of all. (*GM*, p. 409)

The youth of Ramakrishna is recounted by Saradananda as a narrative of the great soul in his "attitude of the devotee" (*sādhaka-bhāva*). During this time Ramakrishna goes through a series of spiritual exercises: in Tantra with the Bhairavi, in the forms of nondualistic Vedantic *sādhanā* (spiritual exercise) with Totapuri, and in certain forms of Sufi meditation with

Govinda Ray, besides his meetings with various religious personalities during his trip to Varanasi and Vrindavan. Ramakrishna is said to have attained mastery (*siddhi*) in each of these forms of religious practice. Saradananda even has a short section on "the extraordinary way in which the Master attained proficiency in the religion founded by Śrī Śrī Īśā" (*L* 2:370–73). The method was a mystical encounter with Christ himself. During one of his conversations with his disciples many years later, Ramakrishna asked them what the Bible said about Christ's physical appearance. The disciples reasoned that being Jewish, he must have been "very fair, with long eyes and an aquiline nose."

> The Master said, "But I saw that the tip of his nose was a little flat. I don't know why I saw him like that." . . .
>
> But we came to know, shortly after the Master passed away, that there were three different descriptions of Jesus' physical features; and according to one of them the tip of his nose was a little flat. (*GM*, p. 297)

All this time, until Ramakrishna took up "the attitude of the teacher" (*guru-bhāva*), he lived his life "free from the influence of Western ideas and ideals" (*GM*, p. 707). Only when he came into contact with Keshabchandra and the Brahmos did he become aware of the spiritual state of the educated sections of society. What he saw was a state of crisis.

> He saw that, although [the Brahmos] were making efforts to realize God, they had deviated from the ancient national ideal of renunciation. His mind, therefore, engaged itself in finding out its cause. It was thus that he became acquainted for the first time with the mass of exotic ideas entering the lives of the people of India because of Western education and training. (*GM*, p. 708)

Ramakrishna decided that behind all this lay some shrewd purpose of the divine will.

> The Master, therefore, perfectly comprehended that it was only owing to the Divine Mother's will that Western ideas and ideals had entered India and that by Her will alone had the Brahmos and other educated communities become mere toys in their hands. . . . The Master said, "Let them accept as much of the immediate knowledge of the seers as is possible for them; the Mother of the universe will bring forward in future such persons as will fully accept that knowledge." (*GM*, p. 709)

Thus it was that Ramakrishna decided to gather around him a circle of young disciples and to initiate them into his religion. In each case, the Master had a yogic vision of the disciple before he actually arrived in Dakshineswar (*GM*, p. 811). From the beginning of 1881, "the all-renouncing devotees, the eternal playmates of the Master in his Lila, began coming to him one by one" (*GM*, p. 711). By 1884, they had all arrived. It was only then that Ramakrishna finally took up his *divyabhāva*, "the attitude of the divine."

The purpose of all this is clear to Saradananda. Had not the Divine Lord promised in the *Gītā* that whenever religion declines, he would assume a human body and manifest his powers? (*GM*, p. 16). Now, when the nation lay enslaved and its brightest minds confused and frustrated, had not such a time arrived?

> Did India, shorn of its glory and reduced to an object of contempt to foreigners, once again arouse the compassion of the Lord to incarnate Himself? That this did happen will become clear on a perusal of the life-story of the great soul, possessed of an infinite urge to do good, which is here recorded. India was once more blessed by the coming, in response to the need of the age, of One who, incarnating Himself as Sri Rama, Sri Krishna and others, renewed the eternal religion again and again. (*GM*, pp. 9–10)

To explain this "purpose of his advent" (*GM*, p. 3), Saradananda recounts the story of Ramakrishna's life as an episode in an eternal play—a story that begins with a dream.

But although the *Līlāprasaṅga* claims to be something like an official biography, it is not the text that is most familiar to generations of avid readers of Ramakrishna literature. That honor is reserved for the *Rāmkṛṣṇa kathāmṛta.* Circulated now in several editions and virtually annual reprints, it is a collection of the Master's "sayings." Ever since its publication in the early years of this century, its five volumes have acted as the principal sourcebook on Ramakrishna.

LANGUAGE

Sumit Sarkar has noted the stylistic peculiarity of the *Kathāmṛta* in the way it combines two radically different linguistic idioms—one, the rustic colloquial idiom spoken by Ramakrishna, and the other, the chaste formality of the new written prose of nineteenth-century Calcutta.[36] The former, for all its rusticity (a "rusticity," we must remember, itself produced by the difference created in the nineteenth century between the new high culture of urban sophistication and everything else that became marked as coarse, rustic, or merely local), was by no means a language that any villager in nineteenth-century Bengal would have spoken, for its use by Ramakrishna shows great conceptual richness, metaphoric power, and dialectical skill. It was the language of preachers and poets in precolonial Bengal, and even when used by someone without much formal learning (such as Ramakrishna), it was able to draw upon the conceptual and rhetorical resources of a vast body of literate tradition. By contrast, the new written prose of late nineteenth-century Calcutta, in what may be called its post-Bankim phase, was distinct not so much as a "development" of earlier narrative forms but fundamentally by virtue of its adoption of a wholly different, that is, modern European, discursive framework. Recent studies have identified the ways in which grammatical models borrowed from the modern European languages shaped the "standard" syntactic forms of modern Bengali prose; other studies have shown similar "modular" influences of rhetorical forms borrowed from English in particular.[37]

The appearance of these formal differences between the two idioms was of course intricately tied to another difference—a difference in the very conceptual and logical apparatus articulated in language. The users of the new Bengali prose not only said things in a new way, they also had new things to say. This was the principal intellectual impetus that led to the rapid flourishing of the modern Bengali prose literature; by the 1880s, when Mahendranath Gupta (1854–1932) was recording his diary entries of Ramakrishna's sayings for what was to become the *Kathāmṛta*, a considerable printing and publishing industry operated in Calcutta (in fact, one of the more important industrial activities in the city), testifying to the creation of both a modern "high culture" and a "print-capitalism," the two sociological conditions that are supposed to activate the nationalist imagination.[38] What is nevertheless intriguing is the quite rapid "standardization" of this prose. The 1850s was still a time when a "standard" form had not appeared; by the 1880s, the "standard" form had come to stay. It is worth speculating whether the sheer proximity of European discursive models—available, palpable, already standardized by more momentous historical processes and hence unquestionably worthy of emulation—had something to do with the astonishing speed with which the entirely new form of narrative prose came to be accepted as "normal" by the English-educated Bengali middle class.

The modular influence was strongest when written prose was employed to discuss subjects that were explicitly theoretical or philosophical. The *Kathāmṛta* is marked not only by the divergence between the "rustic" and the "urban" idioms in Bengali; it is an even more explicitly bilingual text in its repeated employment of English terms, phrases, and quotations. It is remarkable how often Mahendranath introduces with a heading in English sections in which Ramakrishna discusses questions of a philosophical nature: there must be some fifty sections with titles such as "Reconciliation of Free Will and God's Will—of Liberty and Necessity" or "Identity of the Absolute or Universal Ego and the Phenomenal World" or "Problems of Evil and the Immortality of the Soul" or "Philosophy and Scepticism," and so on. Each heading of this kind is followed by a recording of Ramakrishna's own words or a conversation, directly reported, between him and his disciples. Mahendranath, in his self-appointed role of narrator, does not attempt to explicate the sayings of his preceptor, and yet this form of introducing sections serves to create the impression that Ramakrishna is dealing with the same questions that are discussed in European philosophy. Mahendranath also repeatedly translates various philosophical concepts used by Ramakrishna with English terms and inserts them into the text in parentheses or in footnotes. Thus, for instance, when Ramakrishna describes his state of trance as one in which he is unable to count things—*ek duier pār* (literally, "beyond ones and twos")—Mahendranath adds a footnote in English: "The absolute as distinguished from the relative." He explains *Kālī* as "God in His relations with the conditioned" or *Brahma* as "the Unconditioned, the Absolute." When Ramakrishna says *pratyakṣa*, Mahendranath adds in parentheses "perception"; when Ramakrishna says that in a trance *īśvara* does not appear as a *vyakti*, Mahendranath adds "person." A section entitled "Perception of the Infinite" has a footnote saying, "Compare discussion about the order of perception of the Infinite and of the Finite in Max Müller's Hibbert Lectures and Gifford Lectures."

This bilingual dialogue runs through the text, translating the terms of an Indian philosophical discourse into those of nineteenth-century European logic and metaphysics. It is as though the wisdom of an ancient speculative tradition of the East, sustained for centuries not only in philosophical texts composed by the learned but through debates and disquisitions among preachers and mystics, is being made available to minds shaped by the modes of European speculative philosophy. (The invocation of Max Müller is significant.) This dialogue also expresses the desire to assert that the "common" philosophy of "rustic" Indian preachers is no less sophisticated, no less "classical" in its intellectual heritage, than the learned speculations of modern European philosophers: in fact, the former is shown as providing different, and perhaps better, answers to the same philosophical problems posed in European philosophy.[39] (Mahendranath also embellishes some of Ramakrishna's words with quotations in Sanskrit from texts such as the Upaniṣads and the *Gītā*; Ramakrishna himself almost never used Sanskrit aphorisms in his conversations.) But for both narrator and reader of the *Kathāmṛta*, the terrain of European thought is familiar ground—familiar, yet foreign—from which they set out to discover (or perhaps, rediscover) the terrain of the indigenous and the popular, a home from which they have been wrenched. The bilingual discourse takes place within the same consciousness, where both lord and bondsman reside. Contestation and mediation have taken root within the new middle-class mind, a mind split in two.

NARRATIVE TIME

The internal arrangement of each volume of the *Kathāmṛta* is strictly chronological. The book was not originally planned to run into five volumes. The first volume consequently is composed of selections from Mahendranath's diaries in the period from 26 February 1882 to 27 December 1885, beginning with an account of his first meeting with Ramakrishna. The later volumes contain other selections, but covering roughly the same period (vol. 2, 17 October 1882 to 24 April 1886; vol. 3, 5 August 1882 to 13 April 1886; vol. 4, 1 April 1883 to 21 April 1886; vol. 5, 11 March 1882 to 24 September 1885). Each volume has appendixes; those added to volume 5 record some events of 1881 while those in the other volumes deal with conversations between Ramakrishna's disciples after the Master's death in August 1886.

Mahendranath is scrupulous not only in maintaining a chronological order within each volume but also in meticulously recording the date, time, and place of each conversation. He also adds wherever possible a description of the physical surroundings and invariably notes the names of those present at the time. Mahendranath is clearly conscious of the requirements of authentic documentation. And yet, as soon as he passes to the reporting of the Master's sayings, he not only abandons the formal structure of a rational narrative prose, he surrenders himself completely in his journey with Ramakrishna through the fluid space of mythic time, from Rāma, Hanumāna, Bhīṣma, and Yudhiṣṭhira to the ancient sages Nārada, Vaśiṣṭha, or Viśvāmitra, to the apocryphal stories of folklore to Ramakrishna's own spiritual mentors Totāpurī or the Bhairavi to contemporary figures like Keshab Sen or Vidyasagar or Bankimchandra, jumping from one to another, equating, contrasting, connecting, with complete disregard for historical specifics. Mahendranath's careful construction of a narrative grid was designed to authenticate the historical truth of his master's sayings; yet the truth is seized only after it has escaped the grid of historical time.

It is possible, of course, to use the narrative arrangement of materials in the *Kathāmṛta* for a historical-biographical study of Ramakrishna. But as far as the "message" of the *Kathāmṛta* is concerned, the arrangement of the materials does not matter in the least. The chronological arrangement completely defeats any attempt at indicating a progression or thematization. What it produces instead is a repetitiousness: the same arguments, the same stories, even the same jokes, repeated over and over again. Redundancy is, of course, a characteristic element of the structure of self-evidence of mythic truth.

THE PRISONHOUSE OF REASON

For the colonized middle-class mind, caught in its "middleness," the discourse of Reason was not unequivocally liberating. The invariable implication it carried of the historical necessity of colonial rule and its condemnation of indigenous culture as the storehouse of unreason, or (in a stage-of-civilization argument) of reason yet unborn, which only colonial rule would bring to birth (as father, mother, or midwife—which?), made the discourse of Reason oppressive. It was an oppression that the middle-class mind often sought to escape. Bankimchandra Chattopadhyay (1838–94), unquestionably the most brilliant rationalist essayist of the time, escaped into the world not of mythic time but of imaginary history, sliding imperceptibly from the past-as-it-might-have-been to the past-as-it-should-have-been to an invocation of the past-as-it-will-be.[40] So did the most brilliant rationalist defender of "orthodox" tradition—Bhudeb Mukhopadhyay (1827–94), in that remarkable piece of utopian history *Svapnalabdha bhāratbarṣer itihās* (The history of India as revealed in a dream). More common was the escape from the oppressive rigidities of the new discursive prose into the semantic richness and polyphony of ordinary, uncolonized speech. It would be an interesting project to study the ways in which Bengali prose writers have found it so compelling to adopt the device of shifting from an authorial narrative prose to the dramatic forms of direct dialogue. Even more striking is the communicative power of the modern Bengali drama, the least commended on aesthetic grounds by the critics of modern Bengali literature (certainly so in comparison with the novel or the short story or poetry) and yet arguably the most effective cultural form through which the English-educated literati of Calcutta commanded a popular audience (and the one cultural form subjected to the most rigorous and sustained police censorship by the colonial government). Reborn in the middle of the nineteenth century in the shapes prescribed by European theater, the modern Bengali drama found its strength not so much in the carefully structured directedness of dramatic action and conflict as in the rhetorical power of speech. Where written prose marked a domain already surrendered to the colonizer, common speech thrived within its zealously guarded zone of autonomy and freedom.

FEAR

It is important to note that the subordination of the Bengali middle class to the colonial power was based on much more than a mental construct. Hegemonic power is always a combination of force and the persuasive self-evidence of ideology. To the extent that the persuasive apparatus of colonial ideology necessarily and invariably fails to match the requirements of justifying direct political domination, colonial rule is always marked by the palpable, indeed openly demonstrated, presence of physical force.

For the middle-class Bengali babu of late nineteenth-century Calcutta, the figures of the white boss in a mercantile office or a jute mill, the magistrate in court, the officer in the district, the police sergeant or uniformed soldiers and sailors roaming the streets of Calcutta (invariably, it seems, in a state of drunkenness) were not objects of respect and emulation: they were objects of fear.

Consider the following episode from a skit written by Girishchandra Ghosh (1844–1912), the most eminent playwright and producer on the nineteenth-century Calcutta stage and a close disciple of Ramakrishna. This minor farce, *Bellik-bājār*, was first performed at the Star Theater on Christmas Eve of 1886, only a few months after Ramakrishna's death.[41]

The opening scene is set, not without reason, in the Death Registration office at the Nimtala cremation ground in Calcutta. We meet first a doctor and then a lawyer inquiring from a *murdāpharās* (whose business it is to burn dead bodies) about recent cremations. They are practitioners of the new arts of commercialization of death: the first works upon bodies in a state of sickness, prolonging the disease while holding death at bay; the second begins his work after death, entangling surviving relatives in an endless chain of litigation. The colonial city is where people come to make money out of death. The sole official representative here—the registration clerk (who, when we meet him, is, suitably enough, asleep)—has the job of putting into the official accounts the details of every death.

Enter Dokari, himself a recent and lowly entrant into the world of the Calcutta babus, learning to survive by his wits in a city of worldly opportunities. He tells the two gentlemen about the death of a wealthy trader whose only son, Lalit, would be an easy prey for all of them. The three strike a deal and proceed to lure the moneyed young man into the path of expensive living, dubious property deals, and lawsuits. In time, Dokari is predictably outmaneuvered by his more accomplished partners and, thrown out by his wealthy patron, finds himself back on the street. It is

Christmas Eve, and the lawyer and doctor have arranged a lavish party, at Lalit's expense, of course, where they are to deliver upon their unsuspecting victim the coup de grâce. Dokari, roaming the streets, suddenly comes upon three Englishmen and, instinctively, turns around and runs. (The italicized words in the following extracts are in English in the original.)

ENG 1: *Not so fast, not so fast . . .*

They catch hold of Dokari.

DOKARI: Please, saheb! *Poor man*! . . . *License have, thief not.*
ENG 1: *Hold the ankle, Dick. Darkee wants a swing . . .*

They lift him up and swing him in the air.

DOKARI: *My* bones *all another place*, my insides *up down*, *head making thus thus*. [Falls]

. . . .

ENG 2: *Grog-shop*?
DOKARI: Curse in English as much as you please. I don't understand it, so it doesn't touch me.
ENG 2: *A good ale house*?
DOKARI: Let me give it back to you in Bengali. My great-grandson is married to your sister, I'm married to your sister, I'm her bastard. . . .
ENG 3: *Wine shop* . . . sharab ghar . . .

Dokari now realizes what the Englishmen want and remembers the party in Lalit's gardenhouse.

DOKARI: *Yes, sir, your servant, sir. Wine shop here not. Master eat wine? Come garden, very near. . . . Brandy, whiskey, champagne, all, all, fowl, cutlet . . . free, free, come garden, come my back, back me, not beat, come* from my *back*.

The party is a travesty of "enlightened" sociability, with a couple of hired dancing girls posing as the liberated wives of our friends the lawyer and the doctor. A social reformer delivers an impassioned speech on the ignorance and irrationality of his countrymen. As he ends his speech with the words "*Oh! Poor India, where art thou, come to your own country*," Dokari enters with the three Englishmen. The sight of the white men causes immediate panic, the party breaks up in confusion, and the Englishmen settle down to a hearty meal.

A mortal fear of the Englishman and of the world over which he dominated was a constituent element in the consciousness of the Calcutta middle class—in its obsequious homages in pidgin English and foul-mouthed denunciations in Bengali no less than in the measured rhetoric of enlightened social reformers. But fear can also be the source of new strategies of survival and resistance.

WITHDRAWAL FROM KARMA

> MASTER (to Keshab and other Brahmo admirers): You people speak of doing good to the world. Is the world such a small thing? And who are you, pray, to do good to the world? First realize God, see Him by means of spiritual discipline. If He imparts power, then you can do good to others; otherwise not.
>
> A BRAHMO DEVOTEE: Then must we give up our activities [*karma*] until we realize God?
>
> MASTER: No. Why should you? You must engage in such activities as contemplation, singing His praises, and other daily devotions.
>
> BRAHMO: But what about our worldly duties—duties associated with our earning money, and so on?
>
> MASTER: Yes, you can perform them too, but only as much as you need for your livelihood. At the same time, you must pray to God in solitude with tears in your eyes, that you may be able to perform those duties in an unselfish manner. You should say to Him: "O God, make my worldly duties fewer and fewer; otherwise, O Lord, I find that I forget Thee when I am involved in too many activities. I may think I am doing unselfish work [*niṣkāma karma*], but it turns out to be selfish." . . . Sambhu Mallik once talked about establishing hospitals, dispensaries, and schools, making roads, digging public reservoirs, and so forth. I said to him: "Don't go out of your way to look for such works. Undertake only those works that present themselves to you and are of pressing necessity—and those also in a spirit of detachment." It is not good to become involved in too many activities. That makes one forget God. . . . Therefore I said to Sambhu, "Suppose God appears before you; then will you ask Him to build hospitals and dispensaries for you?" (*Laughter*) A lover of God never says that. He will rather say: "O Lord, give me a place at Thy Lotus Feet. Keep me always in Thy company. Give me sincere and pure love [*bhakti*] for Thee."
>
> Karmayoga is very hard indeed. In the Kaliyuga it is extremely difficult to perform the rites enjoined in the scriptures. . . . In the Kaliyuga the best way is bhaktiyoga, the path of devotion—singing the praises of the Lord, and prayer. The path of devotion is the religion [*dharma*] of this age. (*K*, pp. 41–42)[42]

This recurrent message runs through the *Kathāmṛta*. Worldly pursuits occupy a domain of selfish and particular interests. It is a domain of conflict, of domination and submission, of social norms, legal regulations, disciplinary rules enforced by the institutions of power. It is a domain of constant flux, ups and downs of fortune, a domain of greed and of humiliation. It is a domain that the worldly householder cannot do without, but it is one he has to enter because of the force of circumstances over which he has no control. But he can always escape into his own world of consciousness, where worldly pursuits are forgotten, where they have no essential existence. This is the inner world of devotion, a personal relation of *bhakti* (devotion) with the Supreme Being.

The strategy of survival in a world that is dominated by the rich and the powerful is withdrawal. Do not attempt to intervene in the world, do not engage in futile conflict, do not try to reform the world. Those who involve themselves in such activities do so not because they wish to change the world for the better but because they too pursue their particular interests—fame, popularity, power. This is a strong element operating in that part of the middle-class consciousness in which it is submissive, weak, afraid of its fate in the world.

WITHDRAWAL FROM JÑĀNA

Ramakrishna asks Narendranath (later Swami Vivekananda, 1863–1902) and Girish Ghosh to do *vicāra* (debate) in English. The debate starts, not quite in English, but in Bengali interspersed with English words. Narendra talks about the infinite form of God and the incapacity of thought to conceive of that form. Girish suggests that God might also appear in a finite, phenomenal, form. Narendra disagrees.

> Gradually Narendra and Girish become involved in a heated discussion. If God is Infinity, how can He have parts? What did Hamilton say? What were the views of Herbert Spencer, of Tyndall, of Huxley? And so forth and so on.
>
> MASTER (to M.): I don't enjoy these discussions. Why should I argue at all? I clearly see that God is everything; He Himself has become all. I see that whatever is, is God. He is everything; again, He is beyond everything. (*K*, pp. 160–61; *G*, p. 733)

Later, calling Narendra aside, Ramakrishna says,

> As long as a man argues about God, he has not realized Him. You two were arguing. I didn't like it. . . .
>
> The nearer you approach God, the less you reason and argue. When you attain Him, then all sounds—all reasoning and disputing—come to an end. (*K*, p. 163; *G*, p. 735)

Ramakrishna is heard repeating the argument several times in the *Kathāmṛta*. Learning is futile: it produces no true knowledge, only the pride of the learned. While acknowledging the pursuit of knowledge by the Vedantic scholar, he pronounces this an impossible project for the ordinary man in the present age. He is curious about the forms of logical argument in European philosophy and often inquires from his learned disciples about this (including staging the absurd theater of European-style *vicāra* mentioned above), but his impatience soon gets the better of his curiosity.

This attitude strikes a sympathetic chord in his disciples. They are convinced of the limits of science and rational knowledge, of their failure to grasp the truth in its eternal, unchanging essence. Trained in the new schools of colonialism—some, like Narendranath, are in fact highly proficient in several branches of modern European knowledge—they feel oppressed in the prisonhouse of Reason and clamor to escape into the vicāra-less freedom of bhakti.

Mahendranath closes the first volume of the *Kathāmṛta* with a long section on the disputations between Dr. Mahendralal Sarkar (1833–1904) and Ramakrishna's disciples. Dr. Sarkar, the most eminent practitioner in his time of Western medicine in Calcutta and founder of the first Indian institution for modern scientific research, was the only one of those close to Ramakrishna to openly voice his skepticism about Ramakrishna's preaching. (The italicized words in the following extract are in English in the original.)

> DOCTOR: Just because some fisherman [the reference is to Mathuranath Biswas, Ramakrishna's erstwhile patron, who came from a caste of fishermen] accepted all that you say, do you think I will accept you too? Yes, I respect you, I have *regard* for you, as I have *regard* for human beings. . . .
>
> MASTER: Have I asked you to accept?
>
> GIRISH: Has he asked you to accept?
>
> DOCTOR (to the Master): So, you say it's all God's will?
>
> MASTER: That is all that I say. . . .
>
> DOCTOR: If it is God's will, why do you talk so much? Why do you try to preach so much?
>
> MASTER: I talk because He makes me talk. I am the instrument, He is the player.
>
> DOCTOR: Then say you are only an instrument, or else keep quiet. Let God speak.
>
> GIRISH: Think what you will. He makes me do what I do. Can one take *a single step against the Almighty Will*?
>
> DOCTOR: He has given me *free will*. I can contemplate God if I so decide. I can also forget him if I feel like it. . . . I don't say it is completely *free*. It is like a cow tied to a leash. It is free as far as the rope will let it go.
>
> MASTER: Jadu Mallik gave me the same analogy. Is it an English analogy? . . .
>
> GIRISH: How do you know it is *free will*?

DOCTOR: Not by *reason. I feel it.*

GIRISH: *Then I and others feel it to be the reverse.*

. . . The Master and another devotee ask the doctor, "Will you listen to some songs?"

DOCTOR: But then you will start to jump about. You have to keep your bhāva under control. . . .

The doctor tells Mahendranath, "*It is dangerous to him.*" . . .

MASTER: . . . If someone eats the flesh of pigs and still retains bhakti for God, he is a worthy man, and if someone eats the purest food but remains attached to the world . . .

DOCTOR: He is unworthy! But let me say this. The Buddha used to eat pork. Pork causes colic pain, for which the Buddha took opium. Do you know what nirvāṇa is? Drugged by opium, drugged senseless—that's nirvāṇa. . . . (to Girish) Do what you wish, *but do not worship him* [Ramakrishna] *as God.* Why are you spoiling this good man?

GIRISH: What else can we do? He has helped us cross the oceans of worldly living and scepticism. . . .

NARENDRA (to the doctor): We regard him as god. . . . There is a zone between the *man-world* and the *god-world*, where it is difficult to say whether a person is man or god. . . .

DOCTOR: One has to control these feelings. It is not proper to express them in public. No one understands my feelings. *My best friends* think I am devoid of compassion. . . . My son, my wife, even they think I am *hard-hearted*, because my fault is that I don't express my feelings to anyone. . . . My *feelings* get *worked up* even more than yours do. *I shed tears in solitude.* . . .

NARENDRA: Think of this. You have *devoted* your *life* to the cause of *scientific discovery*. You risk your health. The knowledge of God is *the grandest of all sciences*. Why should he [Ramakrishna] not *risk* his *health* for it?

DOCTOR: All religious reformers—Jesus, Chaitanya, Buddha, Muhammad—each one in the end comes out as self-opinionated: "This I have said, this is the final truth!" What sort of attitude is that?

GIRISH: Sir, you are guilty of the same crime. When you say they are self-opinionated, you make the same error.

The DOCTOR stays silent.

NARENDRA: *We offer him worship bordering on divine worship.*

The MASTER laughs like a child. (*K*, pp. 193–205)[43]

Skeptical rationalism, which had strayed into the hostile territory of "feelings" and unquestioning devotion, has been tamed and conquered. Mahendranath can now close his book.

OF WOMAN AND GOLD

What is it that stands between the family man and his quest for God? It is a double impediment, fused into one. *Kāminī-kāñcan*, "woman and gold," "woman-gold": one stands for the other. Together they represent *māyā*, man's attachment to and greed for things particular and transient, the fickle pursuit of immediate worldly interest. Together they stand as figures of the bondage of man.

> MASTER: It is woman-and-gold that binds man [*jīva*] and robs him of his freedom. It is woman that creates the need for gold. For woman one man becomes the slave of another, and so loses his freedom. Then he cannot act as he likes. . . . You can see for yourself the condition in which you live, working for others. All these learned men who have learnt English, passed so many examinations, all they do now is serve their masters who kick them with their boots everyday. The one cause of all this is woman. You marry and settle down in the marketplace; now you cannot get out of the market. You suffer humiliation, the pain of bondage. (*K*, pp. 58–59; *G*, pp. 166–67)[44]

> MASTER: How can a man living in the midst of woman-and-gold realize God? It is very hard for him to lead an unattached life. First, he is the slave of his wife, second, of money, and third, of the master whom he serves. (*K*, p. 374; *G*, p. 710)

This woman who stands as a sign of man's bondage in the world is the woman of flesh and blood, woman in the immediacy of everyday life, with a fearsome sexuality that lures, ensnares, and imprisons the true self of man. It binds him to a pursuit of worldly interests that can only destroy him. The figure of this woman is typically that of the seductress.

> MASTER: Just see the bewitching power of women! I mean women who are the embodiment of *avidyā*, the power of delusion. They fool men. They reduce their men into stupid useless creatures. When I see a man and woman sitting together, I say to myself, "There, they are done for!" (*Looking at M.*) Haru, such a nice boy, is possessed by a witch [*petni*, *pretinī* = a female malignant spirit, presumed in popular demonology to live in trees]. People ask: "Where is Haru? Where is he?" But where do you expect him to be?
>
> They all go to the banyan and find him sitting quietly under it. He no longer has his beauty, power or joy. Ah! He is possessed by the witch that lives in the banyan!
>
> If a woman says to her husband, "Go there," he at once stands up, ready to go. If she says, "Sit down here," immediately he sits down.
>
> A job-seeker got tired of visiting the manager [head babu] in an office. He couldn't get the job. The manager said to him, "There is no vacancy now,

but come and see me now and then." This went on for a long time, and the candidate lost all hope. One day he told his tale of woe to a friend. The friend said, "How stupid you are! Why are you wearing away the soles of your feet going to that fellow? Go to Golap. You will get the job tomorrow." "Is that so?" said the candidate. "I am going right away." Golap was the manager's mistress. The candidate called on her and said: "Mother, I am in great distress. You must help me out. I am the son of a poor brahmin. Where else shall I go for help? Mother, I have been out of work for many days. My children are about to starve to death. I can get a job if you but say the word." Golap said to him, "Child, whom should I speak to?" And she said to herself, "Ah! this poor brahmin boy! He has been suffering so much." The candidate said to her, "I am sure to get the job if you just put in a word about it to the manager." Golap said, "I shall speak to him today and settle the matter." The very next morning a man called on the candidate and said, "You are to work in the manager's office, beginning today." The manager said to his English boss: "This man is very competent. I have appointed him. He will do credit to the firm."

All are deluded by woman-and-gold. (*K*, pp. 524–25; *G*, p. 748)

MASTER: Haripada has fallen into the clutches of a woman of the Ghoshpara sect. He can't get rid of her. He says that she takes him on her lap and feeds him. She claims that she looks on him as the Baby Krishna. I have warned him a great many times. She says that she thinks of him as a child. But this maternal affection soon degenerates into something dangerous.

You see, you should keep far away from woman; then you may realize God. It is extremely harmful to have anything to do with women who have bad motives, or to eat food from their hands. They rob a man of his true being [*sattā*] . . .

You must be extremely careful about women. *Gopāla bhāva*! Pay no attention to such things. The proverb says: "Woman devours the three worlds." Many women, when they see handsome and healthy young men, lay snares for them. That's *gopāla bhāva*! (*K*, pp. 334–35; *G*, p. 603)

The female body is here a representation of the prison of worldly interests, in which the family man is trapped and led to a daily existence of subordination, anxiety, pain, and humiliation, whose only culmination is decay and destruction. The female body hides with the allurements of māyā its true nature, which is nothing but dirt and filth.

MASTER: What is there in the body of a woman? Blood, flesh, fat, gut, worms, urine, shit, all this. Why do you feel attracted to a body like this? (*K*, p. 426, my translation; *G*, p. 113)

The only path for survival for the householder is to reduce one's attachments in the world, to sever oneself and withdraw from the ties of worldly interest, escape into the freedom of a personal relationship of devotion to an absolute power that stands above all temporal and transient powers.

> MASTER: The "I" that makes one a worldly person and attaches one to woman-and-gold is the "wicked I." There is a separation between *jīva* and *ātman* because this "I" stands in between. . . .
>
> Who is this "wicked I"? The "I" which says, "Don't you know who I am? I have so much money! Who is richer than me?" If a thief steals ten rupees, he first snatches the money back, then beats up the thief, then he calls the police and has the thief arrested, sent to prison. The "wicked I" says, "What? Steal ten rupees from me? What insolence!"
>
> . . . if the "I" must remain, let the rascal remain as the "servant I." As long as you live, you should say, "O God, you are the master and I am your servant." Let it stay that way. (*K*, p. 62; *G*, p. 170)

The "wicked I" that works, schemes, oppresses, does violence to others in order to gain a fragmented, transitory power in the world is an "I" that also subjects a part of itself. For every act of domination, there is a corresponding subjection, within the same consciousness. The "servant I," paradoxically, becomes the figure of the free householder, who stoically reduces his subjection in the world to an inessential part of his life.

> MASTER: . . . you must practise discrimination. Woman-and-gold is impermanent. God is the only eternal substance. What does a man get with money? Food, clothes, a dwelling-place—nothing more. It does not get you God. Therefore money can never be the goal of life. This is discrimination. Do you understand?
>
> M.: Yes. I have just read a Sanskrit play called *Probodhacandrodaya*. There it is called discrimination among things [*vastuvicāra*].
>
> MASTER: Yes, discrimination among things. Consider—what is there in money, or in a beautiful body? Discriminate and you will find that even the body of a beautiful woman consists of bones, flesh, fat, and other disagreeable things. Why should men set their minds on such things and forget God? (*K*, p. 19; *G*, p. 82)

The creation of this autonomous domain of freedom in consciousness impels the family man to an everyday routine of nonattached performance of worldly activities, guided by duty (*kartavya*) and compassion (*dayā*), not by the sensual pursuit of *kāma* (desire) or the interested pursuit of *artha* (wealth).

> TRAILOKYA: Where do they have the time? They have to serve the English.
>
> MASTER: Give God your power of attorney. If you place your trust in a good man, does he do you harm? Give Him the responsibility and stop worrying. Do what He has asked you to do. . . .

Of course you have duties. Bring up your children, support your wife, make arrangements for her maintenance in your absence. If you don't do all this, you have no compassion. . . . He who has no compassion is no man.

SUB-JUDGE: How long is one to look after one's children?

MASTER: Until they become self-sufficient. . . .

SUB-JUDGE: What is one's duty towards one's wife?

MASTER: Give her advice on dharma, support her while you are alive. If she is chaste, you will have to provide for her after your death. (*K*, p. 123; *G*, p. 628)

M.: Is it right to make efforts to earn more money?

MASTER: It is alright in a home where there is truth. Earn more money but by proper means. The aim is not to earn, the aim is to serve god. If money can be used to serve god, then there is nothing wrong in that money. (*K*, p. 427; *G*, p. 114)

MASTER: When one has true love for God [*rāgabhakti*], there are no ties of attachment with one's wife or child or kin. There is only compassion. The world becomes a foreign land, a land where one comes to work. Just as one's home is in the village, Calcutta is only a place where one works. (*K*, pp. 64–65; *G*, p. 173)

Absolute freedom in spirit while accepting bondage in a transient world: the strategy is explained through the analogy of the servant-woman.

MASTER: I tell people that there is nothing wrong in the life of the world. But they must live in the world as a maidservant lives in her master's house. Referring to her master's house, she says, "That is our house." But her real home is perhaps in a far-away village. Pointing out her master's house to others, she says, no doubt, "This is our house," but in her heart she knows very well that it doesn't belong to her and that her own home is in a far-away village. She brings up her master's son and says, "My Hari has grown very naughty," or "My Hari doesn't like sweets." Though she repeats "My Hari" with her lips, yet she knows in her heart that Hari doesn't belong to her, that he is her master's son.

So I say to those who visit me: "Live in the world by all means. There is no harm in that. But always keep your mind on God. Know for certain that this house, family and property are not yours. They are God's. Your real home is beside God." (*K*, pp. 104–5; *G*, pp. 456–57)

In fact, with an attitude of nonattachment, the family man can turn his home into a haven for his spiritual pursuits.

MASTER: When you have to fight a war, it is best to fight it from your own fort. You have to fight a war against your senses [*indriya*] and against hunger and thirst. It is best to do all this while remaining in the world. Again, in this age, life depends on food. Suppose you have no food. Then all your thoughts of God will go haywire. . . .

Why should you leave the world? In fact, there are advantages at home. You don't have to worry about food. Live with your wife—nothing wrong in that. Whatever you need for your physical comforts, you have them at home. If you are ill, you have people to look after you. (*K*, p. 122; *G*, p. 627)

But if others in the family deliberately create obstacles in the way of one's spiritual quest, those obstacles would have to be removed.

A DEVOTEE: Suppose someone's mother says to him, "Don't go to Dakshineswar." Suppose she curses him and says, "If you do, you will drink my blood." What then?

MASTER: A mother who says that is no mother. She is the embodiment of *avidyā*. It is not wrong to disobey such a mother. She obstructs the way to God. (*K*, p. 510; *G*, p. 722)

M.: What should one do if one's wife says: "You are neglecting me. I shall commit suicide." What does one do?

MASTER (*in a grave voice*): Give up such a wife. She is an obstacle in the path to God. Let her commit suicide or anything else she likes. A woman who puts obstacles in the way of God is a woman of *avidyā*.

M. moves to one side of the room and stands, leaning against the wall, deep in thought. NARENDRA and the other devotees remain speechless for a while. (*K*, p. 215; *G*, p. 126)

This, however, is extreme. For the most part, the life of a householder can be ordered by means of a suitable *aśramadharma*.

MASTER: The renunciation of woman-and-gold is meant for the sannyasi. . . . [It] is not meant for householders like you. . . . As for you, live with woman in an unattached way, as far as possible. From time to time, go away to a quiet place and think of God. Women must not be present there. If you acquire faith and devotion in God, you can remain unattached. After the birth of one or two children, husband and wife must live like brother and sister, and constantly think of God, so that their minds do not turn to sensual pleasure, so that they do not have any more children. (*K*, p. 177; *G*, p. 866)

For a domestic life of true nonattachment, the figure of woman as temptress, with a threatening sexuality, is turned into the safe, comforting figure of the mother, erased of sexuality.

MASTER: He who has found God does not look upon woman with lust; so he is not afraid of her. He looks at women as so many aspects of the Divine Mother. He worships all women as the Mother herself. (*K*, p. 59; *G*, p. 168)

MASTER: Man forgets God if he is entangled in the world of *māyā* through woman. It is the Mother of the Universe who has assumed the form of *māyā*, the form of woman. One who knows this rightly does not feel like leading the life of *māyā* in the world. But he who realizes that all women are manifestations of the Divine Mother may lead a spiritual life in the world. Without realizing God one cannot truly know what woman is. (*K*, p. 400; *G*, p. 965)

Indeed, this true knowledge of the essence of womanhood would transcend all the distinctions between women in the immediate world and bring out that which is universally true in them. It would enable man to relate to woman without either lust and attachment or fear and disgust.

MASTER: Do I feel disgust for them? No. I appeal to the Knowledge of Brahman. He has become everything; all is Narayana. All *yoni* is *yoni* of the Mother. Then I see no distinctions between a whore and a chaste woman. (*K*, p. 374; *G*, p. 710)

With this knowledge, the family man can live up to a new ideal of masculinity.

The Master is very anxious about Bhabanath who has just got married. Bhabanath is about twenty-three or twenty-four years old.

MASTER (*to Narendra*): Give him a lot of courage.

Narendra and Bhabanath look at the Master and smile. Sri Ramakrishna says to Bhabanath, "Be a hero. Don't forget yourself when you see her weeping behind her veil. Oh, women cry so much—even when they blow their noses! (*Narendra, Bhabanath and M. laugh.*)

"Keep your mind firm on God. He who is a hero lives with woman [*ramaṇī*] but does not engage in sexual relations [*ramaṇ*]." (*K*, p. 401; *G*, pp. 965–66)

There is, in fact, another figure whom Ramakrishna often invokes to describe this state beyond sexuality—the androgynous figure of the female-in-the-male—a transcendence of sexuality achieved by the mystical (or magical) transposition of the attributes of femininity in the male.

MASTER (*to the young man*): A man can change his nature by imitating another's character. By transposing on to yourself the attributes of woman, you gradually destroy lust and the other sensual drives. You begin to behave like women. I have noticed that men who play female parts in the theater speak like women or brush their teeth while bathing—exactly like women. (*K*, p. 623; *G*, p. 176)

MASTER: How can a man conquer the senses? He should assume the attitude of a woman. I spent many days as the handmaid of God. I dressed myself in women's clothes, put on ornaments. . . . Otherwise, how could I have kept my wife with me for eight months? Both of us behaved as if we were the handmaids of the Divine Mother.

I could not call myself "*pu*" [male]. One day I was in an ecstatic mood. My wife asked me, "Who am I to you?" I said, "The Blissful Mother." (*K*, p. 335; *G*, p. 603)

THE ASSERTION OF MASCULINITY

The figure of woman often acts as a sign in discursive formations, standing for concepts or entities that have little to do with women in actuality. Each signification of this kind also implies a corresponding sign in which the figure of man is made to stand for other concepts or entities, opposed to and contrasted with the first. However, signs can be operated upon—connected to, transposed with, differentiated from other signs in a semantic field where new meanings are produced.

The figure of woman as *kāminī* and the identification of this figure with *kāñcan* (gold) produced a combination that signified a social world of everyday transactions in which the family man was held in bondage. In terms of genealogy, the specific semantic content of this idea in Ramakrishna's sayings could well be traced to a very influential lineage in popular religious beliefs in Bengal, in which the female, in her essence of *prakṛti*, the principle of motion or change, is conceived of as unleashing the forces of *pravṛtti*, or desire, to bring about degeneration and death in the male, whose essence of *puruṣa* represents the principle of stasis or rest.[45] (One must, however, be careful, first, not to attribute to this any essentialist meaning characteristic of "Hindu tradition" or "Indian tradition" or even "popular tradition," for it is only one strand in precolonial religious and philosophical thought. Second, we must bear in mind that even this idea of the male and female principles operated within a rich semantic field and was capable of producing in religious doctrines and literary traditions a wide variety of specific meanings.)

But in the particular context of the *Kathāmṛta* in relation to middle-class culture, the figure of woman-and-gold could acquire the status of a much more specific sign: the sign of the economic and political subordination of the respectable male householder in colonial Calcutta. It connoted humiliation and fear, the constant troubles and anxieties of maintaining a life of respectability and dignity, the sense of intellectual confusion and spiritual crisis in which neither the traditional prescriptions of ritual practice nor the unconcretized principles of enlightened rationality could provide adequate guidance in regulating one's daily life in a situation that, after all, was unprecedented in "tradition." The sign, therefore, was loaded with negative meanings: greed, venality, deception, immorality, aggression, violence—the qualifications of success in the worlds both of commerce and of statecraft. The signification, in other words, could work toward a moral condemnation of the wealthy and the powerful. It would also produce a searing condemnation in nationalist mythography of the British imperialist—the unscrupulous trader turned ruthless conqueror.

The figure of woman-and-gold also signified the enemy within: that part of one's own self which was susceptible to the temptations of an ever-unreliable worldly success. From this signification stemmed a strategy of survival, of the stoical defense of the autonomy of the weak encountered in the "message" of Ramakrishna. It involved, as we have seen, an essentialization of the "inner" self of the man-in-the-world and an essentialization of womanhood in the protective and nurturing figure of the mother. This inner sanctum was to be valorized as a haven of mental peace, spiritual security, and emotional comfort: woman as mother, safe, comforting, indulgent, playful, and man as child, innocent, vulnerable, ever in need of care and protection.

But we are dealing here with a middle class whose "middleness" would never let its consciousness rest in stoical passivity. The "hypermasculinity" of imperialist ideology made the figure of the weak, irresolute, effeminate babu a special target of contempt and ridicule.[46] The colonized literati reacted with rage and indignation, inflicting upon itself a fierce assault of self-ridicule and self-irony. No one was more unsparing in this than Bankimchandra.[47]

> By the grace of the Almighty, an extraordinary species of animal has been found on earth in the nineteenth century: it is known as the modern Bengali. After careful investigation, zoologists have concluded that this species displays all the external features of *homo sapiens*. It has five fingers on its hands and feet; it has no tail, and its bones and cranial structure are identical with those of bimanous mammals. As yet, there is no comparable certainty about its inner nature. Some believe that in its inner nature too it resembles humans; others hold that it is only externally human, in its inner nature it is closer to beasts. . . .
>
> Which side do we support in this controversy? We believe in the theory which asserts the bestiality of Bengalis. We have learnt this theory from writers in English newspapers. According to some of these copper-bearded savants, just as the creator took grains of beauty from all of the world's beautiful women to create Tilottama, in exactly the same way, by taking grains of bestiality from all animals, he has created the extraordinary character of the modern Bengali. Slyness from the fox, sycophancy and supplication from the dog, cowardliness from sheep, imitativeness from the ape and volubility from the ass—by a combination of these qualities he has caused the modern Bengali to shine in the firmament of society, lighting up the

horizon, kindling the future hopes of India and attracting the particular affection of the sage Max Müller.[48]

And if this passage strikes one as being too indecisive in choosing between the babu and his European critics as its target of irony, then consider the following, purportedly a prediction by the sage Vaiśampāyana, the all-seeing reciter of the *Mahābhārata*:

> The word "babu" will have many meanings. Those who will rule India in the Kali age and be known as Englishmen will understand by the word a common clerk or superintendent of provisions; to the poor it will mean those wealthier than themselves, to servants the master. . . . Like Viṣṇu the babu will always lie on an eternal bed. Like Viṣṇu again, he will have ten incarnations: clerk, teacher, Brahmo, broker, doctor, lawyer, judge, landlord, newspaper editor and idler. Like Viṣṇu, in every incarnation, he will destroy fearful demons. In his incarnation as clerk, he will destroy his attendant, as teacher he will destroy the student, as station master the ticketless traveller, as Brahmo the poor priest, as broker the English merchant, as doctor his patient, as lawyer his client, as judge the litigant, as landlord his tenants, as editor the innocent gentleman, as idler the fish in the pond. . . . He who has one word in his mind, which becomes ten when he speaks, hundred when he writes and thousands when he quarrels is a babu. He whose strength is one-time in his hands, ten-times in his mouth, a hundred times behind the back and absent at the time of action is a babu. He whose deity is the Englishman, preceptor the Brahmo preacher, scriptures the newspapers and pilgrimage the National Theater is a babu. He who declares himself a Christian to missionaries, a Brahmo to Keshabchandra, a Hindu to his father and an atheist to the Brahman beggar is a babu. One who drinks water at home, alcohol at his friend's, receives abuse from the prostitute and kicks from his boss is a babu. He who hates oil when he bathes, his own fingers when he eats and his mother tongue when he speaks is indeed a babu. . . .
>
> O King, the people whose virtues I have recited to you will come to believe that by chewing *pān*, lying prone on the bed, making bilingual conversation and smoking tobacco, they will reconquer India. (*BR* 2:11–12)

The mode of self-ridicule became a major literary form of expressing the bhadralok's view of himself. And once the moral premises of the autocritique had been stated publicly—the valorization, that is to say, of courage, achievement, control, and just power as the essence of true manliness—the critique of babu effeminacy could be legitimately voiced even by the babu's indigenous "others," that is, by the women in their families and by both men and women of the lower classes. Fiction and drama in late nineteenth-century Bengal are replete with instances of women, from "respectable" families as well as from the urban poor, showing up the pretentiousness, cowardice, and effeminacy of the educated male.

We have then, simultaneously with the enchantment of the middle class with Ramakrishna's mystical play upon the theme of the feminization of the male, an invocation of physical strength as the true history of the nation, an exhortation to educated men to live up to their responsibilities as leaders of the nation, as courageous sons of a mother humiliated by a foreign intruder. Narendranath transformed into Swami Vivekananda is the most dramatic example of this switching of signs, converting Ramakrishna's message of inner devotion into a passionate plea for moral action in the world, turning the attitude of defensive stoicism into a call for vanguardist social and, by implication, political activism. Bankim too used the inherently polysemic possibilities of the construction of social entities as gendered categories by classicizing, in an entirely "modern" way, the ideal of masculinity as standing for the virtues of self-respect, justice, ethical conduct, responsibility, and enlightened leadership and of femininity as courage, sacrifice, inspiration, and source of strength.

Ramakrishna was hardly appreciative of these exhortations of hypermasculinity in the male or of the supposed activization of the masculine-in-the-female. The *Kathāmṛta* has a reference to a meeting between Ramakrishna and Bankim. Ramakrishna had asked Bankim what he thought were the true duties of human beings. Feigning a crass materialism, Bankim replied, "To eat, sleep and have sex." Ramakrishna was scandalized. He said, "What kind of talk is this? You are a real rogue! That's all you think of day and night, and that's what comes out of your mouth" (*K*, p. 191; *G*, p. 891). More interesting is a report on Mahendranath's reading passages from Bankim's novel *Debī Caudhurāṇī* to Ramakrishna.

> M. said: "A young girl—the heroine—fell into the hands of a robber named Bhabani Pathak. Her name had been Praphulla, but the robber changed it to Devi Choudhurani. At heart Bhabani was a good man. He made Praphulla go through many spiritual disciplines; he also taught her how to perform selfless action. He robbed wicked people and with that money fed the poor and helpless. He said to Praphulla, 'I put down the wicked and protect the virtuous.'"
>
> MASTER: But that is the duty of the king!

Mahendranath then read from the novel the section on Praphulla's education, on how she read grammar, poetry, Sāṅkhya, Vedānta, logic.

> MASTER: Do you know what this means? That you cannot have knowledge without learning. This writer and people like him think, "Learning first, God later. To find God you must first have knowledge of books!"

Ramakrishna was thoroughly unconvinced by the emerging middle-class ideal of the "new" woman who would fulfill her vocation as daughter, wife, or mother in respectable urban homes precisely by means of an education that had been denied to "traditional" women or to women of the lower classes.

> M. continued to read: "To provide for all, one has to organize a great deal of labour. One needs a little display, an imposing appearance, a graciousness of living. Therefore Bhabani said, 'A little shopkeeping is necessary.'"
>
> MASTER (*sharply*): Shopkeeping! One speaks as one thinks. Nothing but worldly thoughts, deceiving people—even their words become like that! If one eats radish, one belches radish. Instead of saying "shopkeeping," he could have said, "Act as subject while knowing one is not the subject." (*K*, pp. 362–66; *G*, pp. 683–86)

What is rational and realistic to Bankim becomes immoral worldliness to Ramakrishna; what is true devotion to Ramakrishna becomes hypocrisy to Bankim. Both attitudes were, however, parts of the same consciousness. They came to be reconciled in curious ways, most importantly by an ingenious and not always comfortable separation between, on one plane, the outer and the inner selves, and on another plane, the public and the private selves. The public self of the intelligentsia was its political self—rationalist, modern, expressing itself within the hegemonic discursive domain of enlightened nationalism. The private self was where it retreated from the humiliation of a failed hegemony. Dr. Mahendralal Sarkar was not untypical: the story of his encounter with Ramakrishna tells us a great deal about why, in the public postures of the Bengali intelligentsia to this day, its relationship to Ramakrishna has been both uneasy and shamefaced.

TO RETURN TO MEDIATION

There are three themes in this reading of the *Kathāmṛta* that I will pursue in the rest of this book. All of them have to do with nationalism as a project of mediation.

First is the appropriation of the popular. Mahendranath's favorite description of Ramakrishna is that of the child—laughing, innocent, mischievous, playful. This innocence is not quite pre-adult, but an innocence that has passed through the anxieties and misfortunes of adulthood to return to itself. It is an innocence that contains within itself a wisdom far richer and more resilient than the worldly cunning of worldly adults.

We know this to be the preferred form in which middle-class consciousness desires to appropriate the popular. The popular becomes the repository of natural truth, naturally self-sustaining and therefore timeless. It has to be approached not by the calculating analytic of rational reasoning but by "feelings of the heart," by lyrical compassion. The popular is also the timeless truth of the national culture, uncontaminated by colonial reason. In poetry, music, drama, painting, and now in film and the commercial arts of decorative design, this is the form in which a middle-class culture, constantly seeking to "nationalize" itself, finds nourishment in the popular.

The popular is also appropriated in a sanitized form, carefully erased of all marks of vulgarity, coarseness, localism, and sectarian identity. The very timelessness of its "structure" opens itself to normalization.

The popular enters hegemonic national discourse as a gendered category. In its immediate being, it is made to carry the negative marks of concrete sexualized femininity. Immediately, therefore, what is popular is unthinking, ignorant, superstitious, scheming, quarrelsome, and also potentially dangerous and uncontrollable. But with the mediation of enlightened leadership, its true essence is made to shine forth in its natural strength and beauty: its capacity for resolute endurance and sacrifice and its ability to protect and nourish.

The second theme is that of the classicization of tradition. A nation, or so at least the nationalist believes, must have a past. If nineteenth-century Englishmen could claim, with scant regard for the particularities of geography or anthropology, a cultural ancestry in classical Greece, there was no reason why nineteenth-century Bengalis could not claim one in the Vedic age. All that was necessary was a classicization of tradition. Orientalist scholarship had already done the groundwork for this. A classicization of modern Bengali high culture—its language, literature, aesthetics, religion, philosophy—preceded the birth of political nationalism and worked alongside it well into the present century.

A mode of classicization could comfortably incorporate as particulars the diverse identities in "Indian tradition," including such overtly anti-Brahmanical movements as Buddhism, Jainism, and the various deviant popular sects. A classicization of tradition was, in any case, a prior requirement for the vertical appropriation of sanitized popular traditions.

The real difficulty was with Islam in India, which could claim, within the same classicizing mode, an alternative classical tradition. The national past had been constructed by the early generation of the Bengali intelligentsia as a "Hindu" past, regardless of the fact that the appellation itself was of recent vintage and that the revivalism chose to define itself by a name given to it by "others." This history of the nation could accommodate Islam only as a foreign element, domesticated by shearing its own lineages of a classical past. Popular Islam could then be incorporated in the national culture in the doubly sanitized form of syncretism.

The middle-class culture we have spoken of here was, and still is, in its overwhelming cultural content, "Hindu." Its ability and willingness to extend its hegemonic boundaries to include what was distinctly Islamic became a matter of much contention in nineteenth- and twentieth-century Bengal, giving rise to alternative hegemonic efforts at both the classicization of the Islamic tradition and the appropriation of a sanitized popular Islam.

The third theme concerns the structure of the hegemonic domain of nationalism. Nationalism inserted itself into a new public sphere where it sought to overcome the subordination of the colonized middle class. In that sphere, nationalism insisted on eradicating all signs of colonial difference by which the colonized people had been marked as incorrigibly inferior and therefore undeserving of the status of self-governing citizens of a modern society. Thus, the legal-institutional forms of political authority that nationalists subscribed to were entirely in conformity with the principles of a modern regime of power and were often modeled on specific examples supplied by Western Europe and North America. In this public sphere created by the political processes of the colonial state, therefore, the nationalist criticism was not that colonial rule was imposing alien institutions of state on indigenous society but rather that it was restricting and even violating the true principles of modern government. Through the nineteenth century and into the twentieth, accompanied by the spread of the institutions of capitalist production and exchange, these legal and administrative institutions of the modern state penetrated deeper and deeper into colonial society and touched upon the lives of greater and greater sections of the people. In this aspect of the political domain, therefore, the project of nationalist hegemony was, and in its postcolonial phase, continues to be, to institute and ramify the characteristically modern forms of disciplinary power.

But there was another aspect of the new political domain in which this hegemonic project involved an entirely contrary movement. Here, unlike in Europe in the eighteenth and nineteenth centuries, the public sphere in the political domain, and its literary precursors in the debating societies and learned bodies, did not emerge out of the discursive construction of a social world peopled by "individuals." Nor was there an "audience-oriented subjectivity," by which the new conjugal family's intimate domain became publicly transparent and thus consistent with and amenable to the discursive controls of the public sphere in the political domain.[49] In Europe, even as the distinction was drawn between the spheres of the private and the public, of "man" and "bourgeois" and later of "man" and "citizen," the two spheres were nevertheless united within a single political domain and made entirely consistent with its universalist discourse. In colonial society, the political domain was under alien control and the colonized excluded from its decisive zones by a rule of colonial difference. Here for the colonized to allow the intimate domain of the family to become amenable to the discursive regulations of the political domain inevitably meant a surrender of autonomy. The nationalist response was to constitute a new sphere of the private in a domain marked by cultural difference: the domain of the "national" was defined as one that was different from the "Western." The new subjectivity that was constructed here was premised not on a conception of universal humanity, but rather on particularity and difference: the identity of the "national" community as against other communities.[50] In this aspect of the political domain, then, the hegemonic movement of nationalism was not to promote but rather, in a quite fundamental sense, to resist the sway of the modern institutions of disciplinary power.

The contradictory implications of these two movements in the hegemonic domain of nationalism have been active right through its career and continue to affect the course of postcolonial politics. The process could be described, in Gramscian terms, as "passive revolution" and contains, I think, a demonstration of both the relevance and the insurmountable limits of a Foucauldian notion of the modern regime of disciplinary power.[51] The search for a postcolonial modernity has been tied, from its very birth, with its struggle against modernity.

I will, in the rest of this book, follow these three themes, beginning with the theme of classicization and the imagining of the nation as endowed with a past.

CHAPTER FOUR

The Nation and Its Pasts

"WE MUST HAVE A HISTORY!"

In a series of lectures delivered in Calcutta in 1988, Ranajit Guha discussed the conditions and limits of the agenda developed in the second half of the nineteenth century for "an Indian historiography of India."[1] It was an agenda for self-representation, for setting out to claim for the nation a past that was not distorted by foreign interpreters. Reviewing the development of historiography in Bengal in the nineteenth century, Guha shows how the call sent out by Bankimchandra—"We have no history! We must have a history!"—implied in effect an exhortation to launch the struggle for power, because in this mode of recalling the past, the power to represent oneself is nothing other than political power itself.[2]

Of course, Bankim's observation that "Bengalis have no history" was, strictly speaking, incorrect. In 1880, when he began to write his essays on the history of Bengal,[3] there was a fair amount of historical writing in Bengali. Even Bankim refers, in the book review in which he first sets out his agenda, to "the books in the Bengali language which are being written everyday for the instruction of schoolboys. . . ." His objection was, of course, that these books did not contain the true history of Bengal. What he meant by true history was also clear: it was the memory of the glorious deeds of one's ancestors. "There are a few godforsaken jāti in this world who are unaware of the glorious deeds of their forefathers. The foremost among them is the Bengali." And to emphasize the depth of this shame, Bankim adds, "Even the Oriyas have their history." It is hardly necessary to remind ourselves of the pretensions to cultural superiority of the English-educated intelligentsia of Bengal to realize that for Bankim's readers this would have been a stinging condemnation.

His reason for this reproach was that there was no history of Bengal written by Bengalis themselves. "In our judgment, there is not a single English book which contains the true history of Bengal." Why? Because the English had based their histories of Bengal on the testimonies of foreign Muslim chroniclers; there was no Bengali testimony reflected in those histories. Consequently, Bengalis could not accept them as their own history. "Anyone who uncritically accepts as history the testimony of these lying, Hindu-hating Musalman zealots is not a Bengali."

It is, needless to say, a primary sign of the nationalist consciousness that it will not find its own voice in histories written by foreign rulers and that it will set out to write for itself the account of its own past. What is noteworthy in Bankim's nationalist call to history writing is, first, that whereas he identifies his subject nation sometimes as "Bengali" and at other times as "Indian" (*bhāratavarṣīya*), in both cases he names the foreign ruler and aggressor as the Muslim.[4] Second, the historical consciousness he is seeking to invoke is in no way an "indigenous" consciousness, because the preferred discursive form of his historiography is modern European. Third, in 1880, when Bankim was making his exhortation—"Bengal must have a history, or else there is no hope for it. Who will write it? You will write it, I will write it, all of us will write it. Every Bengali will have to write it"—the numerous books that were being written in Bengali on the history of Bengal and of India, although dismissed by Bankim as "adolescent literature," were actually informed by a historiographic practice that was in no way different from his own. When compared with many other, admittedly less talented, Bengali writers of history of his time, Bankim's views on history were not exceptional.[5]

Some of these writings are contained mainly in school textbooks.[6] None of these books was written by major historians, and none claimed any great originality in historical interpretation. But for that very reason, they are good indicators of the main features of a commonly shared discursive formation within which Indian nationalist historiography made its appearance.

But before I present this material from the middle and late nineteenth century, let me begin with a text from the very early years of the century that demonstrates how a radical transformation was effected in the forms of recounting the political events of the past.

A PURANIC HISTORY

The first three books of narrative prose in Bengali commissioned by the Fort William College in Calcutta for use by young Company officials learning the local vernacular were books of history. Of these, *Rājābali* (1808) by Mrityunjay Vidyalankar was a history of India—the first history of India in the Bengali language that we have in print.[7] Mrityunjay (ca. 1762–1819) taught Sanskrit at Fort William College and was the author of some of the first printed books in Bengali. When he decided to set down in writing the story of "the Rajas and Badshahs and Nawabs who have occupied the throne in Delhi and Bengal," he did not need to undertake any fresh "research" into the subject; he was only writing down an account that was in circulation at the time among the Brahman literati and their landowning patrons.[8] His book was, we might say, a good example of the historical memory of elite Bengali society as exemplified in contemporary scholarship.

The book starts with a precise reckoning of the time at which it is being written.

> In course of the circular motion of time, like the hands of a clock, passing through the thirty *kalpa* such as Pitṛkalpa etc., we are now situated in the Śvetavarāha kalpa. Each kalpa consists of fourteen *manu*; accordingly, we are now in the seventh manu of Śvetavarāha kalpa called Vaivasvata. Each manu consists of 284 *yuga*; we are now passing through the one hundred and twelfth yuga of Vaivasvata manu called Kaliyuga. This yuga consists of 432,000 years. Of these, up to the present year 1726 of the Śaka era, 4,905 years have passed; 427,095 years are left. (*R*, pp. 3–4)

The calendrical system is also precisely noted. For the first 3,044 years of Kaliyuga, the prevailing era (*śaka*) was that of King Yudhiṣṭhira. The next 135 years comprised the era of King Vikramāditya. These two eras are now past.

> Now we are passing through the era of the King called Śālivāhana who lived on the southern banks of the river Narmadā. This śaka will last for 18,000 years after the end of the Vikramāditya era. After this there will be a king called Vijayābhinandana who will rule in the region of the Citrakūṭa mountains. His śaka will last for 10,000 years after the end of the Śālivāhana era.
>
> After this there will be a king called Parināgārjuna whose era will last until 821 years are left in the Kaliyuga, at which time will be born in the family of Gautabrāhmaṇa in the Sambhala country an *avatāra* of Kalkideva. Accordingly, of the six eras named after six kings, two are past, one is present and three are in the future. (*R*, p. 8)

Whatever one might say of this system of chronology, lack of certitude is not one of its faults.

Mrityunjay is equally certain about identifying the geographical space where the historical events in his narrative take place.

> Of the five elements—space [*ākāśa*], air, fire, water and earth—the earth occupies eight *ānā* [half] while the other four occupy two *ānā* [one-eighth] each. . . . Half of the earth is taken up by the seas, north of which is Jambudvipa. . . . There are seven islands on earth of which ours is called Jambudvipa. Jambudvipa is divided into nine *varṣa* of which Bhāratavarṣa is one. Bhāratavarṣa in turn is divided into nine parts [*khaṇḍa*] which are called Aindra, Kaseru, Tāmraparṇa, Gavastimata, Nāga, Saumya, Vāruṇa, Gandharva and Kumārikā. Of these, the part in which the *varṇāśrama* [caste] system exists is the Kumārikākhaṇḍa.

The other parts [of Bhāratavarṣa] are inhabited by the *antyaja* people [those outside caste]. (*R*, pp. 4–6)

Thus *Rājābali* is the history of those who ruled over the earth, in which there are seven islands, of which the one called Jambudvipa has nine parts, of which Bhāratavarṣa is one, and so forth, and so on. Where does this history begin?

In the Satyayuga, the Supreme Lord [*parameśvara*] had planted in the form of an Aśvathva tree a king called Ikṣāku to rule over the earth. The two main branches of this tree became the Sūrya and the Candra *vaṃśa*. The kings born in these two lineages have ruled the earth in the four yuga. Of these, some were able to acquire the greatest powers of dharma and thus ruled over the entire earth consisting of the seven islands. Others had lesser powers and thus ruled over only Jambudvipa or only Bhāratavarṣa or, in some cases, only the Kumārikākhaṇḍa. If a king from one lineage became the emperor [*samrāṭa*], then the king of the other lineage would become the lord of a *maṇḍala*. The accounts of these kings are recorded in the branches of knowledge [*śāstra*] called the Purāṇa and the Itihāsa. (*R*, pp. 6–7)

A few things may be clarified at this point. In Mrityunjay's scheme of history, the rulers on earth are, as it were, appointed by divine will. They enjoy that position to the extent, and as long as, they acquire and retain the powers of dharma. By attaining the highest levels of dharma, one could even become the ruler of the entire earth. In order to distinguish this variety of history writing from that we are more familiar with today, Mrityunjay's narrative can be called a Puranic history. Mrityunjay would not have quarreled with this description, not because he was aware of the distinction, but because *purāṇetihāsa* was for him the valid form of retelling the political history of Bhāratavarṣa.

The discipline of Puranic history cannot be accused of being sloppy in its counting of dynasties and kings. "In the 4,267 years since the beginning of the Kaliyuga, there have been 119 Hindus of different jāti who have become *samrāṭ* on the throne of Delhi" (*R*, p. 10). The count begins with King Yudhiṣṭhira of the *Mahābhārata*, who heads a list of twenty-eight Kṣatriya kings who ruled for a total of 1,812 years. "After this the actual reign of the Kṣatriya jāti ended." Then came fourteen kings of the Nanda dynasty, starting with "one called Mahānanda born of a Kṣatriya father and a Śūdra mother," who ruled for a total of 500 years. "The Rājput jāti started with this Nanda."

After this came the Buddhist kings: "Fifteen kings of the Nāstika faith, from Vīravāhu to Āditya, all of the Gautama lineage, ruled for four hundred years. At this time the Nāstika views enjoyed such currency that the Vaidika religion was almost eradicated."

We then have a curious list of dynasties—nine rulers of the Mayūra dynasty, sixteen of the Yogi dynasty, four of the Bairāgi dynasty, and so on. Of course, there are "the Vikramādityas, father and son, who ruled for ninety-three years." We are also told of "thirteen kings, from Dhī Sena to Dāmodara Sena, of the Vaidya jāti of Bengal who ruled for 137 years and one month"—from, let us remember, "the throne in Delhi"! The rule of the "Chohān Rājput jāti" ends with

> Pṛthorāy who ruled for fourteen years and seven months. . . . This is as far as the empire [*sāmrājya*] of the Hindu kings lasted.
>
> After this began the *sāmrājya* of the Musalman. From the beginning of the empire of the Yavanas to the present year 1726 of the Śaka era, fifty-one kings have ruled for 651 years three months and twenty-eight days. (*R*, pp. 12–13)

What is interesting about this chronology is the way in which its dynastic sequence passes ever so smoothly from the kings of the *Mahābhārata* to the kings of Magadha and ends with the Mughal Emperor Shah Alam II, "of the lineage of Amir Taimur," occupying the throne in Delhi at the time of Mrityunjay's writing. Myth, history, and the contemporary—all become part of the same chronological sequence; one is not distinguished from another; the passage from one to another, consequently, is entirely unproblematical.[9] There is not even an inkling in Mrityunjay's prose of any of the knotty questions about the value of Puranic accounts in constructing a "proper" historical chronology of Indian dynasties, which would so exercise Indian historians a few decades later. Although Mrityunjay wrote at the behest of his colonial masters, his historiographic allegiances are entirely precolonial.

It would therefore be of some interest to us to discover how a Brahman scholar such as Mrityunjay describes the end of "the Hindu dynasties" and the accession to the throne at Delhi of "the Yavana emperors." Curiously, the story of the defeat of Prithviraj Chauhan at the hands of Shihabuddin Muhammad Ghuri takes the form of a Puranic tale.

Prithviraj's father had two wives, one of whom was a demoness (*rākṣasī*) who ate human flesh. She had also introduced her husband into this evil practice. One day the rākṣasī ate the son of the other queen who, taken by fright, ran away to her brother. There she gave birth to a son who was called Pṛthu. On growing up, Pṛthu met his father. At his request, Pṛthu cut off his father's head and fed the flesh to twenty-one women belonging to his jāti. Later, when Pṛthu became king, the sons of those twenty-one women became his feudatories (*sāmanta*). "Because Pṛthu had killed his father, the story of his infamy spread far and wide. Kings who paid tribute to him stopped doing so." In other words, Prithviraj was not a ruler who enjoyed much respect among his subjects.

It was at this time that Shihabuddin Ghuri threatened to attack Prithviraj.

> When the King heard of the threatening moves of the Yavanas, he called a number of scholars learned in the Vedas and said, "Oh learned men! Arrange a sacrifice which will dissipate the prowess and the threats of the Yavanas." The learned men said, "Oh King! There is such a sacrifice and we can perform it. And if the sacrificial block [*yūpa*] can be laid at the prescribed moment, then the Yavanas can never enter this land." The King was greatly reassured by these words and arranged for the sacrifice to be performed with much pomp. When the learned men declared that the time had come to lay the block, much efforts were made but no one could move the sacrificial block to its assigned place. Then the learned men said, "Oh King! What Īśvara desires, happens. Men cannot override his wishes, but can only act in accordance with them. So, desist in your efforts. It seems this throne will be attacked by the Yavanas."

Hearing these words, Prithviraj was greatly disheartened and "slackened his efforts at war." His armies were defeated by Shihabuddin, who arrived triumphantly at Delhi. Then Prithviraj

> emerged from his quarters and engaged Śāhābuddīn in a ferocious battle. But by the grace of Īśvara, the Yavana Śāhābuddīn made a prisoner of Pṛthurājā. On being reminded that Pṛthurājā was son-in-law of King Jayacandra [Jaichand, ruler of a neighboring kingdom, had already collaborated with Muhammad Ghuri], he did not execute him but sent him as a prisoner to his own country of Ghaznin. (*R*, pp. 109–10)

Let us remember that in Mrityunjay's scheme of history, dynasties are founded by the grace of the divine power, and kingdoms are retained only as long as the ruler is true to dharma. The Chauhan dynasty was guilty of such heinous offenses as cannibalism and patricide. That Prithviraj had lost divine favor was already revealed at the sacrificial ceremony. His defeat and the establishment of "Yavana rule" by Muhammad Ghuri were, therefore, acts of divine will.

Half a century later, when Puranic history would be abandoned in favor of rational historiography, this account of the battle of Thanesar would undergo a complete transformation. English-educated Brahman scholars would not accept with such equanimity the dictates of a divine will.

Mrityunjay has a few more things to say about the reasons for the downfall of the Chauhan dynasty. These remarks are prefaced by the following statement: "I will now write what the Yavanas say about the capture of the throne of Delhi by the Yavana Śāhābuddīn"

(*R*, pp. 112–13). Mrityunjay then goes back to the earlier raids into various Indian kingdoms by Nasruddin Sabuktagin, father of Mahmud Ghaznavi.

> When Nāsruddīn came to Hindustan, there was no harmony among the kings of Hindustan. Each thought of himself as the emperor [*bādśah*]; none owed fealty to anyone else and none was strong enough to subjugate the others. On discovering this, the Yavanas entered Hindustan. The main reason for the fall of kingdoms and the success of the enemy is mutual disunity and the tendency of each to regard itself as supreme. When Sekandar Shah [Alexander] had become emperor in the land of the Yavanas, he had once come to Hindustan, but seeing the religiosity and learning of the Brahmans, he had declared that a land whose kings had such advisers [*hākim*] could never be conquered by others. Saying this, he had returned to his country and had never come back to Hindustan. Now there were no more such Brahmans and, bereft of their advice, the kings of this country lost divine grace and were all defeated by the Yavanas. (*R*, pp. 121–22)

Mrityunjay's accounts of the Sultanate and the Mughal periods were very likely based on the Persian histories in circulation among the literati in late eighteenth-century Bengal. It is possible that some of these texts contained comments on the disunity among Indian kings and perhaps even the statement attributed to Alexander. But the argument that it was because of the failings of the Brahmans that the kings strayed from the path of dharma and thus lost the blessings of god was undoubtedly one formulated by Mrityunjay the Brahman scholar. It was the duty of the Brahmans to guide the king along the path of dharma. They had failed in that duty and had brought about the divine wrath which ended the rule of the Hindu kings and established the rule of the Yavanas. Later, as the role of divine intervention in history becomes less credible, this story of the fall acquires in the modern writings the form of a general decay of society and polity.

But this is anticipating. Note, for purposes of comparison, Mrityunjay's account of the destruction by Mahmud Ghaznavi of the temple at Somnath. The main details of the story are the same as those which would appear in later histories, for they all come from Persian sources such as the *Tārīkh-i-Firishta*. But Mrityunjay mentions one "fact" about the idol at Somnath that is never to be mentioned again. "There was a very large sacred idol called Somnath which was once in Mecca. Four thousand years after the time when the Yavanas say the human race was born, this idol was brought by a king of Hindustan from Mecca to its present place" (*R*, p. 129). Mrityunjay's source for this information is uncertain, but it is never to be mentioned again by any Bengali historian.

Two Mughal emperors are subjects of much controversy in nationalist historiography, and Mrityunjay has written about them both. On Akbar, Mrityunjay is effusive. "Since Śrī Vikramāditya, there has never been in Hindustan an emperor with merits equal to those of Akbar Shah" (*R*, p. 195). Apart from having a deep sense of righteousness and performing all his duties in protecting his subjects, Akbar also had, according to Mrityunjay, an additional merit:

> Because of his knowledge of many śāstra, his spiritual views were skeptical of the doctrines of Muhammad and were closer to those of the Hindus. The kings of Iran and Turan often complained about this. . . . He did not eat beef and forbid the slaughter of cows within his fort. To this day, cow-slaughter is prohibited in his fort. (*R*, pp. 191, 194)

On Aurangzeb, on the other hand, Mrityunjay has this to say:

> He became very active in spreading the Muhammadī faith. And he destroyed many great temples. Many ceremonies of the Hindus such as the worship of the sun and of Gaṇeśa had been performed in the fort of the Badshah since the time of Akbar; [Aurangzeb] discontinued these practices and issued new rules invented by himself.

He then adds:

> Although he destroyed many great temples, he was favored by the divine powers at Jvālāmukhī and Lachmanbālā and made sizable grants of land for the maintenance of those temples. He later lived at Aurangabad for twelve years and, on being cursed by a Brahman, died uttering horrible cries of pain. (*R*, p. 221)

Where kings acquire kingdoms and hold power by divine grace, the business of arriving at a verdict on the character of rulers has to be negotiated between kings and gods. The only role that the ordinary *prajā* (subject) has in all this is in bearing the consequences of the actions of these superior entities. Of course, the prajā knows the difference between a good king and a bad one, which is why he praises a ruler such as Akbar. And when Aurangzeb dies "uttering horrible cries of pain," perhaps the prajā shudders a little at the ferocity of divine retribution, but is reassured in the end by the victory of dharma. In all this, however, the prajā never implicates himself in the business of ruling; he never puts himself in the place of the ruler. In recalling the history of kingdoms, he does not look for a history of himself.

If it was ever suggested to Mrityunjay that in the story of the deeds and fortunes of the kings of Delhi might lie the history of a nation, it is doubtful that he would have understood. His own position in relation to his narrative is fixed—it is the position of the prajā, the ordinary subject, who is most often only the sufferer and sometimes the beneficiary of acts of government. It is from that position that he tells the story of Prithviraj's misdeeds or of Akbar's righteousness. But the thought would never have occurred to him that because of the associations of "nationality," he, Mrityunjay Vidyalankar, a Brahman scholar in the employment of the East India Company in Calcutta in the early nineteenth century, might in some way become responsible for the acts of Prithviraj or Akbar. *Rājābali* is not a national history because its protagonists are gods and kings, not peoples. The bonds of "nation-ness" have not yet been imagined that would justify the identification of the historian with the consciousness of a solidarity that is supposed to act itself out in history.

THE PRESENT AS PURANIC HISTORY

It is in his telling of the recent history of Bengal that Mrityunjay's position becomes the clearest. Mrityunjay was born only a few years after the battle of Plassey. The history of those times must have been fresh in popular memory in the years of his boyhood and youth. His condemnation of the misrule of Siraj-ud-daulah is severe: "The violations of dharma multiplied when [the Nawab] abducted the wives, daughters-in-law and daughters of prominent people, or amused himself by cutting open the stomachs of pregnant women or by overturning boats full of passengers" (*R*, pp. 268–69).

When Siraj "attempted to destroy the clan" of Raja Rajballabh, the Raja sought the protection of the English in Calcutta. The English refused to hand him over to the nawab. "Then Nawab Siraj-ud-daulah sowed the seeds of his own destruction by plundering the *kuṭhi* of the Company Bahadur and the town of Calcutta" (*R*, p. 270). The English were forced temporarily to leave Calcutta. After some time,

> [the sahibs] returned to Calcutta and, accepting without a question the estimates of damages suffered in the raid by traders, shopkeepers and residents, compensated all of them. Then, after consulting through Khwaja Petrus the Armenian with leading men such as Maharaj Durlabhram, Bakshi Jafarali Khan, Jagat Seth Mahatabray and his brother Maharaj Swarupchandra, and collecting money and some soldiers, [the English], intending to defend their protégé and holding aloft the flag of dharma, marched to battle at Palasi. (*R*, p. 271)

What happened in the battle is common knowledge. Siraj tried to flee, but was captured.

> Then Miran Sahib, son of Jafarali Khan, without informing Maharaj Durlabhram or anyone else and ignoring the pleas of mercy from a terrified

> Siraj-ud-daulah, carved up the body of the Nawab with his own hands, and putting the dismembered body on top of an elephant, displayed it around the town. Thus, by the will of god, was demonstrated the consequences of such misdeeds as . . . the treacherous murder of Nawab Sarfraz Khan and the secret executions of Alibhaskar and other Maharashtrian sardars and the raping of women by Siraj-ud-daulah. (*R*, p. 276)

Thus, Miran acted in accordance with the divine will and Siraj faced the consequences of his misdeeds. But what happened to Miran in the end? "Thereafter, Nawab Miran was once coming from Azimabad to Murshidabad when at Rajmahal, as a consequence of his having betrayed Nawab Siraj-ud-daulah, he was struck by lightning. Even after his death, lightning struck twice on Nawab Miran's grave." And Mir Jafar? "Nawab Jafarali Khan, on resuming his *subahdari* for two years, died of leprosy after much suffering" (*R*, pp. 281, 289).

It is the force of divine will that acts in history, and in the end it is dharma that is vindicated. This belief frames Mrityunjay's description of the most recent events in the history of Bengal. At the conclusion of his story, he locates himself unhesitatingly as someone seeking the protection of the Company—the same Company that, flying the flag of dharma, had gone to battle with the promise to defend those under its protection.

> When, because of the evil deeds of certain emperors and kings and nawabs, from Viśārad of the Nanda dynasty to Shah Alam and from Nawab Munaim Khan to Nawab Kasemali Khan, this land of Hindustan was facing utter destruction, the Supreme Lord willed that the rule of the Company Bahadur be established. Thus ends this book called Rājataraṅga composed in the Gauḍīya language by Śrī Mṛtyuñjay Śarmā, pandit in the school established by the *baḍa sāheb* [governor-general] who is like the flower and the fruit of the tree which is the Company Bahadur. (*R*, pp. 294–95)

Let us remember, the Company rules by divine will in order to protect its subjects. It remains a constant implication that if that object is not fulfilled and if the subjects are oppressed, then, by divine intervention, the kingdom would pass to someone else and the truth of dharma would be vindicated once again.

MORE MYTHIC HISTORY

This was the form of historical memory before the modern European modes were implanted in the mind of the educated Bengali. In Mrityunjay, the specific form of this memory was one that was prevalent among the Brahman literati in eighteenth-century Bengal. What, then, was the form followed by Bengali Muslim writers? The court chronicles of the Afghan or the Mughal nobility are not of concern here because these were never written in Bengali. The examples of dynastic history written by Bengali Muslim writers show that notions of divine intervention, punishment for misdeeds, and the victory of righteousness are as prominent in them as they were in Mrityunjay. The following text is from 1875, a much later date than those of the Fort William College histories. But it is so prominently marked by the features of the *puthi* literature of the village poets of eastern Bengal and so completely devoid of the influence of modern historical education that we should have no difficulty in assuming that this poet from Barisal was in fact following a form that had been conventional for some time.[10] The dynastic history begins thus:

> How the name of Delhi became Hindustan
> Can be learnt from its kings, from beginning to end.

However, Hindu writers cannot tell the full story.

> The Hindus believe in the four yuga;
> They cannot grasp the full significance.
> Satya, Tretā, Dvāpar and Kali: these are the four yuga
> In which the Hindus ruled with pleasure.

That, presumably, is the story that Hindu writers are best qualified to tell. This poet then gives his list of fifty-nine Muslim kings of Delhi ending with "Shah Alam Bahadur," the last Mughal emperor. It is only a list, composed in verse, with no descriptions of events and no comments on the rulers. Then comes a miraculous event.

> Suddenly by a miracle [*daiva*], the English came to this land
> And defeated the Nawab in battle.
> The English occupied most of the kingdom:
> Since then there is the rule of Maharani Victoria.
> Putting to death Kumar Singh, the Company
> Abolished all *ijārā* and made the land *khās* of the Maharani.

It is curious that the only event of the Revolt of 1857 that is mentioned is the suppression of Kunwar Singh's rebellion. Then there is a panegyric to Queen Victoria and a list of the marvels of modern technology.

> The people are governed with full justice.
> In her reign, the prajā have no complaints.
> Cowries have been abolished; now
> People buy what they need with coins.
> People exchange news through the mail.
> The towns are now lit with gaslights.

The steamer has vanquished the pinnace and the sailboat.
The railway has reduced a week's journey to hours.
In Calcutta they can find out what's happening in England
In a matter of moments—with the help of the wire.
If in court an injustice is done,
Then it is corrected in another court.

But even such a well-ruled kingdom as the Maharani's cannot last forever.

The prajā is fortunate that the Maharani rules now.
What happens after this, I do not know.

In particular, if the British occupy Turkey, then all hell will break loose.

If the Queen comes to rule over Rūm [Turkey],
Then only Mecca and Medina will be left.
There will be despair and anarchy in the land,
And all will lose *jāt* and become one *jāt*.

And then, after a series of cataclysmic events, the day of judgment will arrive.

The Prophet Isā [Jesus] will come down from the sky,
And again the Musalmani faith will appear.
From the east to the west, and from north to south,
The world will be shattered by a terrible storm.
This is how it has been written in the Ayat Kudria
And explained clearly in the Hadis.
When the sun rises in the west,
All the doors of *tauba* will be closed thereafter.
The sun will rise only a few cubits
And will set soon after, and the night will be long.
Each night will stretch for six or seven nights,
And the people will rise only to sleep again. . . .
From the year 1300 Hijri,
And before 1400 is past, let it be known,
Those who are still alive
Will see many unnatural things in this world.

We might compare this with Mrityunjay's prediction: "After this there will be a king called Parināgārjuna whose era will last until 821 years are left in the Kaliyuga, at which time there will be born in the family of Gautabrāhmaṇa in the Sambhala country an *avatāra* of Kalkideva" (*R*, p. 8). There does not seem to be much difference in the mode of historical thinking.

HISTORY AS THE PLAY OF POWER

This framework changed radically as the Bengali literati was schooled in the new colonial education. Now Indians were taught the principles of European history, statecraft, and social philosophy. They were also taught the history of India as it came to be written from the standpoint of modern European scholarship. The Orientalists had, from the last years of the eighteenth century, begun to "recover" and reconstruct for modern historical consciousness the materials for an understanding of Indian history and society. The English-educated class in Bengal, from its birth in the early decades of the nineteenth century, became deeply interested in this new discipline of Indology.

But, curiously enough, the new Indian literati, while it enthusiastically embraced the modern rational principles of European historiography, did not accept the history of India as it was written by British historians. The political loyalty of the early generation of English-educated Bengalis toward the East India Company was unquestioned, and in 1857, when most of northern India was in revolt, they were especially demonstrative in their protestations of loyalty. And yet, by the next decade, they were engaged in open contestation with the colonialist interpretation of Indian history. By the 1870s, the principal elements were already in place for the writing of a nationalist history of India. It is interesting to trace the genealogy of this new history of "the nation."

In 1857–58, with the inauguration of the University of Calcutta, a set of translations was produced in Bengali, for use in schools, of histories of India and of Bengal written by British historians. By then, fifty years had passed after the publication of *Rājābali*, written in Bengali for the instruction of English officers in the history of India. The new translations were meant for the instruction of Bengali students in the history of their country as written by the colonizer.

One volume of J. C. Marshman's *History of Bengal* was translated by Iswarchandra Vidyasagar (1820–91).[11] The other volume was translated at Vidyasagar's request by Ramgati Nyayaratna (1831–94).[12] The latter contains sentences like "Sultan Suja arrived as the *gabharṇar* of Bengal" or "Murshid sent his son-in-law to Orissa as his *ḍepuṭi*," betraying in its use of administrative terminology its source in an English history of Bengal. And at the point where the book ends with the Maratha raids on Bengal in the period of Alivardi Khan, Ramgati feels it necessary to indicate the miraculous transformation that was about to take place.

> At that time the influence of the Marathas was so strong that everyone thought they would become the rulers of the country. But how ineffable is

the greatness of the divine will! Those who had come to this country only as ordinary traders, those who were often on the verge of leaving this country for ever, those who had never even dreamed of becoming rulers of this country—they, the English, ousted Siraj-ud-daulah from the throne of Alivardi and have now become the virtual sovereign of all of India.[13]

Only ten years later, however, in 1869, a book of questions and answers based on the same English textbooks had the following entry:

Q: How did Clive win?
A: If the treacherous Mir Jafar had not tricked the Nawab [Siraj-ud-daulah], Clive could not have won so easily.

Or, the following question about the ethics of English officials:

Q: Was Nandakumar's execution carried out in accordance with justice?
A: His offenses did not in any way deserve the death sentence. It was at the request of the unscrupulous Hastings that Chief Justice Elijah Impey conducted this gross misdeed.[14]

A Bengali textbook of 1872 tells the story of the betrayal of Nawab Siraj-ud-daulah in much greater detail. Siraj, says Kshetranath Bandyopadhyay, was a tyrant, but, contrary to the canard spread by the English, he was not responsible for the "black hole of Calcutta." Yet it was against him that the English conspired. Siraj was suspicious of the loyalties of his general Mir Jafar and made him swear on the Koran. But Mir Jafar betrayed him at Plassey, although his other generals fought valiantly. "If this battle had continued for some time, then Clive would surely have lost. But fortune favored the English, and weakened by the betrayal of Mir Jafar, the Nawab was defeated and Clive was victorious." Kshetranath's hatred is directed particularly against Mir Jafar and Miran. "Mir Jafar was cruel, stupid, greedy and indolent. On becoming the Nawab, he sought to plunder the wealth of prominent Hindus." "Miran was stupid and cruel, a beast among men. He was such an evil character that his oppressions made people forget all the misdeeds of Siraj."[15]

Nawab Mir Kasim too was a victim of betrayal:

[Mir Kasim] scrapped the duties on all goods. Thus all traders, English or Bengali, were treated on an equal footing, and unlike before, when all except the English were discriminated against, now others began to prosper. This angered the English. They began to prepare for war. . . . Mir Kasim's army was undoubtedly the best in Bengal, and yet it never won a single battle. There was a hidden reason for this, which was the treachery of Gargin [Mir Kasim's Armenian general].[16]

Kshetranath also describes the condition of the emperor in Delhi:

> The emperor at this time was in a pitiable condition. Even his capital was under the control of others. He had no throne to sit on. The table at which the English dined became his throne, from which the emperor of all of India offered to the English the *diwani* of three provinces and thirty million subjects. The Emperor of Delhi, whose pomp was once without limit and at whose power the whole of India trembled, was now reduced to a condition that was truly sad.[17]

Not only in gaining an empire, but even in administering one, the English resorted to conspiracy and force. In the period before and after Clive, says Kshetranath, "the English committed such atrocities on the people of this country that all Bengalis hated the name of the English." Because of his intrigues, Hastings "is despised by all and is condemned in history." In 1857, just as the soldiers committed atrocities, so did the English: "At the time of the suppression of the revolt, the English who are so proud of their Christian religion wreaked vengeance upon their enemies by cutting out the livers from the bodies of hanged rebels and throwing them into the fire." Even the end of the mutiny did not bring peace.

> In no age do the poor and the weak have anyone to protect them. When the disorder died down at other places, a huge commotion began in Bengal. In the areas of Bengal where indigo is grown, the English planters became truculent. The cruelties they perpetrated on the poor tenants will prevent them for all time from being counted among human beings.[18]

It was in fact in the course of writing the history of British rule in India that English-educated Bengalis abandoned the criteria of divine intervention, religious value, and the norms of right conduct in judging the rise and fall of kingdoms. The recent history of Bengal demonstrated that kingdoms could be won and, what was more, held by resorting to the grossest acts of immorality. The modern historiography seemed to validate a view of political history as simply the amoral pursuit of *raison d'état*.

The popular textbook of Krishnachandra Ray portrayed the political success of the British in India as the result of a cynical pursuit of power devoid of all moral principles. On Clive's intrigues, he said, "Most people criticize Clive for these heinous acts, but according to him there is nothing wrong in committing villainy when dealing with villains." The new revenue arrangements of 1772 are described as follows:

> "The land belongs to him who has force on his side." It is from this time that the Company stopped being a revenue collector and really became the ruler. If the Emperor [in Delhi] had been strong, there would have been a huge incident over this. But there was nothing left [to the Empire]. Whatever Hastings decided, happened.

The deep hatred we saw in Mrityunjay of Siraj's misrule has disappeared completely in Krishnachandra. In its place, there is a political explanation of his actions. For instance, when the English strengthened their fortifications in Calcutta, Siraj ordered the new constructions demolished. "Which ruler can allow foreigners to build forts within his territory? . . . [Siraj] could not accept any longer that this bunch of traders should suddenly arrive in his kingdom and defy his commands. Humiliated, his anger was now boiling over." Or his role in the so-called black hole incident is explained as follows:

> It must have been an inauspicious moment when Siraj-ud-daulah entered Calcutta. He knew nothing of the black hole deaths and did not order the imprisonment of the English captives. Yet, that became the source of his downfall. Intoxicated by power, he had stepped on a tiger thinking it was only a cat. In the end, it was this error of judgment which led to the loss of his kingdom, his death and the endless misery of his family. Indeed, it was the black hole deaths which created the opportunity for the rise of the English power in India.

The downfall of Siraj is not seen any more as the consequence of immoral acts. It is now the result of an error of judgment: mistaking a tiger for a cat.[19]

History was no longer the play of divine will or the fight of right against wrong; it had become merely the struggle for power. The advent of British rule was no longer a blessing of Providence. English-educated Bengalis were now speculating on the political conditions that might have made the British success impossible.

> If this country had been under the dominion of one powerful ruler, or if the different rulers had been united and friendly towards one another, then the English would never have become so powerful here and this country would have remained under the Musalman kings. Perhaps no one in this country would have ever heard of the English.

The book ends with a list of the benefits of British rule. And yet it is clearly implied that this does not establish its claims to legitimacy: "In any case, whatever be the means by which the English have come to acquire this sprawling kingdom, it must be admitted that infinite benefits have been effected by them to this country."[20] We have almost reached the threshold of nationalist history.

Kshirodchandra Raychaudhuri's book, published in 1876, had this announcement by its author in the preface: "I have written this book for those who have been misled by translations of histories written in English." The extent to which European historiography had made inroadsd into the consciousness of the Bengali literati can be judged from the following comment on relations between the European colonial powers:

> The English and the French have always been hostile towards each other. Just as the conflict between the Mughals and the Pathans is proverbial in India, so is the hostility between the English and the French in Europe. Thus it was beyond belief that in India they would not attack each other and instead drink from the same water.

The book ends with the following sentences:

> Having come to India as a mere trader, the East India Company became through the tide of events the overlord of two hundred million subjects, and the shareholders of the Company, having become millionaires and billionaires, began to institute the laws and customs of foreign peoples. In no other country of the world has such an unnatural event taken place.[21]

ELEMENTS OF A NATIONALIST HISTORY

Earlier I spoke of Mrityunjay's position with respect to the political events he was describing as that of an ordinary subject. The same could be said of the authors of the textbooks I have just mentioned. But these "subjects" were very different entities. In the seventy years that had passed, the creature known as the educated Bengali had been transmuted. Now he had grown used to referring to himself, like the educated European, as a member of "the middle class." Not only was he in the middle in terms of income, but he had also assumed, in the sphere of social authority, the role of a mediator. On the one hand, he was claiming that those who had wealth and property were unfit to wield the power they had traditionally enjoyed. On the other hand, he was taking upon himself the responsibility of speaking on behalf of those who were poor and oppressed. To be in the middle now meant to oppose the rulers and to lead the subjects. Our textbook historians, while they may have thought of themselves as ordinary subjects, had acquired a consciousness in which they were already exercising the arts of politics and statecraft.

Simultaneously, the modern European principles of social and political organization were now deeply implanted in their minds. The English-educated middle class of Bengal was by the 1870s unanimous in its belief that the old institutions and practices of society needed to be fundamentally changed. It is useful to remind ourselves of this fact, because we often tend to forget that those who are called "conservative" or "traditionalist" and who are associated with the movements of Hindu revivalism were also vigorous advocates of the reform and modernization of

Hindu society. Whatever the differences between "progressives" and "conservatives" among the new intellectuals in the nineteenth century, they were all convinced that the old society had to be reformed in order to make it adequate for coping with the modern world.

This becomes clear from reading the most commonplace writings of minor writers in the second half of the nineteenth century. A completely new criterion of political judgment employed in these writings is, for instance, the notion of "impartiality." An 1866 text by an author who is undoubtedly a "traditionalist Hindu" recommends in a chapter titled "The Treatment of Young Women" that "whether indoors or out, no young woman should at any time be left alone and unwatched." Yet, he is opposed to polygamy and the practice of dowry. In another chapter, "The Subject of Political Loyalty," this traditionalist, Tarakrishna Haldar, writes:

> In the days when this country was under the rule of the Hindu jāti, the arbitrariness of kings led to the complete domination by a particular jāti over all the others. That jāti wielded the power to send others to heaven or hell. . . . When the kingdom was in the hands of the Yavanas, they treated all Hindus as infidels. In all respects they favored subjects belonging to their own jāti and oppressed those who were Hindu. . . . The principles of government followed by the British jāti do not have any of these defects. When administering justice, they treat a priest of their own jāti as equal to someone of the lowest occupation in this country, such as a sweeper. . . . No praise is too great for the quality of impartiality of this jāti.[22]

One step further and we get the next argument in nationalist history: the reason Hindu society was corrupt and decadent was the long period of Muslim rule. The following is an extract from a lecture by a certain Bholanath Chakravarti at an Adi Brahmo Samaj meeting in 1876:

> The misfortunes and decline of this country began on the day the Yavana flag entered the territory of Bengal. The cruelty of Yavana rule turned this land to waste. Just as a storm wreaks destruction and disorder to a garden, so did the unscrupulous and tyrannical Yavana jāti destroy the happiness and good fortune of Bengal, this land of our birth. Ravaged by endless waves of oppression, the people of Bengal became disabled and timid. Their religion took distorted forms. The education of women was completely stopped. In order to protect women from the attacks of Yavanas, they were locked up inside their homes. The country was reduced to such a state that the wealth of the prosperous, the honor of the genteel and the chastity of the virtuous were in grave peril.[23]

Half of nationalist history has been already thought out here. In the beginning, the history of the nation was glorious; in wealth, power, learning, and religion, it had reached the pinnacle of civilization. This nation was sometimes called Bengali, sometimes Hindu, sometimes Arya, sometimes Indian, but the form of the history remained the same. After this came the age of decline. The cause of the decline was Muslim rule, that is to say, the subjection of the nation. We do not get the rest of nationalist history in this lecture I have just cited, because although Bholanath Chakravarti talks about the need for the regeneration of national society, he also thinks that its possibility lies entirely in the existence of British rule.

> There are limits to everything. When the oppressions of the Musalman became intolerable, the Lord of the Universe provided a means of escape. . . . The resumption of good fortune was initiated on the day the British flag was first planted on this land. Tell me, if Yavana rule had continued, what would the condition of this country have been today? It must be loudly declared that it is to bless us that īśvara has brought the English to this country. British rule has ended the atrocities of the Yavanas. . . . There can be no comparison between Yavana rule and British rule: the difference seems greater than that between darkness and light or between misery and bliss.[24]

However, even if Bholanath Chakravarti did not subscribe to it, the remainder of the argument of nationalist history was already fairly current. Take, for example, the eighteenth edition, published in 1878, of "The History of India," by Tarinicharan Chattopadhyay.[25] Tarinicharan (1833–97) was a product of colonial education, a professor at Sanskrit College, and a social reformer. His textbooks on history and geography were extremely popular and were the basis for many other lesser-known textbooks. His *History of India* was probably the most influential textbook read in Bengali schools in the second half of the nineteenth century.

In the next chapter, I will recount some of the stories from Tarinicharan's history in order to point out how the materials of Hindu-extremist political rhetoric current in postcolonial India were fashioned from the very birth of nationalist historiography.

CHAPTER FIVE

Histories and Nations

THE CONSTRUCTION OF A CLASSICAL PAST

The first sentence of *Bhāratbarṣer itihās* is striking: "India [*bhāratavarṣa*] has been ruled in turn by Hindus, Muslims and Christians. Accordingly, the history of this country [*deś*] is divided into the periods of Hindu, Muslim and Christian rule [*rājatva*]" (*BI*, p. 1).

This sentence marks the passage from the "history of kings" to the "history of this country." Never again will *Rājābali* be written; from now on, everything will be the "history of this *deś*." This history, now, is periodized according to the distinctive character of rule, and this character, in turn, is determined by the religion of the rulers. The identification here of country (deś) and realm (rājatva) is permanent and indivisible. This means that although there may be at times several kingdoms and kings, there is in truth always only one realm which is coextensive with the country and which is symbolized by the capital or the throne. The rājatva, in other words, constitutes the generic sovereignty of the country, whereas the capital or the throne represents the center of sovereign statehood. Since the country is *bhāratavarṣa*, there can be only one true sovereignty that is coextensive with it, represented by a single capital or throne as its center. Otherwise, why should the defeat of Prithviraj and the capture of Delhi by Muhammad Ghuri signal the end of a whole period of Indian history and the beginning of a new one? Or why should the battle of Plassey mark the end of Muslim rule and the beginning of Christian rule? The identification in European historiography between the notions of country or people, sovereignty, and statehood is now lodged firmly in the mind of the English-educated Bengali.

On the next page follows another example of the modernity of this historiographic practice. "All Sanskrit sources that are now available are full of legends and fabulous tales; apart from the *Rājatarañginī* there is not a single true historical account" (*BI*, p. 2). The criteria of the "true historical account" had been, of course, set by then by European historical scholarship. That India has no true historical account was a singular discovery of European Indology. The thought had never occurred to Mrityunjay. But to Tarinicharan, it seems self-evident.

We then have a description of the inhabitants of India:

> In very ancient times, there lived in India two very distinct communities [*sampradāy*] of people. Of them, one resembled us in height and other aspects of physical appearance. The descendants of this community are now called Hindu. The people of the other community were short, dark and extremely uncivilized. Their descendants are now known as Khas, Bhilla, Pulinda, Sāoṅtāl and other primitive [*jaṅglā*, "of the bush"] jāti. (*BI*, p. 2)

There were others who were the products of the mixing of sampradāy. Thus, the first three varṇa among the Hindus are said to be twice-born, but the Śūdra are not entitled to that status. "This shows that in the beginning the former were a separate *sampradāy* from the latter. The latter were subsequently included in the former community, but were given the status of the most inferior class" (*BI*, p. 4).

The notion of the gradual spread of "the Hindu religion" from the north of the country to the south is also introduced. This spread is the result of the expansion of the realm.

> The south of the country was in the beginning covered by forests and inhabited by non-Hindu and uncivilized jāti. Rāmacandra was the first to hoist the Hindu flag in that part of India. . . . To this day there are many popular tales of the ancient colonization of the south by the Hindus. (*BI*, p. 27)

The image of the hero of the *Rāmāyaṇa* holding aloft the modern symbol of national sovereignty came easily to the mind of this English-educated Bengali Brahman a hundred years ago, although the votaries of political Hinduism today would probably be embarrassed by the suggestion that Rama had subdued the inhabitants of southern India and established a colonial rule.

Since there is a lack of authentic sources, the narrative of ancient Indian history is necessarily fragmentary. Gone is the certitude of Mrityunjay's dynastic lists; Tarinicharan states quite clearly the limits to a rational reconstruction of the ancient past.

> European historians have proved by various arguments that the battle of Kurukṣetra took place before the fourteenth century B.C. For a long period after the battle of Kurukṣetra, the historical accounts of India are so uncertain, partial and contradictory that it is impossible to construct from them a narrative. (*BI*, pp. 16–17)

The narrative he does construct is not particularly remarkable, because he follows without much amendment the history of ancient India as current among British writers on the subject. The only interesting comment in these chapters of Tarinicharan's book is the one he makes on Buddhism:

> [The Buddha] became a great enemy of the Hindu religion, which is why Hindus describe him as an atheist and the destroyer of dharma. Nevertheless, the religion founded by him contains much advice of the highest spiri-

> tual value. He did not admit anything that was devoid of reason [*yukti*]. No matter how ancient the customs of a jāti, if stronger reasons can be presented against the traditional views, then the opinions of at least some people are likely to change. (*BI*, p. 17)

The reasonableness of the religious views of Buddhism is not denied. On the contrary, Buddhism is presented as a rationalist critique from within "the Hindu religion." Otherwise, in accordance with the criterion of periodization, the period of the Buddhist rulers would have had to be classified as a separate period of ancient Indian history. Now it is given a place within the "Hindu period."

Although the historical sources for the ancient period are said to be fragmentary and unreliable, on one subject there seems to be no dearth of evidence: "the civilization and learning of the ancient Indians." This is the title of chapter 6 of Tarinicharan's book. The main argument is as follows:

> What distinguishes the giant from the dwarf or the mighty from the frail is nothing compared to the difference between the ancient and the modern Hindu. In earlier times, foreign travellers in India marvelled at the courage, truthfulness and modesty of the people of the Arya *vaṃśa*; now they remark mainly on the absence of those qualities. In those days Hindus would set out on conquest and hoist their flags in Tatar, China and other countries; now a few soldiers from a tiny island far away are lording it over the land of India. In those days Hindus would regard all except their own jāti as *mleccha* and treat them with contempt; now those same *mleccha* shower contempt on the descendants of Aryans. Then the Hindus would sail to Sumatra and other islands, evidence of which is still available in plenty in the adjacent island of Bali. Now the thought of a sea voyage strikes terror in the heart of a Hindu, and if anyone manages to go, he is immediately ostracized from society. (*BI*, p. 32)

Ancient glory, present misery: the subject of this entire story is "us." The mighty heroes of ancient India were "our" ancestors, and the feeble inhabitants of India today are "ourselves." That ancient Indians conquered other countries or traded across the seas or treated other people "with contempt" is a matter of pride for "us." And it is "our" shame that "the descendants of Aryans" are today subordinated to others and are the objects of the latter's contempt. There is a certain scale of power among the different peoples of the world; earlier, the people of India were high on that scale, while today they are near the bottom.

Not only physical prowess but the achievements of ancient Indians in the field of learning were also universally recognized.

> In ancient times, when virtually the whole world was shrouded in the darkness of ignorance, the pure light of learning shone brightly in India. The

> discoveries in philosophy which emanated from the keen intellects of ancient Hindus are arousing the enthusiasm of European scholars even today. (*BI*, p. 33)

Note that the opinion of European scholars in this matter is extremely important to Tarinicharan. In fact, all the examples he cites on the excellence of ancient Indian learning—in the fields of astronomy, mathematics, logic, and linguistics—were discoveries of nineteenth-century Orientalists. By bringing forward this evidence, Tarinicharan seems to be suggesting that although Europeans today treat Indians with contempt because of their degraded condition, Indians were not always like this, because even European scholars admit that the arts and sciences of ancient India were of the highest standard. This evidence from Orientalist scholarship was extremely important for the construction of the full narrative of nationalist history.

That Tarinicharan's history is nationalist is signified by something else. His story of ancient glory and subsequent decline has a moral at the end: reform society, remove all of these superstitions that are the marks of decadence, and revive the true ideals of the past. These false beliefs and practices for which Indians are today the objects of contempt did not exist in the past because even Europeans admit that in ancient times "we" were highly civilized.

> Today we find Hindu women treated like slaves, enclosed like prisoners and as ignorant as beasts. But if we look a millennium and a quarter earlier, we will find that women were respected, educated and largely unconstrained. Where was child marriage then? No one married before the age of twenty-four. (*BI*, p. 33)

Ancient India became for the nationalist the classical age, while the period between the ancient and the contemporary was the dark age of medievalism. Needless to say, this pattern was heartily approved by European historiography. If the nineteenth-century Englishman could claim ancient Greece as his classical heritage, why should not the English-educated Bengali feel proud of the achievements of the so-called Vedic civilization?

NARRATIVE BREAK

The chapter "The Civilization and Learning of the Ancient Indians" closes Tarinicharan's history of ancient India. He then takes the reader outside India—to Arabia in the seventh century. Why should it be necessary, in discussing a change of historical periods in twelfth-century India, to begin the description from seventh-century Arabia? The answer to this question is, of course, obvious. But implicit in that answer is an entire ensemble of assumptions and prejudices of nineteenth-century European historiography.

> Muhammad gave to his followers the name *musalman*, that is, the faithful, and to all other humans the name *kafir* or infidel. . . . Directing his followers to take the sword in order to destroy the *kafir*, he said that God had ordained that those Muslims who die in the war against false religion will go to paradise and live in eternal pleasure in the company of doe-eyed nymphs. But if they run away from battle, they will burn in hell. The Arab jāti is by nature fearless and warlike. Now, aroused by the lust for plunder in this world and for eternal pleasure in the next, their swords became irresistible everywhere. All of Arabia came under Muhammad's control and only a few years after his death the Muslim flag was flying in every country between Kabul and Spain. Never before in history had one kingdom after another, one land after another, fallen to a conqueror with the speed at which they fell to the Muslims. It was impossible that such people, always delirious at the prospect of conquest, would not covet the riches of India. (*BI*, pp. 36–37)

The ground is being prepared here for the next episode that will result from the clash of this distinct history of the Muslims with the history of Indians. This distinct history originates in, and acquires its identity from, the life of Muhammad. In other words, the dynasty that will be founded in Delhi at the beginning of the thirteenth century and the many political changes that will take place in the subsequent five centuries are not to be described merely as the periods of Turko-Afghan or Mughal rule in India; they are integral parts of the political history of Islam.

The actors in this history are also given certain behavioral characteristics. They are warlike and believe that it is their religious duty to kill infidels. Driven by the lust for plunder and the visions of cohabiting with the nymphs of paradise, they are even prepared to die in battle. They are not merely conquerors, but "delirious at the prospect of conquest" (*digvijayonmatta*), and consequently are by their innate nature covetous of the riches of India.

It is important for us at this point to note the complex relation of this new nationalist historiography to the histories of India produced by British writers in the nineteenth century. While James Mill's *History of British India*, completed in 1817, may have been "the hegemonic textbook of Indian history" for European Indology,[1] for the first nationalist historians of India it represented precisely what they had to fight against. Mill did not share any of the enthusiasm of Orientalists such as William Jones for the philosophical and literary achievements of ancient India. His condemnation of the despotism and immorality of Indian civilization was total, and even his recognition of "the comparative superiority of Islamic civilisation" did not in any significant way affect his judgment that until the arrival of British rule, India had always been "condemned to semi-barbarism and the miseries of despotic power."[2] Nationalist history in India could be born only by challenging such an absolute and comprehensive denial of all claims to historical subjectivity.[3]

Far more directly influential for the nationalist school texts we are looking at was Elphinstone's *History of India* (1841). This standard textbook in Indian universities was the most widely read British history of India until Vincent Smith's books were published in the early twentieth century. The reason why nationalist readers found Elphinstone more palatable than Mill is not far to seek. As E. B. Cowell, who taught in Calcutta and added notes to the later editions of Elphinstone's *History*, explained in a preface in 1866, a "charm of the book is the spirit of genuine hearty sympathy with and appreciation of the native character which runs though the whole, and the absence of which is one of the main blemishes in Mr. Mill's eloquent work."[4] In this spirit of sympathy, Elphinstone wrote entire chapters in his volume called "Hindús" on "Philosophy," "Astronomy and Mathematical Science," "Medicine," "Language," "Literature," "Fine Arts," and "Commerce." He also began his volume on "Mahometans" with a chapter called "Arab Conquests A.D. 632, A.H. 11–A.D. 753, A.H. 136," whose first section was "Rise of the Mahometan Religion."

Another source often acknowledged in the Bengali textbooks is the series called *The History of India as Told by Its Own Historians*.[5] Compiled by Henry Elliot, and edited and published after his death by John Dowson between 1867 and 1877, these eight volumes comprise translated extracts from over 150 works, principally in Persian, covering a period from the ninth to the eighteenth centuries. It was a gigantic example of the privilege claimed by modern European scholarship to process the writings of a people supposedly devoid of historical consciousness and render into useful sources of history what otherwise could "scarcely claim to rank higher than Annals." The technical qualities of the scholarship of Elliot and Dowson were to be questioned in subsequent decades,[6] but with the substitution of English for Persian as the language of the state, it was through their mediation that the Persian sources of Indian history would now become available to the modern literati in Bengal.

The assumptions which regulated the selection and translation of these sources were quite explicitly stated by Elliot:[7]

> In Indian Histories there is little which enables us to penetrate below the glittering surface, and observe the practical operation of a despotic Government. . . . If, however, we turn our eyes to the present Muhammadan kingdoms of India, and examine the character of the princes, . . . we may fairly

> draw a parallel between ancient and modern times. . . . We behold kings, even of our own creation, slunk in sloth and debauchery, and emulating the vices of a Caligula or a Commodus. . . . Had the authors whom we are compelled to consult, pourtrayed their Caesars with the fidelity of Suetonius, instead of the more congenial sycophancy of Paterculus, we should not, as now, have to extort from unwilling witnesses, testimony to the truth of these assertions. . . . The few glimpses we have, even among the short Extracts in this single volume, of Hindús slain for disputing with Muhammadans, of general prohibitions against processions, worship, and ablutions, and of other intolerant measures, of idols mutilated, of temples razed, of forcible conversions and marriages, of proscriptions and confiscations, of murders and massacres, and of the sensuality and drunkenness of the tyrants who enjoined them, show us that this picture is not overcharged, and it is much to be regretted that we are left to draw it for ourselves from out of the mass of ordinary occurrences.

The fact that even Hindu writers wrote "to flatter the vanity of an imperious Muhammadan patron" was, Elliot thought, "lamentable": "there is not one of this slavish crew who treats the history of his native country subjectively, or presents us with the thoughts, emotions and raptures which a long oppressed race might be supposed to give vent to." Elliot also drew for his readers the conclusions from his presentation of these extracts:

> They will make our native subjects more sensible of the immense advantages accruing to them under the mildness and equity of our rule. . . . We should no longer hear bombastic Bábús, enjoying under our Government the highest degree of personal liberty, and many more political privileges than were ever conceded to a conquered nation, rant about patriotism, and the degradation of their present position. If they would dive into any of the volumes mentioned herein, it would take these young Brutuses and Phocions a very short time to learn, that in the days of that dark period for whose return they sigh, even the bare utterance of their ridiculous fantasies would have been attended, not with silence and contempt, but with the severer discipline of molten lead or empalement.

Ironically, when the young Brutuses and Phocions did learn Elliot's lessons on Muhammadan rule, their newly acquired consciousness of being "a long oppressed race" did not stop with a condemnation of Islamic despotism; it also turned against British rule itself.

In the second half of the nineteenth century, European Indological scholarship seemed to have agreed that the history of Hinduism was one of a classical age—for some the Vedic civilization, for others the so-called Gupta revival in the fourth to the seventh centuries—followed by a medieval decline from the eighth to the eighteenth centuries.[8] For some, this decline was itself the reason why the country fell so quickly to the Muslim invaders. In any case, the theory of medieval decline fitted in nicely with the overall judgment of nineteenth-century British historians that "Muslim rule in India" was a period of despotism, misrule, and anarchy[9]—this, needless to say, being the historical justification for colonial intervention.

For Indian nationalists in the late nineteenth century, the pattern of classical glory, medieval decline, and modern renaissance appeared as one that was not only proclaimed by the modern historiography of Europe but also approved for India by at least some sections of European scholarship. What was needed was to claim for the Indian nation the historical agency for completing the project of modernity. To make that claim, ancient India had to become the classical source of Indian modernity, while "the Muslim period" would become the night of medieval darkness. Contributing to that description would be all the prejudices of the European Enlightenment about Islam. Dominating the chapters from the twelfth century onward in the new nationalist history of India would be a stereotypical figure of "the Muslim," endowed with a "national character": fanatical, bigoted, warlike, dissolute, and cruel.

MUSLIM TYRANNY, HINDU RESISTANCE

The story that begins with the birth of Islam in Arabia does, of course, shift to India, but this happens in stages. Tarinicharan gives long descriptions of the Arab invasions of Sind and the successive raids by Mahmud Ghaznavi into different Indian kingdoms, all of which take place well before the establishment of the so-called Slave dynasty in Delhi in the early thirteenth century. These descriptions trace a common pattern that can be clarified by looking at three examples: Tarinicharan's accounts of the invasion of Sind by Muhammad Ibn Kasim, of Mahmud Ghaznavi's attack on Punjab, and of the victory of Muhammad Ghuri at Thanesar.

Muhammad Kasim began his war on Dahir, the king of Sind, in 712.

> Fortune favored him. A ball of fire thrown by his soldiers struck King Dahir's elephant which panicked and fled from the battlefield. Dahir's troops, thinking that their king had given up the battle, fell into disarray. Later it will be seen that even when Indians had every chance of victory, similar misfortunes often led to their defeat at the hands of the Muslims. (*BI*, p. 38)[10]

It must be noted that what Tarinicharan calls "fortune" (*daiva*) and "misfortune" (*durddaiva*) are not the same as the daiva that was divine intervention in Mrityunjay's narrative. Misfortune here is mere accident, a matter of chance. There is no suggestion at all of retribution for immoral conduct. It is the misfortune not of kings, but of "Indians" that despite deserving to win, they have repeatedly lost because of accidents.

> Finally, after displaying much heroism, [King Dahir] was killed at the hands of the enemy. His capital was besieged, but Dahir's wife, displaying a courage similar to her husband's, continued to defend the city. In the end, food supplies ran out. Deciding that it was preferable to die rather than submit to the enemy, she instructed the inhabitants of the city to make necessary arrangements. Everyone agreed; everywhere, pyres were lit. After the immolations [of the women], the men, completing their ablutions, went out sword in hand and were soon killed by the Muslims. (*BI*, p. 38)[11]

Similar stories of defeat in battle appear later. Two features are worth notice: one, the courage of Hindu women in resisting aggression, and the other, the death in battle of Hindu men as a ritualized form of self-sacrifice. Thus appear such narrative indexes as "everywhere, pyres were lit" and "completing their ablutions . . . killed by the Muslims." The corresponding index for Muslim soldiers is "driven by the prospect of cohabiting with doe-eyed nymphs . . . etc." The contrast is significant.

Tarinicharan tells another story about Kasim that is part of the same narrative structure.

> On completing his conquest of Sind, Kasim was preparing to drive further into India when the resourcefulness of a woman became his undoing. Among the women who were captured in war in Sind were two daughters of King Dahir. They were not only of high birth but were also outstandingly beautiful. Kasim thought they would make appropriate presents for the Khalifa and accordingly sent them to his master. The ruler of the Muslims was bewitched by the beauty of the elder daughter and began to look upon her with desire. At this, she burst into tears and said, "It is a pity that I am not worthy of receiving the affections of someone like you, because Kasim has already sullied my dharma." Hearing of this act of his servant, the Khalifa was enraged and ordered that Kasim be sown in hide and brought before him. When this order was carried out, the Khalifa showed Kasim's corpse to the princess. Eyes sparkling with delight, she said, "Kasim was entirely innocent. I had made the allegation only in order to avenge the deaths of my parents and the humiliation of their subjects." (*BI*, p. 39)[12]

To the courage of Hindu women is added another element: intelligence. And parallel to the story of self-sacrifice is created another story: vengeance on the enemy for the death of one's kin.

Let us move to the beginning of the eleventh century and the period of Mahmud of Ghazna. "Of all Muslims, it was his aggressions which first brought devastation and disarray to India, and from that time the freedom of the Hindus has diminished and faded like the phases of the moon" (*BI*, p. 41). Tarinicharan mentions some of Mahmud's qualities such as courage, foresight, strategic skill, and perseverance, but ignores the fact, discussed in Elphinstone, that Mahmud was also a great patron of arts and letters. "Although he was endowed with these qualities, he was also a great adherent, at least in public, of the Musalman religion, a bitter opponent of the worship of idols and an unyielding pursuer of wealth and fame" (*BI*, p. 42). This was another alleged trait of the Muslim character: where faith in Islam was a reason for war, it was not true faith but only an apparent adherence to religion.

Mahmud moved against King Anandapal of the Shahiya dynasty.

> "The Muslims are determined to destroy the independence of all of India and to eradicate the Hindu religion. If they conquer Lahore, they will attack other parts of the country. It is therefore a grave necessity for all to unite in suppressing the *mleccha* forces." Saying this, the King [Elphinstone writes the name as Anang Pál, as does Tarinicharan] sent emissaries to all the principal Hindu kings. His appeal did not go unheeded. The kings of Delhi, Kanauj, Ujjain, Gwalior, Kalinjar and other places joined with Anangapal. Masses of troops arrived in Punjab. Worried by this sudden increase in the strength of the opposition, Mahmud decided, for reasons of safety, to halt near Peshawar. The Hindu forces increased daily. Hindu women from far away sold their diamonds, melted down their gold ornaments and sent supplies for war. (*BI*, pp. 43–44)[13]

King Anandapal is unlikely to have had the historical foresight to anticipate that the fall of Lahore to Mahmud would lead to "the destruction of the independence of all of India." Needless to say, these are Tarinicharan's words. But by putting them on the lips of the ruler of Punjab, he turns this story into a war of the Hindu jāti: "the kings joined with Anangapal," "the Hindu forces increased daily," "Hindu women from far away sent supplies," and so forth. But then came the inevitable stroke of misfortune. "A fire-ball or a sharp arrow flung from the Musalman camp struck the elephant of the Hindu commander Anangapal. The elephant, with the king on its back, fled from the field of battle. At this, the Hindu soldiers fell into disarray" (*BI*, p. 44).

This episode too ends with a story of vengeance, but this time of another variety: "The king of Kanauj, who had collaborated with Mahmud, became an object of hatred and contempt in the community of Hindu kings. Hearing this, the ruler of Ghazni entered India for the tenth time to help his protégé. But well before his arrival, the king of Kalinjar performed the execution of the king of Kanauj" (*BI*, p. 46). Needless to say, this too was a ritual; hence, it was not just an execution, but the "performance of an execution."

On Muhammad Ghuri, Tarinicharan says that his soldiers were

> inhabitants of the hills, hardy and skilled in warfare. By comparison, the Hindu kings were disunited and their soldiers relatively docile and undisciplined. Consequently, it was only to be expected that Muhammad would win easily. But that is not what happened. Virtually no Hindu ruler surrendered his freedom without a mighty struggle. In particular, the Rajahpūta were never defeated. The rise, consolidation and collapse of Muslim rule have been completed, but the Rajahpūta remain free to this day. (*BI*, p. 53)

Not only did the Hindu kings not submit without resistance, but after the first attack by Muhammad, they even "chased the Muslims away for twenty *kroś* [forty miles]" (*BI*, p. 54). On his second attack, the treachery of Jaichand and the unscrupulousness of Muhammad led to the defeat of Prithviraj. This account by Tarinicharan bears no resemblance at all to the narratives of Mrityunjay. There is also a story of revenge at the end. A hill tribe Tarinicharan calls "Gokṣur" (Elphinstone calls them "a band of Gakkars") had been defeated by Muhammad; one night, some of them managed to enter his tent and kill the Sultan in revenge.

With the establishment of the Sultanate, the story of the oppression of Hindus by intolerant rulers will be repeated a number of times. For instance, Sikandar Lodi:

> Sekendar prohibited pilgrimage and ritual bathing in the Ganga and other sacred rivers. He also destroyed temples at many places. A Brahman who had declared that "The Lord recognizes every religion if followed sincerely" was called before Sekendar, and when he refused to discard his tolerant views was executed by the cruel ruler. When a Musalman holy man criticized the ban on pilgrimage, the king was enraged and shouted, "Rascal! So you support the idolaters?" The holy man replied, "No, that is not what I am doing. All I am saying is that the oppression by rulers of their subjects is unjust." (*BI*, p. 83)[14]

Tarinicharan's barbs are the sharpest when they are directed against Aurangzeb. "Arāñjib was deceitful, murderous and plundered the wealth of others" (*BI*, p. 220). "His declaration of faith in the Musalman religion only facilitated the securing of his interests. . . . In truth, Arāñjib would never forsake his interests for reasons of religion or justice" (*BI*, p. 173). On the other hand, Tarinicharan has praise for Akbar, although his reasons are interesting.

> Akbar attempted to eradicate some irrational practices prescribed in the Musalman religion. He also tried to stop several irrational practices of the Hindus. He prohibited the ordeal by fire, the burning of widows against their wishes and child-marriage. He also allowed the remarriage of widows. . . .

> Orthodox Muslims were strongly opposed to him because of his liberal views on religion. Many called him an atheist. (*BI*, p. 141)

Thus, it was not his impartiality in matters of religion but his use of the powers of the state to reform both the Hindu and the Muslim religions that makes Akbar worthy of praise.

The issue of the alliance of certain Hindu kings with Muslim rulers comes up again in the context of Akbar's policy. Thus, on the subject of the marriages of Rajput princesses with Mughals:

> The Rajahpūta who consented to such marriages became particular favorites of the emperor. Far from regarding such marriages as humiliating and destructive of jāti, all Rajahpūta kings, with the exception of the ruler of Udaipur, felt themselves gratified and honored by them. But the king of Udaipur broke off all ties with these Yavana-loving kings. For this reason, the lineage of Udaipur is today honored as the purest in caste among the Rajahpūta. Other kings consider it a great privilege to have social transactions with him. (*BI*, pp. 125–26)

OTHER CLAIMS TO A NATIONAL PAST

Not only was Tarinicharan's book reprinted every year, it also served as a model for many other textbooks.[15] One such is called "Questions and Answers on the History of India." Written by Saiyad Abdul Rahim of Barisal, it follows Tarinicharan very closely, but with a few significant amendments.

First, Abdul Rahim writes the story of the Aryans differently: "The Hindus are not the original inhabitants of India. They came from the west of the river Sindhu and became inhabitants of India by the force of arms."[16] Where Tarinicharan had written "the non-Aryans were included in the Arya *sampradāy*," or "the Aryans established colonies" or "planted the Hindu flag," the description is now changed to "became inhabitants of India by the force of arms."

In the remaining part of the historical narrative, Abdul Rahim does not deviate from Tarinicharan. Thus: "Between Muhammad Ghaznavi and Muhammad Ghori, the latter caused greater harm to the Hindus, because whereas Muhammad Ghaznavi only looted and plundered, Muhammad Ghori robbed the Hindus of the precious treasure of independence." Or, "The benevolent [*mahātmā*] Akbar had scrapped the *jiziya* tax; the wicked [*durātmā*] Arañjib reinstated it." Indeed, in answer to a question, there is even an explanation, echoing Tarinicharan, that "the reason for the collapse of the Mughal empire was the bigotry and oppression of Arañjib."[17]

The change comes with the very last question in the book.

> TEACHER: What lesson have you drawn from your reading of the history of Musalman rule?
>
> STUDENT: Arya! This is what I have learnt for certain by reading the history of Musalman rule. To rule a kingdom is to destroy one's life both in this world and in the next. To rule, one must give up for all time the god-given gifts of forgiveness and mercy. How lamentable it is that one must, for the sake of a kingdom, redden the earth with the blood of one's own brother in whose company one has spent so many years of one's childhood. Oh kingdom! I have learnt well from the history of Musalman rule how you turn the human heart into stone. For your sake, to kill one's parents or one's brothers and sisters, or even to sacrifice the great treasure of religion, seems a matter of little concern. Oh kingdom, how bewitching are your powers of seduction![18]

In spite of having plowed through his book, this student of Tarinicharan has clearly developed little appreciation for the charms of *raison d'état.* Where Saiyad Abdul Rahim writes in his own words, we can still hear the voice of Mrityunjay's prajā.

But we will not hear it for much longer. If there is no place for Islam in the classical heritage of Indian culture, then, in the new mode of historiography, it is going to be thought of as constituting an alternative and different classical tradition. Writing a biography of the Prophet in 1886, Sheikh Abdar Rahim cites, like Tarinicharan, the authority of European scholars to make his claim: "Islam has been far more beneficial to the human jāti than the Christian religion. Philosophy and science were first taken to the European continent from the Musalman of Asia and the Moors of Spain. . . . The Musalman of Spain were the founders of philosophy in Europe." He also refutes the false accusations against Islam by Europeans:

> All the biographies of the Prophet Muhammad which hitherto have been written in the Bengali language are incomplete. Especially since they have followed English books on the subject, they are in many respects unsuitable for Musalman readers. People of other religions have falsely accused Muhammad of spreading his religion by the sword; a perusal of this book will show how little truth there is in that charge.

Further, the assessment made by Hindu authors on the history of Muslim rule in India is denied: "Although some Musalman rulers have oppressed people on grounds of religion, these were acts contrary to religion and must not lead to a charge against Islam itself."[19]

In the last decade of the nineteenth century, the journal *Mihir o sudhākar*, edited by the same Abdar Rahim, would call for, using almost the same rhetoric as Bankim's *Bañgadarśan* in the previous decade, the writing of "a national history appropriate for the Musalman of Bengal." Responding to that call, Abdul Karim (1863–1943) would write the history of Muslim rule in India,[20] and Ismail Husain Siraji (1880–1931) the historical ballad *Anal prabāha*.[21] These writers were clearly imbued with the ideas of a modern English-educated middle class. They were highly conscious of their role as leaders of the people, in this case of the Muslim prajā of Bengal. They would not end their books with the lament "Oh kingdom, how bewitching are your powers of seduction!"

On the contrary, Abdul Karim chose to write his history of Muslim rule in India in the belief that a true account of the glorious achievements of the Muslims in India would produce a better appreciation of their heroism, generosity, and love of learning and create greater amity between Hindus and Muslims (*BMRI*, preface). The narrative structure he adopts is, however, exactly the same as that used by the British historians he condemns. The story of Muslim rule in India begins with the birth of Muhammad, the conversion of Arabs to the new monotheistic religion, their "abandonment of false beliefs, false customs and superstition" and their "acceptance of true religion and morality," and the new feelings among them of fraternity and unity. All this enabled the Arabs to become "a jāti of unprecedented power" (*BMRI*, p. 11).

However, beginning with the accounts of the early Arab incursions into Sind, Abdul Karim takes great care to point out that the Arab military commanders were punctilious in following the codes of honor and justice in warfare.

> [Muhammad Kasim] captured the fort and killed all men bearing arms, but spared all merchants, artisans and ordinary people. . . . Muhammad then wrote to Hejaz to ask whether the Hindus should be allowed to follow their own religion. Hejaz wrote back to say: "Now that they have accepted our suzerainty and agreed to pay taxes to the Khalifa, they must be protected by us and their life and property secured. They are hereby allowed to worship their own gods." (*BMRI*, pp. 40-41)

On the account of Mahmud Ghaznavi's destruction of the Somnath idol, Abdul Karim comments: "Modern historians think that this account is completely fictitious. . . . Since Mahmud adopted the honorific title of 'The Destroyer of Idols,' the Persian historians decided to turn Mahmud's raid of the Somnath temple into a story of his religious fervor" (*BMRI*, p. 59).

Abdul Karim is scrupulous in distinguishing between just and honorable conduct of the affairs of state, as approved by Islam, and religious bigotry, to be condemned at all times. Thus Sikandar Lodi, he says, had an extremely narrow and intolerant view of religion and was oppressive toward Hindus (*BMRI*, p. 151). In all this, his concern clearly was to repudiate the slander that it was a characteristic of Islam as a religion and of Muslims as rulers to be violent, intolerant, and oppressive toward others. This, he suggests, is a calumny spread by European historians; if one were only to listen to Muslim historians telling the story of their own past, it would promote the self-esteem of Muslims as a people and elicit the respect of others toward Islamic civilization and tradition. The structure of this historiographic response was, of course, no different from what Bankim had suggested for the nationalist past.

HISTORY AS THE SOURCE OF NATIONHOOD

Discussing the identification in Bankim's agenda of the national past with a Hindu past, Ranajit Guha has suggested that there is an inconsistency here.[22] Although Bankim urged that one must reclaim one's own history which, moreover, was a history of power (*bāhubal*), he confined the memory of that struggle for power entirely to the pre-British past. In spite of enumerating the conditions for the historical liberation of a subject nation from colonial rule, he refrained from announcing that the struggle for power be launched against British colonialism. All he tells his readers are stories of the struggle of the Hindu jāti against its Muslim rulers. "The excision of colonial rule from the history of *bahubol*, hence the exclusion of *bahubol* from the history of colonial rule, prevented the agenda for an alternative historiography from being put into effect even as it was formulated and urged with such fervour."[23]

If we read Bankim alongside the other less notable history writers of his time, we find, first, that although much less sophisticated, the other writers held more or less the same views on historiography. Second, their writings are also marked by the same inconsistency referred to by Guha. Third, to explain this inconsistency, even if we say in the case of Bankim that the real struggle for power had already been posed against the British although it could not be declared openly,[24] we cannot say the same for the other writers. Because in the 1880s, a number of Bengali writers were announcing quite openly that the struggle for an independent historiography and the struggle for independent nationhood were both to be waged against colonialism. The difficulty is that by colonial rule, they meant both British rule and Muslim rule. In both cases, the object of national freedom was the end of colonial rule; in both cases, the means was a struggle for power. There was no inconsistency in their agenda.

It is remarkable how pervasive this framework of nationalist history became in the consciousness of the English-educated Hindu middle class in Bengal in the late nineteenth century. In their literary and dramatic productions as well as in their schools and colleges, this narrative of national history went virtually unchallenged until the early decades of the twentieth century.

The idea that "Indian nationalism" is synonymous with "Hindu nationalism" is not the vestige of some premodern religious conception. It is an entirely modern, rationalist, and historicist idea. Like other modern ideologies, it allows for a central role of the state in the modernization of society and strongly defends the state's unity and sovereignty. Its appeal is not religious but political. In this sense, the framework of its reasoning is entirely secular. A little examination will show that compared to Mrityunjay's historiography, which revolved around the forces of the divine and sacred, Tarinicharan's is a wholly secular historiography.

In fact, the notion of "Hindu-ness" in this historical conception cannot be, and does not need to be, defined by any religious criteria at all. There are no specific beliefs or practices that characterize this "Hindu," and the many doctrinal and sectarian differences among Hindus are irrelevant to its concept. Indeed, even such anti-Vedic and anti-Brahmanical religions as Buddhism and Jainism count here as Hindu. Similarly, people outside the Brahmanical religion and outside caste society are also claimed as part of the Hindu jāti. But clearly excluded from this jāti are religions like Christianity and Islam.

What then is the criterion for inclusion or exclusion? It is one of historical origin. Buddhism or Jainism are Hindu because they originate in India, out of debates and critiques that are internal to Hinduism. Islam or Christianity come from outside and are therefore foreign. And "India" here is the generic entity, with fixed territorial definitions, that acts as the permanent arena for the history of the jāti.

What, we may ask, is the place of those inhabitants of India who are excluded from this nation? There are several answers suggested in this historiography. One, which assumes the centrality of the modern state in the life of the nation, is frankly majoritarian. The majority "community" is Hindu; the others are minorities. State policy must therefore reflect this preponderance, and the minorities must accept the leadership and protection of the majority. This view, which today is being propagated with such vehemence in postcolonial India by Hindu-extremist politics, actually originated more than a hundred years ago, at the same time Indian nationalism was born.

Consider the utopian history of Bhudeb Mukhopadhyay, written in 1876.[25] The army of Ahmad Shah Abdali is engaged in battle with the Maratha forces in the fields of Panipat. A messenger from the Maratha commander comes to Ahmad Shah and says that although the Muslims had always mistreated the Hindus, the Hindus were prepared to forgive. "'You may return home unhindered with all your troops. If any Musalman living in India wishes to go with you, he may do so, but he may not return within five years.'"

This is, of course, "the history of India as revealed in a dream": Ahmad Shah therefore says:

> "Go to the Maharashtrian commander and tell him that . . . I will never attack India again."
>
> Hearing this, the messenger saluted [Ahmad Shah] and said, ". . . I have been instructed to deliver another message. All Musalman nawabs, subahdars, zamindars, jagirdars, etc. of this country who choose not to accompany you may return immediately to their own estates and residences. The Maharashtrian commander has declared, 'All previous offenses of these people have been condoned.'"

There is then held a grand council of all the kings of India in which the following proposal is made:

> Although India is the true motherland only of those who belong to the Hindu jāti and although only they have been born from her womb, the Muslims are not unrelated to her any longer. She has held them at her breast and reared them. The Muslims are therefore her adopted children.
>
> Can there be no bonds of fraternity between two children of the same mother, one a natural child and the other adopted? There certainly can; the laws of every religion admit this. There has now been born a bond of brotherhood between Hindus and Muslims living in India. . . .
>
> Now all will have to unite in taking care of our Mother. But without a head, no union can function. Who among us will be our leader? By divine grace, there is no room left for debate in this matter. This throne which has been prepared for Raja Ramchandra . . . will never be destroyed. There, behold the wise Badshah Shah Alam coming forward to hand over of his own accord his crown, and with it the responsibility of ruling over his empire, to Raja Ramchandra.

Thus, the Mughal emperor hands over his throne to the Maratha ruler Ramchandra. "As soon as the assembly was dissolved and everyone rose from their seats, no one was able to see Shah Alam again. Seated on the throne of Delhi was Raja Ramchandra of the dynasty of Shivaji, on his head the crown given to him by Shah Alam."

It may be mentioned that in this imaginary council a constitution is then promulgated more or less along the lines of the German Reich, with strongly protectionist economic policies that succeed, in this anticolonial utopia, in keeping the European economic powers firmly in check.

The second answer, which also made the distinction between majority and minority "communities," is associated with what is called the politics of "secularism" in India. This view holds that in order to prevent the oppression of minorities by the majority, the state must enact legal measures to protect the rights and the separate identities of the minorities. The difficulty is that the formal institutions of the state, based on an undifferentiated concept of citizenship, cannot allow for the separate representation of minorities. Consequently, the question of who represents minorities necessarily remains problematic, and constantly threatens the tenuous identity of nation and state.

There was a third answer in this early nationalist historiography. This denied the centrality of the state in the life of the nation and instead pointed to the many institutions and practices in the everyday lives of the people through which they had evolved a way of living with their differences. The writings of Rabindranath Tagore in his post-Swadeshi phase are particularly significant in this respect. The argument here is that the true history of India lay not in the battles of kings and the rise and fall of empires but in this everyday world of popular life whose innate flexibility, untouched by conflicts in the domain of the state, allowed for the coexistence of all religious beliefs.

The principal difficulty with this view, which has many affinities with the later politics of Gandhism, is its inherent vulnerability to the overwhelming sway of the modern state. Its only defense against the historicist conception of the nation is to claim for the everyday life of the people an essential and transhistorical truth. But such a defense remains vulnerable even within the grounds laid by its own premises, as is shown rather interestingly in Rabindranath's hesitation in this matter. Reviewing Abdul Karim's history of Muslim rule in India, Rabindranath remarks on the reluctance of Hindus to aspire to an achievement of power and glory which would lead them to intervene in the lives of other people and on their inability to cope with those who do.[26] The political history of Islam and, more recently, the history of European conquests in the rest of the world show, he says, that people who have world-conquering ambitions hide under the edifice of civilized life a secret dungeon of ferocious beastliness and unbridled greed. Compared to this, it often seems preferable to lie in peace in a stagnant pool, free from the restlessness of adventure and ambition.

> But the fortifications put up by the *śāstra* have failed to protect India and conflicts with other peoples have become inevitable. We are now obliged to defend our interests against the greed of others and our lives against the violence of others. It would seem to be advisable then to feed a few pieces of flesh to the beast which lies within us and to have it stand guard outside our doors. At the very least, that would arouse the respect of people who are powerful.[27]

None of these answers, however, can admit that the Indian nation as a whole might have a claim on the historical legacy of Islam. The idea of the singularity of national history has inevitably led to a single source of Indian tradition, namely, ancient Hindu civilization. Islam here is either the history of foreign conquest or a domesticated element of everyday popular life. The classical heritage of Islam remains external to Indian history.

The curious fact is, of course, that this historicist conception of Hindu nationalism has had few qualms in claiming for itself the modern heritage of Europe. It is as rightful participants in that globalized domain of the modern state that today's contestants in postcolonial India fight each other in the name of history.

SUPPRESSED HISTORIES

There was a fourth answer, so unclear and fragmented that it is better to call it only the possibility of an answer. It raises doubts about the singularity of a history of India and also renders uncertain the question of classical origins. This history does not necessarily assume the sovereignty of a single state; it is more confederal in its political assumptions.

Surprisingly, there is a hint of this answer in Bankim's own writings.[28] "Just because the ruler is of a different jāti does not mean that a country is under subjection." Indeed, it was Bengal under the independent sultans that Bankim regarded as the birthplace of the renaissance in Bengali culture.

> History tells us that a principal consequence of subjection is that the intellectual creativity of a subject jāti is extinguished. Yet the intellect of the Bengali shone more brightly during the reign of the Pathans. . . . Never before and never after has the face of Bengal lit up more brightly than in these two hundred years. (*BR*, p. 332)

> How did we come upon this *renaissance*? Where did this sudden enlightenment in the intellectual life of the jāti come from?. . . How was this light extinguished? (*BR*, p. 339)[29]

> It was Emperor Akbar, upon whom we shower praises, who became Bengal's nemesis. He was the first to make Bengal a truly subject country. . . . The Mughal is our enemy, the Pathan our ally. (*BR*, p. 332)

There is a great disjuncture here between the history of India and the history of Bengal. The putative center of a generically sovereign state, coextensive with the nation, also becomes uncertainly located. Bankim notes that the Aryans appeared in Bengal at a much later date; does this weaken the claims of the Bengali upon the classical heritage of the Aryans?

> Many will think that the claims of Bengal and Bengalis have now become less formidable, and that we have been slandered as a jāti of recent origin. We who flaunt our ancient origins before the modern English have now been reduced to a modern jāti.
>
> But it is hard to see why there should be anything dishonorable in all this. We still remain descendants of the ancient Arya jāti: no matter when we may have come to Bengal, our ancestors are still the glorious Aryans. (*BR*, p. 326)

But, on the other hand, the question is raised: who of the Bengalis are Aryans? What is the origin of the Bengali jāti? Bankim looked for answers to these questions in a long essay, "The Origins of the Bengalis." The "scientific" evidence he accumulated in support of his arguments will now seem extremely dubious, and this is now one of his least remembered essays. But its conclusion was not very comfortable for the writing of a singular history of the Indian nation.

> The English are one jāti, the Bengalis are many jāti. In fact, among those whom we now call Bengali can be found four kinds of Bengalis: one, Aryan; two, non-Aryan Hindu; three, Hindu of mixed Aryan and non-Aryan origin; and four, Bengali Musalman. The four live separately from one another. At the bottom of Bengali society are the Bengali non-Aryans, mixed Aryans and Bengali Muslims; the top is almost exclusively Aryan. It is for this reason that, looked from the outside, the Bengali jāti seems a pure Aryan jāti and the history of Bengal is written as the history of an Aryan jāti. (*BR*, p. 363)

Elements of this alternative history can be found not only in Bankim but in other writers as well. Rajkrishna Mukhopadhyay, whose book provided the occasion for Bankim's first comments on the history of Bengal, observed that unlike in other parts of India, Islam did not spread in Bengal by the sword.[30] Krishnachandra Ray compares the British period with that of Sultani or Nawabi rule and notes that in the latter "there was no hindrance to the employment in high office of people of this country."[31] And the process of "nationalization" of the last nawab of Bengal, which reached its culmination in Akshaykumar Maitreya's *Sirājuddaulā* (1898), has already been noted.

The question is whether these two alternative forms of "national" history—one, a history of the *bhāratavarṣīya*, assuming a classical Aryan past and centered in northern India, and the other of Bengalis of many jāti, derived from uncertain origins—contained in the divergences in their trajectories and rhythms the possibility of a different imagining of nationhood. It is difficult now to explore this possibility in positive terms, because the second alternative in the pair has been submerged in the last hundred years by the tidal wave of historical memory about Arya-Hindu-Bhāratavarṣa. But the few examples considered here show that it would be impossible, according to this line of thinking, to club Pathan and

Mughal rule together and call it the Muslim period, or to begin the story of the spread of Islam in Bengal with "Muhammad instructed his followers to take up the sword and destroy the infidels."

It might be speculated that if there were many such alternative histories for the different regions of India, then the center of Indian history would not need to remain confined to Aryavarta or, more specifically, to "the throne of Delhi." Indeed, the very centrality of Indian history would then become largely uncertain. The question would no longer be one of "national" and "regional" histories: the very relation between parts and the whole would be open for negotiation. If there is any unity in these alternative histories, it is not national but confederal.

But we do not yet have the wherewithal to write these other histories. Until such time that we accept that it is the very singularity of the idea of a national history of India which divides Indians from one another, we will not create the conditions for writing these alternative histories.

CHAPTER SIX

The Nation and Its Women

THE PARADOX OF THE WOMEN'S QUESTION

The "women's question" was a central issue in the most controversial debates over social reform in early and mid-nineteenth-century Bengal—the period of its so-called renaissance. Rammohan Roy's historical fame is largely built around his campaign against the practice of the immolation of widows, Vidyasagar's around his efforts to legalize widow remarriage and abolish Kulin polygamy; the Brahmo Samaj was split twice in the 1870s over questions of marriage laws and the "age of consent." What has perplexed historians is the rather sudden disappearance of such issues from the agenda of public debate toward the close of the century. From then onward, questions regarding the position of women in society do not arouse the same degree of public passion and acrimony as they did only a few decades before. The overwhelming issues now are directly political ones—concerning the politics of nationalism.

How are we to interpret this change? Ghulam Murshid states the problem in its most obvious, straightforward form.[1] If one takes seriously, that is to say, in their liberal, rationalist and egalitarian content, the mid-nineteenth-century attempts in Bengal to "modernize" the condition of women, then what follows in the period of nationalism must be regarded as a clear retrogression. Modernization began in the first half of the nineteenth century because of the penetration of Western ideas. After some limited success, there was a perceptible decline in the reform movements as popular attitudes toward them hardened. The new politics of nationalism "glorified India's past and tended to defend everything traditional"; all attempts to change customs and life-styles began to be seen as the aping of Western manners and were thereby regarded with suspicion. Consequently, nationalism fostered a distinctly conservative attitude toward social beliefs and practices. The movement toward modernization was stalled by nationalist politics.

This critique of the social implications of nationalism follows from rather simple and linear historicist assumptions. Murshid not only accepts that the early attempts at social reform were impelled by the new nationalist and progressive ideas imported from Europe, he also presumes that the necessary historical culmination of such reforms in India ought to have been, as in the West, the full articulation of liberal values in social institutions and practices. From these assumptions, a critique of nationalist ideology and practices is inevitable, the same sort of critique as that of the colonialist historians who argue that Indian nationalism was nothing but a scramble for sharing political power with the colonial rulers; its mass following only the successful activization of traditional patron-client relationships; its internal debates the squabbles of parochial factions; and its ideology a garb for xenophobia and racial exclusiveness.

Clearly, the problem of the diminished importance of the women's question in the period of nationalism deserves a different answer from the one given by Murshid. Sumit Sarkar has argued that the limitations of nationalist ideology in pushing forward a campaign for liberal and egalitarian social change cannot be seen as a retrogression from an earlier radical reformist phase.[2] Those limitations were in fact present in the earlier phase as well. The renaissance reformers, he shows, were highly selective in their acceptance of liberal ideas from Europe. Fundamental elements of social conservatism such as the maintenance of caste distinctions and patriarchal forms of authority in the family, acceptance of the sanctity of the *śāstra* (scriptures), preference for symbolic rather than substantive changes in social practices—all these were conspicuous in the reform movements of the early and mid-nineteenth century.

Following from this, we could ask: How did the reformers select what they wanted? What, in other words, was the ideological sieve through which they put the newly imported ideas from Europe? If we can reconstruct this framework of the nationalist ideology, we will be in a far better position to locate where exactly the women's question fitted in with the claims of nationalism. We will find, if I may anticipate my argument in this chapter, that nationalism did in fact provide an answer to the new social and cultural problems concerning the position of women in "modern" society, and that this answer was posited not on an identity but on a difference with the perceived forms of cultural modernity in the West. I will argue, therefore, that the relative unimportance of the women's question in the last decades of the nineteenth century is to be explained not by the fact that it had been censored out of the reform agenda or overtaken by the more pressing and emotive issues of political struggle. The reason lies in nationalism's success in situating the "women's question" in an inner domain of sovereignty, far removed from the arena of political contest with the colonial state. This inner domain of national culture was constituted in the light of the discovery of "tradition."

THE WOMEN'S QUESTION IN "TRADITION"

Apart from the characterization of the political condition of India preceding the British conquest as a state of anarchy, lawlessness, and arbitrary despotism, a central element in the ideological justification of British colonial rule was the criticism of the "degenerate and barbaric" social customs of the Indian people, sanctioned, or so it was believed, by the religious tradition. Alongside the project of instituting orderly, lawful, and rational procedures of governance, therefore, colonialism also saw itself as performing a "civilizing mission." In identifying this tradition as "degenerate and barbaric," colonialist critics invariably repeated a long list of atrocities perpetrated on Indian women, not so much by men or certain classes of men, but by an entire body of scriptural canons and ritual practices that, they said, by rationalizing such atrocities within a complete framework of religious doctrine, made them appear to perpetrators and sufferers alike as the necessary marks of right conduct. By assuming a position of sympathy with the unfree and oppressed womanhood of India, the colonial mind was able to transform this figure of the Indian woman into a sign of the inherently oppressive and unfree nature of the entire cultural tradition of a country.

Take, for example, the following account by an early nineteenth-century British traveler in India:

> at no period of life, in no condition of society, should a woman do any thing at her mere pleasure. Their fathers, their husbands, their sons, are verily called her protectors; but it is such protection! Day and night must women be held by their protectors in a state of absolute dependence. A woman, it is affirmed, is never fit for independence, or to be trusted with liberty . . . their deity has allotted to women a love of their bed, of their seat, and of ornaments, impure appetites, wrath, flexibility, desire of mischief and bad conduct. Though her husband be devoid of all good qualities, yet, such is the estimate they form of her moral discrimination and sensibilities, that they bind the wife to revere him as a god, and to submit to his corporeal chastisements, whenever he chooses to inflict them, by a cane or a rope, on the back parts. . . . A state of dependence more strict, contemptuous, and humiliating, than that which is ordained for the weaker sex among the Hindoos, cannot easily be conceived; and to consummate the stigma, to fill up the cup of bitter waters assigned to woman, as if she deserved to be excluded from immortality as well as from justice, from hope as well as from enjoyment, it is ruled that a female has no business with the texts of the Veda—that having no knowledge of expiatory texts, and no evidence of law, sinful woman must be foul as falsehood itself, and incompetent to bear witness. To them the fountain of wisdom is sealed, the streams of knowledge are dried up; the springs of individual consolation, as promised in their religion, are guarded and barred against women in their hour of desolate sorrow and parching anguish; and cast out, as she is, upon the wilderness of bereavement and affliction, with her impoverished resources, her water may well be spent in the bottle; and, left as she is, will it be a matter of wonder that, in the mo-

> ment of despair, she will embrace the burning pile and its scorching flames, instead of lengthening solitude and degradation, of dark and humiliating suffering and sorrow?[3]

An effervescent sympathy for the oppressed is combined in this breathless prose with a total moral condemnation of a tradition that was seen to produce and sanctify these barbarous customs. And of course it was suttee that came to provide the most clinching example in this rhetoric of condemnation—"the first and most criminal of their customs," as William Bentinck, the governor-general who legislated its abolition, described it. Indeed, the practical implication of the criticism of Indian tradition was necessarily a project of "civilizing" the Indian people: the entire edifice of colonialist discourse was fundamentally constituted around this project.

Of course, within the discourse thus constituted, there was much debate and controversy about the specific ways in which to carry out this project. The options ranged from proselytization by Christian missionaries to legislative and administrative action by the colonial state to a gradual spread of enlightened Western knowledge. Underlying each option was the liberal colonial idea that in the end, Indians themselves must come to believe in the unworthiness of their traditional customs and embrace the new forms of civilized and rational social order.

I spoke, in chapter 2, of some of the political strategies of this civilizing mission. What must be noted here is that the so-called women's question in the agenda of Indian social reform in the early nineteenth century was not so much about the specific condition of women within a specific set of social relations as it was about the political encounter between a colonial state and the supposed "tradition" of a conquered people—a tradition that, as Lata Mani has shown in her study of the abolition of *satīdāha* (immolation of widows),[4] was itself produced by colonialist discourse. It was colonialist discourse that, by assuming the hegemony of Brahmanical religious texts and the complete submission of all Hindus to the dictates of those texts, defined the tradition that was to be criticized and reformed. Indian nationalism, in demarcating a political position opposed to colonial rule, took up the women's question as a problem already constituted for it: namely, as a problem of Indian tradition.

THE WOMEN'S QUESTION IN NATIONALISM

I described earlier the way nationalism separated the domain of culture into two spheres—the material and the spiritual. The claims of Western civilization were the most powerful in the material sphere. Science, technology, rational forms of economic organization, modern methods of statecraft—these had given the European countries the strength to subjugate the non-European people and to impose their dominance over the whole world. To overcome this domination, the colonized people had to learn those superior techniques of organizing material life and incorporate them within their own cultures. This was one aspect of the nationalist project of rationalizing and reforming the traditional culture of their people. But this could not mean the imitation of the West in every aspect of life, for then the very distinction between the West and the East would vanish—the self-identity of national culture would itself be threatened. In fact, as Indian nationalists in the late nineteenth century argued, not only was it undesirable to imitate the West in anything other than the material aspects of life, it was even unnecessary to do so, because in the spiritual domain, the East was superior to the West. What was necessary was to cultivate the material techniques of modern Western civilization while retaining and strengthening the distinctive spiritual essence of the national culture. This completed the formulation of the nationalist project, and as an ideological justification for the selective appropriation of Western modernity, it continues to hold sway to this day.

The discourse of nationalism shows that the material/spiritual distinction was condensed into an analogous, but ideologically far more powerful, dichotomy: that between the outer and the inner. The material domain, argued nationalist writers, lies outside us—a mere external that influences us, conditions us, and forces us to adjust to it. Ultimately, it is unimportant. The spiritual, which lies within, is our true self; it is that which is genuinely essential. It followed that as long as India took care to retain the spiritual distinctiveness of its culture, it could make all the compromises and adjustments necessary to adapt itself to the requirements of a modern material world without losing its true identity. This was the key that nationalism supplied for resolving the ticklish problems posed by issues of social reform in the nineteenth century.

Applying the inner/outer distinction to the matter of concrete day-to-day living separates the social space into *ghar* and *bāhir*, the home and the world. The world is the external, the domain of the material; the home represents one's inner spiritual self, one's true identity. The world is a treacherous terrain of the pursuit of material interests, where practical considerations reign supreme. It is also typically the domain of the male. The home in its essence must remain unaffected by the profane activities of the material world—and woman is its representation. And so one gets an identification of social roles by gender to correspond with the separation of the social space into ghar and bāhir.

Thus far we have not obtained anything that is different from the typical conception of gender roles in traditional patriarchy. If we now find continuities in these social attitudes in the phase of social reform in the nineteenth century, we are tempted to label this, as indeed the liberal historiography of India has done, as "conservatism," a mere defense of traditional norms. But this would be a mistake. The colonial situation, and the ideological response of nationalism to the critique of Indian tradition, introduced an entirely new substance to these terms and effected their transformation. The material/spiritual dichotomy, to which the terms *world* and *home* corresponded, had acquired, as noted before, a very special significance in the nationalist mind. The world was where the European power had challenged the non-European peoples and, by virtue of its superior material culture, had subjugated them. But, the nationalists asserted, it had failed to colonize the inner, essential, identity of the East, which lay in its distinctive, and superior, spiritual culture. Here the East was undominated, sovereign, master of its own fate. For a colonized people, the world was a distressing constraint, forced upon it by the fact of its material weakness. It was a place of oppression and daily humiliation, a place where the norms of the colonizer had perforce to be accepted. It was also the place, as nationalists were soon to argue, where the battle would be waged for national independence. The subjugated must learn the modern sciences and arts of the material world from the West in order to match their strengths and ultimately overthrow the colonizer. But in the entire phase of the national struggle, the crucial need was to protect, preserve, and strengthen the inner core of the national culture, its spiritual essence. No encroachments by the colonizer must be allowed in that inner sanctum. In the world, imitation of and adaptation to Western norms was a necessity; at home, they were tantamount to annihilation of one's very identity.

Once we match this new meaning of the home/world dichotomy with the identification of social roles by gender, we get the ideological framework within which nationalism answered the women's question. It would be a grave error to see in this, as liberals are apt to in their despair at the many marks of social conservatism in nationalist practice, a total rejection of the West. Quite the contrary: the nationalist paradigm in fact supplied an ideological principle of *selection*. It was not a dismissal of modernity but an attempt to make modernity consistent with the nationalist project.

DIFFERENCE AS A PRINCIPLE OF SELECTION

It is striking how much of the literature on women in the nineteenth century concerns the threatened Westernization of Bengali women. This theme was taken up in virtually every form of written, oral, and visual communication—from the ponderous essays of nineteenth-century moralists, to novels, farces, skits and jingles, to the paintings of the *paṭuā* (scroll painters). Social parody was the most popular and effective medium of this ideological propagation. From Iswarchandra Gupta (1812–59) and the *kabiyāl* (songsters) of the early nineteenth century to the celebrated pioneers of modern Bengali theater—Michael Madhusudan Dutt (1824–73), Dinabandhu Mitra, Jyotirindranath Tagore (1849–1925), Upendranath Das (1848–95), Amritalal Bose (1853–1929)—everyone picked up the theme. To ridicule the idea of a Bengali woman trying to imitate the ways of a *memsāheb* (and it was very much an idea, for it is hard to find historical evidence that even in the most Westernized families of Calcutta in the mid-nineteenth century there were actually any women who even remotely resembled these gross caricatures) was a sure recipe calculated to evoke raucous laughter and moral condemnation in both male and female audiences. It was, of course, a criticism of manners, of new items of clothing such as the blouse, the petticoat, and shoes (all, curiously, considered vulgar, although they clothed the body far better than the single length of sari that was customary for Bengali women, irrespective of wealth and social status, until the middle of the nineteenth century), of the use of Western cosmetics and jewelry, of the reading of novels, of needlework (considered a useless and expensive pastime), of riding in open carriages. What made the ridicule stronger was the constant suggestion that the Westernized woman was fond of useless luxury and cared little for the well-being of the home. One can hardly miss in all this a criticism—reproach mixed with envy—of the wealth and luxury of the new social elite emerging around the institutions of colonial administration and trade.

Take, for example, a character called "Mister Dhurandhar Pakrashi," whose educated wife constantly calls him a "fool" and a "rascal" (in English) and wants to become a "lady novelist" like Mary Correlli. This is how their daughter, Phulkumari, makes her entrance:

PHULKUMARI: Papa! Papa! I want to go to the races, please take me with you.

DHURANDHAR: Finished with your tennis?

PHULKUMARI: Yes, now I want to go to the races. And you have to get me a new bicycle. I won't ride the one you got me last year. And my football is torn: you have to get me another one. And Papa, please buy me a self-driving car. And also a nice pony. And please fix an electric lamp in my drawing-room; I can't see very well in the gaslight.

DHURANDHAR: Nothing else? How about asking the Banerjee Company to rebuild this house upside down, ceiling at the bottom and floor on top?

PHULKAMARI: How can that be, Papa? You can't give me an education and then expect me to have low tastes?[5]

Or take the following scene, which combines a parody of the pretensions to Westernized manners of the reformists with a comment on their utter impotence against the violence and contempt of the British. A group of enlightened men, accompanied by their educated wives, are meeting to discuss plans for "female emancipation" when they are interrupted by three English soldiers called—yes!—James, Frederick, and Peter. (Most of the scene is in English in the original.)

JAMES: What is the matter? my dear—something cheering seems to take place here?

UNNATA BABU: Cheering indeed, as ninety against twenty—a meeting for the Hindu female liberty.

JAMES: A meeting for the Hindu female liberty? A nice thing indeed amidst poverty.

FREDERICK: Who sit there, both males and females together?

PETER: These seem to be the Hindu Heroes, met to unveil their wives' veiled nose.

FREDERICK: Nose alone won't do—if eyes and head be set to full liberty, Hindu ladies are sure to be the objects of curiosity.

PETER: Curiosity, nicety, and charity too.

UNNATA BABU: This is offensive—this is offensive.

JAMES: Nothing offensive—nothing offensive.

UNNATA BABU: Go hence, ye foreigners. Why come here, ye vain intruders?

JAMES: To dance, to sing and to feast—
With our rising cousins of the East.

He takes Unnata Babu's wife by her hand, sings and dances with her, and then kisses her.

UNNATA BABU [Catches JAMES by the hand]: Leave her, leave her. She is my wife, my married wife.

JAMES [Throws UNNATA to the ground]:
O! thou nigger of butter and wax made,
Dared come, my hand to shake!
If Jupiter himself with his thunder-bolt in hand,
Comes to fight us, we will here him withstand.
[Takes out his sword]
Look, look, here is my sword.
Come, please, stain it with your blood.
[FREDERICK and PETER also take out their swords]
Strike him, strike the devil right and left,
We both better strike the rest.

The English soldiers make their exit with the following words to Unnata's wife:

JAMES: . . . O! pretty poor lady! We good-bye,
Pray you—go, go forward—
Wait upon, and guard your husband,
A treacherous, bloody coward.[6]

The literature of parody and satire in the first half of the nineteenth century clearly contained much that was prompted by a straightforward defense of existing practices and outright rejection of the new. The nationalist paradigm had still not emerged in clear outline. In hindsight, this period—from Rammohan to Vidyasagar—appears as one of great social turmoil and ideological confusion among the literati. And then a new discourse, drawing from various sources, began to form in the second half of the century—the discourse of nationalism.

In 1851, for instance, a prize essay on "Hindu female education" marshalled evidence that women's education was encouraged in ancient India and that it was not only not harmful but positively beneficial for women to be educated.[7] It went into numerous practical considerations on how women from respectable families could learn to read and write without any harm to their caste or their honor. In 1870, however, a tract on the duties of wives was declaring that the old prejudices about women's education had virtually disappeared. "Now the times are such that most people believe that . . . by educating women the condition of the country will improve and that there will be happiness, welfare and civilized manners in social life."[8]

The point of the new discussions was to define the social and moral principles for locating the position of women in the "modern" world of the nation. Take, for example one of the most clearly formulated tracts on the subject: Bhudeb Mukhopadhyay's *Pāribārik prabandha* (Essays on the family), published in 1882. Bhudeb states the problem in his characteristic matter-of-fact style:

> Because of the hankering for the external glitter and ostentation of the English way of life . . . an upheaval is under way within our homes. The men learn English and become *sahibs*. The women do not learn English but nevertheless try to become *bibis*. In households which manage an income of a hundred rupees, the women no longer cook, sweep or make the bed . . . everything is done by servants and maids; [the women] only read books, sew carpets and play cards. What is the result? The house and furniture get untidy, the meals poor, the health of every member of the family is ruined; children are born weak and rickety, constantly plagued by illness—they die early.
>
> Many reform movements are being conducted today; the education of women, in particular, is constantly talked about. But we rarely hear of those great arts in which women were once trained—a training which if it had still

been in vogue would have enabled us to tide over this crisis caused by injudicious imitation. I suppose we will never hear of this training again.[9]

The problem is put here in the empirical terms of a positive sociology, a genre much favored by serious Bengali writers of Bhudeb's time. But the sense of crisis he expresses was very much a reality. Bhudeb is voicing the feelings of large sections of the newly emergent middle class of Bengal when he says that the very institutions of home and family were threatened under the peculiar conditions of colonial rule. A quite unprecedented external condition had been thrust upon us; we were forced to adjust to those conditions, for which a certain degree of imitation of alien ways was unavoidable. But could this wave of imitation be allowed to enter our homes? Would that not destroy our inner identity? Yet it was clear that a mere restatement of the old norms of family life would not suffice; they were breaking down because of the inexorable force of circumstance. New norms were needed, which would be more appropriate to the external conditions of the modern world and yet not a mere imitation of the West. What were the principles by which these new norms could be constructed?

Bhudeb supplies the characteristic nationalist answer. In an essay entitled "Modesty," he talks of the natural and social principles that provide the basis for the feminine virtues.[10] Modesty, or decorum in manner and conduct, he says, is a specifically human trait; it does not exist in animal nature. It is human aversion to the purely animal traits that gives rise to virtues such as modesty. In this aspect, human beings seek to cultivate in themselves, and in their civilization, spiritual or godlike qualities wholly opposed to the forms of behavior which prevail in animal nature. Further, within the human species, women cultivate and cherish these godlike qualities far more than men. Protected to a certain extent from the purely material pursuits of securing a livelihood in the external world, women express in their appearance and behavior the spiritual qualities that are characteristic of civilized and refined human society.

The relevant dichotomies and analogies are all here. The material/spiritual dichotomy corresponds to animal/godlike qualities, which in turn corresponds to masculine/feminine virtues. Bhudeb then invests this ideological form with its specifically nationalist content:

In a society where men and women meet together, converse together at all times, eat and drink together, travel together, the manners of women are likely to be somewhat coarse, devoid of spiritual qualities and relatively prominent in animal traits. For this reason, I do not think the customs of such a society are free from all defect. Some argue that because of such close association with women, the characters of men acquire certain tender and spiritual qualities. Let me concede the point. But can the loss caused by

> coarseness and degeneration in the female character be compensated by the acquisition of a certain degree of tenderness in the male?

The point is then hammered home:

> Those who laid down our religious codes discovered the inner spiritual quality which resides within even the most animal pursuits which humans must perform, and thus removed the animal qualities from those actions. This has not happened in Europe. Religion there is completely divorced from [material] life. Europeans do not feel inclined to regulate all aspects of their life by the norms of religion; they condemn it as clericalism. . . . In the Arya system there is a preponderance of spiritualism, in the European system a preponderance of material pleasure. In the Arya system, the wife is a goddess. In the European system, she is a partner and companion.[11]

The new norm for organizing family life and determining the right conduct for women in the conditions of the modern world could now be deduced with ease. Adjustments would have to be made in the external world of material activity, and men would bear the brunt of this task. To the extent that the family was itself entangled in wider social relations, it too could not be insulated from the influence of changes in the outside world. Consequently, the organization and ways of life at home would also have to be changed. But the crucial requirement was to retain the inner spirituality of indigenous social life. The home was the principal site for expressing the spiritual quality of the national culture, and women must take the main responsibility for protecting and nurturing this quality. No matter what the changes in the external conditions of life for women, they must not lose their essentially spiritual (that is, feminine) virtues; they must not, in other words, become essentially Westernized. It followed, as a simple criterion for judging the desirability of reform, that the essential distinction between the social roles of men and women in terms of material and spiritual virtues must at all times be maintained. There would have to be a marked *difference* in the degree and manner of Westernization of women, as distinct from men, in the modern world of the nation.

A GENEALOGY OF THE RESOLUTION

This was the central principle by which nationalism resolved the women's question in terms of its own historical project. The details were not, of course, worked out immediately. In fact, from the middle of the nineteenth century right up to the present day, there have been many controversies about the precise application of the home/world, spiritual/material, feminine/masculine dichotomies in various matters concerning the everyday life of the "modern" woman—her dress, food, manners, education, her role in organizing life at home, her role outside the home. The concrete problems arose out of the rapidly changing situation, both external and internal, in which the new middle-class family found itself; the specific solutions were drawn from a variety of sources—a reconstructed "classical" tradition, modernized folk forms, the utilitarian logic of bureaucratic and industrial practices, the legal idea of equality in a liberal democratic state. The content of the resolution was neither predetermined nor unchanging, but its form had to be consistent with the system of dichotomies that shaped and contained the nationalist project.

The new woman defined in this way was subjected to a *new* patriarchy. In fact, the social order connecting the home and the world in which nationalists placed the new woman was contrasted not only with that of modern Western society; it was explicitly distinguished from the patriarchy of indigenous tradition, the same tradition that had been put on the dock by colonial interrogators. Sure enough, nationalism adopted several elements from tradition as marks of its native cultural identity, but this was now a "classicized" tradition—reformed, reconstructed, fortified against charges of barbarism and irrationality.

The new patriarchy was also sharply distinguished from the immediate social and cultural condition in which the majority of the people lived, for the "new" woman was quite the reverse of the "common" woman, who was coarse, vulgar, loud, quarrelsome, devoid of superior moral sense, sexually promiscuous, subjected to brutal physical oppression by males. Alongside the parody of the Westernized woman, this other construct is repeatedly emphasized in the literature of the nineteenth century through a host of lower-class female characters who make their appearance in the social milieu of the new middle class—maidservants, washer women, barbers, peddlers, procuresses, prostitutes. It was precisely this degenerate condition of women that nationalism claimed it would reform, and it was through these contrasts that the new woman of nationalist ideology was accorded a status of cultural superiority to the Westernized women of the wealthy parvenu families spawned by the colonial connection as well as to common women of the lower classes. Attainment by her own efforts of a superior national culture was the mark of woman's newly acquired freedom. This was the central ideological strength of the nationalist resolution of the women's question.

We can follow the form of this resolution in several specific aspects in which the life and condition of middle-class women have changed over the last one hundred years or so. Take the case of female education, that contentious subject that engaged so much of the attention of social reformers in the nineteenth century.[12] Some of the early opposition to the opening of schools for women was backed by an appeal to tradition, which supposedly prohibited women from being introduced to bookish learning, but this argument hardly gained much support. The real threat was seen to lie in the fact that the early schools, and arrangements for teaching women at home, were organized by Christian missionaries; there was thus the fear of both proselytization and the exposure of women to harmful Western influences.[13] The threat was removed when in the 1850s Indians themselves began to open schools for girls. The spread of formal education among middle-class women in Bengal in the second half of the nineteenth century was remarkable. From 95 girls' schools with a total attendance of 2,500 in 1863, the figures went up to 2,238 schools in 1890 with a total of more than 80,000 students.[14] In the area of higher education, Chandramukhi Bose (1860–1944) and Kadambini Ganguli (1861–1923) were celebrated as examples of what Bengali women could achieve in formal learning: they took their bachelor of arts degrees from the University of Calcutta in 1883, before most British universities agreed to accept women on their examination rolls. Kadambini then went on to medical college and became the first professionally schooled woman doctor.

The development of an educative literature and teaching materials in the Bengali language undoubtedly made possible the quite general acceptance of formal education among middle-class women. The long debates of the nineteenth century on a proper "feminine curriculum" now seem to us somewhat quaint, but it is not difficult to identify the real point of concern. Much of the content of the modern school education was seen as important for the "new" woman, but to administer it in the English language was difficult in practical terms, irrelevant because the central place of the educated woman was still at home, and threatening because it might devalue and displace that central site where the social position of women was located. The problem was resolved through the efforts of the intelligentsia, which made it a fundamental task of the national project to create a modern language and literature suitable for a widening readership that would include newly educated women. Through textbooks, periodicals, and creative works, an important force that shaped the new literature of Bengal was the urge to make it accessible to women who could read only one language—their mother tongue.

Formal education became not only acceptable but, in fact, a requirement for the new *bhadramahilā* (respectable woman) when it was demonstrated that it was possible for a woman to acquire the cultural refinements afforded by modern education without jeopardizing her place at home, that is, without becoming a memsāheb. Indeed, the nationalist construct of the new woman derived its ideological strength from making the goal of cultural refinement through education a personal challenge for every woman, thus opening up a domain where woman was an autonomous subject. This explains to a large extent the remarkable degree of enthusiasm among middle-class women themselves to acquire and use for themselves the benefits of formal learning. They set this goal for themselves in their personal lives and as the objects of their will: to achieve it was to achieve freedom.[15] Indeed, the achievement was marked by claims of cultural superiority in several different aspects: superiority over the Western woman for whom, it was believed, education meant only the acquisition of material skills to compete with men in the outside world and hence a loss of feminine (spiritual) virtues; superiority over the preceding generation of women in their own homes who had been denied the opportunity of freedom by an oppressive and degenerate social tradition; and superiority over women of the lower classes who were culturally incapable of appreciating the virtues of freedom.

It is this particular nationalist construction of reform as a project of both emancipation and self-emancipation of women (and hence a project in which both men and women had to participate) that also explains why the early generation of educated women themselves so keenly propagated the nationalist idea of the "new woman." Recent historians of a liberal persuasion have often been somewhat embarrassed by the profuse evidence of women writers of the nineteenth century, including those at the forefront of the reform movements in middle-class homes, justifying the importance of the so-called feminine virtues. Radharani Lahiri, for instance, wrote in 1875: "Of all the subjects that women might learn, housework is the most important. . . . Whatever knowledge she may acquire, she cannot claim any reputation unless she is proficient in housework."[16] Others spoke of the need for an educated woman to develop such womanly virtues as chastity, self-sacrifice, submission, devotion, kindness, patience, and the labors of love. The ideological point of view from which such protestations of "femininity" (and hence the acceptance of a new patriarchal order) were made inevitable was given precisely by the nationalist resolution of the problem, and Kundamala Debi, writing in 1870, expressed this well when she advised other women

> If you have acquired real knowledge, then give no place in your heart to *memsāheb*-like behavior. That is not becoming in a Bengali housewife. See how an educated woman can do housework thoughtfully and systematically in a way unknown to an ignorant, uneducated woman. And see how if God had not appointed us to this place in the home, how unhappy a place the world would be.[17]

Education then was meant to inculcate in women the virtues—the typically bourgeois virtues characteristic of the new social forms of "disciplining"—of orderliness, thrift, cleanliness, and a personal sense of responsibility, the practical skills of literacy, accounting, hygiene, and the ability to run the household according to the new physical and economic conditions set by the outside world. For this, she would also need to have some idea of the world outside the home, into which she could even venture as long as it did not threaten her femininity. It is this latter criterion, now invested with a characteristically nationalist content, that made possible the displacement of the boundaries of the home from the physical confines earlier defined by the rules of purdah to a more flexible, but nonetheless culturally determinate, domain set by the *differences* between socially approved male and female conduct. Once the essential femininity of women was fixed in terms of certain culturally visible spiritual qualities, they could go to schools, travel in public conveyances, watch public entertainment programs, and in time even take up employment outside the home. But the "spiritual" signs of her femininity were now clearly marked—in her dress, her eating habits, her social demeanor, her religiosity.

The specific markers were obtained from diverse sources, and in terms of their origins, each had its specific history. The dress of the bhadramahilā, for instance, went through a whole phase of experimentation before what was known as the brāhmikā sari (a form of wearing the sari in combination with blouse, petticoat, and shoes made fashionable in Brahmo households) became accepted as standard for middle-class women.[18] Here too the necessary differences were signified in terms of national identity, social emancipation, and cultural refinement—differences, that is to say, with the memsāheb, with women of earlier generations, and with women of the lower classes. Further, in this as in other aspects of her life, the spirituality of her character had also to be stressed in contrast with the innumerable ways men had to surrender to the pressures of the material world. The need to adjust to the new conditions outside the home had forced upon men a whole series of changes in their dress, food habits, religious observances, and social relations. Each of these capitulations now had to be compensated for by an assertion of spiritual purity on the part of women. They must not eat, drink, or smoke in the same way as men; they must continue the observance of religious rituals that men were finding difficult to carry out; they must maintain the cohesiveness of family life and solidarity with the kin to which men could not now devote much attention. The new patriarchy advocated by nationalism conferred upon women the honor of a new social responsibility, and by associating the task of female emancipation with the historical goal of sovereign nationhood, bound them to a new, and yet entirely legitimate, subordination.

As with all hegemonic forms of exercising dominance, this patriarchy combined coercive authority with the subtle force of persuasion. This was expressed most generally in the inverted ideological form of the relation of power between the sexes: the adulation of woman as goddess or as mother. Whatever its sources in the classical religions of India or in medieval religious practices, the specific ideological form in which we know the "Indian woman" construct in the modern literature and arts of India today is wholly and undeniably a product of the development of a dominant middle-class culture coeval with the era of nationalism. It served to emphasize with all the force of mythological inspiration what had in any case become a dominant characteristic of femininity in the new construct of "woman" standing as a sign for "nation," namely, the spiritual qualities of self-sacrifice, benevolence, devotion, religiosity, and so on. This spirituality did not, as we have seen, impede the chances of the woman moving out of the physical confines of the home; on the contrary, it facilitated it, making it possible for her to go into the world under conditions that would not threaten her femininity. In fact, the image of woman as goddess or mother served to erase her sexuality in the world outside the home.

There are many important implications of this construct. To take one example, consider an observation often made: the relative absence of gender discrimination in middle-class occupations in India, an area that has been at the center of demands for women's rights in the capitalist West. Without denying the possibility that there are many complexities that lie behind this rather superficial observation, it is certainly paradoxical that, whereas middle-class employment has been an area of bitter competition between cultural groups distinguished by caste, religion, language, and so on, in the entire period of nationalist and postcolonial politics in India, gender has never been an issue of public contention. Similarly, the new constitution of independent India gave women the vote without any major debate on the question and without there ever having been a movement for women's suffrage at any period of nationalist politics in India. The fact that everyone assumed that women would naturally have the vote indicates a complete transposition of the terms in which the old patriarchy of tradition was constituted. The fixing by nationalist ideology of masculine/feminine qualities in terms of the material/spiritual dichotomy does not make women who have entered professional occupations competitors to male job seekers, because in this construct there are no specific cultural signs that distinguish women from men in the material world.

In fact, the distinctions that often become significant are those that operate *between* women in the world outside the home. They can mark out women by their dress, eating habits (drinking/smoking), adherence to religious marks of feminine status, behavior toward men, and so on, and classify them as Westernized, traditional, low-class (or subtler variations on those distinctions)—all signifying a deviation from the acceptable norm. A woman identified as Westernized, for instance, would invite the ascription of all that the "normal" woman (mother/sister/wife/daughter) is not—brazen, avaricious, irreligious, sexually promiscuous—and this not only from males but also from women who see themselves as conforming to the legitimate norm, which is precisely an indicator of the hegemonic status of the ideological construct. An analogous set of distinctions would mark out the low-class or common woman from the normal. (Perhaps the most extreme object of contempt for the nationalist is the stereotype of the Anglo-Indian *ṭṅyāś*—Westernized and common at the same time.) Not surprisingly, deviation from the norm also carries with it the possibility of a variety of ambiguous meanings—signs of illegitimacy become the sanction for behavior not permitted for those who are "normal"—and these are the sorts of meaning exploited to the full by, for instance, the commercial media of film, advertising, and fashion. Here is one more instance of the displacement in nationalist ideology of the construct of woman as a sex object in Western patriarchy: the nationalist male thinks of his own wife/sister/daughter as "normal" precisely because she is not a "sex object," while those who could be "sex objects" are not "normal."

ELEMENTS OF A CRITIQUE OF THE RESOLUTION

I end this chapter by pointing out another significant feature of the way in which nationalism sought to resolve the women's question in accordance with its historical project. This has to do with the one aspect of the question that was directly political, concerning relations with the state. Nationalism, as we have noticed before, located its own subjectivity in the spiritual domain of culture, where it considered itself superior to the West and hence undominated and sovereign. It could not permit an encroachment by the colonial power in that domain. This determined the characteristically nationalist response to proposals for effecting social reform through the legislative enactments of the colonial state. Unlike the early reformers from Rammohan to Vidyasagar, nationalists of the late nineteenth century were in general opposed to such proposals, for such a method of reform seemed to deny the ability of the nation to act for itself even in a domain where it was sovereign. In the specific case of reforming the lives of women, consequently, the nationalist position was firmly based on the premise that this was an area where the nation was acting on its own, outside the purview of the guidance and intervention of the colonial state.

We now get the full answer to the historical problem I raised at the beginning of this chapter. The reason why the issue of "female emancipation" seems to disappear from the public agenda of nationalist agitation in the late nineteenth century is not because it was overtaken by the more emotive issues concerning political power. Rather, the reason lies in the refusal of nationalism to make the women's question an issue of political negotiation with the colonial state. The simple historical fact is that the lives of middle-class women, coming from that demographic section that effectively constituted the "nation" in late colonial India, changed most rapidly precisely during the period of the nationalist movement—indeed, so rapidly that women from each generation in the last hundred years could say quite truthfully that their lives were strikingly different from those led by the preceding generation. These changes took place in the colonial period mostly outside the arena of political agitation, in a domain where the nation thought of itself as already free. It was after independence, when the nation had acquired political sovereignty, that it became legitimate to embody the idea of reform in legislative enactments about marriage rules, property rights, suffrage, equal pay, equality of opportunity, and so on. Now, of course, the women's question has once again become a political issue in the life of the nation-state.

Another problem on which we can now obtain a clearer perspective is that of the seeming absence of any autonomous struggle by women themselves for equality and freedom. We would be mistaken to look for evidence of such struggle in the public archives of political affairs, for unlike the women's movement in nineteenth- and twentieth-century Europe or America, the battle for the new idea of womanhood in the era of nationalism was waged in the home. We know from the evidence left behind in autobiographies, family histories, religious tracts, literature, theater, songs, paintings, and such other cultural artifacts, that it was the home that became the principal site of the struggle through which the hegemonic construct of the new nationalist patriarchy had to be normalized. This is the real history of the women's question whose terrain our genealogical investigation into the nationalist idea of "woman" has identified. The nationalist discourse we have heard so far is a discourse *about* women; women do not speak here. In the next chapter, we will explore the problem of enabling women in recent Indian history to speak for themselves.

The location of the state in the nationalist resolution of the women's question in the colonial period has yet another implication. For sections of the middle class that felt themselves culturally excluded from the formation of the nation and that then organized themselves as politically distinct groups, their relative exclusion from the new nation-state would act as a further means of displacement of the legitimate agency of reform. In the case of Muslims in Bengal, for instance, the formation of a new middle class was delayed, for reasons we need not go into here. Exactly the same sorts of ideological concerns typical of a nationalist response to issues of social reform in a colonial situation can be seen to operate among Muslims as well, with a difference in chronological time.[19] Nationalist reforms do not, however, reach political fruition in the case of the Muslims in independent India, because to the extent that the dominant cultural formation among them considers the community excluded from the state, a new colonial relation is brought into being. The system of dichotomies of inner/outer, home/world, feminine/masculine are once again activated. Reforms that touch upon what is considered the inner essence of the identity of the community can be legitimately carried out only by the community itself, not by the state. It is instructive to note how little institutional change has been allowed in the civil life of Indian Muslims since independence and to compare the degree of change with that in Muslim countries where nationalist cultural reform was a part of the successful formation of an independent nation-state. The contrast is striking if one compares the position of middle-class Muslim women in West Bengal today with that of neighboring Bangladesh.

The continuance of a distinct cultural "problem" of the minorities is an index of the failure of the Indian nation to effectively include within its body the whole of the demographic mass that it claims to represent. The failure becomes evident when we note that the formation of a hegemonic "national culture" was *necessarily* built upon the privileging of an "essential tradition," which in turn was defined by a system of exclusions. Ideals of freedom, equality, and cultural refinement went hand in hand with a set of dichotomies that systematically excluded from the new life of the nation the vast masses of people whom the dominant elite would represent and lead, but who could never be culturally integrated with their leaders. Both colonial rulers and their nationalist opponents conspired to displace in the colonial world the original structure of meanings associated with Western liberal notions of right, freedom, equality, and so on. The inauguration of the national state in India could not mean a universalization of the bourgeois notion of "man."

Indeed, in setting up its new patriarchy as a hegemonic construct, nationalist discourse not only demarcated its cultural essence as distinct from that of the West but also from that of the mass of the people. It has generalized itself among the new middle class, admittedly a widening class and large enough in absolute numbers to be self-reproducing, but is situated at a great distance from the large mass of subordinate classes. My analysis of the nationalist construction of woman once again shows how, in the confrontation between colonialist and nationalist discourses, the dichotomies of spiritual/material, home/world, feminine/masculine, while enabling the production of a nationalist discourse which is different from that of colonialism, nonetheless remains trapped within its framework of false essentialisms.

CHAPTER SEVEN

Women and the Nation

THE TROUBLE WITH THEIR VOICES

If there is one theme that dominates the new literature which emerged in Bengal in the nineteenth century, it is the theme of change. Everything was changing; nothing was likely to remain the same. Prolonged and bitter debates ensued about how best to cope with all this change. But at bottom the assumption was shared that the force working to alter the very foundations of society was both overwhelming and alien: the source of change itself lay outside and beyond control. It is important to remember this when considering the emergence of a "modern" consciousness of the self under colonial conditions.

The question of the "new woman" was, like other contemporary social issues, formulated, as we have just seen, as a question of coping with change. But who was to do the coping? Bankimchandra, the most eminent literary figure in Bengal in the late nineteenth century, wrote in the early 1870s an essay comparing the virtues and faults of women of an older age with those of women of modern times.[1] Bankim began the essay by declaring that in all societies it was men who always laid down the ways in which women must behave. "Self-interested men are mindful of the improvement of women only to the extent that it furthers their self-interest; not for any other reason." There was, consequently, no confusion in Bankim's mind about the social agency in question when considering the character of women. If the modern woman differed from her predecessors, she did so as the result of social policies pursued by men; men's attitudes and actions were on trial here.

Bankim then goes on to list the virtues and defects of the "new" woman compared with those of the "traditional." It is a familiar list, reproduced, embellished, and canonized in succeeding decades in the prodigious nationalist literature on women. In the past, women were uneducated, and therefore coarse, vulgar, and quarrelsome. By comparison, modern women have more refined tastes. On the other hand, whereas women were once hardworking and strong, they were now lazy and fond of luxury, unmindful of housework, and prone to all sorts of illnesses. Further, in the olden days women were religious. They were faithful to their husbands, hospitable to guests, and charitable to the needy. They genuinely believed in the norms of right conduct. Today, if women do these things, they do so more because of fear of criticism than because they have faith in dharma.

Bankim may have felt that despite his initial remarks about the responsibility of men as lawmakers of society, the essay was likely to be read as a criticism of women themselves, whether traditional or modern. In the subsequent issue of the journal in which the essay appeared, Bankim appended three letters, supposedly written by women in response to the article. All three complained that women had been treated unfairly by the author. The first retaliated with a list of accusations against the educated male.

> Alright, we are lazy. But what about you? . . . You work only because the English have tied you to the millstone. . . . We have no bonds of religion, you say. And you? You are ever fearful of religion because it is like a noose around your neck: one end of the rope is held by the owner of the liquor-store and the other by the prostitute.

The second argued that the defects of the modern woman had been produced only by the "virtues" of the modern man.

> Yes, by your virtues, not by your faults. If only you had not loved us so much, we would not have had so many defects. We are lazy because you have made us so contented. . . . We are unmindful of guests because we are so mindful of our husbands and children. . . . And, finally, are we not afraid of religion? In truth, it is only because we are afraid of religion that we dare not tell you what we should. You are our only religion. We are so afraid of you that we have no fear of any other religion. . . . If this is a crime against religion, then it is both your fault and your virtue. And if you do not mind being asked a question by this prattling female—"You are our teachers, we are your disciples: what religion do you teach us?" . . . Oh shame! Don't spread tales about your slaves!

The third correspondent offered to exchange places with the modern male. "Come indoors and take charge of the house. Let us go out to work. Slaves for seven hundred years, and still you pride yourselves on your masculinity! Aren't you ashamed?"[2]

I mention this essay by Bankim at the very beginning of my discussion of women's writings about themselves not only to remind us that the hegemonic discourse which framed these writings—the discourse of anticolonial nationalism—was in its core a male discourse, but also to point out the capacity of this discourse to appropriate discordant, marginal, and critical voices. In Bankim's case, the device was self-irony. The strand of nationalist thinking Bankim represented sought to create a national leadership in the image of ideal masculinity—strong, proud, just, wise, a protector of the righteous, and a terror to the mischievous. Relentlessly, he poured scorn and ridicule on an educated elite that, he thought, was failing to live up to this ideal. Self-irony was the mode by which he could, as a member of this inadequate elite, expose to itself its own weaknesses, even by assuming the voices of its "others"—those of the illiterate, the poor and the "mad," and also those of women.[3] The form was used widely. Indeed, fiction and drama in late nineteenth-century Bengal are full of instances of women, from "respectable" families as well as from the urban poor, using the rhetorical skills of "common" speech and the moral precepts of "common" sense to show up the pretentiousness and hypocrisy of the educated male. We must not overlook the hegemonic possibilities of this internalized critique: it could, up to a point, retain its own legitimacy and appropriate both feminine and popular ridicule simply by owning up to them.[4]

The question is: Up to what point? Or rather, in which discursive field? Within what sort of boundaries? We cannot find a historically nuanced answer to this question unless we think of the field of discourse as one of contention, peopled by several subjects, several consciousnesses. We must think of discourse as situated within fields of power, not only constituting that field but also constituted by it. Dominance here cannot exhaust the claims to subjectivity, for even the dominated must always retain an aspect of autonomy. Otherwise, power would cease to be a relation; it would no longer be constituted by struggle.

If nationalist ideology in late nineteenth-century Bengal legitimized the subjection of women under a new patriarchy, its history must be a history of struggle. The difficulty which faces historians here is that by working from the conventional archives of political history, women appear in the history of nationalism only in a "contributive" role.[5] All one can assert here is that women *also* took an active part in nationalist struggle, but one cannot identify any autonomous subjectivity of women and from that standpoint question the manner in which the hegemonic claims of nationalist culture were themselves fashioned.

My argument is that because of the specific conditions of colonial society, this history is to be found less in the external domain of political conflict and more in the "inner" space of the middle-class home. Fortunately, there exists something of an archive for us to delve into: a series of autobiographies by educated women who wrote about their lives and their struggles in this eventful period of modern Indian history. I propose to present here a reading of five such autobiographies, beginning with a woman who was born in the first decade of the nineteenth century and ending with one who reached middle age in the first decade of the twentieth.

The autobiography would seem to be obvious material for studying the emergence of "modern" forms of self-representation. Unfortunately, here too the colonial condition works to displace the points of application of the usual critical apparatus. Historians of Bengali literature conventionally agree that the modern forms of the biography and the autobiography made their appearance in Bengal sometime in the middle of the nineteenth century because of the emergence of a new concept of the "individual" among the English-educated elite.[6] Yet, despite the continued popularity of the genre, it is difficult to explain why the facts of social history and the development of new cultural norms for the collective life of the nation, rather than the exploration of individuality and the inner workings of the personality, constitute the overwhelming bulk of the material of these life stories. The first comprehensive social history of nineteenth-century Bengal was written in the form of a biography of a social reformer,[7] while the foremost political leader of Bengal at the turn of the century entitled his autobiography *A Nation in Making*.[8] The "new individual," it would seem, could represent the history of his life only by inscribing it in the narrative of the nation.

Not unexpectedly, autobiographies of women have characteristics rather different from those of men. It is not simply that women's life stories are concerned more with the domestic than with the public sphere, a feature often noticed in women's autobiographies of the modern period in all countries. Nor is it a particular characteristic that the self-discovery of female identity acknowledges "the real presence and recognition of another consciousness" and that "the disclosure of female self is linked to the identification of some 'other.'"[9] In a fundamental sense, all identity has to be disclosed by establishing an alterity.[10] Men's autobiographies, it seems to me, do the same: the difference lies in the textual strategies employed. In the case of the women's autobiographies discussed here, the most striking feature is the way in which the very theme of disclosure of self remains suppressed under a narrative of changing times, changing manners, and customs, and changing values.

When the first autobiographies came to be written in the second half of the nineteenth century by men who had achieved eminence in the new public life of colonial Bengal, the most common title given to these works was the *ātmacarit*. While this was meant to stand as a literal translation of the English word *autobiography,* it also carried, more significantly, an allusion to the entire body of *carita* literature of the classical and medieval eras in which the lives of kings and saints were recorded. *Buddhacarita* by Aśvaghoṣa and *Harṣacarita* by Bāṇa are perhaps the most well known examples of a whole genre of religious and secular hagiographic writings in Sanskrit, whereas the *Caitanyacaritāmṛta* (1615) is the most distinguished of numerous carit writings in Bengali in the two centuries preceding the colonial age. While the more obvious hagiographic conventions were quickly abandoned in the new biographical literature of the nineteenth century, the idea of the carit as the life of an illustrious man, told either by himself or by others, clearly persisted even in its modern sense.

Women's life stories were not given the status of carit. Of some twenty or so autobiographies I have seen of nineteenth-century Bengali women, not one is called an *ātmacarit*.[11] This, in fact, gives us a clue to the nature of women's autobiographical writings in this period: these were not simply variants on men's autobiographical writings but constituted a distinct literary genre. The most common name by which they were described was the *smṛtikathā*: "memoirs," or more accurately, "stories from memory." What held these stories together into a single narrative was not the life history of the narrator or the development of her "self" but rather the social history of the "times." The most commonly employed narrative device was the contrast: "In those days . . ."/"Nowadays . . ." The stories told were those of everyday life in the "inner" part of the house inhabited by women, of rituals and celebrations, of births, deaths, and marriages, of the sudden interruptions of everyday routine by calamitous events, and, of course, of how everything was so different "nowadays." It is not surprising that the first systematic surveys of women's autobiographical writings have treated this material principally as a source for reconstructing the social history of nineteenth-century Bengal,[12] and a recent book-length study of women's autobiographies has carried out this exercise much more elaborately.[13]

What made the narrative history of domestic life particularly suitable as a "feminine" literary genre was the belief, inculcated, needless to say, by male guardians of literary conventions, that this required little more than the retelling from memory of impressions left by direct personal experience. One did not have to have the imaginative power or stylistic flair of the poet or the novelist in order to tell one's smṛtikathā: anyone could do it. The immediacy, directness, and indeed the very artlessness of the form was seen to make it appropriate for an authentic "feminine" literary voice. When Charulata, the heroine of Rabindranath Tagore's story "The Broken Nest" (made into a film by Satyajit Ray), first tried her hand at writing, she began with an essay called "The August Clouds" but soon discovered that it read too much like another essay called "The July Moon," written by her brother-in-law Amal. She then proceeded to write about the Kālī temple in the village in which she had lived as a child. Tagore approved of this change in Charu's style: "Although in the early part her writing was cluttered by the excessively ornamental style of Amal, it soon acquired a simplicity and charm of its own, filled as it now was with the richness of a rural idiom."[14]

The genre, in short, did not require the author to express her "self" or examine the development of her personality. It was not the telling of an exemplary life, not even of a life of any importance: to this day, it is useful to remember, there are fewer biographies of Bengali women written by others than there are autobiographies. The genre required the writer only to tell her readers, mainly women from a younger generation, how the everyday lives of women had changed. This allowed the questions to be raised: How are we to cope with this change? In what ways must we change ourselves? These were, of course, the central questions of nationalist discourse. However, in this particular case, the discourse enabled a more specific question to be asked—and answered: How must women behave in these changing times?

To discover how educated women of the nineteenth century answered this question, we will now look at some of their own writings. We will listen to their own words, but we will also do well to remember that sovereignty over language, a tricky business under the best of circumstances, is doubly vitiated for those who were subordinated, at one and the same time, to colonialism as well as to a nationalist patriarchy.

BEFORE ENLIGHTENMENT

Shanta Nag, who came from a generation of middle-class women whose mothers were already educated, tells the story of how she learned to read the alphabet. It was sometime around the turn of the century. Her mother would sit across the table teaching her elder brother and she would stand beside her, silently watching the proceedings. In a few months, without anybody suspecting it, she had learned to read the first two books of the Bengali primer. The only difficulty was that in order to read, she had to hold the book upside down.[15] Of course, by her time the education of women had become normal practice in middle-class homes in Bengal, and she herself would have learned the alphabet and gone to school as a matter of routine. But the sense of acquiring a skill that was really meant for somebody else seems to have stayed with these early generations of educated women.

Nowhere is this more poignant than in the story of Rassundari Debi (1809–1900). For her, learning to read and write was nothing less than a lifelong struggle. She had been born in a wealthy, landed family and the village school was located in one of the buildings on the estate. When she was eight, her uncle sent her to this school, where, for the next two years, she sat everyday on the floor, the only girl in a roomful of boys, and was taught the Bengali alphabet, some arithmetic, and some Persian (which had still not been replaced by English as the language of bureaucracy). The teacher was an Englishwoman.[16] Rassundari does not tell us this, but we know from other sources that during this brief spell in the early nineteenth century, Christian missionary women attempted to educate Indian girls, first in schools and then in their homes.[17] The attempt had to be given up rather quickly because the idea of women being exposed to Christian influences seemed far too threatening to the men of their families, and it was only in the latter half of the century, when Indians themselves began to open schools for women and to produce what was considered a suitable modern educational literature in Bengali, that the practice of middle-class girls going to school would become legitimate.

In the meantime, Rassundari's education came to an abrupt halt when she was ten because the building in which her school was housed was destroyed in a fire.[18] It is doubtful how far her education would have progressed in any case, because at the age of twelve, in accordance with the prevailing custom, she was given in marriage.

From then on, her life was enclosed by the daily performance of her household duties. After the death of her mother-in-law a few years later, she had to take on the entire burden of running the house. She cooked three times a day for about thirty members of the household. She gave birth to twelve children, of whom seven died in her lifetime. Her responsibilities in the family would not allow her to go anywhere. Even when she did, to visit her husband's relatives on weddings and other ritual occasions, she would be accompanied on the boat by two guards, two maids, and ten or fifteen other people, and, "like a prisoner on parole," would have to return in a couple of days. Rassundari particularly lamented her failure to visit her mother before she died.

> I tried in so many ways to go and see my mother, but I was not fated to do so. This is not a matter of small regret to me. Oh Lord, why did you give birth to me as a human being? Compared to all the birds and beasts and other inferior creatures in this world, it is a rare privilege to be granted a human birth. And yet, despite this privilege, I have failed grievously in my duty. Why was I born a woman? Shame on my life! . . . If I had been my mother's son and known of her imminent death, no matter where I happened to be, I would have flown to her side like a bird. Alas, I am only a bird in a cage.[19]

Had this been all there was to Rassundari's life, it would have been no different from those of thousands of other women in upper-caste landed families in early nineteenth-century Bengal, and we would have had no opportunity to read about it in her own words. Fortunately, she nursed a secret dream. She was always a devout woman, and sometime in her late youth she had a longing to read the religious epics and the lives of the great saints. She did not so much as dare look at even a piece of paper that had been written on, for fear of adverse comments, but every day, she tells us, she would pray to her god: "Oh Lord, give me learning, so that I can read books. . . . If you do not teach me, who will?"[20] And yet, she did not know how this impossible feat would be accomplished.

The way was shown to her in a dream.

> One day, in my sleep, I dreamt I had opened a copy of the *Caitanya-bhāgavat* and was reading it. As soon as I woke up, my body and mind were filled with delight. I closed my eyes and again thought of the dream, and realized what a precious gift I had received. . . . I said to myself, "How remarkable! I have never seen a copy of the *Caitanya-bhāgavat* and would not recognize it even if I saw one. And yet, there I was reading it in my dream." . . . Every day I had asked the Almighty, "Teach me to read. I want to read books." The Almighty had not taught me to read, but had now given me the power to read books in my dream. I was delighted and thanked the Almighty.[21]

Rassundari, however, was to be blessed even more generously. That very day, while she was busy in the kitchen, her husband came in looking for their eldest son and said to him, "This is my *Caitanya-bhāgavat*. Keep it here somewhere. I'll send for it later." Rassundari waited until no one was around, removed a page of the unbound manuscript, and hid it in her room. Later, she tried to read it and discovered that so many years after her brief period of schooling, she could not recognize most of the letters. She then stole a page on which her son had practiced his alphabets, and for months thereafter, whenever she was alone, she would compare the two pieces of paper and, painfully and in absolute secrecy, teach herself to read.

Over the next couple of years, she worked her way through the *Caitanya-bhāgavat*. No one in the household, except a few trusted maids, knew of her accomplishment. But Rassundari had perceived the existence of a whole new world that still seemed out of her reach.

> My mind seemed to have acquired six hands. With two of them, it wanted to do all the work of the household so that no one, young or old, could find fault with me. With two others, it sought to draw my children close to my heart. And with the last two, it reached out for the moon. . . . Has anyone held the moon in her hands? . . . And yet, my mind would not be convinced; it yearned to read the *purāṇa*.[22]

Rassundari gathered up courage and shared her secret with her widowed sisters-in-law. To her surprise, not only did they not reprimand her, but in fact eagerly conspired to start a secret reading circle, arranging to procure books from the outer quarters of the house and setting up an elaborate warning system to prevent discovery.[23]

In time, when her sons were grown, it was no longer necessary to keep up the secrecy. In any case, the times had also changed, and men of her son's generation looked upon the education of women as a virtue. It was with the assistance of her sons that Rassundari learned to read the printed book and later on to write.[24]

Rassundari thought of her achievement as a divine gift. In fact, her testimony is quite unique in the collection we are looking at for the utterly sincere way in which it tells the story of a life shaped entirely by the inscrutable whims and fancies of a divine power, including the dreams and miraculous coincidences in which that power revealed its presence. It could well be a fragment, paraphrased in the prose of the nineteenth century, from the devotional literature of an earlier era. All subjectivity is attributed here to a divine agency, and Rassundari recounts her toil and sorrow—"the burden of three lives thrust into one"—only as the story of a fate assigned to her. I should also mention that she notes with great satisfaction the good fortune of women younger than her, for "the Lord of the Universe has now made new rules for everything. Women today do not have to suffer. . . . Nowadays parents take great care to educate their daughters. I feel very pleased when I see this."[25]

Before we leave Rassundari to move on to the life histories of women whose beliefs were shaped more directly by the sensibilities of this "modern" world, we must note the way in which her story was given a place in the autobiographical literature of Bengal. When her book was published in the early decades of this century, it was introduced with two forewords—one by the dramatist Jyotirindranath Tagore and the other by the pioneering historian of Bengali literature Dineshchandra Sen (1866–1939). Jyotirindranath saw in her writing "a simple and unselfconscious charm" and noted in particular the fact that "it was her thirst for religious knowledge which drove her to learn to read and write."[26]

Dineshchandra saw in it "a true portrait of the traditional Hindu woman," "the original picture of the long-suffering, compassionate Bengali woman." He remarked on the tendency in modern literature to focus on woman exclusively as the subject of romantic love, which produced, he says, a very incomplete picture of the Hindu woman who was, after all, also a mother, daughter, sister, sister-in-law, daughter-in-law, and mistress of the household and "had to earn credit in all of these roles before she would be praised by society." Rassundari's life was a model of such traditional virtues.[27] Of course, the social norms within which she led her life were often oppressive, but those were the undesirable aspects of tradition which had to be reformed.

Nationalists of the twentieth century saw in Rassundari's story only a confirmation of their construction of the true essence of Indian womanhood: self-sacrificing, compassionate, spiritual, and possessing great resources of emotional strength drawn from personal faith and devotion. This essence, they thought, needed to be recovered from the morass of bigotry and superstition into which tradition had fallen, and reform and education could accomplish this. What they did not recognize was that Rassundari's struggle emanated from a consciousness that was yet uncolonized by the Enlightenment. She submitted to as well as resisted a patriarchy that was premodern; her strategies of resistance also sprang out of traditions that far predated the advent of "women's education" as an agenda of nationalist reform. Above all, the intervention of nationalist male reformers was not required to set Rassundari's consciousness into motion.[28] Indeed, in her time, the nationalist project had not even begun. Only later did nationalism appropriate her story into its own prehistory.

If I might stay with this transitional period a little longer, I would like to bring in here the story of Saradasundari Debi (1819–1907). Saradasundari was married at the age of nine into one of the most prominent families of colonial Calcutta. Ramkamal Sen, her father-in-law, was, as I mentioned before in another context, a close associate of English traders and officials and although very much an advocate of Western education, he was also concerned with the preservation of religious orthodoxy. Saradasundari's husband had been educated into the new world, and every night, in the secrecy of their bedroom, he would teach her to read and rite.[29] She, however, became a widow when she was still a young woman, and later in her life, while she could still read, she had lost her ability to write. The account we are reading was dictated by her to a younger male relative.

The story she tells us is one of suffering—the suffering of a widow with small children surrounded by male relatives intent on defrauding her of her property. Her main responsibility in the world was toward her children—giving her sons a good education and arranging for the marriage of her daughters. Whenever she could, she sought to escape the sufferings of the world by going on pilgrimage. She too was a devout woman, and the happiest episodes in the story that she tells occur in her journeys away from home.

Once again, this is a life that might have been led by numerous other upper-caste women of her time. What prompted her amanuensis to record Saradasundari's story was the fact that her son Keshabchandra Sen was one of the most charismatic leaders of the religious reform movement in Bengal in the second half of the nineteenth century. It is as the life history of Keshab's mother that Saradasundari's autobiography found a place in the archives of Bengali literature.[30]

And it is in this respect that her account reveals traces of the struggle inside urban homes caught in the vortex of cultural reform. Unlike Rassundari, Saradasundari is much more self-conscious about her religiosity. She talks about her joy and fulfillment in the many pilgrimages she made in her life, and yet she also expresses a sense of guilt.

> I felt then that I was being virtuous. I would not feel the same way now. I was a little childish then. Even now, I go on pilgrimages, but not to earn religious merit. I go only out of love, in the same way that I have love for my children and those who are my own. But I do not believe that I will gain salvation by going on pilgrimages. . . . I had this obsession for religion and a strong urge to see the holy places. Even now I perform many kinds of worship, but all from the same feeling [of love]. I believe in my heart that there is only one God and unless I worship Him I will never find salvation. I cannot say with certainty that people never achieve salvation if they worship the deities with form [*sākār*], but I do know that they achieve it if they worship the formless God [*nirākār*] and that my own salvation depends upon His grace.

Those who know the social history of Bengal in this period will immediately hear in these words resonances of that contentious debate between monotheistic Brahmo reformers and the defenders of Hindu orthodoxy. Living in an orthodox family, and yet the proud mother of a son celebrated for his radical religious views, Saradasundari was clearly caught in a conflict that was not of her own making. She had, therefore, to speak in two voices—one recalling with gratitude and joy her visits to the great Vaishnav temples of India and her miraculous visions of the deity, and the other asserting her role as Keshab Sen's mother. It would be presumptuous on our part to declare one of the two as her true voice; what was true was her struggle to make both voices her own.

> I had to suffer a great deal because [Keshab] became a Brahmo. I had to bear with much insult . . . and ill treatment. There was not a day when I did not cry. . . . There were times when even I thought that Keshab was doing wrong. I do not think so anymore. . . . I sought advice from my *guru*. He told me, "If your son accepts this new religion, he will become a great man. People will flock to him. Don't worry about this anymore." I was calmed by his words.[31]

It should not be surprising to notice that for this early generation of women from the new middle class of Bengal, the presence of society and religion as a set of regulatory practices appeared in the immediacy of family and kin relations converging upon the home. So did the presence of new currents in the outside world, including the presence of the West itself, appear in the person of a male member of the family, usually the husband or a son. The great conflicts over social reform in a public domain peopled exclusively by males were thus transmitted into the lives of women inside their homes. Women, consequently, had to devise strategies to cope with the new demands made upon their loyalties and their desires. If Saradasundari seems painfully torn between a conventional devotion which gave her solace in an oppressive world and a rational religion preached by her radical son, we have another testimony which suggests a resolution of this dilemma. Significantly, this occurs in the case of a woman who was able to escape the daily surveillance of the extended family and live a life with her modernist husband, as it were, outside the reaches of "society."

THE NEW WOMEN

Kailasbasini Debi (1830–95) was the wife of Kishorichand Mitra (1822–73), a prominent figure among the social reformers of the mid-nineteenth century.[32] Kishorichand was an employee of the East India Company and held important administrative positions in the district towns of Bengal and Bihar. For several years of her married life, therefore, Kailasbasini lived alone with her husband, away from home, in company bungalows and houseboats. Her husband taught her to read and write Bengali and some English as well. Later, when he settled down in Calcutta, Kishorichand built a garden house in the outskirts of the city, where Kailasbasini would often live with her husband and daughter.

In marked contrast to the other stories we have heard so far, Kailasbasini talks of her married life as one of happiness. She looked from a critical distance at the traditional life of the family she had left behind but that was always waiting for her out there. She was horrified by the unhygienic and degrading conditions in which women in traditional homes were confined at childbirth and regretted that other women she knew did not have the benefits of enlightened teaching which her husband had given her.[33] She was quite conscious of the way in which her husband had assiduously molded her thoughts and beliefs, and was grateful for it. Most of these views were rationalist, in the way in which rationalist arguments were used in the nineteenth century to supply instrumental justifications for traditional beliefs and customs. Thus, Kailasbasini says, echoing her husband, widows are traditionally restricted to a hard life devoid of luxury in order to make them unattractive to men, so that they do not become objects of their lust. Meat eating is regarded as polluting because India is a warm country in which meat is bad for the health. Idolatry meets the need to provide a practical religion for ignorant people who find it difficult to conceive of an abstract, formless God.[34]

There is no question that Kailasbasini saw herself as both more fortunate than and superior to other women around her. She was happy in the formative company of her enlightened husband. When he was away on tour, she tells us with a stunning simile, she spent her time "like Robinson Crusoe, eating, sleeping, reading, sewing, teaching my daughter and writing this journal."[35]

And yet, even for someone so free from the rigors of customary regulation and so happily enveloped by an entirely new conjugal tutelage, Kailasbasini required strategies to protect herself against the consequences of her husband's reformist projects.

> I do not believe in the rituals of Hindu orthodoxy, but I follow all of them. For I know that if I relax my hold, my husband will give up the Hindu religion altogether. My closest relatives are Hindus and I can never abandon them. For this reason, I scrupulously follow all the rules of the Hindu religion.
>
> I have this great fear that no one will accept food from my hands. That would be a shame worse than death. As it is, my husband eats out [without observing ritual regulations]; if I too join him, it would be a calamity.
>
> . . . Since I follow the Hindu rules, I have no problems, no matter what my husband does. That is the religion of the Bengalis, which is why those who are clever do not believe in it. But I never say this to my husband, although I know it would please him to no end if he heard it from me.[36]

I wish to suggest that we have here a moment where a strategy worked out within the space of the emergent nationalist middle-class home anticipated the form of a more general strategy which political nationalism would later attempt to use in order to make the solidarity of cultural communities compatible with the requirements of the modern state. A neat separation between a private sphere of diverse individuals residing in bourgeois patriarchal families and a public sphere inhabited by homogeneous citizens was not available to Indian nationalism. The rational-bureaucratic form of the modern state brought to India by the colonial power was premised precisely upon the denial of citizenship to colonized Indians. The strategy, therefore, had to use another distinction—between the spiritual or the inner, on the one hand, and the material or the outer, on the other. The latter was a ground surrendered to the colonial power; the former was where nationalism began to fashion its claims to hegemony. Kailasbasini, speaking from within this emergent middle-class home, is not telling us that religious beliefs and practices are private matters and that what is important for the life of the nation is the public behavior of its citizens. On the contrary, she has discovered that the practices of the outside world which men have to get used to are in the end inconsequential, since what truly matters in the life of the nation are practices in the inner space of community life. Here it is the duty of women to hold fast to the religious practices of the community: even "private" beliefs are of no consequence. Her strategy mirrors a crucial move in the cultural politics of nationalism.

The home, I suggest, was not a complementary but rather the original site on which the hegemonic project of nationalism was launched.

Women from the new middle class in nineteenth-century India thus became active agents in the nationalist project—complicit in the framing of its hegemonic strategies as much as they were resistant to them because of their subordination under the new forms of patriarchy.

To return to Kailasbasini: the apparent stability of the manner in which she chose to reconcile the conflicting demands on her loyalty was undoubtedly made possible by the fortuitous distance between her conjugal home and the effective center of her social life. The situation was to be repeated in the cases of many middle-class families of the Bengali diaspora that spread out into the cities and towns of northern India with the expansion of colonial administration in the second half of the nineteenth century. But in her case at least, the fragility of an individual solution worked out in the peripheries of society was exposed rather tragically. In 1873, when Kailasbasini was in her early forties, her husband died.

> I took the name "widow." When I hear that name, it is as though lightning strikes my heart. Oh Lord, why have you given me this name? How long am I to live with it? I will not be able to bear the suffering. I hope this name soon vanishes into dust. What a terrible name! My heart trembles at its very sound.[37]

Those are the last words in Kailasbasini's diary. As far as we know, she never wrote again.[38]

The project of cultural reform which nationalist ideology placed on the agenda in the second half of the nineteenth century did, however, provide the resources for women to turn personal misfortune into a new social identity. This becomes clear in the story of Prasannamayi Debi (1857–1939). Born in an upper-caste landed family, Prasannamayi was married at the age of ten to a husband who turned out to be mentally deranged. After she had made two brief visits to her in-laws, her father refused to send her back, and from the age of fourteen Prasannamayi lived for the rest of her life with her parents and brothers. Her father was committed to the cause of reform and arranged not only to give the best possible education to his sons, many of whom were later to reach positions of eminence in their respective professions, but also to educate his daughter at home.

From a very young age, Prasannamayi showed signs of literary talent. Because of her father's literary and musical interests, the family was part of a cultural circle that included some of the most prominent literary figures of the time. Prasannamayi was not only allowed to listen to these discussions but encouraged to take an active part in them. Often she would read aloud her own poetry in these distinguished gatherings. Even as a young woman, her writings began to be published regularly in major literary magazines, and she soon came out with her own books of poems.

Indeed, she became quite a celebrity as a woman who had overcome a personal tragedy caused by the retrograde custom of child marriage and gone on to make a name for herself as a writer. Protected and encouraged by a circle of male relatives and friends that, in the late nineteenth century, was now far more self-assured about its cultural project, Prasannamayi became an exemplary figure, standing for all the virtues claimed on behalf of the "new woman."

We know about the tragedy of Prasannamayi's marriage from other sources;[39] she herself tells us absolutely nothing about it. In ninety-one pages of detailed description of domestic life in her childhood and youth and of dozens of relatives and acquaintances, she does not once mention her husband. All that she says about her experience of married life is that when she first arrived at her in-laws, dressed in the new fashion with petticoat and jacket and surrounded by rumors about her ability to read and write, she was regarded with great curiosity as "the English bride" (*mem bau*), and when she innocently made a display of her accomplishments, including a demonstration on the concertina, she was rebuked by her mother-in-law (*PK*, p. 44). She allows herself only one comment on the custom of hypergamous *kulīn* marriage, of which she was a victim: "avaricious *kulīn* parents," she says, "in their desire to preserve the reputation of their lineages, did not consider the uncertain consequences of giving their daughters in marriages of this sort, although many of these incompatible marriages led to much unhappiness. But it was difficult suddenly to break with a social custom" (*PK*, p. 37). She mentions the fact that several other women in her family had suffered because of such marriages, but then adds: "It is best that this unfortunate history remains unknown to the public [*janasamāj*]" (*PK*, p. 89).

Thus, even as the new form of the conjugal family was being institutionalized within the middle class in Bengal, and its normative ideals produced discursively in the social reform debates and imaginatively in the new fictional and poetical literature, a whole set of differentiations of the inside/outside was also being put in place in order to demarcate those aspects of family life which could be spoken of and those which could not. It is not the case, therefore, that a sphere of the intimate was created, peopled by privatized individuals with subjectivities "oriented toward an audience."[40] Rather, the sphere of the intimate, even when it was subjected to a reformist critique on ethical or aesthetic grounds, was nevertheless declared a subject that could not be spoken of "in public." It was a fiercely guarded zone lodged deep inside the precincts of community life; even its memory could not be revealed in the open arena of the janasamāj.

There is only one place where Prasannamayi slips from her objective narrative of social history to allow us a glimpse into the domain where women in her situation had to wage the struggle for identity and recognition. This occurs when she talks of Indumati, the widowed daughter of the reformer Ramtanu Lahiri (1813–98). "This remarkable woman," she says, "was born only to teach the world the duty of love, to demonstrate that the purpose of human life is not indulgence, but sacrifice—the sacrifice of the pleasures and desires of youth to the cause of service to others." But she also knew Indumati as a friend, and in their friendship, both found the means to forget the immediate world.

> I cannot explain now how wonderful it was to forget ourselves completely. From morning to evening and then late into the night, we would talk, and time would fly past us. This was no political conspiracy, nor was it a discussion on some scientific problem. It was only the dream-like imagination and the pain of unfulfilled desire of two people inexperienced in the ways of the world. All the feelings and scenes that went into the making of this imagined world were products of our minds, bearing no relationship at all to the world of phenomenal things. (*PK*, p. 55)

Apart from this brief slippage, the rest of Prasannamayi's story is a model of nationalist social history written from the standpoint of the "new woman." She is critical of the irrationality and superstitiousness of many religious beliefs and customs.[41] She is horrified by the excesses of caste discrimination and is hopeful that the extreme rigidities of the system will be gradually weakened. "All must join in bringing about the welfare of the nation. We cannot live separately anymore. All must join in worshipping the Mother" (*PK*, p. 71). She is grateful to her father, her brothers, and their circle of friends for the guidance and encouragement they gave her in fashioning a completely new role as a woman with an identity in public life. Her view on contemporary history is entirely one of the legitimacy of reform and national progress. On the other hand, she bemoans the fact that English education was leading to so much superficial aping of Western manners and the negligence of what was good in tradition: "Young people today can recite by heart the names of [Admiral] Nelson's ancestors but do not know the names of their own grandparents" (*PK*, p. 51). And she affirms without question the essential identity of woman as faithful wife and exemplary mother:

> My mother, Srimati Magnamayi Debi, was very patriotic. Her love for her country was without comparison. Every grain of Indian sand was to her like a speck of gold. . . . Her immediate deity was her husband. Always abiding by the commands of her husband, she built her life according to an ideal and taught her children to follow that ideal. (*PK*, p. 14)

If we are to take a linear view of history as progress, then our journey that began with Rassundari in the early decades of the nineteenth century has reached its fulfillment with Prasannamayi at the close of the century. For in Prasannamayi, the nationalist idea of the "new woman" as a hegemonic construct would seem to have been actualized; her struggle has been completely encapsulated in the project to produce the nation—everything else is erased from public memory.

THE WOMEN LEFT OUT

If I stop my culling of these archives at this point, the principal course of the narrative will have thus described a linear movement. Needless to say, this is not an accident. I have deliberately chosen and arranged the four texts in such a way as to produce exactly that effect. My object was to trace through these supposedly self-revelatory texts the genealogy of the nationalist construct of the "new woman." I could, of course, have read the same texts in the opposite direction, against the grain, as texts that show the marks of resistance to a hegemonizing discourse; I have, even in this account, pointed out several of these marks. But I wish to retain up to this point the smooth linearity of my story, if only to emphasize once more the powers of a hegemonizing nationalism to take in its stride a whole range of dissenting voices.

We have therefore a linear narrative. The nationalist will read this as a movement from bondage to emancipation; the feminist critic of nationalism will read it as a movement from one kind of bondage to another. In order now to mess up the picture and forestall both of these closures, I will continue my story a little further and bring in the autobiography of Binodini.[42]

Binodini (1863–1941) was perhaps the most celebrated actress on the Calcutta stage in the last decades of the nineteenth century. This position of the professional actress was itself a creation of the new educated middle-class culture, supplying a need produced by the requirements of the new public theater modeled on European lines. Yet it was a need that was difficult to fulfill within the norms of respectability laid down for women. The solution devised by the early generation of theater producers was to recruit young women from among the city's prostitutes and train them in the modern techniques of the dramatic arts. It became a remarkable educative project in itself, producing women schooled in the language and sensibilities of a modernist literati who learned to think of themselves as professional career artists and yet were excluded from respectable social life by the stigma of immoral living. Binodini's life as a professional actress was produced by these contradictions of the new world of middle-class cultural production.

She was brought into the theater at the age of ten; when she was eighteen, she was at the peak of her career; at twenty-three, she decided to leave the stage. The autobiography she wrote and published when she was forty-nine describes the thirteen years of her professional life as a historical sequence of events, but everything before and after exists as though in a zone of timelessness. As a child, she was brought up in a Calcutta slum, in a household characterized by the absence of adult males. In her autobiography, she talks about the environment of the slum with considerable distaste, and remembers herself as a child looking upon her neighbors "with fear and surprise" and hoping she would never have to face such contempt.[43] She had been told of her marriage at the age of five or six, and there was a boy in the neighborhood whom others referred to as her husband.[44] Whether this might have become a significant event in her life can only be speculated upon, because everything changed when her mother agreed to give her to the theater as a child actress on a monthly salary.

For a girl eleven or twelve years old, training to become a professional actress was hard work. But then again, being in the theater was also like living in a large family. Binodini saw her identity as an actress entirely in terms of her place within this family of artistes. She submitted to its rules, did all that was required of her with dedication, and brought fame and popularity to the theaters she worked for. It is only when we locate this collective site where she grounded her identity and into which she poured out her feelings of loyalty—the extended family transposed on to the artificially constructed world of the middle-class professional theater, which to her was the very real surrogate for society itself—that we begin to see the significance of the central theme of Binodini's autobiography: betrayal.

Binodini had been driven by the belief that the shame of being a woman of ill repute would be removed by her dedication and accomplishments as an artist. Indeed, her acceptance of a position of concubinage to various wealthy patrons seemed to her to be justified by the greater cause of art. She desperately needed to believe in the solidarity and well-being of her surrogate family, for it was only there that she could lead a life of worth and dignity. When her theater company faced a crisis, she even agreed, at considerable personal risk, to become the mistress of a wealthy businessman who was prepared to finance the founding of a new theater only if he could have in exchange the famous Miss Binodini. She was led to believe that her "brothers and sisters" in the company would express their gratitude to her by naming their new theater after her. When this did not happen, she felt betrayed.[45] This was the first of a series of betrayals with which Binodini marks out for us the story of her life.

Trained in the language and sensibilities of the new middle-class culture, Binodini, we can well imagine, felt an intense desire to believe in the emancipatory claims made on behalf of the "new woman." Her life in the theater had introduced her to Greek tragedy and Shakespeare, to the new humanism of Michael Madhusudan Dutt, Bankimchandra, and Dinabandhu Mitra, and to the fervently nationalist representations by Girishchandra Ghosh of Hindu mythology and religious history. When she realized that she could be transformed only to fulfill the cultural needs of a class claiming to represent the nation but would not be given the place of respectability that the class had set aside for its own women, she learned not to believe anymore.

> Ever since I was thrust into the affairs of the world in my adolescence, I have learnt not to trust. The responsibility for this lies with my teachers, my social position and myself. But what is the use of apportioning blame? The distrust remains. . . . How deeply rooted it is in my heart will become clear from the events of my life. . . . And it is impossible to uproot it! I realize that faith is the basis of peace, but where is that faith?[46]

Something, Binodini felt, had been promised to her in return for her dedication to the ideals and disciplines she had been taught. If the enlightened virtues of respectable womanhood meant conformity to a new set of disciplinary rules, she was prepared to conform. Yet respectability was denied to her. She had a daughter whom she wanted to send to school; no school would have her. When the daughter died, she felt she had been betrayed once more.[47]

In late middle age, when she decided to write down the story of her life "to blacken white sheets of paper with the stigma of my heart,"[48] she asked her teacher, Girishchandra Ghosh, to write a foreword to her book. Girish did, but Binodini did not like what her teacher wrote. Girish in fact sought to apply the classic appropriating strategy, pointing out "the great moral lesson in the insignificant life of an ordinary prostitute. . . . On reading this autobiography, the pride of the pious will be curbed, the self-righteous will feel humble, and the sinner will find peace." He went on to comment on "the aspersions" cast by Binodini on the guardians of society. "Rather than emphasizing the didactic aspects of her art, she has tried to tell her own story. The concealing of the personal which is the essence of the technique of writing an autobiography has been compromised." Girish recognized that Binodini had her reasons to feel bitter, "but such bitter words are best left out of one's own life-story. For the reader whose sympathy [Binodini] must expect will refuse to give it when he encounters such harshness."[49]

Binodini, as I said, was not satisfied with this foreword and insisted that her teacher and the greatest actor on the Calcutta stage write "a true account" of all that had happened. The revised version never came, because a few months later Girish Ghosh died. To Binodini, this was another betrayal. "My teacher had told me, 'I will write the foreword before

I die.' . . . But it was not in my fate. . . . By leaving the foreword unfinished, my teacher taught me once more that all that one wishes in life is not fulfilled."[50]

The most heartbreaking betrayal, however, came in Binodini's attempt to build a life of her own outside the theater. For thirty years, from about the time she left the stage, she lived with a gentleman from one of the wealthiest and most respected families in the city. She put into this relationship all her feelings of loyalty and devotion and felt free, loved, respected, and cared for. What she did not realize was the inevitable fragility of the arrangement, because individual patronage, no matter how sincere, could hardly overcome the boundaries of a newly constructed world of the dominant that could only claim to speak on her behalf but never recognize her as its constituent part. Lying on his deathbed, the worthy gentleman made her a promise: "If I have devotion and faith in God, if I have been born in a virtuous family, you will never have to beg for protection." Death, however, rendered him powerless to fulfill his promise. His family, one can guess, did not feel in the least bit obliged to recognize an embarrassing relationship. Binodini was betrayed once more.

Ignoring the advice and admonitions of all her teachers, therefore, Binodini in turn felt that she was under no obligation to hide her deep-rooted skepticism about the verities of customary belief and convention. Determined to tell "her own story," she violated every canon of the feminine smṛtikathā and wrote down what amounted to her indictment of respectable society in the form of a series of letters addressed to her deceased lover. Perhaps her very marginality enabled her to assert this autonomy over her own words. With bitter irony, she wrote in her preface to the book:

> Hindu men and women, I take it, believe with complete sincerity in heaven and hell, in birth and rebirth. . . . Although he [her lover] is no longer on earth, he must be in heaven, from where he can see all that has happened to me and can feel the pain in my heart—if, that is, the Hindu religion is true and the gods are true; if, that is, birth and rebirth are true.[51]

Before we close our narrative of the nationalist transition, therefore, we need to remind ourselves of Binodini's story. For it tells us once more that the story of nationalist emancipation is necessarily a story of betrayal. Because it could confer freedom only by imposing at the same time a whole set of new controls, it could define a cultural identity for the nation only by excluding many from its fold; and it could grant the dignity of citizenship to some only because the others always needed to be represented and could not be allowed to speak for themselves. Binodini reminds us once more that the relations between the people and the nation, the nation and the state, relations which nationalism claims to have resolved once and for all, are relations which continue to be contested and are therefore open to negotiation all over again.

A PESSIMISTIC AFTERWORD

Having written this nicely inconclusive last sentence, I am struck by doubt. The sentence promises further episodes in the story of women and nationalism, and I feel I have succeeded in avoiding a closure. Have I?

In a recent article, Edward Said has spoken of "an incipient and unresolved tension" in the contest "between stable identity as it is rendered by such affirmative agencies as nationality, education, tradition, language and religion, on the one hand, and all sorts of marginal, alienated or . . . anti-systemic forces on the other." This tension, he says, "produces a frightening consolidation of patriotism, assertions of cultural superiority, mechanisms of control, whose power and ineluctability reinforce . . . the logic of identity."[52]

Said is thinking of "the cruel, insensate, shameful violence" that has taken place so often in the name of patriotic affirmation of identity in the Middle East. I am thinking of the equally shameful violence that has become virtually endemic in India in the matter of political relations between religious or linguistic communities. I therefore find myself in agreement with Said when he says, "it must be incumbent upon even those of us who support nationalist struggle in an age of unrestrained nationalist expression to have at our disposal some decent measure of intellectual refusal, negation and skepticism."

But then he says: "It is at precisely that nexus of committed participation and intellectual commitment that we should situate ourselves to ask *how much* identity, *how much* positive consolidation, *how much* administered approbation we are willing to tolerate in the name of our cause, our culture, our state." And here I begin once again to have doubts. Are we still trying to sort out that old liberal problem of "good nationalism" versus "bad nationalism"? Must it be our argument that a little bit of identity and positive consolidation and administered approbation is all for the good, but beyond a point they are intolerable? It is hard for me to accept this, because I have long argued against the posing of this kind of liberal paradox.[53]

One of the ways of avoiding the paradox is to question and reproblematize the all-too-easy identification, claimed by every nationalist state ideology, of the state with the nation and the nation with the people. As an act of intellectual skepticism, this might well involve risks that are more than intellectual. But speaking now only of effects in the intellectual domain, one important effect will be, I think, the somewhat startling discovery that the most powerful and authentic historical achievements of anticolonial nationalism were often won outside the political battlefield and well before the actual contest for political power was settled. This discovery will open up once more the question of who led and who followed, and of when it all began. It will introduce, in short, an agenda to rewrite the history of nationalism with different actors and a different chronology. It will also demonstrate that the culturally creative forms of anticolonial nationalism seeking to establish a zone of hegemony outside the intervention of the colonial state cannot be covered by the "modular" forms of nationalism produced in Europe or the Americas.

What is crucial, however, is for us to be able to show the many risky moments in this narrative of anticolonial nationalism, the alternative sequences that were suppressed, the marks of resistance that were sought to be erased. Much intellectual work of dissent in postcolonial countries is today performing precisely this task. It is arguing that the history of the transition from colonial to postcolonial regimes is highly problematical, that the promise of national emancipation was fulfilled, if not fraudulently, then certainly by the forcible marginalization of many who were supposed to have shared in the fruits of liberation. Indeed, the opening up of the whole problematic of the national project within and outside the domain of the state makes it possible for us now to make the radical suggestion that the cultural history of nationalism, shaped through its struggle with colonialism, contained many possibilities of authentic, creative, and plural development of social identities that were violently disrupted by the political history of the postcolonial state seeking to replicate the modular forms of the modern nation-state. We too, like Binodini, have a story to tell of betrayal.

My doubts are about the effectiveness of this critique. Having to survive in a world pulverized by the concentrated violence of the Gulf War, I cannot, I am afraid, share Said's easy optimism in "scholarship and politics from a world viewpoint, past domination, toward community."[54] It is the very biculturalism of intellectuals in postcolonial countries—a necessary biculturalism that they must work hard to acquire—which enables them to see through the sham and hypocrisy of today's myths of global cooperation. For us, it is hard to imagine a plausible state of the world in which our relation to the dominant structures of scholarship and politics will be anything other than adversarial.

It would be dishonest, therefore, to claim that the critique of nationalism is easy. Rather, the more realistic tactic is not to underestimate nationalism's capacity to appropriate, with varying degrees of risk and varying degrees of success, dissenting and marginal voices. I must, for the sake of truthfulness, note here that Binodini today is an honored name in the public history of the theater in Bengal. Her life as a story of struggle and betrayal is a popular subject for plays and films, and the official liberality of the new domain of the postcolonial state does not allow any judgment of sexual morality to affect the esteem accorded to her as an artist.

In the public sphere within the new domain of the state? Yes. In the ethical domain of the community? Doubtful. Only a few months ago, I came across in a Calcutta daily a brief letter. A leading actress of yesteryear, now in her seventies and honored with several state awards, was complaining about an article in the newspaper on a deceased actor in which she had been mentioned as his "close friend and companion." "At the age of 78, do I have to prove by a letter in a newspaper," she asked, "that Nirmalendu Lahiri was my husband and that I bore four of his children? Yes, there was certainly friendship between me and Mr Lahiri, just as there was a relationship of disciple to master. But this is my first and last word: I was his first wife and the mother of his children."[55]

The ethical domain of nationalism remains very much a contested terrain.

CHAPTER EIGHT

The Nation and Its Peasants

THE MODERN STATE AND THE PEASANTRY

The relationship between the modern state and a peasantry is ambiguous and shot through with tension. In Western Europe, the institutionalization of a modern regime of power coincides with or follows a process of the extinction of the peasantry. Even in France, where it survived as a significantly large mass of the population in the second half of the nineteenth century, the peasantry was associated with such supposedly aberrant political phenomena as Bonapartism and had to be systematically disciplined and transformed into "Frenchmen."[1] Hegel, we know, assigned to the class of peasants—the "substantial class"—an ambiguous position in civil society: it was a part of the class structure produced by the "system of needs" but had an ethical life that was only immediate. Even when agriculture was conducted "on methods devised by reflective thinking, i.e. like a factory," Hegel would allow a member of this class only to accept "unreflectively what is given to him." The agricultural class had "little occasion to think of itself" and was "inclined to subservience."[2] Further east, the peasantry figured for more than half a century as the hub of a fierce debate between populists and Marxists over its role in a revolutionary Russia. This debate also highlighted the controversy, known in one form or the other everywhere in Europe, between modernizers who thought of peasants as embodying all that was backward and premodern and those modern critics of modernity, especially romantics, who saw in a peasantry the rapidly vanishing virtues of simplicity, naturalness, and cultural authenticity. In the end, the matter was settled in Russia by the elimination of the peasantry under the collectivization program of the 1930s.

In the agrarian societies of the colonial East, peasants of course became the repositories of all of those cultural presuppositions that allegedly made those societies incapable of modern self-government and hence justified the paternal authoritarianism of Western colonial rule. In India, the colonial mind thought of Indian peasants as simple, ignorant, exploited by landlords, traders, and moneylenders, respectful of authority, grateful to those in power who cared for and protected them, but also volatile in temperament, superstitious and often fanatical, easily aroused by agitators and troublemakers from among the Indian elite who wanted to use them for their narrow political designs. Indian nationalists, not surprisingly, shared similar assumptions. For them, too, the peasants were simple and ignorant, unaware of the fact that their poverty was the result of the exploitative nature of colonial rule and therefore in need of being woken up to a new consciousness, of being guided and led into effective political action by a nationalist organization. This was a necessary task if the opposition to colonial rule was to acquire the form of a mass movement, but it was also a difficult and dangerous task because the ignorance and volatility of the peasantry could easily lead it astray. In thus proceeding toward their opposed political objectives—located, however, within the same historical career of the modern state—both colonial and nationalist politics thought of the peasantry as an object of their strategies, to be acted upon, controlled, and appropriated within their respective structures of state power.

What does the history of anticolonial struggles in India tell us about the relation between the nation and the peasantry? It is now reasonably clear that contrary to the claims of both colonialist and nationalist historiographies, neither the competitive factional interests of Indian elite groups nor the efforts of the Congress leadership to arouse an all-embracing nationalist consciousness among the entire people can explain the dynamics of the involvement of the peasantry in anticolonial movements. Indeed, several studies published in the 1970s and the early 1980s on the course of the Congress movement among peasants in different parts of India have shown, some explicitly and others implicitly, the existence of a structure of duality in the nationalist mass movement.[3] A coming together of two domains of politics seems to have occurred. On the one hand was the domain of the formally organized political parties and associations, moving within the institutional processes of the bourgeois state forms introduced by colonial rule and seeking to use their representative power over the mass of the people to replace the colonial state by a bourgeois nation-state. On the other hand was the domain of peasant politics where beliefs and actions did not fit into the grid of "interests" and "aggregation of interests" that constituted the world of bourgeois representative politics. Seen from the former domain, the latter could appear only as the realm of spontaneity, which was of course nothing more than the acknowledgment that the specific determinants of the domain of peasant political activity remained incomprehensible from the standpoint of bourgeois politics.

Specifically, two major aspects of the mass movement of nationalism were brought out by these studies. First, the meeting of these two domains of politics was marked by an unresolved contradiction. There was undoubtedly a coming together of the two domains, so that the organization, ideology, and programs of the formally constituted political domain underwent considerable transformation with the entry of a mass peasant element, just as the peasantry too became aware of an entirely new world of political issues, languages, leaders, and forms of action. And yet the very union of these two domains was of a form which required that they be kept apart. While the nationalist leadership sought to mobilize the peasantry as an anticolonial force in its project of establishing a nation-state, it was ever distrustful of the consequences of agitational politics among the peasants, suspicious of their supposed ignorance and backward consciousness, careful to keep their participation limited to the forms of bourgeois representative politics in which peasants would be regarded as a part of the nation but distanced from the institutions of the state. On the other hand, while peasants became aware of the hitherto unknown world of nationalist agitation, they made sense of it not in terms of the discursive forms of modern bourgeois politics but rather by translating it into their own codes, so that the language of nationalism underwent a quite radical transformation of meaning in the peasant domain of politics.[4] The meeting of the two domains did not therefore mean that the first domain was able to absorb and appropriate its other within a single homogeneous unity; the unity itself remained fragmented and fraught with tension.

The second aspect of the meeting of the two domains was that it did not bring about a linear development of the consciousness of the peasantry into a new sense of nationhood. While peasants in different parts of India became aware, albeit in varying degrees, of the realities of nationalist politics, their participation in it seemed to be marked by radical breaks and often reversals, for spells of militant anticolonial action by peasants were often followed by bitter sectarian strife, sometimes in the course of a single movement, and at other times by spells of apparently inexplicable quiescence. Both of these aspects of peasant participation in nationalist politics seemed to point in the same direction: the need for a critique of both colonialist and nationalist historiographies by bringing in the peasantry as a subject of history, endowed with its own distinctive forms of consciousness and making sense of and acting upon the world on its own terms.

PEASANT INSURGENTS OF COLONIAL INDIA

The problem was formulated specifically by Ranajit Guha, using the material on peasant insurgency in the period immediately preceding that of nationalist mass movements.[5] From the series of peasant revolts in colonial India between 1783 and 1900, Guha undertook to isolate the ideological invariants of peasant consciousness and their relational unity—that is to say, its paradigmatic form. He began by assuming that the domination and exploitation under which the peasant lived and worked existed within a relation of power. There was thus an opposed pair: on the one side, the dominators (the state or the landlords or moneylenders), and on the other, the peasants. A relational opposition of power necessarily meant that the dominated had to be granted their own domain of subjectivity, where they were autonomous, undominated. If it were not so, the dominators would, in the exercise of their domination, wholly consume and obliterate the dominated. Dominance then would no longer exist within a social relation of power with its own conditions of reproduction. In this specific case, therefore, the peasantry had to be granted its autonomous domain.

Where was one to locate this domain? If domination is one aspect of this relation of power, its opposed aspect must be resistance. The dialectical opposition of the two gives this relation its unity. This opposition also creates the possibility for a movement within that relation, and thus makes it possible for there to be a history of the relation of dominance and subordination. In searching for the characteristic form of the autonomous domain of peasant consciousness, Guha was led to a study of the aspect of resistance. This did not mean that resistance was more important, or more true, than domination. On the contrary, by placing the forms of peasant consciousness within a dialectical relation of power, peasant consciousness would be assigned its proper theoretical value: its significance was to be established only in relation to its other, namely, the consciousness of the dominator.

If resistance was the aspect of the power relation through which the peasantry expressed its distinct and autonomous identity, as opposed to that of its dominators, where were we to find it in the historical material available to us? Precisely in the material on peasant insurgency, where the insurgent consciousness left its imprint on that of its dominator, and where the dominator was forced expressly to "recognize" its other. Thus the inquiry into the characteristic forms of peasant consciousness became in Guha a study of the elementary aspects of peasant insurgency. The study of peasant insurgency was, in other words, a methodological procedure by which one obtained an access into peasant consciousness, expressed through its resistance at the point of insurgency and recognized as an antagonistic force in the historical records prepared by the dominant classes. The instituted knowledge of society, as it exists in recorded history, is the knowledge obtained by the dominant classes in their exercise of power. The dominated, by virtue of their very powerlessness, have no means of recording their knowledge within those instituted processes, except as an object of the exercise of power. Thus, Guha used the colonial discourse of counterinsurgency to read, as a mirror image, the discourse of insurgency.

He identified six "elementary aspects," as he called them, of the insurgent peasant consciousness: negation, ambiguity, modality, solidarity, transmission, and territoriality. The insurgent consciousness was, first of all, a "negative consciousness," in the sense that its identity was expressed solely through an opposition, namely, its difference from and antagonism to its dominators. It was an identity whose limits were fixed by the very conditions of subordination under which the peasantry lived and worked; only the relations were inverted. The signs of domination, such as the imposition of taxes or rent or of the power to punish, now became the targets of resistance. A characteristic feature of peasant rebellions was the urge of the oppressed to assert his resistance to authority "not in terms of his own culture but his enemy's." Second, the forms of resistance involved a high degree of ambiguity. Precisely because relations of domination were inverted at the moment of insurgency, the signs of rebellion were liable to be misread by the rulers who would fail to distinguish them from such "normal" signs of aberrant behavior as crime. But unlike crime, "rebellions are necessarily and invariably public and communal events"; "crime and insurgency derive from two very different codes of violence." Third, insurgent peasant movements had their characteristic modalities or forms. On the one hand, the political and yet innately negative character of inverting the dominant relations of power took the form of destroying the signs of authority, such as the police station or the landlord's rent-collection office or the moneylender's house. Specifically for the case of colonial India, Guha identified four forms of destruction: wrecking, burning, eating, and looting. On the other hand, the negativity of the insurgent consciousness of the peasant was also expressed in the setting up of a rebel authority, in the inverted image of the authority that it replaced, equally public in character and with its own powers to impose sanctions and levies on the community. Fourth, the self-definition of the insurgent peasant, his awareness of belonging to a collectivity that was separate from and opposed to his enemies, lay in the aspect of solidarity. Its specific expression varied from rebellion to rebellion, sometimes even from one phase to another within the same rebellion. Often it was expressed in terms of ethnicity or kinship or some such affinal category. Sometimes one can read in it the awareness of a class. But solidarity was the total expression of the communal character of an insurgency. Fifth, within the solidarity thus defined, the message of insurgency was transmitted with an ease and rapidity that the ruling classes often found bewildering, but this too had its characteristic channels. Rumor, for instance, was one such channel, in which the source of a message was anonymous and unknown and which involved no distinction between the communicator and his audience. Absolutely transitive, rumor, as distinct from news, was "an autonomous type of popular discourse." Finally, the solidarity of an insurgent peasantry also occupied a specific geographical space. The limits of this geographical space were determined, on the one hand, negatively by the rebel's perception of the geographical spread of the enemy's authority, that is to say, by a principle of exclusion, and on the other, positively by a notion of the ethnic space occupied by the insurgent community, that is, by the principle of solidarity. The intersection of these two spaces defined the territoriality of the insurgency.

THE NOTION OF COMMUNITY

In all these aspects that Guha identified, there is a single unifying idea that gives to peasant insurgency its fundamental social character: the notion of community. Every aspect expresses itself in its specific political forms through the principle of community. Whether through the negatively constituted character of the forms and targets of insurgent action, defined by applying the criterion of "we" and "they," or whether through the rebel's self-definition of the territorial space of insurgency, a principle of community gives to all these specific aspects their fundamental constitutive character as the purposive political acts of a collective consciousness. This principle, again, enables us to read from the actions of a rebellious peasantry at the moment of insurgency the total constitutive character of a peasant consciousness, to relate those actions to the forms of everyday social existence of the peasantry.

It is important to stress this point, because what the principle of community as the characteristic unifying feature of peasant consciousness does is directly place it at the opposite pole to a bourgeois consciousness. The latter operates from the premise of the individual and a notion of his interests (or, in more fashionable vocabulary, his preferences). Solidarities in bourgeois politics are built up through an aggregative process by which individuals come together into alliances on the basis of common interests (or shared preferences). The process is quite the opposite in the consciousness of a rebellious peasantry. There solidarities do not grow because individuals feel they can come together with others on the basis of their common individual interests: on the contrary, individuals are enjoined to act within a collectivity because, it is believed, bonds of solidarity that tie them together already exist. Collective action does not flow from a contract among individuals; rather, individual identities themselves are derived from membership in a community.

The implication is that peasant consciousness cannot be understood in its own constitutive aspects if we continue to reduce it to the paradigm of bourgeois rationality. We must grant that peasant consciousness has its own paradigmatic form, which is not only different from that of bourgeois consciousness but in fact its very other. This central theoretical proposition is brought out by Guha's book, and it poses a basic challenge to the methodological procedures followed not only by bourgeois economists and sociologists (including those of the Chayanovian and "moral economy" varieties) searching for the "rational peasant" (however defined), but also by many Marxist scholars writing on the agrarian question.

This notion of community cannot be immediately assigned a single determinate value based on a determinate social institution such as totemism or caste or religious denomination. The boundaries or forms of solidarity in peasant rebellions have no single determinate character that can be directly deduced either from its immediate socioeconomic context or from its cultural world. On the contrary, the cultural apparatus of signs and meanings—the language, in the broadest sense—available to a peasant consciousness, far from being narrow and inflexible, is capable of a vast range of transformations to enable it to understand, and to act within, varying contexts, both of subordination and of resistance. It is precisely this ability that makes insurgency the purposeful political work of a deliberate and active insurgent consciousness. Without it, this consciousness could in fact be "objectivized" easily, by reducing it to its determinate institutional form—tribe, caste, religious denomination, locality, whatever. Such a reductionism grossly underestimates, and in fact misunderstands, the ideological resilience and innovativeness of peasant consciousness.

THE CONCRETE FORMS OF COMMUNITY

Guha, therefore, has proposed a paradigmatic form of the insurgent peasant consciousness. Its contours are drawn from a reading of the material on peasant revolts in colonial India from the point of view of the peasant as an active and conscious subject of history. But because of his objective of isolating an invariant structural form, in line with the structuralism inherent in his method, he has not attempted to give us a *history* of this consciousness as a movement of self-transformation. Rather, having found an access into the structural form of this consciousness in its aspect of autonomy, he has given us a basis to ask the appropriate questions about its history.

The first area where this interrogation can begin is precisely that which binds together the structure of peasant consciousness as described by Guha, namely, the community. We have seen that Guha, quite correctly, does not give to this community any immediately determinate content; or rather, to put it more accurately, while he describes the community in the historical context of a particular peasant rebellion in the relevant terms of clan, tribe, caste, village, and so forth, he leaves the theoretical conceptualization of the community in peasant consciousness as a formal construct, abstract and empty. It is necessary now to attempt to give to this crucial concept its proper theoretical content. We already have something to go on. We know, for instance, that the identification of the enemy in peasant revolts, the separation of the "they" from the "we," occurs within a framework where distinct communities are seen as being in antagonistic relation with each other. The same framework of communities provides room for the establishment of solidarities and alliances on the side of the rebels (and, for that matter, on the side of the enemy), and even of collaboration and treachery. The alliances are not seen as the result of contracts based on common interests; rather, they are believed to be the necessary duty of groups bound together by mutual bonds of kinship: "You are our brothers. Do join with all expedition." This invitation of the first group of rebels in the Rangpur uprising of 1783 to the peasants of neighboring villages was, in fact, the standard form of insurgent alliance in peasant rebellions all over India. It applied even in the case of a perceived breach of mutual duty; this was no breach of contract. When the villagers of Kallas wrote to those of Akola blaming them for breaking the solidarity of the movement during the Deccan Revolt of 1875, they did not appeal to a mutuality of interest. Rather, they said, "It is wrong of you people to keep communication with persons who are deemed as excluded from the community of the village. . . . As we consider Kallas and Akola as one village, we have made the above suggestions to you."

We also know that the boundaries of solidarity, the line separating the "we" from the "they," can shift according to changing contexts of struggle. Pandey has given us an account of how a strife between Rajput landlords and Muslim weavers in a small town in Uttar Pradesh in the middle of the nineteenth century quickly changed into the solidarity of the entire town in its defense against outside attack and back again to internal strife, all within the space of a few weeks, without any apparent sign that the people of the town saw anything anomalous in these rapid changes in the boundaries of solidarity. Hardiman, Sarkar, and Chatterjee have also considered this problem of shifting boundaries of solidarity in terms of the changing context of struggle.[6] What is necessary now is to formulate the concept of community within a set of systematic relationships signifying the mutual identity and difference of social groups.

In the Indian context, the system of castes seems to represent an obvious paradigmatic form for signifying identity and difference. On the one hand, castes are mutually separate as though they were distinct species of natural beings, and on the other, they are mutually bound together as parts, arranged hierarchically, within a social whole. In traditional social anthropology, to the extent that these relations were seen as constituting a system, the dominant view has been that it provides a framework for harmonizing the mutual interdependence of separate groups through the inculcation of a set of shared values about the unity of the system as a whole.[7] What is not recognized is the equally systematic nature of the rejection of the supposedly "shared" values by groups that are inferior in caste ranking. There seems to be ample evidence to enable us to ground the system of castes within the totality of power relations, because the changing relations between castes and the periodic attempts to redefine the content of ethical conduct in the Indian religions bear the signs of a continuing struggle, and its temporary resolutions, within social relations of domination and subordination. In short, we have here the possibility of linking a history of peasant struggle with a *history* of the caste system, and through it, with a history of religious beliefs and practices. I will consider this issue at length in the next chapter.

There are strong reasons to suspect that the system of castes operates as a paradigmatic form not merely in the domain of relations between jātis within the fold of the Brahmanical religion; it is probably the case that it is the general cultural form of conceptualizing and ordering the relations of identity and difference between several kinds of social groupings. Significantly, the word *jāti* in most Indian languages can be used to designate not merely caste, but caste agglomerations, tribes, race, linguistic groups, religious groups, nationalities, nations. Anthropologists have, of course, often noted the existence of caste or caste-like forms not only among religious groups such as Buddhists, Jains, or the medieval devotional sects that emerged in opposition to the Brahmanical religion, but also among Indian Muslims and Christians. But this point is of a more general significance: the extent to which a caste-like system provides the cultural form for conceptualizing relations of domination, as well as of resistance, between social groups needs to be examined in its concreteness.

Apart from this question of identifying the boundaries of the community in varying contexts of struggle, there is the other aspect of the internal structure of the community in peasant consciousness. It is clear that the notion of community, especially among the nontribal agrarian population, is not egalitarian, even in the matter of rights in the basic means of production, namely, land. For most parts of India, in the sector of settled peasant cultivation, something like a fifth or more of the population, belonging to the lowest castes, have never had any recognized rights in land. But the unity of a community was nevertheless established by recognizing the rights of subsistence of all sections of the population, albeit a differential right entailing differential duties and privileges. The point then is that the notion of community as itself a differentiated unity operates not merely between peasants as a community and their dominators, but between peasants themselves. The full range of possibilities of alliances and oppositions, with the boundaries of community shifting with changing contexts of struggle, may then be said to operate in relations between sections of the peasantry. The point goes against a populist idealization of the peasantry as an egalitarian and harmonious community, free from internal dissention and struggle.

AN INDIAN HISTORY OF PEASANT STRUGGLE

Following Guha, the argument of the *Subaltern Studies* group of historians has been that by studying the history of peasant rebellions from the point of view of the peasant as an active and conscious subject of history, one obtains an access into that aspect of his consciousness where he is autonomous, undominated. One thereby has the means to conceptualize the unity of that consciousness as grounded in a relationship of power, namely, of domination and subordination. Peasant consciousness, then, is a contradictory unity of two aspects: in one, the peasant is subordinate, where he accepts the immediate reality of power relations that dominate and exploit him; in the other, he denies those conditions of subordination and asserts his autonomy. It has also been argued that the community is the space where this contradictory unity of peasant consciousness makes its appearance. So far, the community has been characterized only in the abstract and formal sense. But there is sufficient historical material to begin a more concrete conceptualization of the community, itself differentiated, as the *site* of peasant struggle, where respective rights and duties are established and contested.

Already this gives us a path of investigation that is likely to deviate from the conventional ways of studying peasant revolts in Europe. In fact, I will argue that what the recent debates about the role of the peasantry in the nationalist movement lead to is a project to write an Indian history of peasant struggle.[8] In principle, this is a different project from that of a history of peasant struggles in India. The semantic difference signifies a quite radical difference in the approach to historiography. The latter stands for an arrangement of the historical material on peasant struggles in India according to a framework in which the fundamental concepts and analytical relations are taken as given, established in their generality by the forms of a universal history (for example, the theory of transition from feudalism to capitalism, or modernization theory, or the theory of world systems, or the theory of the moral economy of the peasant, and so on). The former seeks to discover in that material the forms of an immanent historical development, fractured, distorted, and forced into the grid of "world history" only by the violence of colonialism. The framework of this other history does not take as given its appointed place within the order of a universal history, but rather submits the supposedly universal categories to a constant process of interrogation and contestation, modifying, transforming, and enriching them. The object is not to resume the course of a precolonial history by erasing from historical memory and present reality the experience of colonialism: this would be not only archaic and utopian, it would in fact be reactionary even to pretend that this is possible. Rather, the task is to ground one's historical consciousness in the immanent forms of social development that run through Indian history and from that standpoint to engage our colonial experience in a process of struggle—negating and superseding that experience by appropriating it on one's own terms.

This agenda implies the relegation of the universal categories of social formations into a temporary state of suspension, or rather a state of unresolved tension. But this again is a task fundamental to the historian's practice. The relation between history and the theoretical disciplines of the social sciences is necessarily one where the structural neatness of the latter is constantly disturbed and refashioned by the intransigent material of the former. The plea for an Indian history of peasant politics, then, is also one that calls for the historian to take up his or her proper role as agent provocateur among social scientists.

A calumny was spread by European writers on India in the eighteenth and nineteenth centuries to the effect that because of the lack of a historical consciousness among Indians, there existed next to no material on Indian history, save a few court chronicles, hagiographies, and genealogical tables of questionable veracity. This misrepresentation ought not to be attributed solely to the malicious intentions of the colonial mind to tarnish the character of a conquered people. There were more profound difficulties with the very conception of history as a form of knowledge in post-Enlightenment Europe. Judged from the European standpoint, the overwhelming mass of material out of which the institutions and practices of social relations among the Indian people were fashioned, and which survived as palpable evidence of a living past, was simply not recognized as valid historical material. All evidence that did not fit into the linear order of progression of state forms defined by principalities, kingdoms, and empires was relegated to the exotic, timeless domain of Indian ethnology, where history played only a marginal role.

We now know that the situation is quite the opposite. The variety of structural forms of social relations in India, the intricacy of their interconnections, the multiple layers and degrees of differentiation, the ideological forms of identity and difference, and the long course of the historical evolution of these forms through social struggle are stamped on the living beliefs and practices of the people. In its sheer vastness and intricacy, this material is incomparably richer than what is contained in the received histories of Europe, a fact that the efflorescence of modern anthropology in the period after World War II has brought home to the European consciousness. In fact, the recent attempts to exhume a "popular history" of Europe from the rubble of a dead past have been provoked precisely by this challenge thrown by the new sciences of anthropology and linguistics, working on the material of non-European societies, to the accepted dogmas of post-Enlightenment European knowledge.

Now that there is a much greater eagerness to face up to this evidence as historical material, its very richness forces us to throw up our hands and declare that it is much too complex. Every practicing social scientist of India will confess to this feeling of inadequacy and helplessness. For colonial ethnographers, this was evidence of the orderless mélange that was the mysterious Orient, and for colonial administrators, additional proof of the historical necessity to impose linearity and order on an ungovernable society. For Indian nationalists, this was evidence of the greatness of the indigenous tradition which was capable, they said, of absorbing diverse social forms into a single unity without destroying the marks of difference. Needless to say, the colonial view tended to emphasize the inherent disorderliness of Indian society and its lack of a united consciousness, while the nationalists glorified the absorptive capacity without taking notice of the considerable internal struggles that marked the process of absorption.

For those of us who face up to this problem today, the feeling of unmanageable complexity is, if we care to think of it, nothing other than the result of the inadequacy of the theoretical apparatus with which we work. Those analytical instruments were fashioned primarily out of the process of understanding historical developments in Europe. When those instruments now meet with the resistance of an intractably complex material, the fault surely is not of the Indian material but of the imported instruments. If the day comes when the vast storehouse of Indian social history will become comprehensible to the scientific consciousness, we will have achieved along the way a fundamental restructuring of the edifice of European social philosophy as it exists today.

The second point of strength of the Indian material on peasant struggle arises, curiously enough, from an apparent weakness. There is a common tendency to regard the evidence of open revolts of the peasantry in India as insignificant when compared to the historical experience of medieval Europe or to that of neighboring China. One must, however, be careful in judging the nature of this insufficiency. It has sometimes been suggested, for instance, that a history of peasant insurgency in India is a nonstarter because there has never been a peasant revolt in India which was anything more than local and brief. The fact is, first of all, that the number of such "local" revolts is quite considerable, and from about the seventeenth century, through the period of British rule and right up to the contemporary period of the postcolonial state, the accounts of several hundred peasant revolts from all over the country exist in the historical records. Second, what appears to be only "localized" in the context of a vast country like India may often be found to involve a territory and a rebel population larger than those in even the most famous peasant revolts in European history. The crucial difference lies elsewhere. It is undoubtedly true that peasant revolts in India do not seem to have the same political impact on the evolution of state forms or on legal-proprietary relations as they do in Europe or China.[9] An important reason for this is that dominance in Indian society was not exercised exclusively, or even primarily, through the legal forms of sovereign power embodied in the institutions of the state or of feudal estates. Consequently, resistance was not restricted only to the domain of legal-political relations. The study of peasant struggles in India must therefore encompass a field of social relations far wider than what is conventionally regarded as appropriate in European history. Once again, therefore, what the Indian material calls for is an opening up and restructuring of the received disciplinary boundaries for the study of peasant movements.

THE MOVEMENT OF CONSCIOUSNESS

The immediate implications for the project of an Indian history of peasant politics is, first, that the domain of legal-political relations constituted by the state cannot be regarded as the exclusive, perhaps not even the principal, site of peasant struggle. Second, the domain of community will appear as intricately differentiated and layered, with a structural form that affords far greater flexibility, and hence strategic opportunities for both peasants and the dominant classes, in the making of alliances and oppositions than in the "peasant community" in feudal Europe. Third, in the long intervals between open, armed rebellions by peasants or the spread of the great heterodox religious movements, one is likely to notice, if one looks for it, a continuing and pervasive struggle between peasants and the dominant classes in everyday life. The forms of such struggle will range from absenteeism, desertion, selective disobedience, sabotage, and strikes to verbal forms such as slander, feigned ignorance, satire, and abuse—the "Brechtian forms of class struggle," as James Scott has described them.[10] The storehouse of popular culture in India has preserved an enormously rich collection of the material and ideological artifacts of such everyday forms of peasant protest, which have never been incorporated into the study of the processes of subordination and resistance within which Indian peasants have lived and struggled.

This brings us to our final, and crucial, question. If our objective is to write the history of peasant struggle in the form of a history of peasants as active and conscious agents, then their consciousness must also have a history. Their experience of varying forms of subordination, and of resistance, their attempts to cope with changing forms of material and ideological life both in their everyday existence and in those flashes of open rebellion, must leave their imprint on consciousness as a process of learning and development. Some like Scott have sought to privilege the everyday forms of resistance over those of open rebellion because the former are supposedly more enduring and, in the long run, more effective in their slow and almost imperceptible transformation of the conditions of subordination. It may be premature to dismiss this argument on a priori grounds, but the fact remains that the domain of the quotidian, which is also the domain of the seeming perpetuity of subordination, is circumscribed by a limit beyond which lies the extraordinary, apocalyptic, timeless moment of a world turned upside down. It is the historical record of those brief moments of open rebellion which gives us a glimpse of that undominated region in peasant consciousness and enables us to see the everyday and the extraordinary as parts of a single unity in historical time.

To push the point a little further, we could argue that it is always the specter of an open rebellion by the peasantry which haunts the consciousness of the dominant classes in agrarian societies and shapes and modifies their forms of exercise of domination. This was true of the colonial state in the period of British rule in India, just as it is true today, notwithstanding the establishment of universal adult franchise. Of course, the nature and forms of domination of peasants have changed quite fundamentally in the last hundred years or so. The older forms of feudal extraction and ties of bondage have been replaced to a large extent by new forms of extraction mediated through the mechanisms of the market and of fiscal policies. These changes themselves have not come about solely through reforms at the top; a whole series of peasant struggles from the days of colonial rule have acted upon the structures of domination in order to change and modify them. Even the new political institutions of representative government, struggling to give political form to the material of social relations of a large agrarian country, are themselves being shaped into figures that would be unrecognizable in the liberal democracies of the West. To give one example, the phenomenon of massive and uniform swings in the vote across large regions, which has been a characteristic of several recent elections in India, is of a magnitude and geographical spread unknown in Western liberal democracies and inexplicable in terms of the normal criteria of voting behavior. Do we see in this the form of an insurgent peasant consciousness which, having learned in its own way the mechanisms of the new system of power, is now expressing itself through entirely novel methods of political action?

An Indian history of peasant struggle will tell us a great deal more than simply the story of medieval peasant rebellions. For it is a history that constitutes our living and active present. It is a history that will tell us why when peasants identified the colonial state as their enemy, as they did in 1857 or 1942, they could be so much more radical and thoroughgoing in their opposition than their more enlightened compatriots. It is a history that will educate those of us who claim to be their educators. Indeed, an Indian history of peasant struggle is a fundamental part of the real history of our people; the task is for the Indian historian to perceive in this a consciousness of his or her own self.

CHAPTER NINE

The Nation and Its Outcasts

THE SYNTHETIC THEORY OF CASTE

If there was one social institution that, to the colonial mind, centrally and essentially characterized Indian society as radically different from Western society, it was the institution of caste. All arguments about the rule of colonial difference, and hence about the inherent incapacity of Indian society to acquire the virtues of modernity and nationhood, tended to converge upon this supposedly unique Indian institution.

In responding to this charge, Indian nationalists have adopted, broadly speaking, one of two strategies. The first is to deny the suggestion that caste is essential to the characterization of Indian society. This position has been especially favored by the nationalist left as well as by Marxists. Caste, according to this argument, is a feature of the superstructure of Indian society; its existence and efficacy are to be understood as the ideological products of the specific precapitalist social formations that have made their appearance in Indian history. With the supersession of these precapitalist formations, caste too would disappear. One implication of this argument is that by its refusal to ascribe to caste any fundamental significance, it is able to uphold without qualification the legal-political principles of the modern state, to dispute the rule of colonial difference in the public sphere, and to boldly advocate the cultural project of modernity.

Its difficulty as a nationalist argument, however, is that by wholeheartedly embracing all of the claims made on behalf of Western modernity and advocating them for modern India, it leaves little room for disputing on empirical grounds the colonialist criticism of India as a degenerate, caste-ridden society. By explaining the innumerable instances of caste practices as ideological manifestations of a premodern social formation, it seems to condemn virtually the entire corpus of traditional cultural institutions in India, both elite and popular. Such undifferentiated advocacy of the "modern" does not sit too well on claims about the identity of the "national." The case is made worse by a growing evidence that the spread of capitalist economic activities or of modern education does not necessarily bring about an end to caste practices. Even such a historically perspicuous observer as D. D. Kosambi, after noting in 1944 that "it is not necessarily true that caste will disappear with modern means of production any more than the feudal ideology disappeared from Japanese society with modern machinery," was driven to add:

> With the development of the country as a whole [in the period following the decline of Buddhism], and the foundation of its basic economy on the village unit with the family as a sub-unit, the progressive function of caste may be said to have ended, so that caste itself must thereafter attempt to be static. . . . Thus it is that so much of Indian philosophy and literature, which went on developing, had to take the religious path. This "opium of the people" was needed if life were to be worth living. . . . Without thinking of the consequences of their action, our philosophers followed this pattern, which will have to be discarded when the productive system of the country reaches a stage of maturity.[1]

The second strategy seeks to avoid these difficulties by retaining caste as an essential element of Indian society. The presence of a caste system, the assertion goes, makes Indian society essentially different from the Western. What is denied, however, in this nationalist argument is the charge that caste is necessarily contradictory to, and incompatible with, a modern and just society. This is achieved by distinguishing between the empirical-historical reality of caste and its ideality. Ideally, the caste system seeks to harmonize within the whole of a social system the mutual distinctness of its parts. This is a requirement for any stable and harmonious social order; the caste system is the way this is achieved in India.

This enormously influential nationalist argument has been addressed at different levels. Gandhi used to argue that the empirical reality of caste discrimination and even its sanction in the religious texts had "nothing to do with religion."[2] The ideal fourfold *varṇa* scheme was meant to be a noncompetitive functional division of labor and did not imply a hierarchy of privilege. This idealism found a metaphysical exposition in Sarvepalli Radhakrishnan, who asserted that the varṇa scheme was a universal form of the organic solidarity of the individual and the social order.[3] Since then, successive generations of Indian sociologists, working with increasingly detailed and sophisticated ethnographic materials, have propounded the idea that there is a systematic form to the institutionalized practices of caste, that this system is in some sense fundamental to a characterization of Indian society, and that it represents a way of reconciling differences within a harmonious unity of the social order.[4]

Of the two strategies, one contains a critique of the other. Both, however, accept the premise of modernity, the former espousing it to condemn caste as an oppressive and antiquated institution inconsistent with a modern society, the latter asserting that caste in its ideal form is not oppressive and not inconsistent with the aspirations of individuality within the harmony of a unified social order. The former could be said to represent the pure theory of universal modernity; the latter, its genealogy running deep into the traditions of Orientalist scholarship, upholds a theory of Oriental exceptionalism. As nationalist arguments, both adopt the externally given standpoint of bourgeois equality to criticize the empirical reality of caste practices and to advocate modernist reform. As for their overall framing devices, the former argument, of course, has available to it the entire Western discourse on modernity; the latter, on the other hand, has to construct a special theory, in this case the synthetic theory of caste, which however has the same form as any synthetic theory of "the unity of Indian society."

REQUIREMENTS OF AN IMMANENT CRITIQUE OF CASTE

I wish to state here the requirements for a critique of the synthetic theory of caste that does not rely on an external standpoint.[5] These, in other words, will be the requirements for an immanent critique of caste. By implication, these will also give us the general form for an immanent critique of all synthetic theories about "the unity of Indian society."

1. The starting point is the *immediate* reality of caste, namely the diversity of particular jātis with specific characteristics. Each jāti can be shown to have its particular quality: on the one hand a definition-by-self that is the positive characteristic which identifies the jāti as itself, and on the other a definition-for-another by which other jātis are distinguished from it. Any particular qualitative criterion that is supposed to identify a jāti will imply both the positive and the negative definitions. Thus, if the Chamar is identified as a caste that disposes of dead cattle, this definition-by-self immediately implies a definition-for-another, namely that other castes (at least, some other castes) do not have this occupation. It is thus that distinctions and classifications by quality can be made among jātis.

Now, these distinctive qualities of particular castes are finite and hence alterable. We have innumerable examples of the qualitative marks of particular jātis varying both regionally and over time. We also know that there is a multiplicity of qualitative criteria which can serve to distinguish jāti from jāti. The finiteness of quality is negated by a definition-for-self of caste that shows the diverse individual castes to be many particular forms, distinguished by quantity, of one universal measure of caste. To give an example from another scientific field, particular commodities are immediately distinguishable from one another by a variety of finite qualities, but a definition-for-self of commodity, namely value, enables us to order by quantity, that is, exchange value, the entire range of particular commodities. Similarly, we can make determinate distinctions by quantity between all castes if we have a similar definition-for-self of caste. The most powerful candidate in sociological literature for this definition of "casteness" is hierarchy. According to this argument, hierarchy fixes a universal measure of "casteness" so that, at any given time and place, the immediate qualitative diversity of jātis can be ordered as a quantitative ranking in a scale of hierarchy. The universal measure appears for each particular caste as a determinate position, quantitatively fixed (higher/lower) and hence comparable, in the hierarchy of all castes. Thus the move is made from the unintelligibility of immediate diversity to an identification of the *being-for-self* of caste. Now it is possible to identify *determinate* castes, here and now, as an ordered set, unambiguous and noncontradictory, at least in principle. In fact, like the Maître de Philosophie telling M. Jourdain that he had been speaking prose all his life without knowing it, this is precisely what Louis Dumont tells us in chapter 2 of *Homo Hierarchicus*: he uses the substantive material of caste ethnology to fix the determinate being of castes.[6]

2. Dumont does something more, which also happens to be the next step in our immanent critique of caste. The being-for-self of caste, namely hierarchy, can be shown to imply a contradictory *essence*. As soon as we try to arrange the determinate, here-and-now evidence of the ethnological material in a sequence of change, we will discover in place of the immediacy of being the reflected or mediated self-identity of caste on the one hand and a self-repulsion or difference on the other. Dumont identifies from within the immediacy of caste practices a contradictory essence, mediated by ideology (or religion), namely, the opposition between purity and pollution. While the need to maintain purity implies that the castes must be kept separate (thus, Brahmans cannot engage in the polluting occupations of menial castes), it also necessarily brings the castes together (since Brahmans cannot do without the menial castes if their economic services are to be provided). The unity of identity and difference—in this case, vide Dumont, the unity of purity and pollution—gives us the *ground* of caste as a totality or system. The being of caste is here shown as mediated; its existence is now relative in terms of its interconnections with other existents within the totality of the ground. Dumont devotes the greater part of his book to defending his case that the unity of the opposites purity and pollution provides adequate ground for defining the totality of caste relations as a system.

Once grounded, the immediate relation in the system of castes will appear as the relation between the whole and the parts. Only the parts have independent being, but the relations between the parts themselves are the result of the contradictory unity of identity and difference. The parts can be held together only if they are mediated into self-relation within the whole of the system by *force*. In Dumont's treatment, the force that holds together the different castes within the whole of the caste system is the ideological force of *dharma*. The construct of dharma assigns to each jāti its place within the system and defines the relations between jātis as the simultaneous unity of mutual separateness and mutual dependence.

The movement of force must make apparent the process of uniting the essence of a system with its existence. Here, Dumont's claim is categorical. The central argument of his work is that the ideological force of dharma does in fact unite the mediated being of caste with its ideality. Thus the ideal construct of dharma is actualized in the immediacy of social institutions and practices. This claim is central not merely in Dumont; it must in fact be central to all synthetic constructions of the theory of caste, for all such theories must claim that the conflicting relations between the differentiated parts of the system (namely, jātis) are effectively united by the force of dharma so that the caste system as a whole can continue to reproduce itself. I have chosen to use Dumont's book as the most influential and theoretically sophisticated construction of the synthetic theory of caste.

3. In order to make a critique of the ideology of caste, then, we must show that this process of actualization necessarily contains a contradiction. We must show, in other words, that the unification of the essence of caste with its existence through the movement of the force of dharma is inadequate and one-sided; it is a resolution that reveals its falsity by concealing the contradiction within it. This is the crucial step in the critique of caste. By locating our critique at this level, where the claim that the mediated being of caste (that is to say, its ideality) has been actualized in immediate social reality is brought under critical examination, we look at caste neither as base nor as superstructure but precisely as the level of social reality that claims to unite the two. If this claim can be shown to be false, that is, if the idea of caste can be shown to be *necessarily* at variance with its actuality, we will have the elementary means for an immanent critique of caste.

Dumont traverses the first two stages of this dialectic without attempting to move to the third. It is at the third stage that this critique of Dumont must be grounded. There may of course be several inaccuracies or incorrect statements in Dumont's delineation of the movement in the first two stages. To point these out is undoubtedly justified, and many commentators in the last two decades have done so, but these do not amount to a critique of Dumont, for it is theoretically possible to modify the actual contents of *Homo Hierarchicus* to yield a more correctly constituted Dumont-type construction. The critique must consist in showing the inherent plausibility and justification of the transition from the second to the third stage—and that move will destroy the central claim of

Dumont (or of any synthetic construction of that type) that ideality lies united with actuality in the immediate reality of caste.

Interestingly, Dumont seems to be aware of this line of attack, and in his 1979 preface has attempted to fortify his position against it by declaring that the anthropologist's construction of a global ideology can never hope to "cover without contradiction the entire field of its application" and must, at every stage, leave a certain irreducible residue in the observed object. The demand for an ideology that is "identical in its breadth and content to the reality as lived" is the demand of idealism, "and it is surprising to see it formulated by the same critics who have reproached us in the name of empiricism for granting too much importance to ideas and values." He then states his own position, now suitably modified: "At the most general level, what our conclusion means is that hierarchical ideology, like egalitarian ideology, is not perfectly realized in actuality, or, in other terms does not allow direct consciousness of all that it implies."[7] One could, of course, say to Dumont that he cannot have it both ways. But let us refrain from raising this obvious objection and point out instead that the matter is not simply one of the *empirical* residue of unexplained observations. Our objection will be that any Dumont-like construction of the ideology of caste will be necessarily at variance with its actuality because the unification is contested *within* the "observed object," that is to say, within the immediate system of castes.

We may also note here that Dumont himself acknowledges that he has confined himself to the first two stages of the movement I have delineated above: his object, he says, is to "understand" the caste system, not to criticize it. Speaking—necessarily—from within the system of castes, I cannot, unfortunately, afford this anthropologist's luxury, notwithstanding the fact that many Indian anthropologists, in the mistaken belief that this is the only proper scientific attitude to culture, have presumed to share the same observational position with their European teachers. Dumont further says that his is a study of "structure," not of "dialectic." The oppositions within his structure do not "produce" anything; they are static and not surpassed through a "development"; the global setting of the structure is given once and for all.[8] I am, of course, looking for contradictions that are dialectical, where oppositions are surpassed through negation, producing a developed unity and, once again, a new set of contradictions. I do not, however, agree with Dumont that the dialectical method is necessarily "synthetic." It is rather the Dumont-type method of "structure," where the whole is a "structural" rather than a "dialectical" whole, which, when applied to immediate phenomena bearing the unexamined content of history, becomes profoundly "synthetic" in its assertion that all oppositions are necessarily contained within a global unity "given once and for all."

DUMONT DISINTERRED

It would be redundant here to attempt a review of the contents of such a well-known work as *Homo Hierarchicus*. I propose instead to rearrange the materials of a criticism of Dumont by Dipankar Gupta in terms of the framework outlined above and then assess what remains to be done for an adequate critique to emerge.[9]

Gupta's central criticism of Dumont consists in questioning the latter's claim that the essence of caste lies in a continuous hierarchy along which castes can be ordered in terms of relative purity. Gupta's counterargument is that the essence of caste lies in differentiation into separate and discrete endogamous jātis; the attribute of hierarchy is a property that does not belong to the essence of caste, and in any case, where hierarchy exists it is not purity/pollution that is the necessary criterion.

A little reflection will show that, put in this form, the criticism cannot be sustained. The discreteness of separate endogamous jātis is of course the most obvious aspect of the immediate phenomenon of caste. When this separateness is seen as based on qualitative differences, we necessarily have for each jāti its being-by-self and being-for-another, involving, in this case, the ascription of the natural differences of biological species on an order of cultural differentiation. Every recognized qualitative attribute of a jāti serves to establish its *natural* difference from other jātis, and this difference is upheld above all in the rule of endogamy, which lays down that the natural order of species must not be disturbed. Kane notes the agreement of all medieval *dharmaśāstra* texts on this point and cites the *Sūtasaṃhitā*, which states explicitly that the "several castes are like the species of animals and that caste attaches to the body and not to the soul."[10] The point, however, is that as soon as these discrete jātis are recognized as particular forms belonging to the same class of entities, that is to say, they are all recognized as *castes*, the finiteness of discrete qualities will be negated by a being-for-self of caste embodying the universal measure of "casteness." Dumont identifies this universal measure as one of having a place in the hierarchy of castes. In relation to this being-for-self, particular castes can only be distinguished from one another by quantity, namely their relative place in that hierarchy. An ordering among determinate castes will then be necessarily implied. (Continuity is not, strictly speaking, necessary, even in Dumont's scheme: an unambiguous and transitive ranking by quantity is all that is required.) Gupta's criticism here is misplaced, for the critique of Dumont's method cannot be sustained at the level of the determinate being of caste.

Gupta, however, makes another set of criticisms that is far more promising. There is not one caste ideology, he says, but several, sharing some principles in common but articulated at variance and even in opposition to one another. Now, this criticism is leveled at the essence of caste as identified by Dumont. We have seen already that Dumont locates the essence of caste on the religious ground defined by the opposition purity/pollution and claims that the force of dharma unites the determinate parts (the separate jātis) into a whole. To establish this claim, however, Dumont has first to dispose of a rather serious problem that arises in establishing the unity of the actuality of the institutions and practices of caste with its ideality. This problem has to do with the fact that the actual rankings of caste take variable forms in space (regional caste systems) and in time (caste mobility) and, further, that these specific orderings are not necessarily consistent with an ideal ordering in terms of purity/pollution. Dumont attempts to solve this problem, first, by positing an absolute separation between *dharma* and *artha*, and then asserting the absolute superiority of the former, the domain of ideology, to the latter, the domain of power. This enables him to allow power (economic, political) to play a residual role in the actual ranking of castes; specifically, the quantitative criterion of hierarchical ordering becomes a weighted numeraire where purity/pollution is the only variable allowed to fix the two extreme poles of the scale of ranking, while power variables are allowed to affect the ordering in the middle.

There is something inelegant in this solution offered by Dumont, and a large number of his critics have produced both textual and practical evidence to show that his assertion here is doubtful.[11] But Gupta's criticism that there is not one caste ideology (dharma) but several has the potential, if adequately theorized, for a more serious critique of Dumont. If substantiated, it would amount to the assertion that the very universality of dharma as the ideality of caste is not generally acknowledged by every part of the system of castes. This criticism would hold even if Dumont's specific characterization of dharma is modified to take care of the factual inaccuracies; in other words, the criticism would hold for any synthetic theory of caste.

To develop these criticisms into a theoretical critique of Dumont one would need to show: (1) that the immediate reality of castes represents the appearance not of one universal ideality of caste, but of several which are not only at variance but often in opposition; (2) that the universal dharma which claims to be the force binding the parts of the system into a whole is a one-sided construction; (3) that this one-sided ideality succeeds in its assertion of universality not because of the self-conscious unity of subject and object in each individual part but because of the effectiveness of a relation of domination and subordination; and (4) that the fragmented and contradictory consciousnesses represent an actuality that can be unified only by negating the one-sided ideality of the dominant construction of dharma.

Let me state the implications of this project. I am suggesting, first, that there is in popular beliefs and practices of caste an implicit critique which questions the claim of the dominant dharma to unify the particular jātis into a harmonious whole and which puts forward contrary claims.[12] Second, just as the effectiveness of the claims of the one dharma is contingent upon the conditions of power, so also are the possibilities and forms of the contrary claims conditioned by those relations of power. Third, in their deviance from the dominant dharma, the popular beliefs draw upon the ideological resources of given cultural traditions, selecting, transforming, and developing them to cope with new conditions of subordination but remaining limited by those conditions. Finally, the negativity of these contrary claims is an index of their failure to construct an alternative universal to the dominant dharma and is thus the mark of subalternity; the object of our project must be to develop, make explicit, and unify these fragmented oppositions in order to construct a critique of Indian tradition that is at the same time a critique of bourgeois equality.

What I have identified here are therefore the requirements for an immanent critique of caste ideology. The critique itself cannot be sustained unless one can address the corpus of caste ethnology right up to our contemporary times from this standpoint. I cannot claim any such expertise for myself. All I can attempt here is a brief illustrative exercise to show some of the possibilities of this approach. The interested reader may wish to compare my approach with Dumont's treatment of the same problem in his essay "World Renunciation in Indian Religions."[13] Whereas Dumont treats the series of oppositions—life in the world/life of the renouncer, group religion/disciplines of salvation, caste/individual—as having been unified within the "whole" of Hinduism by integration at the level of doctrinal Brahmanism and by toleration at the level of the sects, I will offer a different interpretation that treats these oppositions as fundamentally unresolved—unified, if at all, not at the level of the self-consciousness of "the Hindu" but only within the historical contingencies of the social relations of power.

THE DHARMA OF THE MINOR SECTS

The so-called minor religious sects of Bengal commanded, at various points of time between the seventeenth and nineteenth centuries, the following of quite a major section of the population of Bengal. Ramakanta Chakrabarty has compiled a list of fifty-six heterodox sects of this kind, many of which survive to this day.[14] Of these, the Bāul, the Jaganmohinī, the Kartābhajā, the Kiśorībhajā, the Sāhebdhanī, and a few others are relatively well known, the Kartābhajā in particular attracting much attention for its easy syncretism from the Calcutta intelligentsia in the nineteenth century, and the Bāul, of course, having been granted the status of an export item in the Festival of India circuit. Most of these sects are broadly classified as Vaiṣṇava or semi-Vaiṣṇava, but it is heterodoxy that is the hallmark of their status as "minor sects." Besides the general presence of what is loosely described as Sahajiyā Vaiṣṇavism, observers have variously noted the strong doctrinal and ritual influence on these sects of Buddhist Sahajiyā ideas, of "left" Tantric practices, of the religion of the Nāth cults, of Sufi doctrines, and of the Dharma cult of lower Bengal. The other crucial characteristic is that their following was predominantly, though not always exclusively, among the lower castes.

If one situates the rise of these cults in relation to the history of Vaiṣṇavism in Bengal, the crucial development that has to be noticed is the systematic introduction of caste practices in the religious and social life of orthodox Vaiṣṇavas. Ramakanta Chakrabarty suggests that caste rules began to be strictly applied after the historic festival held in Kheturi (Rajshahi) sometime between 1576 and 1582, which was attended by representatives of nearly a hundred Vaiṣṇava groups from all over Bengal.[15] The Kheturi council laid down the doctrinal and ritual framework of what was to become the dominant orthodoxy of Gauḍīya Vaiṣṇavism, based on canons prescribed by the *gosvāmīs* of Vrindavan.[16] The attempt, as Hitesranjan Sanyal suggests, may have been on the one hand to provide doctrinal respectability to a relatively unsophisticated popular religious movement by engaging in the discourse of Puranic Brahmanism and the great systems of Vaiṣṇava religious thought, and on the other to create the forms of practical religion that would integrate the diverse Sahajiyā Vaiṣṇava cults into the main trend of the bhakti movement.[17]

But soon enough, the differentiated forms of social identity and distinction appeared in the body of the Vaiṣṇava *sampradāy*. In contrast with the earlier phase of the movement, when several prominent non-Brahman Vaiṣṇava gurus such as Narahari Sarkar, Narottam Datta, and Rasikananda had Brahman disciples, or unlike the "neo-Brahman" phase, when some Vaiṣṇavas such as the followers of Shyamananda Pal in Midnapore began to wear the sacred thread irrespective of caste, the new orthodoxy that grew up frowned upon such practices. Indeed, the emphasis now was against indiscriminate proselytization, and the highest status was accorded among Vaiṣṇavas to the Brahman *kulaguru*, who acted as initiator and spiritual guide to a small number of respectable upper-caste families. Gradually, a clearly recognized social distinction emerged between high-caste Gauḍīya Vaiṣṇava householders and the low-caste *jāt baiṣṇab* (that is, Vaiṣṇava by caste), who were for all practical purposes regarded by the former as outcastes. Indeed, a whole series of stereotypes of the jāt baiṣṇab, combining the familiar prejudices of caste impurity with aspersions on their sexual morality, emerged to condemn the low-caste converts beyond the pale of the orthodox Gauḍīya Vaiṣṇava sampradāy. The sexual aspersions, in particular, derived from the simplicity of the marriage ceremony practiced by the followers of most minor sects, which explicitly rejected the ritual injunctions of the *smṛti*; upper-caste Vaiṣṇavas refused to regard these as proper weddings. Further, the sects were looked down upon for the refuge they often provided to widows and abandoned women; it was believed that the women were engaged in illicit liaisons with cult followers and used in orgiastic rituals, and the ranks of the sect were swelled by the children of such unsanctified unions.[18]

Seen from the standpoint of the history of Vaiṣṇavism in Bengal, this imposition of more or less orthodox caste practices on the Vaiṣṇava movement was part of the same process that gave rise to the deviant sects. As historians have pointed out, it was a situation where, after a spell of substantial mobility and readjustment of positions mostly in the middle rungs of the caste hierarchy in Bengal, and a significant process of incorporation of tribal populations in the peripheral regions into some form of Puranic religious practice,[19] the dominant ideological need was to reproduce a stable structure of social divisions within a harmonious whole. A universalizing religion such as Vaiṣṇavism could justify itself only by accommodating those differences within itself. The points of historical interest for us, therefore, are first the doctrinal and practical means by which this was attempted, and second the marks of unresolved and continuing conflict that this process of unification bears.

"The assertion of Brahmanical dominance," says Ramakanta Chakrabarty, "in a religious movement which was rooted in mysticism, and which was anti-caste and anti-intellectual, inevitably led to the growth of deviant orders."[20] He then gives an account of the origins, mostly in the eighteenth century, of some of these orders that were usually founded by Vaiṣṇavas from the "untouchable" Śūdra castes and that usually had a following among the trading and artisanal castes, the untouchables, and sometimes tribals converted to the new faith.

In talking about the doctrinal beliefs and ritual practices of these sects, the usual description offered is "eclecticism." Thus: "The spread of Vaiṣṇavism among the low castes strengthened eclectic tendencies. Eclecticism was produced by a combination of circumstances."[21] Chakrabarty lists some of these: the secret practice by Vaiṣṇava gurus of Tantric worship while openly professing Vaiṣṇavism; the continued respect for folk gods and goddesses among Vaiṣṇava converts; the obeisance paid to Kṛṣṇa, Rādhā, and Caitanya by non-Vaiṣṇava medieval poets, even Muslim poets, and in non-Vaiṣṇava temple art; and the participation of non-sectarians, including Muslims, in Vaiṣṇava festivals. But to characterize these faiths as eclectic is, of course, nothing more than to acknowledge that they cannot be classified under one or the other of the well-known and dominant theological systems. It is, as a matter of fact, merely to recognize that the existence of these sects is itself evidence of an unstable layering in popular consciousness of material drawn from diverse dominant as well as subordinate traditions, the only principle of unity being the contradictory one of simultaneous acceptance and rejection of domination. To characterize the particular structure of this consciousness, we must identify in the particular historical conjuncture the specific form of this contradictory unity.

What were the doctrinal means used by Vaiṣṇavism to construct the unity of an internally divided community? In the post-Caitanya phase, the fundamental devotional attitude of bhakti was itself explicated along two lines. On the one hand, the more orthodox strand following upon the canonical strictures of the Vrindavan gosvāmīs insisted on the performance by ordinary devotees of *vaidhi*, or ritually sanctioned, bhakti. The *Haribhaktivilāsa* of Gopala Bhaṭṭa Gosvāmin became the authoritative text for this form of Vaiṣṇava devotion, and it went a long way in reconciling the ideal of Vaiṣṇava love with the ritual norms of Brahmanical caste practices. On the other hand, Gauḍīya Vaiṣṇavas also granted doctrinal sanction to what was called *rāgānuga* bhakti, which had a more mystical form and which was said to originate in an unbearable desire or thirst for God in the being of the devotee. Although the forms of rāgānuga devotion soon acquired their own disciplinary modes of practice, and the orthodox school insisted that they could be open only to a select few, the important point was that these forms were not required to conform to scriptural injunctions or institutional arrangements. This was the first mode of doctrinal differentiation by which the religion of Vaiṣṇavism in Bengal would try to unify its fold of believers. It provided a means by which Vaiṣṇava householders could retain their allegiance to the faith while participating in the ritual procedures of social and personal life as laid down in the śāstra, whereas the deviant orders of the *sahajiyā sādhak* could also proclaim to their followers the esoteric connection between their pursuit of ecstatic bhakti and the doctrinal principles of the main body of the movement.

The second mode of differentiation was provided in the forms and methods of Vaiṣṇava worship. It took some time, and a fair amount of debate, for the idea of Caitanya as an incarnation of Kṛṣṇa to be firmly fixed, and even then much controversy followed about a suitable hagiology that would replicate the divine deeds at Vrindavan with those at Nabadwip, a matter complicated further by the Gauḍīya doctrine of Caitanya as the dual incarnation of Kṛṣṇa as well as Rādhā. But the crucial concept that gained predominance within the Bengal school of Vaiṣṇavism and that enabled a wide variety of forms of devotional worship to be doctrinally unified was the theory of *parakīyā* love. Sashibhusan Das Gupta has shown how the celebration in Vaiṣṇava thought of the extramarital love of Kṛṣṇa and Rādhā was appropriated into the forms of an earlier tradition in Bengal of yogic practices leading to the state of *mahāsukha* or *sahaja* as conceived in Tantric Buddhism.[22] But the important point for us is that even in this process of transformation, the doctrine of parakīyā love became internally differentiated. While it was generally acknowledged that the *līlā* of Kṛṣṇa and Rādhā was the means by which Kṛṣṇa in his active, worldly, quality-infused form of *bhagavāna* realized the unity of his ultimate nature, or *svarūpa-śakti*, in the form of an infinite state of love or bliss, the attitude of the Vaiṣṇava devotees to this sport of the gods came to be structured in a differentiated form.

The Gauḍīya orthodoxy (or at least that section of it which subscribed to the superiority of parakīyā over svakīyā love) insisted that the *rādhābhāva*, or the attitude of worship of Kṛṣṇa as a married woman for her lover, was proper only to Srī Caitanya himself. For his devotees, the prescribed attitude of worship was that of the *sakhī* or the *mañjarī*, who comprised a differentiated circle of female companions of the divine couple and whose task it was to act as reverential accomplices, attendants, and voyeurs to the sacred union. In time, especially in the post-Kheturi phase, the orthodox prescription to devotees was to adopt the mañjarī mode of worship, for only by choosing to serve as the humble attendant could one eliminate from one's person all traces of *puruṣābhimāna*, which was proper only to Kṛṣṇa and not to a true Vaiṣṇava devotee. For the latter, the eternal sport of *nityavṛndāvana* was only a memory to be cherished, contemplated, and ritually remembered in daily life.[23] This prescription seems to have opened a way for personal peace and harmony through a devout religiosity but only at the cost of an all-suffering social quiescence.

The deviant Sahajiyā orders, however, turned their affiliation to parakīyā worship in a wholly contrary direction. They subscribed to the doctrine of eternal love as represented in the līlā of Kṛṣṇa and Rādhā in nityavṛndāvana and called it the state of *sahaja*, or supreme bliss, but argued that it was possible for mortal men and women living in a gross material world to make the transition to the state of supreme love through a disciplined process of spiritual culture, or *sādhan*. The Sahajiyā supplemented the orthodox doctrine of bhakti with a theory of *āropa*, that is, the attribution of divinity to mortal men and women, and thus effected its transformation into a fundamentally different doctrine. The argument now was that the *svarūpa*, or true spiritual self, resided within the physical form (*rūpa*) of every human being and had to be realized in its developed and perfect state without denying or annihilating his or her physical existence. Indeed, it is human love, moving from the gross forms of carnal desire through successive stages of spiritual development, that finally attains the perfect and infinite forms of divine love while retaining and subsuming within it the earlier forms. Through such a process of sādhan, it is possible for men and women to realize the svarūpa of Kṛṣṇa and Rādhā in their own selves.

As a doctrine this was heretical, and the actual procedures of parakīyā love practiced by the various Sahajiyā sects were looked upon by "respectable" Vaiṣṇava householders as unclean and disreputable. Sometimes there were fairly violent attempts at suppression, such as in the *pāṣaṇḍīdalan* diatribes launched by the defenders of Brahmanical orthodoxy and in the unrelenting campaigns by the Islamic orthodoxy to suppress the various *marfati* sects, particularly the Bāul. At other times they were allowed to exist, but as degraded orders on the peripheries of normal social life. Nevertheless, the possibility of a doctrinal attachment between the domain of the regular and orthodox on the one hand and that of the degraded and deviant on the other, through an appropriation of one or the other meaning of the inherently polysemic concepts which sought to unify the field of dogma and ritual, meant that on either side the unity, however tenuous, of the whole could be emphasized when required, just as the irreconcilability of differences could also be asserted if necessary.

The question of identity or difference, one dharma or many, then becomes not so much a matter of judging the inherent strength of the synthetic unification proclaimed by a dominant religion. Any universalist religion will bear in its essence the contradictory marks of identity and difference, the parts being held together in a whole by an ideological force that proclaims, with varying degrees of effectiveness, its unity.[24] The question, rather, becomes a historical one of identifying the determinants that make this unity a matter of *contingency*.

It will be apparent from the histories of the minor sects that the varying intensities of their affiliation with the larger unity, the degree of "eclecticism," the varying measures and subtleties in emphasizing their difference and their self-identity reveal not so much the desire to create a new universalist system but rather varying strategies of survival, and of self-assertion. The Bāuls openly proclaim their unconventionality and rejection of scriptural injunctions, both Brahmanical and Islamic, but live as mendicants outside society. They talk of love and the divine power that resides in all men and women and thus engage philosophically in the discourses both of Vaiṣṇavism and Sufism, yet are marked out as unorthodox and deviant, not a proper part of the congregation. They enthrall their audiences by singing, with much lyricism, subtlety, and wit, of the "man of the heart" and the "unknown bird" that flies in and out of the cage which is the human body, but practice their own disciplines of *sādhan* and worship in secret, under the guidance of the *murshid*.[25] Of sects that live on among a lay following of ordinary householders, most do not display any distinct sect-marks on the person of the devotee, so that in their daily lives the sectarians are largely indistinguishable from others. What they offer to their followers, as in the case of the Kartābhajā or the Sāhebdhanī, is a congregational space defined outside the boundaries of the dominant religious life, outside caste society or the injunctions of the *sharī'ah*, but a space brought into active existence only periodically, at thinly attended weekly meetings with the *mahāśay* or the *fakir* and at the three or four large annual festivals where sectarians perform the prescribed duties of allegiance to their preceptor and their faith, while numerous others come just as they would to any religious fair—to eat and drink, listen to the music, pick up a few magic cures for illnesses and disabilities, and generally to collect one's share of virtue that is supposed to accrue from such visits. The sect leaders preach, often in language that conceals under its surface imagery an esoteric meaning open only to initiates, doctrines that talk of their rejection of the Vedas and of caste, of idolatry and sastric or *shariati* ritual, but the greater their sect's reach across the caste hierarchy, the less strident is their critical tone and the more vapid their sentiments about the sameness of all faiths. The Kartābhajā, for instance, originated in the eighteenth century from a founder who was probably Muslim, but the sect was organized in its present form in the early nineteenth century by a prosperous Sadgop family. It has retained its following among the middle and lower castes, and in particular draws a very large number of women, especially widows, to its festivals, but a fair number of upper-caste people have also been initiated into the faith. Not surprisingly, a distinction has been innovated between the *vyavahārik*, the practical social aspect of the life of the devotee, and the *pāramārthik*, the supreme spiritual aspect, the former virtually becoming marked as a ground of inevitable compromise and surrender to the dominant norms of society and the latter the secret preserve of autonomy and self-assertion.[26]

All of these, then, are strategies devised within a relationship of dominance and subordination, and they take on doctrinal or ritual attributes and acquire different values according to the changing contingencies of power. But in all their determinate manifestations in particular historical circumstances, they are shaped by the condition of subalternity. I now propose to discuss the case of a minor sect whose historical effectiveness in propagating a deviant religion for the lowest castes seems to have been particularly unsuccessful: let us see if even this rather extreme case of "failure" tells us something about the strategies of resistance and assertion.

A TEACHER AMONG THE HĀḌI

Along with the Ḍom, the Hāḍi is an archetypal *antaja* caste of Bengal. It is not particularly numerous in Nadia district, where in 1931 it constituted only about 0.02 percent of all untouchable castes and was considerably fewer in number than the Bāgdi, Muchi, Namaśūdra, or Mālo, which comprised the bulk of the 30 percent or so of the Hindu population of that district which was classifiable as untouchable.[27] But it stands as a cultural stereotype of the lowest among the low; thus, for instance, when a Chittagong saying ridicules the proclivity among low castes to assert mutual superiority in ranking, it illustrates the fact precisely by picking out the Hāḍi and the Ḍom: "The Ḍom thinks he is purer than the HāḌi, the HāḌi thinks he is purer than the Ḍom."[28] Risley classifies the Hāḍi as "a menial and scavenger class of Bengal Proper," with whom no one will eat and from whom no one will accept water.[29] The Hāḍis have priests of their own and are forbidden from entering the courtyards of the great temples. In the nineteenth century, they sometimes had tenancy rights in land as occupancy or nonoccupancy *raiyats*, but were mostly day laborers in agriculture, their traditional occupations the tapping of date-palm trees, making bamboo implements, playing musical instruments at weddings and festivals, carrying palanquins, serving as syces, and scavenging. The removal of nightsoil was confined exclusively to the Methar subcaste. Risley reports that the Hāḍis also preferred infant marriage and permitted both divorce and the remarriage of widows, although the synonymous caste of Bhuiṅmāli in Dacca did not at that time allow the latter.

James Wise tells a story about the Dacca Bhuiṅmāli.[30] They were, they say, Śūdras originally and were once invited along with all other castes to a feast given by the goddess Pārvatī. On seeing the goddess, a guileless Bhuiṅmāli remarked: "If I had such a beautiful woman in my house, I would cheerfully perform the most menial offices for her." Śiva overheard the remark, took the Bhuiṅmāli up on his word, gave him a beautiful wife, and made him her sweeper for life. A Dacca proverb makes the comment that the Bhuiṅnmāli is the only Hindu ever to be degraded for love of garbage.

Balarām Hāḍi, founder of the Balarāmī sect, was born in Meherpur in Nadia sometime around 1780.[31] In his youth he was employed as a watchman at the house of the Malliks, the Vaidya zamindars of Meherpur.[32] It is said that among the employees of the Malliks, a number of Bhojpuri Brahmans worked as guards and servants, with whom Balaram spent a lot of his time, listening to recitations from Tulsidas's *Rāmāyaṇa* and other devotional compositions. At this time there occurred one night a theft of some valuable jewelry with which the family deity of the Malliks was adorned. Balaram was suspected to have been involved in the crime and, by the order of his employer, was tied to a tree and severely beaten. Mortified by this, Balaram left Meherpur and did not return to his village for the next twenty years or more. He is said to have wandered about in the company of religious men, and when he came back to Meherpur to found his sect, he was fifty years old and a mendicant.

Balaram was illiterate but was credited with a quick wit and an unusual flair for the use of words. The Hāḍis, he used to say, did not have any of the taints with which the Brahmans had stigmatized them; just as the Gharāmi was one who built houses (*ghar*), so was the Hāḍi one who had created *hāḍ*—the bones with which all living beings are made. Akshaykumar Datta relates an apocryphal story that illustrates rather well Balaram's reputed facility with argumentation:

> Balaram had gone to bathe in the river, when he saw some Brahmans offering *tarpaṇ* to their ancestors. Imitating their actions, he too began to throw water on the river-bank. One of the Brahmans asked him, "Balai, what do you think you are doing?" Balaram answered, "I am watering my field of spinach." The Brahman asked, "Your field of spinach? Here?" Balaram replied, "Well, your ancestors aren't here either. If you think that the water you pick up and throw back into the river reaches your ancestors, then why shouldn't the water I throw on the river-bank reach my fields?"[33]

Balaram emerged as a religious leader sometime in the 1830s. Writing in the 1890s, some three decades after Balaram's death, Jogendra Nath Bhattacharya reported that the sect had a following of about twenty thousand people.[34] Collective memory within the sect has it that at some point in his life as a preacher, Balaram was invited by one of his disciples to Nischintapur in the Tehatta area of Nadia (not far from the infamous fields of Plassey), where he set up another center of activity. Sudhir Chakrabarti gives a list of twelve of his direct disciples, all of whom were low-caste (Muchi, Namaśūdra, Jugi, Hāḍi, Māhiṣya, and Muslim), and three were women described as "earning their livelihood by begging."[35] Balaram also had a female companion, described variously as his wife or his *sevikā* (attendant),[36] who later came to be known as Brahmamātā. She was Mālo by caste and ran the Meherpur center after Balaram's death, while the Nischintapur center was run by a Māhiṣya disciple called Tinu Mandal. Unlike the Sahajiyā Vaiṣṇava sects, the Balarāmīs do not have a guru-disciple structure in their order: the various centers are run by leaders called *sarkār*, but the post is not necessarily hereditary. Until a few decades ago, there were about a dozen active centers in various villages in Nadia. At present, most are in a decrepit state, although a few centers survive in Burdwan, Bankura, and Purulia, where two or three large festivals are held every year.

Like many other religious leaders who have been invested with the attributes of divinity, Balaram too has been the subject of myths that give to the story of his birth an aura of extraordinariness. It is said that at the time of his father's wedding the astrologers had predicted that the son born of this marriage would be the last in the lineage. When the wife became pregnant she concealed the fact from everyone else. One afternoon a small child with a full growth of hair and beard suddenly dropped from the ceiling and, miraculously, the woman found her womb empty. She wrapped the child in a piece of cloth and quietly left it in the jungle. But she had a sister who lived in the next village. Balaram visited her in her dream. The next morning she came to the jungle and found the child lying under a tree, protected by two tigers. She took him away with her. The foster mother found work in the house of a landlord, and when Balaram grew up to be a young boy, he was employed to tend the landlord's cattle.

The birth was miraculous, and the story has a certain resemblance with that of the cowherd Kṛṣṇa, brought up by his aunt in Vrindavan. One day the landlord Jiban Mukherjee was visited by his family guru and the boy Balaram was asked to accompany him to the river Bhairav, where the guru was to bathe. It was here that the aforementioned conversation between Balaram and the Brahmans supposedly took place, and the story goes on to assert that Balaram did in fact perform the miracle of sending the river water to a distant field. Greatly impressed by this feat, the Brahman guru came back and reprimanded his landlord disciple for employing a person with such miraculous powers as a mere servant. Balaram then asked that he be allowed to go back to the jungle from where he had come. Jiban Mukherjee donated a small piece of forest land to Balaram, and it was there that he set up his *ākhḍā*.[37]

Not all Brahmans, however, were quite so generous in acknowledging Balaram's spiritual merits. The Brahman landlord of Nischintapur, for instance, greatly resented Balaram's growing influence over his tenants. One afternoon, while Balaram was away, the landlord arranged to set fire to the Nischintapur ākhḍā. When Balaram was told of this he remarked, "He who sets fire to my house destroys his own." Saying this, he left Nischintapur and in three long steps was ten miles away in Meherpur. Apparently, it began to rain from that moment, and it did not let up for the next nine days. Huge cracks appeared on the land surrounding the zamindar's barnhouse, and by the time the rain stopped, the entire barn had been swallowed by an enormous crater. The place is now called the "barnhouse lake."

Balaram's teachings, not surprisingly, were directed against the Vedas, the ritual injunctions of the śāstra, and the practices of caste. J. N. Bhattacharya, in his brief account of Balaram's sect, makes the remark: "The most important feature of his cult was the hatred that he taught his followers to entertain towards Brahmans."[38] He also forbade them to display any distinctive marks of their sect or, significantly, to utter the name of any deity when asking for alms. The mantras they were asked to chant were in plain Bengali, devoid even of the ornamental semblance of an *oṃ* or a Tantric *hrīṃ klīṃ ślīṃ*, and without the hint of an esoteric subtext. When Balaram died, his body was neither cremated nor buried nor thrown in the water; on his instructions, it was simply left in the forest to be fed to other living creatures. For a few generations after Balaram, the sect leaders were buried after death or their bodies thrown into the river, but now the śāstric procedure of cremation is generally followed.

The sectarian ideology of the Balāhāḍis pitted itself not only against the dominant Brahmanical religion, it also demarcated itself from the religion of the Vaiṣṇavas. Their songs refer with much derision to the practices of the Sahajiyā—their fondness for food, drink, sex, and intoxicants, their obsession with counting the rosary, indeed their very existence as vagabonds without habitation or kin. They laugh at the Gauḍīya dogma of complete servility of the devotee and retort: "Why should I stoop so low when Hāḍirām is within me?" Ridiculing the concept of Caitanya as the dual incarnation of Kṛṣṇa and Rādhā, they ask, "If Caitanya is Kṛṣṇa, then why does he cry for him? If it is the Rādhā in him that cries, then Caitanya is only half a being. Who is the complete being? Hāḍirām, of course. It is for him that Caitanya cries, for Caitanya can never find him. The perfect being appeared not in Nabadwip but in Meherpur."[39]

The songs of the Balarāmī breathe the air of sectarianism. Boastful, aggressive, often vain, they produce the impression of an open battle waged on many fronts. There is little that is secretive about the ways of the sect. Although its following consisted overwhelmingly of low-caste and poor laboring people, there are none of the esoteric practices associated with the Sahajiyā cults. Perhaps the absence of prosperous householders among them made it unnecessary for the Balarāmīs to conceal their defiance of the dominant norms—after all, who cared what a few Hāḍis or Mālos proclaimed in their own little circles? As far as "respectable" people were concerned, these untouchables were not particularly good religionists anyway—indeed, in a certain sense, incapable of good religion. It was their very marginality that may have taken the sting out of their revolt against subordination, and by asserting the unrelenting negativity and exclusiveness of their rebellious faith, they condemned themselves to eternal marginality.

THE GENEALOGY OF INSUBORDINATION

But the defiance was not without conceit. It would be worth our while to delve into some of the mythic material with which the Balarāmīs constructed their faith in order to address the question raised before: How do the contingencies of power determine the form and the outcome of rebellions against the dominance of a dharma that proclaims its universality?

Among the myths is a very curious and distinctive account of the origin of the species, which the Balarāmīs call their *jātitattva*. It seems that in the earliest age, the *ādiyug*, there was nothing: this was, so to speak, time before creation. In the next, the *anādi yug*, were created plants. In the third age, the *divya yug*, there was only Hāḍirām—and no one else. From his *hāi* (yawn) was created Haimabatī, the first female, and from her the first gods, Brahmā, Viṣṇu, and Śiva, who would direct the course of the sacred and profane histories in the *satya*, *tretā*, *dvāpar*, and *kali* ages spoken of in the Purāṇas. This historical time of the four ages is described in the Balarāmī songs as a trap, a vicious snare that binds people to Vedic and Puranic injunctions. The quest for Hāḍirām is to find in one's mortal life the path of escape into that mythic time before history when the Hāḍi was noble, pure, and worthy of respect.

The form of this creation myth is the same as that which occurs in most of the popular cult literature of Bengal, the archetypal form of which is to be found in the *Śūnyapurāṇa*.[40] There too we find an age before all ages, when there was nothing and the supreme lord moved about in a vacuum. The lord then creates out of his compassion another personality called Nirañjana, out of whose yawn is born the bird Uluka. From the lord's sweat is born Ādyāśakti, primordial energy in the form of a woman. From Ādyāśakti are born the three gods Brahmā, Viṣṇu, and Śiva. In the Balarāmī cosmogony, not only does Hāḍirām take the place of Nirañjana, but he seems to usurp the powers of the supreme lord as well.

Specifically, however, there is in the story of Haimabati's birth a more direct and yet curiously unacknowledged element of borrowing. The literature of the Nāth cults of northern and eastern Bengal tells the legend of how at the time of creation Śiva came out of the mouth of the primordial lord, while out of the lord's *hāḍ*, or bone, was born Hāḍipā.[41] When Śiva decided to take Gaurī, the mother of the earth, as his wife and come down to earth, Hāḍipā, along with the other siddha Mīnanāth, accompanied them as their attendants. Hāḍipā, however, expressed his willingness to accept even the occupation of a sweeper if he could have as wife a woman as beautiful as Gaurī, and Śiva ordained that he live on earth as a Hāḍi in the company of the queen Maynāmatī.[42] Hāḍipā was later to be celebrated in the Nāth literature as the preceptor of the great *siddha* Gopīcandra.

The similarity between this creation myth, hallowed in a much more well-known tradition in Bengal's folk literature, and the one held by the Balarāmīs, strongly suggests that Balarām in fact picked it up in order to assert a sacred origin of the Hāḍi. It is not surprising that a further transposition should be introduced into the Nāth legend in order to give Hāḍirām himself the status of the originator of the human species. What is remarkable, however, is that this source of the myth in a fairly well-established strand of popular religious tradition is entirely unacknowledged. There is nothing in the Balarāmī beliefs that claims any affiliation with the Nāth religion or with any other tradition of Śaiva religious thought.

All that is conceded is a somewhat desultory recognition that of the three sons of Haimabatī, Śiva went a little farther than his brothers Brahmā and Viṣṇu along the path of worship that led to Hāḍirām: he counted all of the 108 bones created by the latter and still wanders about, wearing a necklace of bones around his neck and singing the praises of Hāḍirām.[43] Of the other two sons of Haimabatī, we get, in the third generation in the line of Brahmā's eldest daughter Ghāmkāñcanī,[44] two brothers called Ājir Methar and Bhusi Ghoṣ, the Methar being a subcaste of the Hāḍi but the most degraded among them, while Ghoṣ is probably the Goālā caste, which is a "touchable" Śūdra caste, higher in status than both the Methar and the Hāḍi. Viṣṇu's section is more colorful, for in the line of his second daughter, Muchundarī Kālī, we get Hāoyā and Ādam, of whom are born two sons, Hābel and Kābel. Undoubtedly, we have here the Old Testament story of the genesis as related in the Koran—that is, Haw'wa (Eve) and Adam and their sons Habil (Abel) and Qabil (Cain)—slotted in the fourth and fifth generations of the human species. In Hābel's line, we then get four jātis—Sheikh, Saiyad, Mughal, and Pathan, the four traditional classificatory groups among Indian Muslims—and in Kābel's line we get Nikiri, Jolā (low-status Muslim fishermen and weaver castes), and, believe it or not, Rajput.[45] Of Viṣṇu's third child, Musuk Kālī, are born three sons. The eldest, Parāśar, is a sage and he fathers eleven children, namely, goat, tiger, snake, vulture, mouse, mosquito, elephant, horse, cat, camel, and monkey! The youngest son, Ṛṣabh, is also a *muṇi* (sage) and from his grandsons originate thirteen Brahman groups, whose names are Dobe, Cobe, Pāṭhak, Pānḍe, Teoyāri, Miśir, and so forth—the most recognizable names here are those of Bihar and Uttar Pradesh Brahmans, and none is a Bengali name. (Perhaps we ought to recall Balarām's early association with Bhojpuri Brahmans in the house of his landlord employer.) The Bengali Brahmans originate in a particularly degraded section, for Pāṭhak had two children, Vṛṣa (bull) and Meṣa (sheep), one born of an untouchable Bede woman and the other of an untouchable Bāgdi woman. From them originate all of the Brahman lineages of Bengal, such as Bhāṭije, Bāḍije, Mukhuje, Gaṅgāl, Ghuṣāl, Bāgji, Lahaḍī, Bhādariyā, and so forth.

There is much more in this extraordinary genealogical tree whose meanings are not transparent to the uninitiated; even the present-day leaders of the cult cannot explain many of the references. The ramifications of Balarām's jātitattva, inasmuch as it attempts to define a new set of relations between various existent social groups, are for the most part unclear. What is clear, however, is first that the scheme continues to undertake the classification of social groups in terms of the natural division into species, and it does this to a great extent by transforming the relations between elements within a popularly inherited mythic code; and second that by overturning the hierarchical order of the Puranic creation myths, it pushes the very ideality of the dominant scheme of caste to a limit where it merges with its opposite. Balarām's jātitattva does not assert that there are no jātis or differences between social groups akin to the differences between natural species. Rather, by raising the Hāḍi to the position of the purest of the pure, the self-determining originator of differentiations within the genus, and by reducing the Brahman to a particularly impure and degenerate lineage, it subverts the very claim of the dominant dharma that the actual social relations of caste are in perfect conformity with its universal ideality.

Without, of course, asserting a new universal. That mark is imprinted on the consciousness of the yet unsurpassed limit of the condition of subalternity. The conceit shown in the construction of Balarām's jātitattva is a sign of conscious insubordination. But there is no trace in it of a self-conscious contest for an alternative social order.

Or are we being too hasty in our judgment?

THE BODY AS THE SITE OF APPROPRIATION

Caste attaches to the body, not to the soul. It is the biological reproduction of the human species through procreation within endogamous caste groups that ensures the permanence of ascribed marks of caste purity or pollution. It is also the physical contact of the body with defiling substances or defiled bodies that mark it with the temporary conditions of pollution, which can be removed by observing the prescribed procedures of physical cleansing. Further, if we have grasped the essence of caste, the necessity to protect the purity of his body is what forbids the Brahman from engaging in acts of labor that involve contact with polluting material and, reciprocally, requires the unclean castes to perform those services for the Brahman. The essence of caste, we may then say, requires that the laboring bodies of the impure castes be reproduced in order that they can be subordinated to the need to maintain the bodies of the pure castes in their state of purity. All the injunctions of dharma must work to this end.

When popular religious cults deviate from the dogma of the dominant religion, when they announce the rejection of the Vedas, the śāstric rituals or caste, they declare a revolt of the spirit. But the conditions of power which make such revolts possible are not necessarily the same as those that would permit a practical insubordination of laboring bodies. To question the ideality of caste is not directly to defy its immediate reality.

It is not as though this other battle has not been waged. Let us leave aside those high points of popular protest which take the explicit political forms of insurgency: these have received a fair amount of attention from historians, their general features have been examined, and their historical limits broadly delineated. We are also not considering here those particular or individual instances of disobedience, whether demonstrative or covert, which undoubtedly occur in the daily life of every village in India. Instead, let us turn our eyes to the practical aspects of the religious life of the deviant cults we have been talking about. All of these are fundamentally concerned with the body. The Sahajiyā cults practice the forms of bodily worship that do not respect the dictums of either the śāstra or the sharī'ah. But they can be conducted only in secret, under the guidance of the guru, and their principles can be propagated only in the language of enigma. Where they seek an open congregation, it takes the antistructural form of the *communitas* of periodic and momentary religious festivals. And yet there is, underlying it all, the attempt to define a claim of proprietorship over one's own body, to negate the daily submission of one's body and its labor to the demands made by the dominant dharma and to assert a domain of bodily activity where it can, with the full force of ethical conviction, disregard those demands. Notice, therefore, the repeated depiction of the body in the songs of dehatattva not simply as a material entity but as an artifact—not a natural being at all but a physical construct. The body is a house, or a boat, or a cart, or a weaver's loom, or a potter's wheel, or any of countless other instruments or products of labor that remain at the disposal and use of one who possesses them. But the very secretiveness of those cult practices, the fact that they can be engaged in only, as it were, outside the boundaries of the social structure, sets the limit to the practical effectiveness of the claim of possession; not surprisingly, it draws upon itself the charge of licentiousness.

The practical religion of the Balāhāḍis takes a different form. Their sectarianism is not, as we have seen, secretive, nor is it primarily conceived as a set of practices engaged in beyond the margins of social life. Rather, their forms of worship involve a self-disciplining of the body in the course of one's daily social living. Here too the body is an artifact, but it can be used by its owner with skill and wisdom or wasted and destroyed by profligacy. The specific forms of self-discipline, as far as one can gather from the material supplied by Sudhir Chakrabarti, again seem to bear close resemblance with the *haṭhayoga* practices of the Nāth cults. The main principle is that of *ulṭasādhanā*, which involves yogic exercises that produce a regressive or upward movement in the bodily processes. It is believed that in the normal course, the force of *pravṛtti* or activity and change moves in a downward direction, taking the body along the path of decay and destruction. The aim of self-discipline is to reverse this process by moving it in the upward direction of *nivṛtti*, or rest. More specifically, the bodily practices involve the retention of the *bindu* or *śukra* (semen) and prevention of its waste. The Balāhāḍi literature does not, of course, prescribe the full range of haṭhayoga practices, which can be performed only in strict celibacy, with a view to reaching the perfect *siddha* state of immortality.[46] What it does, however, is lay down a sort of new *āśramadharma* for its adherents—a graded series of states of bodily discipline that can be attempted in the course of a mortal, and social, life.

The lowest state is that of *bodhitan*, where the body is completely a prisoner of impulses and base desires. It is a state where one does not even will an escape from the debilitating demands of the "four ages"—that snare of historical time in which all the forces of activity and change work toward the bondage and annihilation of free life. To us, this appears to be a state characterized by the mindless pursuit of instant pleasure, although the Balarāmī would put this as its opposite. The body, he would say, is here completely under the sway of *man*, that is, of mind that is the repository of impulse and desire. In bodhitan, the body is not its own; it is the state of alienation of the body from itself. Indeed, this bodily state becomes the representation of that condition of the laboring classes which provokes such remarks as "The Hāḍi's Lakṣmī finds her way into the Śunḍi's [liquor seller's] house."[47] The passage of the body from this state to that of eyotan is the crucial transition for a Balarāmī householder. In *eyotan*, the bodily processes are under the control of its owner. The semen is preserved and spent only for procreation.[48] This, in this world of representations where the body stands as microcosm for the universe, is the daily affirmation of a proprietorship constantly threatened. If the purity and perfection of the body can be controlled from within itself, nothing external can pollute it. For most lay followers of the sect, this is as far as their sādhan is expected to go. For the fortunate few, a successful life in eyotan is followed by the state of *nityan*, where there is complete unconcern for the world. This is a stage of life spent outside the bonds of family and kin. The final and most perfect state of sādhan is that of *khāstan*. It is a state of complete freedom and hence of unconditioned proprietorship over one's bodily existence, for, as the Balarāmīs say, the prajā of khāstan are entities such as light, air, sky, fire, or water, which do not pay a rent to anyone for their earthly existence. This is a state that only Balarām was able to attain.

What are we to say of this? There are unmistakable signs here of a consciousness alienated from the dominant dharma but apparently bound to nothing else than its spirit of resolute negativity. Its practical defeat too is borne out by the facts of social history. Yet, is there not here an implicit, barely stated, search for a recognition whose signs lie not outside but within one's own self? Can one see here the trace of an identity that is defined not by others but by oneself? Perhaps we have allowed ourselves to be taken in too easily by the general presence of an abstract negativity in the autonomous domain of subaltern beliefs and practices and have missed those marks, faint as they are, of an immanent process of criticism and learning, of selective appropriation, of making sense of and using on one's own terms the elements of a more powerful cultural order. We must, after all, remind ourselves that subaltern consciousness is not merely structure, characterized solely by negativity; it is also history, shaped and developed through a changing process of interaction between the dominant and the subordinate. Surely it would be wholly contrary to our project to go about as though only the dominant culture has a life in history and subaltern consciousness is eternally frozen in its structure of negation.

THE IMPLICIT AND THE EXPLICIT

We must, however, be careful to avoid the easy, mechanical transposition of the specifics of European history. The specific forms of immanent development necessarily work with a definite cultural content. It seems quite farfetched to identify in the criticisms of caste among the deviant religions the embryo of a Protestant ethic or an incipient urge for bourgeois freedom. What we have is a desire for a structure of community in which the opposite tendencies of mutual separateness and mutual dependence are united by a force that has a greater universal moral actuality than the given forms of the dominant dharma. For want of a more concrete concept of praxis, we may call this desire, in an admittedly abstract and undifferentiated sense, a desire for *democratization*, where rights and the application of the norms of justice are open to a broader basis of consultation, disputation, and resolution.

Every social form of the community, in the formal sense, must achieve the unity of mutual separateness and mutual dependence of its parts. The system of castes, we have seen, makes this claim, but its actuality is necessarily in disjunction with its ideality. The external critique of caste, drawn from the liberal ideology of Europe, suggests that a legal framework of bourgeois freedom and equality provides an alternative and, in principle, more democratic basis for this unification. This has been the formal basis of the constitutional structure of the postcolonial state in India. And yet the practical construction of this new edifice out of the given cultural material has been forced into an abandonment of its principles from the very start—notice, for instance, the provisions of special reservations on grounds of caste.[49] The new political processes have, it would seem, managed to effect a displacement of the unifying force of dharma but have replaced it with the unifying concept of "nation" as concretely embodied in the state. What has resulted is not the actualization of bourgeois equality at all but rather the conflicting claims of caste groups (to confine ourselves to this particular domain of social conflict), not on the religious basis of dharma but on the purely secular demands of claims upon the state. The force of dharma, it appears, has been ousted from its position of superiority, to be replaced with a vengeance by the pursuit of artha, but, pace Dumont, on the basis again of caste divisions. On the one hand, we have the establishment of capitalist relations in agricultural production in which the new forms of wage labor fit snugly into the old grid of caste divisions.[50] On the other hand, we have the supremely paradoxical phenomenon of low-caste groups asserting their very backwardness in the caste hierarchy to claim discriminatory privileges from the state, and upper-caste groups proclaiming the sanctity of bourgeois equality and freedom (the criterion of equal opportunity mediated by skill and merit) in order to beat back the threat to their existing privileges. This was evidenced most blatantly in the violent demonstrations over the adoption of so-called Mandal Commission recommendations by the government of India in 1990. What are we to make of these conflicting desires for democratization?

There is no alternative for us but to undertake a search, both theoretical and practical, for the concrete forms of democratic community that are based neither on the principle of hierarchy nor on those of bourgeois equality. Dumont's posing of the principles of *homo hierarchicus* against those of *homo equalis* is a false, essentialist, positing of an unresolvable antinomy. We must assert that there is a more developed universal form of the unity of separateness and dependence that subsumes hierarchy and equality as lower historical moments.

The point is to explicate the principles and to construct the concrete forms of this universal. In Indian politics the problem of unifying the opposed requirements of separateness and dependence has been concretely addressed only at the level of the structure of federalism, a level where the problem is seen as permitting a territorial resolution. The attempt has had dubious success. In other domains, of which caste is a prime example, politics has drifted from one contentious principle to another (bourgeois equality, caste-class correlation, discriminatory privileges for low castes through state intervention, etc.) without finding adequate ground on which it can be superseded by a new universal form of community.

But, and this has been my somewhat Gramscian argument in this chapter, there does exist a level of social life where laboring people in their practical activity have constantly sought in their "common sense" the forms, mediated by culture, of such community. The problem of politics is to develop and make explicit what is only implicit in popular activity, to give to its process of mediation the conditions of sufficiency. The point, in other words, is to undertake a criticism of "common sense" on the basis of "common sense";[51] not to inject into popular life a "scientific" form of thought springing from somewhere else, but to develop and make critical an activity that already exists in popular life.

CHAPTER TEN

The National State

PLANNING FOR PLANNING

In August 1937, the Congress Working Committee at its meeting in Wardha adopted a resolution recommending "to the Congress Ministries the appointment of a Committee of Experts to consider urgent and vital problems the solution of which is necessary to any scheme of national reconstruction and social planning. Such solution will require extensive survey and the collection of data, as well as a clearly defined social objective."[1] The immediate background to this resolution was the formation by the Congress, under the new constitutional arrangements, of ministries in six (later eight) provinces of India and the questions raised, especially by the Gandhians (including Gandhi himself) about the responsibility of the Congress in regulating (more precisely, restricting) the growth of modern industries. The Left within the Congress sought to put aside this nagging ideological debate by arguing that the whole question of Congress policy toward industries must be resolved within the framework of an "all-India industrial plan," which this committee of experts would be asked to draw up. Accordingly, Subhas Chandra Bose in his presidential speech at the Haripura Congress in February 1938 declared that the national state "on the advice of a Planning Commission" would adopt "a comprehensive scheme for gradually socializing our entire agricultural and industrial system in the sphere of both production and appropriation." In October that year, Bose summoned a conference of the Ministers of Industries in the Congress ministries and soon after announced the formation of a National Planning Committee (NPC) with Jawaharlal Nehru as chairman. Of the fifteen members of the committee, four (Purushottamdas Thakurdas, A. D. Shroff, Ambalal Sarabhai, and Walchand Hirachand) were leading merchants and industrialists, five were scientists (Meghnad Saha, A. K. Saha, Nazir Ahmed, V. S. Dubey, and J. C. Ghosh), two were economists (K. T. Shah and Radhakamal Mukherjee)—three, if we include M. Visvesvaraya, who had just written a book on planning—and three had been invited on their political credentials (J. C. Kumarappa the Gandhian, N. M. Joshi the labor leader, and Nehru himself). The Committee began work in December 1938.

The National Planning Committee, whose actual work virtually ceased after about a year and a half, following the outbreak of the war, the resignation of the Congress ministries, and finally Nehru's arrest in October 1940, was nevertheless the first real experience the emerging state leadership of the Congress, and Nehru in particular, had with working out the idea of "national planning." Before making a brief mention of the actual contents of the discussions in that committee, let us take note of the most significant aspects of the *form* of this exercise.

First, planning appeared as a form of determining *state* policy, initially the economic policies of the provincial Congress ministries, but almost immediately afterward the overall framework of a coordinated and consistent set of policies of a national state that was already being envisioned as a concrete idea. In this respect, planning was not only a part of the anticipation of power by the state leadership of the Congress, it was also an anticipation of the concrete forms in which that power would be exercised within a national state. Second, planning as an exercise in state policy already incorporated its most distinctive element: its constitution as a body of *experts* and its activity as one of the technical evaluation of alternative policies and the determination of choices on "scientific" grounds. Nehru, writing in 1944–45, mentioned this as a memorable part of his experience with the NPC: "We had avoided a theoretical approach, and as each particular problem was viewed in its larger context, it led us inevitably in a particular direction. To me the spirit of cooperation of the members of the Planning Committee was particularly soothing and gratifying, for I found it a pleasant contrast to the squabbles and conflicts of politics."[2]

Third, the appeal to a "committee of experts" was in itself an important instrument in resolving a political debate that, much to the irritation of the emerging state leadership of the Congress, still refused to go away. This leadership, along with the vast majority of the professional intelligentsia of India, had little doubt about the central importance of industrialization for the development of a modern and prosperous nation. Yet the very political strategy of building up a mass movement against colonial rule had required the Congress to espouse Gandhi's idea of machinery, commercialization, and centralized state power as the curses of modern civilization, thrust upon the Indian people by European colonialism. It was industrialism itself, Gandhi argued, rather than the inability to industrialize, that was the root cause of Indian poverty. This was, until the 1940s, a characteristic part of the Congress rhetoric of nationalist mobilization. But now that the new national state was ready to be conceptualized in concrete terms, this archaic ideological baggage had to be jettisoned. J. C. Kumarappa brought the very first session of the NPC to an impasse by questioning its authority to discuss plans for industrialization. The national priority as adopted by the Congress, he said, was to restrict and eliminate modern industrialism. Nehru had to intervene and declare that most members of the Committee felt that large-scale industry ought to be promoted as long as it did not "come into conflict with the cottage industries." Emphasizing the changed political context in which the Congress was working, Nehru added significantly: "Now that the Congress is, to some extent, identifying itself with the State it cannot ignore the question of establishing and encouraging large-scale industries. There can be no planning if such planning does not include big industries . . . [and] it is not only within the scope of the Committee to consider large-scale industries, but it is incumbent upon it to consider them." Kumarappa kept up his futile effort for a while after virtually every other member disagreed with his views and finally dropped out. Gandhi himself did not appreciate the efforts of the NPC, or perhaps he appreciated them only too well. "I do not know," he wrote to Nehru, "that it is working within the four corners of the resolution creating the Committee. I do not know that the Working Committee is being kept informed of its doings. . . . It has appeared to me that much money and labour are being wasted on an effort which will bring forth little or no fruit."[3] Nehru in turn did not conceal his impatience with such "visionary" and "unscientific" talk and grounded his own position quite firmly on the universal principles of historical progress: "We are trying to catch up, as far as we can, with the Industrial Revolution that occurred long ago in Western countries."[4]

The point here is not so much whether the Gandhian position had already been rendered politically inviable, so that we can declare the overwhelming consensus on industrialization within the NPC as the "reflection" of an assignment of priorities already determined in the political arena outside. Rather, the very institution of a process of planning became a means for the determination of priorities on behalf of the "nation." The debate on the need for industrialization, it might be said, was politically resolved by successfully constituting planning as a domain outside "the squabbles and conflicts of politics." As early as the 1940s, planning had emerged as a crucial institutional modality by which the state would determine the material allocation of productive resources within the nation: a modality of political power constituted outside the immediate political process itself.

THE RATIONALITY OF THE NEW STATE

Why was it necessary to devise such a modality of power that could operate both inside and outside the political structure constructed by the new postcolonial state? An answer begins to appear as soon as we discover the logic by which the new state related itself to the "nation." For the emerging state leadership (and as the bearer of a fundamental ideological orientation, this group was much larger than simply a section of the leaders of the Congress, and in identifying it, the usual classification of Left and Right is irrelevant), this relation was expressed in a quite distinctive way. By the 1940s, the dominant argument of nationalism against colonial rule was that the latter was impeding the further development of India: colonial rule had become a historical fetter that had to be removed before the nation could proceed to develop. Within this framework, therefore, the economic critique of colonialism as an exploitative force creating and perpetuating a backward economy came to occupy a central place. One might ask what would happen to this late nationalist position if (let us say, for the sake of argument) it turned out from historical investigation that by every agreed criterion foreign rule had indeed promoted economic development in the colony. Would that have made colonialism any more legitimate or the demand for national self-government any less justified? Our nationalist would not have accepted a purely negative critique of colonial rule as sufficient and would have been embarrassed if the demand for self-rule was sought to be filled in by some primordial content such as race or religion. Colonial rule, he would have said, was illegitimate not because it represented the political domination by an alien people over the indigens: alienness had acquired the stamp of illegitimacy because it stood for a form of *exploitation* of the nation (the drain of national wealth, the destruction of its productive system, the creation of a backward economy, etc.). Self-government consequently was legitimate because it represented the historically necessary form of national development. The economic critique of colonialism then was the foundation from which a positive content was supplied for the independent national state: the new state represented the only legitimate form of exercise of power because it was a necessary condition for the development of the nation.

A developmental ideology then was a constituent part of the self-definition of the postcolonial state. The state was connected to the people-nation not simply through the procedural forms of representative government; it also acquired its representativeness by directing a program of economic development on behalf of the nation. The former connected, as in any liberal form of government, the legal-political sovereignty of the state with the sovereignty of the people. The latter connected the sovereign powers of the state directly with the economic well-being of the people. The two connections did not necessarily have the same implications for a state trying to determine how to use its sovereign powers. What the people were able to express through the representative mechanisms of the political process as their will was not necessarily what was good for their economic well-being; what the state thought important for the economic development of the nation was not necessarily what would be ratified through the representative mechanisms. The two criteria of representativeness, and hence of legitimacy, could well produce contradictory implications for state policy.

The contradiction stemmed from the very manner in which a developmental ideology needed to cling to the state as the principal vehicle for its historical mission. "Development" implied a linear path, directed toward a goal, or a series of goals separated by stages. It implied the fixing of priorities between long-run and short-run goals and conscious choice between alternative paths. It was premised, in other words, upon a *rational* consciousness and will, and insofar as "development" was thought of as a process affecting the whole of society, it was also premised upon *one* consciousness and will—that of the whole. Particular interests needed to be subsumed within the whole and made consistent with the general interest. The mechanisms of civil society, working through contracts and the market, and hence defining a domain for the play of the particular and the accidental, were already known to be imperfect instruments for expressing the general. The one consciousness, both general and rational, could not simply be assumed to exist as an abstract and formless force, working implicitly and invisibly through the particular interests of civil society. It had to, as Hegel would have said, "shine forth," appear as an existent, concretely expressing the general and the rational.

Hegel has shown us that this universal rationality of the state can be concretely expressed at two institutional levels—the bureaucracy as the universal class and the monarch as the immediately existent will of the state. The logical requirement of the latter was taken care of, even under the republican constitutional form adopted in India, by the usual provisions of embodying the sovereign will of the state in the person of the Head of State. In meeting the former requirement, however, the postcolonial state in India faced a problem that was produced specifically by the form of the transition from colonial rule. For various reasons that were attributed to political contingency (whose historical roots we need not explore here), the new state chose to retain in a virtually unaltered form the basic structure of the civil service, the police administration, the judicial system, including the codes of civil and criminal law, and the armed forces as they existed in the colonial period. As far as the normal executive functions of the state were concerned, the new state operated within a framework of rational universality, whose principles were seen as having been contained (even if they were misapplied) in the preceding state structure. In the case of the armed forces, the assertion of unbroken continuity was rather more paradoxical, so that even today one is forced to witness such unlovely ironies as regiments of the Indian Army proudly displaying the trophies of colonial conquest and counterinsurgency in their barrack rooms or the Presidential Guards celebrating their birth two hundred years ago under the governor-generalship of Lord Cornwallis! But if the ordinary functions of civil and criminal administration were to continue within forms of rationality that the new state had not given to itself, how was it to claim its legitimacy as an authority that was specifically different from the old regime? This legitimacy, as we have mentioned before, had to flow from the nationalist criticism of colonialism as an alien and unrepresentative power that was exploitative in character and from the historical necessity of an independent state that would promote national development. It was in the universal function of "development" of national society as a whole that the postcolonial state would find its distinctive content. This was to be concretized by the embodiment within itself of a new mechanism of developmental administration, something the colonial state, because of its alien and extractive character, had never possessed. It was in the administration of development that the bureaucracy of the postcolonial state was to assert itself as the universal class, satisfying in the service of the state its private interests by working for the universal goals of the nation.

Planning therefore was the domain of the rational determination and pursuit of those universal goals. It was a bureaucratic function, to be operated at a level above the particular interests of civil society, and institutionalized as such as a domain of policy-making outside the normal processes of representative politics and of execution through a developmental administration. But as a concrete bureaucratic function, it was in planning above all that the postcolonial state would claim its legitimacy as a single will and consciousness—the will of the nation—pursuing a task that was both universal and rational: the well-being of the people as a whole.

In its legitimizing role, therefore, planning, constituted as a domain outside politics, was to become an instrument of politics. If we then look at the process of politics itself, we will discover the specific ways in which planning would also become implicated in the modalities of power.

PLANNING AND IMPLEMENTING

We could first describe the political process in its own terms and then look for the connections with the process of planning. But this would take us into a lengthy excursion into a wholly different field. Let us instead start with the received understanding of the planning experience in India and see how the political process comes to impinge upon it.

Chakravarty has given us a summary account of this experience from within the theoretical boundaries of development planning.[5] From this perspective, the political process appears as a determinate and changing existent when the question arises of "plan implementation." Chakravarty discusses the problems of plan implementation by treating the "planning authorities" as the central directing agency, firmly situated outside the political process itself and embodying, one might justifiably say, the single, universal, and rational consciousness of a state that is promoting the development of the nation as a whole.[6] An implementational failure, Chakravarty says, occurs when (*a*) the planning authorities are inefficient in gathering the relevant information; (*b*) they take so much time to respond that the underlying situation has by then changed, and (*c*) the public agencies through which the plans are to be implemented do not have the capacities to carry them out and the private agencies combine in "strategic" ways to disrupt the expectations about their behavior that the planners had taken as "parametric." Chakravarty adds that the last possibility—that of strategic action by private actors—has greatly increased in recent years in the Indian economy.

Let us look a little more closely at this analysis. What does it mean to say that plans may fail because of the inadequacy of the information planners use? The premise here is that of a separation between the planner on the one hand and the objects of planning on the other, the latter consisting of both physical resources and human economic agents. "Information" is precisely the means through which the objects of planning are constituted for the planner: they exist "out there," independently of his consciousness, and can appear before it only in the shape of "information." The "adequacy" of this information then concerns the question of whether those objects have been constituted "correctly," that is to say, constituted in the planner's consciousness in the same form as they exist outside it, in themselves. It is obvious that on these terms an entirely faultless planning would require in the planner nothing less than omniscience. But one should not use the patent impossibility of this project to turn planning into a caricature of itself. While the epistemological stance of apprehending the external objects of consciousness in their intrinsic and independent truth continues, as is well known, to inform the expressly declared philosophical foundations of the positive sciences, including economics, the actual practice of debates about planning are more concerned with those objects as they have been constituted by the planning exercise itself. Thus, if it is alleged that planners have incorrectly estimated the demand for electricity because they did not take into account the unorganized sector, the charge really is that whereas the "unorganized sector" was already an object of planning since it was *known* that it too was a consumer of electricity, it had not been explicitly and specifically constituted as an object since its demand had not been estimated.

The point about all questions of "inadequate information" is not whether one knows what the objects of planning are: if they are not known, the problem of information cannot arise. The question is whether they have been explicitly specified as objects of planning.

It is here that the issues of the modalities of knowledge and implementation become central to the planning exercise. All three conditions that Chakravarty mentions as leading to faulty implementation concern the ways in which the planner, representing the rational consciousness of the state, can produce a knowledge of the objects of planning. In this sense, even the so-called implementing agencies are the objects of planning, for they represent not the will of the planner but determinate "capacities": a plan that does not correctly estimate the capacities of the implementing agencies cannot be a good plan. Consequently, these agencies—bureaucrats or managers of public enterprises—become entities that act in determinate ways according to specific kinds of "signals," and the planner must know these in order to formulate his plan. The planner even needs to know how long his own machinery will take to implement a plan, or else the information on the basis of which he plans may become obsolete.

If one is not to assume omniscience on behalf of the planner, how is this information ever expected to be "adequate"? Here the rationality of planning can be seen to practice a self-deception—a necessary self-deception, for without it, planning could not constitute itself. Planning, as the concrete embodiment of the rational consciousness of a state promoting economic development, can proceed only by constituting the objects of planning as objects of knowledge. It must *know* the physical resources whose allocation is to be planned, it must *know* the economic agents who act upon those resources, *know* their needs, capacities, and propensities, *know* what constitutes the signals according to which they act, *know* how they respond to those signals. When the agents relate to each other in terms of power, that is, in relations of domination and subordination, the planner must *know* the relevant signals and capacities. This knowledge would enable him to work upon the total configuration of power itself, use the legal powers of the state to produce signals and thereby affect the actions of agents, play off one power against another to produce a general result in which everybody would be better off. The state as a planning authority can promote the universal goal of development by harnessing within a single interconnected whole the discrete subjects of power in society. It does this by turning those subjects of power into the objects of a single body of knowledge.

Here the self-deception occurs. For the rational consciousness of the state embodied in the planning authority does not exhaust the determinate being of the state. The state is also an existent as a site at which the subjects of power in society interact, ally, and contend with one another in the political process. The specific configuration of power that is constituted within the state is the result of this process. Seen from this perspective, the planning authorities themselves are objects for a configuration of power in which others are subjects. Indeed, and this is the paradox that a "science" of planning can never unravel from within its own disciplinary boundaries, the very subjects of social power which the rational consciousness of the planner seeks to convert into objects of its knowledge by attributing to them discrete capacities and propensities can turn the planning authority itself into an object of their power. Subject and object, inside and outside—the relations are reversed as soon as we move from the domain of rational planning, situated outside the political process, to the domain of social power exercised and contested within that process. When we talk of the state, we must talk of both of these domains as its constituent field, and situate one in relation to the other. Seen from the domain of planning, the political process is only an external constraint, whose strategic possibilities must be known and objectified as parameters for the planning exercise. And yet even the best efforts to secure "adequate information" leave behind an unestimated residue, which works imperceptibly and often perversely to upset the implementation of plans. This residue, as the irreducible, negative, and ever-present "beyond" of planning, is what we may call, in its most general sense, politics.

THE POLITICS OF PLANNING: PART ONE

Let us return to history, this time of more recent vintage. Chakravarty says that in the early 1950s, when the planning process was initiated in India, there was a general consensus on a "commodity-centered" approach.[7] That is to say, everyone agreed that more goods were preferable to less goods and a higher level of capital stock per worker was necessary for an improved standard of living. Obviously, the central emphasis of development was meant to be placed on accumulation. But this was not all; in the specific context in which planning was taken up in India, accumulation had to be reconciled with legitimation. "Adoption of a representative form of government based on universal adult suffrage did have an effect on the exercise of political power, and so did the whole legacy of the national movement with its specifically articulated set of economic objectives." These two objectives—accumulation and legitimation—produced two implications for planning in India. On the one hand, planning had to be "a way of avoiding the *unnecessary rigours* of an industrial transition in so far as it affected the masses resident in India's villages." On the other hand, planning was to become "a positive instrument for *resolving conflict* in a large and heterogeneous subcontinent."[8] What did these objectives mean in terms of the relation between the state and the planning process?

In the classical forms of capitalist industrialization, the originary accumulation required the use of a variety of coercive methods to separate a large mass of direct producers from their means of production. This was the "secret" of the so-called primitive accumulation, which was not the result of the capitalist mode of production but its starting point; in a concrete historical process, it meant "the expropriation of the agricultural producer, of the peasant, from the soil."[9] The possibility and limits of originary accumulation were set by the specific configuration in each country of the political struggle between classes in the precapitalist social formation,[10] but in each case a successful transition to capitalist industrialization required that subsistence producers be "robbed of all their means of production and of all the guarantees of existence afforded by the old feudal arrangements." Whatever the political means adopted to effect this expropriation of direct producers, and with it the destruction of precapitalist forms of community concretely embodying the unity of producers with the means of production, they could not have been legitimized by any active principle of universal representative democracy. (It is curious that in the one country of Europe where a "bourgeois" political revolution was carried out under the slogan of liberty, equality, and fraternity, the protection of small-peasant property after the Revolution meant the virtual postponement of industrialization by some five or six decades.)

Once in place, accumulation under capitalist production proper could be made legitimate by the equal right of property and the universal freedom of contract on the basis of property rights over commodities. Originary accumulation having already effected the separation of the direct producer from the means of production, labor-power was now available as a commodity owned by the laborer, who was entitled to sell it according to the terms of a free contract with the owner of the means of production. As a political ideology of legitimation of capitalist accumulation, this strictly liberal doctrine of "freedom," however, enjoyed a surprisingly short life. By the third and fourth decades of the nineteenth century, when the first phase of the Industrial Revolution had been completed in Britain, the new context of political conflict made it necessary to qualify "freedom" by such notions as the rights to subsistence, to proper conditions of work, and to a decent livelihood. In time, this meant the use of the legal powers of the state to impose conditions on the freedom of contract (on hours of work, on minimum wage, on physical conditions of work and living) and to curtail the free enjoyment of returns from the productive use of property (most importantly by the taxation on higher incomes to finance public provisions for hygiene, health, education, etc.). While this may be seen as consistent with the long-term objectives of capitalist accumulation, on the ground that it facilitated the continued reproduction of labor-power of a suitable concretized quality, it must also be recognized as a political response to growing oppositional movements and social conflict. As a political doctrine of legitimation this meant, first, the creation of a general content for social good that combined capitalist property ownership with the production of consent through representative political processes and, second, the determination of this content not mediately through the particular acts of economic agents in civil society but directly through the activities of the state. The course of this journey from the strictly liberal concept of "freedom" to that of "welfare" is, of course, coincidental with the political history of capitalist democracy in the last century and a half. What we need to note here is the fact that as a universal conception of the social whole under capitalist democracy, the elements of a concept of "welfare" had already superseded those of pure freedom and were available to the political leadership in India when it began the task of constructing a state ideology.

The "unnecessary rigors" of an industrial transition, consequently, meant those forms of expropriation of subsistence producers associated with originary accumulation which could not be legitimized through the representative processes of politics. This was, our planner would say, a parametric condition set by the political process at the time when planning began its journey in India. Yet, accumulation was the prime task if industrialization was to take place. Accumulation necessarily implied the use of the powers of the state, whether directly through its legal and administrative institutions or mediately through the acts of some agents with social power over others, to effect the required degree of dissociation of direct producers from their means of production. As Chakravarty himself says, the development model first adopted in India was a variant of the Lewis model, with a "modern" sector breaking down and superseding the "traditional" sector, the two significant variations being that the modern sector itself was disaggregated into a capital goods and a consumer goods sector and that the major role in the modern sector was assigned to a development bureaucracy instead of to capitalists.[11] Despite these variations, the chosen path of development still meant conflicts between social groups and the use of power to attain the required form and rate of accumulation. Since the "necessary" policies of the state that would ensure accumulation could not be left to be determined solely through the political process, it devolved upon the institution of planning, that embodiment of the universal rationality of the social whole standing above all particular interests, to lay down what in fact were the "necessary rigors" of industrialization. Given its location outside the political process, planning could then become "a positive instrument for resolving conflict" by determining, within a universal framework of the social good, the "necessary costs" to be borne by each particular group and the "necessary benefits" to accrue to each. But who was to use it in this way as a "positive instrument"? We have still to address this question.

The specific form in which this twin problem of planning—accumulation with legitimation—was initially resolved, especially in the Second and Third Five-Year Plans, is well known. There was to be a capital-intensive industrial sector under public ownership, a private industrial sector in light consumer goods, and a private agricultural sector. The first two were the "modern" sectors, which were to be financed by foreign aid, low-interest loans, and taxation of private incomes mainly in the second sector. The third sector was seen as being mainly one of petty production, and it was there that a major flaw of this development strategy was to appear. It has been said that the Second and Third Plans did not have an agricultural strategy at all, or even if they did, there was gross overoptimism about the long-term ability of traditional agriculture to contribute to industrialization by providing cheap labor and cheap food.[12] The problem is often posed as one of alternative planning strategies, with the suggestion that if suitable land reforms had been carried out soon after independence, a quite different development path might have been discovered that would have avoided the "crisis" in which the planning process found itself in the middle of the 1960s. The difficulty with this suggestion, if we are to look at it from a political standpoint, is precisely the confusion it entails regarding the effective relation between the whole and the parts, the universal and the particulars, in the acts of a state promoting and supervising a program of planned capitalist development. To discover the nature of this relation, we need to look upon planned industrialization as part of a process of what may be called the "passive revolution of capital."

PASSIVE REVOLUTION

Antonio Gramsci has talked of the "passive revolution" as one in which the new claimants to power, lacking the social strength to launch a full-scale assault on the old dominant classes, opt for a path in which the demands of a new society are "satisfied in small doses, legally, in a reformist manner"—in such a way that the political and economic position of the old feudal classes is not destroyed, agrarian reform is avoided, and the popular masses especially are prevented from going through the political experience of a fundamental social transformation.[13] Gramsci, of course, treats this as a "blocked dialectic," an exception to the paradigmatic form of bourgeois revolution he takes to be Jacobinism. It now seems more useful to argue, however, that as a historical model, passive revolution is in fact the general framework of capitalist transition in societies where bourgeois hegemony has not been accomplished in the classical way.[14] In "passive revolution," the historical shifts in the strategic relations of forces between capital, precapitalist dominant groups, and the popular masses can be seen as a series of contingent, conjunctural moments. The dialectic here cannot be assumed to be blocked in any fundamental sense. Rather, the new forms of dominance of capital become understandable, not as the immanent supersession of earlier contradictions, but as parts of a constructed hegemony, effective because of the successful exercise of both coercive and persuasive power, but incomplete and fragmented at the same time because the hegemonic claims are fundamentally contested within the constructed whole.[15] The distinction between "bourgeois hegemony" and "passive revolution" then becomes one in which, for the latter, the persuasive power of bourgeois rule cannot be constructed around the universal idea of "freedom"; some other universal idea has to be substituted for it.[16]

In the Indian case, we can look upon "passive revolution" as a process involving a political-ideological program by which the largest possible nationalist alliance is built up against the colonial power. The aim is to form a politically independent nation-state. The means involve the creation of a series of alliances—within the organizational structure of the national movement, between the bourgeoisie and other dominant classes—and the mobilization, under this leadership, of mass support from the subordinate classes. The project is a reorganization of the political order, but it is moderated in two quite fundamental ways. On the one hand, it does not attempt to break up or transform in any radical way the institutional structures of "rational" authority set up in the period of colonial rule. On the other hand, it also does not undertake a full-scale assault on all precapitalist dominant classes; rather, it seeks to limit their former power, neutralize them where necessary, attack them only selectively, and in general bring them round to a position of subsidiary allies within a reformed state structure. The dominance of capital does not emanate from its hegemonic sway over "civil society." On the contrary, it seeks to construct a synthetic hegemony over the domains of both civil society and the precapitalist community. The reification of the "nation" in the body of the state becomes the means for constructing this hegemonic structure, and the extent of control over the new state apparatus becomes a precondition for further capitalist development. It is by means of an interventionist state, directly entering the domain of production as mobilizer and manager of investable "national" resources, that the foundations are laid for industrialization and the expansion of capital. Yet the dominance of capital over the national state remains constrained in several ways. Its function of representing the "national-popular" has to be shared with other governing groups and its transformative role restricted to reformist and "molecular" changes. The institution of planning, as we have seen, emerges in this process as the means by which the "necessity" of these changes is rationalized at the level not of this or that particular group but of the social whole.

For the development model adopted in India, the modern sector is clearly the dynamic element. Industrialization as a project emanated from the particular will of the modern sector; the "general consensus" Chakravarty refers to was in fact the consensus within this modern sector. But this will for transformation had to be expressed as a general project for the "nation," and this could be done by subsuming within the cohesive body of a single plan for the nation all of those elements which appeared as "constraints" on the particular will of the modern sector. If land reform was not attempted in the 1950s, it was not a "fault" of planning, nor was it the lapse of a squeamish "political will" of the rulers. It was because at this stage of its journey the ideological construct of the "passive revolution of capital" consciously sought to incorporate within the framework of its rule not a representative mechanism solely operated by individual agents in civil society but entire structures of precapitalist community taken in their existent forms. In the political field, this was expressed in the form of the so-called vote banks, a much-talked-about feature of Indian elections in the 1950s and 1960s, by which forms of social power based on landed proprietorship or caste loyalty or religious authority were translated into "representative" forms of electoral support. In the economic field, the form preferred was that of "community development," in which the benefits of plan projects meant for the countryside were supposed to be shared collectively by the whole community. That the concrete structures of existent communities were by no means homogeneous or egalitarian but were in fact built around precapitalist forms of social power was not so much ignored or forgotten as tacitly acknowledged, for these were precisely the structures through which the "modernizing" state secured legitimation for itself in the representative processes of elections. It is therefore misleading to suggest as a criticism of this phase of the planning strategy that the planners "did not realize the nature and dimension of political mobilization that would be necessary to bring about the necessary institutional changes" to make agriculture more productive.[17] Seen in terms of the political logic of passive revolution, what the strategy called for precisely was promoting industrialization without taking the risk of agrarian political mobilization. This was an essential aspect of the hegemonic construct of the postcolonial state: combining accumulation with legitimation while avoiding the "unnecessary rigors" of social conflict.

Rational strategies pursued in a political field, however, have the unpleasant habit of producing unintended consequences. Although the objective of the Indian state in the 1950s was to lay the foundations for rapid industrialization without radically disturbing the local structures of power in the countryside, the logic of accumulation in the "modern" sector could not be prevented from seeping into the interstices of agrarian property, trade, patterns of consumption, and even production. It did not mean a general and radical shift all over the country to capitalist farming, but there were clear signs that agrarian property had become far more "commoditized" than before, that even subsistence peasant production was deeply implicated in large-scale market transactions, that the forms of extraction of agricultural surplus now combined a wide variety and changing mix of "economic" and "extra-economic" power, and that a steady erosion of the viability of small-peasant agriculture was increasing the ranks of marginal and landless cultivators. Perhaps there were conjunctural reasons why the "food crisis" should have hit the economic, and immediately afterward the political, life of the country with such severity in the mid-1960s. But it would not be unwarranted to point out a certain inevitability of the logic of accumulation breaking into an agrarian social structure that the politics of the state was unwilling to transform.

Other consequences of this phase of planned industrialization under state auspices were to be of considerable political significance.

THE POLITICS OF PLANNING: PART TWO

The object of the strategy of passive revolution was to *contain* class conflicts within manageable dimensions, to control and manipulate the many dispersed power relations in society to further as best as possible the thrust toward accumulation. But conflicts surely could not be avoided altogether. And if particular interests collided, mobilizations based on interests were only to be expected, specially within a political process of representative democracy. In fact, the very form of legitimacy by electoral representation, insofar as it involves a *relation* between the state and the people, implies a mutual recognition by each of the organized and articulate existence of the other, the general on the one hand and the particular on the other. Mobilizations, consequently, did take place, principally as oppositional movements and in both the electoral and nonelectoral domains. The response of the state was to subsume these organized demands of particular interests within the generality of a rational strategy.

The form of this strategy is for the state to insist that all conflicts between particular interests admit of an "economic" solution—"economic" in the sense of allocations to each part that are consistent with the overall constraints of the whole. Thus, a particular interest, whether expressed in terms of class, language, region, caste, tribe, or community, is to be recognized and given a place within the framework of the general by being assigned a priority and an allocation relative to all the other parts. This, as we have seen before, is the form that the single rational consciousness of the developmental state must take—the form of planning. It is also the form that the political process conducted by the state will seek to impose on all mobilizations of particular interests: the demands therefore will be for a reallocation or a reassignment of priorities relative to other particular interests.

It is curious to what extent a large variety of social mobilizations in the last two decades have taken both this "economic" form and the form of demands upon the state. Mobilizations that admit of demographic solidarities defined over territorial regions can usually make this claim within the framework of the federal distribution of powers. This claim could be for greater shares of the federating units from out of the central economic pool, or for a reallocation of the relative shares of different federating units, or even for a redefinition of the territorial boundaries of the units or the creation of new units out of old ones. On the one hand, we therefore have a continuous process of bargaining between the union and the states over the distribution of revenues, which such statutory bodies as the Finance Commissions seek to give an orderly and rational form, but which inevitably spills over into the disorderly immediacy of contingent political considerations, such as the compulsions of party politics, electoral advantage, or the pressures of influential interest lobbies, and which takes the form of an ever-growing series of ad hoc allocations that defy rational and consistent justification. On the other hand, we also have many examples of demands for the creation of new states within the federal union. While the solidarities over which these demands are defined are cultural, such as language or ethnic identity, the justification for statehood inevitably carries with it a charge of economic discrimination within the existing federal arrangements and is thus open to political strategies operating within the "economic" framework of distribution of resources between the center and the states.

For mobilizations of demographic sections that cannot claim representative status of territorial regions, the demands made upon the state are nevertheless also of an "economic" form. These include not only the demands made by the organizations of economic classes but also by social segments such as castes or tribes or religious communities. Examples of the management of class demands of this kind are, of course, innumerable and form the staple of the political economy literature. They affect virtually all aspects of economic policy-making and include taxation, pricing, subsidies, licensing, wages, and the like. But for the economic demands of "ethnic" sections too, the state itself has legitimized the framework by qualifying the notion of citizenship with a set of special protections for culturally underprivileged and backward groups (lower castes, tribes) or minority religious communities. The framework has virtually transformed, to repeat a point made in the previous chapter, the nature of caste movements in India over the last fifty years from movements of lower castes claiming higher ritual status within a religiously sanctified cultural hierarchy to the same castes now proclaiming their ritually degraded status in order to demand protective economic privileges in the fields of employment or educational opportunities. In response, the higher castes, whose superiority has historically rested upon the denial of any notion of ritual equality with lower castes, are now defending their economic privileges precisely by appealing to the liberal notion of equality and by pointing out the economic inefficiencies of special protection.

The point could therefore be made here that the centrality which the state assumes in the management of economic demands in India is not simply the result of the large weight of the public sector or the existence of state monopolies, as is often argued.[18] Even otherwise, a developmental state operating within the framework of representative politics would necessarily require the state to assume the role of the central allocator if it has to legitimize its authority in the political domain.

THE AMBIGUITIES OF LEGITIMATION

There is no doubt that the fundamental problematic of the postcolonial state—furthering accumulation in the modern sector through a political strategy of passive revolution—has given rise to numerous ambiguities in the legitimation process. In the field of economic planning, these ambiguities have surfaced in the debates over the relative importance of market signals and state commands, over the efficiency of the private sector and the inefficiency of the state sector, over the growth potential of a relatively "open" economy and the technological backwardness of the strategy of "self-reliance," and over the dynamic productive potential of a relaxation of state controls compared with the entrenchment of organized privileges within the present structure of state dominance. It is not surprising that in these debates, the proponents of the former argument in each opposed pair have emphasized the dynamic of accumulation while those defending the latter position have stressed the importance of legitimation (although there have been arguments, increasingly less forceful over recent years, that defend the latter on the grounds of accumulation as well). We need not go into the details of these debates here, for they have now become the staple of political discussion in India with the adoption by the government of the "open market" policy prescriptions of international financial agencies. What should be pointed out, however, is, first, that these ambiguities are *necessary* consequences of the specific relation of the postcolonial developmental state with the people-nation; second, that it is these ambiguities which create room for maneuver through which the passive revolution of capital can proceed; and third, that these ambiguities cannot be removed or resolved within the present constitution of the state.

Let me briefly illustrate this point. Given the political process defined by the Indian state, the ambiguities of legitimacy are expressed most clearly in the mechanisms of representation. As far as the modern sector is concerned, particular interests are organized and represented in the well-known forms of interest groups: the variety of permanent associations of industrialists, merchants, professionals, and workers as well as temporary agitational mobilizations based on specific issues. Demands compete in this sector, and the state may use both coercive and persuasive powers to allocate relative priorities in satisfying these demands. But the overall constraint here is to maintain the unity of the modern sector as a whole, for that, as we have seen before, stands forth within the body of the state as the overwhelmingly dominant element of the nation. The unity of the modern sector is specified in terms of a variety of criteria encompassing the domains of industrial production, the professional, educational, and service sectors connected with industrial production, and agricultural production outside the subsistence sector, and also embracing the effective demographic boundaries of the market for the products of the modern sector. The identification of this sector cannot be made in any specific regional terms, nor does it coincide with a simple rural/urban dichotomy. But because of its unique standing as a particular interest that can claim to represent the dynamic aspect of the nation itself, the entire political process conducted by the state, including the political parties that stake their claims to run the central organs of the state, must work toward producing a consensus on protecting the unity of the modern sector. Any appearance of a fundamental lack of consensus here will resonate as a crisis of national unity itself. Thus the political management of economic demands requires that a certain internal balance—an acceptable parity—be maintained between the several fractions within the modern sector. Seen from this angle, the analysis of the "political economy" of Indian planning as a competitive game between privileged pressure groups within a self-perpetuating modern sector will appear one-sided,[19] for it misses the fundamental ambiguity of a state process that must further accumulation while legitimizing the modern sector itself as representative of the nation as a whole.

Indeed, more profound ambiguities appear in the relations between the modern sector and the rest of the people-nation. On the one hand, there is the system of electoral representation on a territorial basis in the form of single-member constituencies. On the other hand, competing demands may be voiced not only on the basis of permanent interest-group organizations but also as mobilizations building upon pre-existing cultural solidarities such as locality, caste, tribe, religious community, or ethnic identity. It would be wrong to assume that no representative process works here. Rather, the most interesting aspect of contemporary Indian politics is precisely the way in which solidarities and forms of authority deriving from the precapitalist community insert themselves into the representational processes of a liberal electoral democracy. This allows, on the one hand, for organizations and leaders to appear in the domain of the state process claiming to represent this or that "community," and for groups of people threatened with the loss of their means of livelihood or suffering from the consequences of such loss to use those representatives to seek the protection, or at least the indulgence, of the state. On the other hand, the state itself can manipulate these "premodern" forms of relations between the community and the state to secure legitimacy for its developmental role.

An instance of the latter is the shift from the earlier strategy of "community development" to that of distributing "poverty removal" packages directly to selected target groups among the underprivileged sections. This strategy, developed during Indira Gandhi's regime in the 1970s, allows for the state to use a political rhetoric in which intermediate rungs of both the social hierarchy (local power barons, dominant landed groups) and the governmental hierarchy (local officials and even elected political representatives) can be condemned as obstacles in the way of the state trying to extend the benefits of development to the poor and to directly present the package of benefits to groups of the latter as a gift from the highest political leadership.[20] From the standpoint of a rational doctrine of political authority, these forms of legitimation doubtless appear as premodern, harking back to what sociologists would call "traditional" or "charismatic" authority. But the paradox is that the existence, the unity, and indeed the representative character of the modern sector as the leading element within the nation has to be legitimized precisely through these means.

There is the other side to this relation of legitimation: the ambiguous image of the state in popular consciousness. If, as we have seen in chapter 8, it is true that the state appears in popular consciousness as an external and distant entity, then, depending upon the immediate perception of local antagonisms, the state could be seen either as an oppressive intruder in the affairs of the local community or as a benevolent protector of the people against local oppressors. The particular image in which the state appears is determined contextually. But this again opens up the possibility for the play of a variety of political strategies of which the story of modern Indian politics offers a vast range of examples.

Such ambiguities show up the narrow and one-sided manner in which the "science" of planning defines itself—a necessary one-sidedness, for without it, the singular rationality of its practice would not be comprehensible to itself. From its own standpoint, planning will address the inefficiency and wastage of the public sector, the irrationality of choosing or locating projects purely on grounds of electoral expediency, the granting of state subsidies in response to agitational pressure. The configuration of social powers in the political process, on the other hand, will produce these inefficient and irrational results that will go down in the planning literature as examples of implementational failures. Yet, in the process of projecting the efficiency of productive growth as a rational path of development for the nation as a whole, the particular interests in the modern sector must shift on to the state the burden of defraying the costs of producing a general consent for their particular project. The state sector, identified as the embodiment of the general, must bear these social costs of constructing the framework of legitimacy for the passive revolution of capital.

What I have tried to show is that the two processes—one of "rational" planning and the other of "irrational" politics—are inseparable parts of the very logic of this state that is conducting the passive revolution. The paradox in fact is that it is the very "irrationality" of the political process which continually works to produce legitimacy for the rational exercise of the planner. While the planner thinks of his own practice as an instrument for resolving conflict, the political process uses planning itself as an instrument for producing consent for capital's passive revolution.

It is not surprising then to discover that the rational form of the planning exercise itself supplies to the political process a rhetoric for conducting its political debates. *Growth* and *equity*—both terms are loaded with potent rhetorical ammunition which can serve to justify as well as to contest state policies that seek to use coercive legal powers to protect or alter the existent relations between social groups. I have shown how the very form of an institution of rational planning located outside the political process is crucial for the self-definition of a developmental state embodying the single universal consciousness of the social whole. I have also shown how the wielders of power can constrain, mold, and distort the strategies of planning in order to produce political consent for their rule. What is science in the one domain becomes rhetoric in the other; what is the rational will of the whole in the one becomes the contingent agglomeration of particular wills in the other. The two together—this contradictory, perennially quarrelsome, and yet ironically well-matched couple—constitute the identity of the developmental state in India today.

CHAPTER ELEVEN

Communities and the Nation

KAMALAKANTA had been called in as a witness in court in a case of petty theft. Both magistrate and counsel were eager to get on to his testimony, but the preliminaries were proving to be difficult, since Kamalakanta, with the extreme analytical skills found only among the mad, had raised a series of unanswerable objections to the oath he was required to take. Finally, those difficulties had somehow been overcome and the identity of the witness was being recorded.

The lawyer then asked him, "What jāti are you?"

K: Am I a jāti?
LAWYER: What jāti do you belong to?
K: To the Hindu jāti.
LAWYER: Oh, come now! What varṇa?
K: A very very dark varṇa.
LAWYER: What the hell is going on here! Why did I have to call a witness like this? I say, do you have *jāt*?
K: Who can take it from me?

The magistrate saw that the lawyer was getting nowhere. He said, "You know there are many kinds of jāti among the Hindus, such as Brahman, Kayastha, Kaibarta. Which one of these jāti do you belong to?"

K: My lord! All this is the lawyer's fault! He can see I have the sacred thread around my neck. I have said my name is Chakravarti. How am I to know that he will still not be able to deduce that I am a Brahman?

The magistrate wrote, "Caste: Brahman."[1]

Those who know Kamalakanta will recall how, in Bankim's trenchant narration, he shows up, with his madman's logic, the utter madness of all the claims to rationality made on behalf of colonial reason.[2] In this particular piece, Bankim uses Kamalakanta's uncolonizable voice to mock the trappings of colonial justice, including the way in which it required an unambiguous classification of caste to locate and fix the identity of the colonial subject. Kamalakanta here does not dwell very long on the ambiguities that the "modern" forms of social knowledge face when confronted with a term such as *jāti*. But we can already guess that those ambiguities will, in fact, be literally endless.

THE MANIFOLD USES OF JĀTI

Consider the ways in which the word *jāti* can be used in any modern Indian language. I take as an example the word as used in Bengali. Pick up any standard Bengali dictionary and look through the entries under *jāti*. (It would be useful to remember that these dictionaries themselves have been compiled according to European models so as to conform to the requirements of "modern" forms of knowledge.) It will first give the Sanskrit etymology of the word: √*jan* (to originate, to be born) + *ti*, a noun that literally means "birth," "origin." This will be followed typically by at least a dozen different senses in which the word can be used. Jnanendramohan Das, for instance, lists, among others, the following:

1. *jāti* as origin, such as Musalman by birth, Vaiṣṇav by birth, a beggar by birth [*jātite musalmān*, *jātbhikhāri*]
2. classes of living species, such as human *jāti*, animal *jāti*, bird *jāti*, etc.
3. *varṇa* following from classifications according to *gūṇa* and *karma*, such as Brahman, etc.
4. *vaṃśa*, *gotra*, *kula* [lineage, clan], such as Arya *jāti*, Semitic *jāti*
5. human collectivities bound by loyalty to a state or organized around the natural and cultural characteristics of a country or province [Jnanendramohan adds in English "nation; race"], such as English, French, Bengali, Punjabi, Japanese, Gujarati, etc.[3]

Let us pass over the other, technical, uses of the word in logic, grammar, music, rhetoric, and the like, and concentrate on these—its uses as a category of social classification. Haricharan Bandyopadhyay lists most of the above uses but adds, curiously, to (3)—the sense in which *jāti* is used to denote "caste" in Indian sociology—a derivation from the Persian *zat*.[4] Jnanendramohan too takes note of this alternative derivation but restricts it to the non-Sanskritic word *jāt*, presumed to be a corruption of *jāti* and used in Bengali in all of the first three senses. Finally, in order to clarify our criteria for translation (since, in this particular case, we are discussing the terms of political discourse in India in the English language), let us note that a Sanskrit-Bengali-English trilingual dictionary gives as the English equivalents of *jāti* the following: "species, caste, birth, family, universals."[5]

Between (1) and (5) above, the range of meanings available to the word *jāti* is immense. It is not surprising that Kamalakanta in court should have found it so easy to play around with the word. Indeed, he could have gone on endlessly, describing himself as belonging to the human jāti, the Indian jāti, the Bengali jāti, the jāti of madmen, even (one suspects, with some degree of pride) the jāti of opium addicts. One could, obviously and without any contradiction, belong to several jāti, not simultaneously but contextually, invoking in each context a collectivity in which membership is not a matter of self-interested individual choice or contractual agreement but an immediate inclusion, originary, as it is by birth. We should not be surprised therefore when political discourse permits the imagining of collective solidarities to slide from one particular form to another, each activated contextually but proclaiming each time a bond of kinship, a natural bond that unites all who share the same origin and who therefore must share the same destiny.

Consider the form of imaginative construction of large political solidarities through the union of several jāti. Let us recall a text we have already discussed in an earlier chapter. Bhudeb Mukhopadhyay is giving us his picture of the nationalist utopia emerging out of a counterfactual past.[6] In the grand council that meets after the new emperor of India has been crowned, the following proposal is made:

> Although India is the true motherland only of those who belong to the Hindu jāti and although only they have been born from her womb, the Musalmans are not unrelated to her any longer. She has held them at her breast and reared them. Musalmans are therefore her adopted children.
>
> Can there be no bonds of fraternity between two children of the same mother, one a natural child and the other adopted? There certainly can; the laws of every religion admits this. There has now been born a bond of brotherhood between Hindus and Musalmans living in India.

Remember that for Bhudeb Indian nationalism is synonymous with Hindu nationalism. But he is also a nationalist of a perfectly modern kind, because in this imaginary council a constitution is promulgated more or less along the lines of the German Reich, with strongly protectionist economic policies which succeed, in this anticolonial utopia, in keeping the European economic powers at bay. Yet in order to think of a nation that includes both Hindu and Musalman jāti, albeit under the leadership of Hindus, Bhudeb has to use the language of kinship.

Nevertheless, this imputation of kinship is clearly contextual. Bhudeb would have been horrified if, for instance, someone had appealed to these imputed affinal ties to make a case, let us say, for marriage between Hindus and Muslims or, for that matter, for eating the same food. Identities and solidarities within the language of jāti are contextually defined. The language affords the possibility of imagining new bonds of affinity, but it does this precisely by imposing restrictions on their free flow. There are no substantive affinities that define identity regardless of context.

It is political discourse of the "modern" kind which insists that these collectivities have a fixed, determinate, form, and, if there are several to which an individual can belong, that there be a priority among them, so that it becomes imperative to ask: "Are you a Muslim first or a Bengali first?" "Are you a Bengali first or an Indian first?" Since these are questions that recur constantly in contemporary political discourse in India, we must ask what it is that seeks to erase the contextuality of a concept such as jāti and give it the fixity that was demanded of Kamalakanta in court.

COMMUNITIES: FUZZY AND ENUMERATED

Sudipta Kaviraj has recently argued that a fundamental change effected in the discursive domain of modern politics in the colonial period was the impoverishment of the earlier "fuzzy" sense of the community and an insistence upon the identification of community in the "enumerable" sense.[7] Earlier, communities were fuzzy, in the sense that, first, a community did not claim to represent or exhaust all the layers of selfhood of its members, and second, the community, though definable with precision for all practical purposes of social interaction, did not require its members to ask how many of them there were in the world. The colonial regime, once firmly in place in the second half of the nineteenth century, sought to fashion the conceptual instruments of its control over an alien population precisely by enumerating the diverse communities that, in the colonial imagination, constituted the society over which it had been destined by History to rule. Bernard Cohn, in a well-known piece, has shown how caste and religion became established both conceptually and instrumentally as the "sociological keys" to the numerical description of Indian society.[8] That this classificatory scheme did not reside exclusively in the colonial imagination is also documented by Cohn, because it shaped in turn the subsequent forms of mobilization seeking representation in the state domain—representation, that is, by caste or religion.

To us, situated on this side of the divide represented by postcolonial politics and poststructuralist theory, the move by a colonial power toward the enumeration of Indian society by ethnic communities seems almost natural. One of the fundamental elements in the colonial conceptualization of India as a "different" society was the fixed belief that the population was a mélange of communities. As discussed in an earlier chapter, the conservative opinion said to have dominated imperial policy in the post-Mutiny decades considered this an irredeemable racial characteristic: it was foolish to think that Western education would somehow improve the moral quality of a colonized people and turn them into individuals fit to inhabit a liberal-democratic society. If the colonial state was to seek legitimacy, it had to do so by picking out and bringing over to its side the "natural leaders" of the various communities. This theory of representation informed even the constitutional reforms of the late colonial period.

Mature colonial thought adopted this fairly obvious position because, after all, it could not countenance the idea that subject peoples might constitute, in the same way that advanced people did, a singular and true political community such as the nation. At the same time, if "communities" rather than "nation" were what characterized this society, those communities had to be singular and substantive entities in themselves, with determinate and impermeable boundaries, so insular in their differences with one another as to be incapable of being merged into larger, more modern political identities.

Nationalists, of course, rejected this presumptuous postulate that India could never become a nation. What is curious is the way in which, despite the establishment of a postcolonial regime, an underlying current of thinking about the sociological bases of Indian politics continues to run along channels excavated by colonial discourse. The most obvious example of this is the notion of majority and minority communities defined in terms of criteria such as religion, language, or tribe and applied over a variety of territorial units ranging from a part of a district to the country itself. The other example is the continued preoccupation with precise calculations of proportionality in demands both for and against "reservations," not only for the statutorily designated Scheduled Castes and Tribes but also for that contentious category of "backward castes." And finally, although caste enumerations have been banished from the schedules of the census in independent India, it is remarkable how tenaciously political discourse clings on to the idea of representation by enumerable communities: virtually every discussion on Indian elections looks for supportive evidence in the complicated political arithmetic of caste and communal alliances, calculations taken seriously into account even in the electoral strategies of parties and candidates. Therefore, even if we dismiss the sociological view that declares India to be a mere collection of discrete communities as a peculiarly colonial construct, we are apparently still left with a brand of postcolonial politics whose discursive forms are by no means free of that construct.

"COMMUNITY" IN POSTCOLONIAL POLITICS

I think, however, that there has been a transformation in the terms of political discourse. It would be too facile to make the criticism that all our forms of modern politics are merely the unfortunate legacy of colonialism. It is true, of course, that the fuzziness which enabled a wide variety of solidarities ranging from subcaste to gender to nation to be encompassed under the single rubric of jāti has come under great strain when those solidarities have been forcibly inserted into the grid of the modern regime of power. On the other hand, it is also true that the modern disciplinary regime in India is itself limited and conditioned by the numerous resistances to its hegemonic sway. The result has been an unresolved tension through which the twin constituents of political discourse within the modern domain—one, the categories of the liberal-democratic state produced theoretically in the West, and the other, the categories that made up the Orientalist construction of India—are continuously being re-created in ever more unrecognizable forms.

In the days when the nation was being produced imaginatively without the actual shape of a state, many possibilities of communities that colonial knowledge would have declared as radically distinct came together into large political solidarities. The period of the Khilafat-Noncooperation movement (1919–22) is an obvious instance. Conventional historiography often explains this solidarity as the result of a conscious policy of "alliance" pursued especially by Gandhi and the Ali brothers. However, as our example from Bhudeb's utopian history showed, the idiom of love and kinship in which the nationalist imagination sought to cast the relation between the Hindu jāti and the Muslim jāti can hardly be said to belong to a discourse of group interests and alliances, even when, as in Bhudeb's case, the partnership between different jātis was not on the basis of equality.

More interesting are the instances of sanctions imposed by such political collectivities upon those suspected of deviating from community norms. Ranajit Guha has recently discussed the significance of the "social boycott" that was a widespread phenomenon at the time of the Swadeshi movement in Bengal in 1905–9.[9] The forms of punishment traditionally imposed for violation of caste rules were at this time imposed on those accused of violating the injunctions of the "nation"—offenses such as trading in foreign goods or collaborating with government officials, for instance. Even in the rhetoric of the topmost leaders of the movement, the slide from one sense of *jāti* to another seemed fairly unproblematical. Hitesranjan Sanyal's researches among participants of the Noncooperation or the Civil Disobedience movements in Midnapore showed how persuasively, almost with the transparency of the self-evident, the concept of the nation, be it jāti, or *deś*, "the country," was made tangible in the concreteness of an imagined network of kinship extending outward from the local structures of community.[10]

I do not believe that the imaginative possibilities afforded by the fuzziness of the community have disappeared from the domain of popular political discourse. On the contrary, I suspect that with the greater reach of the institutions and processes of the state into the interiors of social life, the state itself is being made sense of in the terms of that other discourse, far removed from the conceptual terms of liberal political theory. The notions of representation and the legitimation of authority, for instance, have taken on a set of meanings in the popular domain of contemporary

Indian politics that would be impossible to describe, let alone justify, in the terms of a theory of interest aggregation or of the rationalization of authority. Our helplessness in understanding processes such as the elections since 1977 or the sudden rise and demise of "ethnic" movements or the inexplicable fluctuations in the authority of particular political leaders seems largely due to the fact that we lack a theoretical language to talk about this domain of popular political discourse.

That this lack is critical is shown by the responses in the domain of "high" discourse to this process of increasing interpenetration of the two domains of politics. There have been, it seems to me, two principal responses, both enabled by the play between the "pure" theory of the modern state and the theory of Oriental exceptionalism. One response involves the reassertion of the universal truth of the pure theory. Thus, claims are being made all over again on behalf of the citizen as a rational individual, transacting public business in accordance with calculations of rational interest and keeping "culture" tucked away within the confines of private belief. There are similar claims about the need to separate politics and ethnicity, politics and religion.

In one sense, these claims are paradoxical. Thus, when the "secular" historian asserts that although medieval rulers may often have acted to inflict damage upon the institutions or followers of a rival religion, there was nothing "religious" about this—it was all "politics"—the claim also empties the domain of politics of that culturally rooted sense of moral solidarity that the same historian would need to uphold when talking, for instance, of the struggle of the "nation" against colonial rule. On the other hand, this same "modernist" discourse would allow the argument to be made that the policy of "reservations" by caste is divisive because it is prompted only by sectional political interests and is harmful for such general national concerns as merit and efficiency. Our modern discourse, it would seem, has to insist that although "politics" may at times be good for the nation, at other times it is best abjured.

There is a further irony. The assertion of a zone of pure politics, while rejecting the colonialist dogma that Indian society is unfit to have a modern state, acknowledges at the same time that the cultural realities in the domain of mass politics can only pollute and corrupt the rational processes of the state. Whether it is communalism or casteism, nepotism or power brokerage, thoughtless populism or the absence of a work ethic, the impact of the popular domain is seen as bearing the mark of an impurity.

Take as an example a recent collection of essays on the politics of caste.[11] The list of writers is a fairly representative sample of the strands of thinking among social scientists writing in Bengali today. (Let me add, since I do not wish to suggest a false standpoint of distance, that this list includes my name as well.) The title of the volume is significant, for it announces itself as a book on the politics of *jātpāt*, not just caste but "casteism," and not only casteism but the entire gamut of divisive politics based on religion, language, or ethnicity. *Jātpāt* is a curious word. A very recent entrant into the vocabulary of politics, it cannot be found in any standard Bengali dictionary. It has probably made its way into the lexicon of Bengali journalism and social science from Hindi,[12] and in its use within this sophisticated discourse of rationality and progress, it carries a double imprint of corruption. *Jāt* itself, according to our lexicographers, is a corruption of *jāti* (or else it is derived from the Persian); *jātpāt* pushes it even further into the dark recesses of the "cow belt" or the "deep south," where they practice a politics so arcane and medieval that progressive Bengalis can only throw up their hands in despair.

The word *jātpāt* also enables one to hierarchize the many senses of *jāti*. *Jāti* can now be given a proper place within the modern discursive formation by reserving its use to the "good" community, namely, the nation. The other senses will then connote undesirable forms of community, evidence of the cultural backwardness of the people and describable as the politics of jātpāt.

The other response in the domain of "high" discourse involves the assertion that all the forms of the modern state in India today represent the unwelcome intrusion of the West and that "traditional" institutions, if allowed to function freely, are still capable of devising adequate instruments for the harmonious functioning of large collectivities.[13] This is the theory of Oriental exceptionalism turned around, for it argues, first, that the Orient can create its own brand of modernity and, second, that the Orient could not care less if its modernity qualifies as modern or not by the criteria of the West. What the argument overlooks is the depth to which the processes of the modern state have taken root in the contemporary history of India. It is not the origins but the process of domestication of the modern state in India that is at issue; one does not, unfortunately, have the option of sending this state back to its origins.

THE MODERN STATE AND CIVIL SOCIETY

We can see then that to sort out these problems of correspondence between the terms of discourse in the domains of elite and popular politics, we need to confront the central question of the modern state and its mechanisms of normalization that seek to obliterate the fuzziness of communities. I will end by raising this rather large question, which we have encountered several times, in one form or another, during the course of this book.

The crux of the matter concerns the presumed emergence in Western Europe of a domain of civil society and its continued autonomous existence, sometimes in opposition to and at other times supportive of the state. What is this civil society? In a recent essay, Charles Taylor has distinguished between three different senses in which civil society can be identified in the European political tradition:[14]

1. In a minimal sense, civil society exists where there are free associations, not under the tutelage of state power.
2. In a stronger sense, civil society only exists where society as a whole can structure itself and coordinate its actions through such associations which are free of state tutelage.
3. As an alternative or supplement to the second sense, we can speak of civil society wherever the ensemble of associations can significantly determine or inflect the course of state policy.

He then spells out five distinct ideas that historically contributed to the production in Europe of a concept of civil society separate from the idea of the state:

A. The medieval idea that society is not identical with its political organization and that political authority is only one organ among others.
B. The Christian idea of the Church as an independent society.
C. The development within feudalism of a legal notion of subjective rights.
D. The growth in medieval Europe of relatively independent, self-governing cities.
E. The secular dualism of the medieval polity in which a monarch ruled with the intermittent and uncertain support of a body of Estates.

Taylor then describes how these ideas were brought together in two quite distinct ways by Locke and Montesquieu, respectively, to produce two different conceptualizations of the state-civil society relation.

In Locke, (A) is interpreted to mean that society is created before government, through a first contract by which individuals in the state of nature give themselves a society. This society then sets up government as a trust. The implication is that if government should violate its trust, society would recover its freedom against government. (B) is given the meaning of a prepolitical community constituted by a natural law received from God. This now becomes the foundation for subjective rights in (C): no positive law can be valid if it contravenes these rights. This particular combination of (A), (B), and (C) produces in Locke the notion of a civil society distinguished from political authority, in which much that is valuable and creative in social life, especially in the sphere of social production, is seen as belonging to the domain of civil society, outside the direction or intervention of the political authority. We can immediately notice the centrality of this notion in the ideological self-representation of English capitalism.

Montesquieu, on the other hand, since he does not presume a prepolitical natural community, does not need to appeal to either (A) or (B). For him, society and political authority are coeval. In order to establish his antiabsolutist doctrine, he brings together (C), (D), and (E) in a form that enables him to distinguish between central political authority on the one hand and a set of entrenched rights, defended by citizens who have a republican sense of patriotic virtue, on the other. His view of society then is that of a balance between two elements, neither prior to the other, which remain as it were in perpetual but creative tension, seeking always to achieve that equilibrium in which both retain their identities without destroying each other.

What is significant in this distinction drawn by Taylor between the two streams of thinking leading to the state/civil society opposition, represented by Locke and Montesquieu, respectively, is the element they share in common. Element (C)—the notion of subjective rights—plays the crucial role in establishing both the distinction between as well as the unity of state and civil society in both these antiabsolutist doctrines. I think this commonality is important especially because of the way in which the history of these two streams of political thinking in Europe becomes implicated in another history: the history of capital. I will return to this point later.

In the meantime, let us note another curious feature shared by both streams. Both Locke and Montesquieu defend subjective rights by appealing to a notion of community. In Locke, this is straightforward. Subjective rights have their source in the prepolitical natural community God creates for mankind: (C) is grounded in (B). People in the state of nature are already constituted as "subjects" by the community of natural law, even before the emergence of society. They can, therefore, proceed, as already constituted "individuals," to create through mutual contracts first society and then government, and thereby establish the institutions for the defense of their subjective rights. In Montesquieu, although (C) is related in institutional terms to the equilibrating forces contained in (D) and (E), the ultimate defense of subjective rights is *vertu*, the patriotic spirit of citizens who "feel shame in obeying any order which derogates from their code" and who "defend the laws to the death against internal and external threats." One would be justified, it seems to me, to think of *vertu* as that sense of community, which is not prior to the establishment of political authority but coeval with it, which nevertheless regards itself as having an identity distinct from that of the political authority.

Why else would the defense of subjective rights against royal encroachment be "patriotic"?

Subjective rights and the grounding of those rights in community—these are the two features that are common to the otherwise different arguments made by Locke and Montesquieu. The problems that appear in the subsequent history of the state-civil society relation in Europe are, I think, fundamentally shaped by divergences in conceptualizing the relation between rights and community. These divergences are framed within two extreme positions: on the one hand, abolishing community altogether and thinking of rights as grounded solely in the self-determining individual will, and on the other, attributing to community a single determinate form, delegitimizing all other forms of community. This subsequent history, I will argue, is intricately tied with the history of capital.

CIVIL SOCIETY AND COMMUNITY

The two streams represented by Locke and Montesquieu were brought together in its most celebrated form by Hegel. Yet, as Taylor notes, the two "sit uneasily together" in Hegel's new concept of civil society. Let me explore the source of this tension in Hegel.

Hegel, as we know, strenuously resisted the line of argument that preferred to think of the state as having been founded by contract. Contracts follow from the accidental, and entirely contingent, agreements among individual wills. They properly belong to the domain of the "system of needs" but are too fickle to be the basis of Right itself. Hegel also would not admit that the family, that first elementary moment of social life, was founded on contract. To admit this would mean having to recognize that members of a family, whether adults or children, might have rights against each other and even the right to dissociate from or dissolve the family at will. That would make the primary elements of social life subject to the transient and utterly chaotic accidents of contingent agreements. Contracts, for Hegel, belong neither to the domain of the state nor to that of the family; their place is in civil society.

How, then, is the family formed? Hegel, as we know, begins the *Philosophy of Right* by first establishing subjective will in abstract right. But when he moves to the actualizing of subjective will in the concreteness of "ethical life," he grounds the first moment—the family—in "love," which is precisely the free surrender of will and personality. The family is ethical mind "in its natural or immediate phase," where it "is specifically characterized by love, which is mind's feeling of its own unity. . . . One is in it not as an independent person but as a member."[15] I quote some of the other things Hegel has to say about this "natural or immediate phase" of ethical life because I prefer to read these passages as a suppressed narrative of community, flowing through the substratum of liberal capitalist society, which those who celebrate the absolute and natural sovereignty of the individual will refuse to recognize. Hegel says:

> Love means in general terms the consciousness of my unity with another, so that I am not in selfish isolation but win my self-consciousness only as the renunciation of my independence and through knowing myself as the unity of myself with another and of the other with me. Love, however, is feeling, i.e. ethical life in the form of something natural. . . . The first moment in love is that I do not wish to be a self-subsistent and independent person and that, if I were, then I would feel defective and incomplete. The second moment is that I find myself in another person, that I count for something in me. Love, therefore, is the most tremendous contradiction; the Understanding cannot resolve it since there is nothing more stubborn than this point of self-consciousness which is negated and which nevertheless I ought to possess as affirmative. Love is at once the propounding and the resolving of this contradiction. As the resolving of it, love is unity of an ethical type.

> The right of the family properly consists in the fact that its substantiality should have determinate existence. Thus it is a right against externality and against secessions from the family unity. On the other hand, to repeat, love is a feeling, something subjective, against which unity cannot make itself effective. The demand for unity can be sustained, then, only in relation to such things as are by nature external and not conditioned by feeling.[16]

Hegel, of course, restricts this substantial unity to the nuclear family, in which it finds its determinate existence as a right against externality and secession in, first, the family property, and second, the male head of the family—husband and father. In doing this, Hegel leads himself into a precarious position, for no matter how hard he tries to resist the idea of the family as based on a contractual agreement in which the members retain their individual rights against each other, he cannot prevent the tide of individualism from seeping into the representations of marriage and inheritance even in the positive law of modern Western societies. Reading these passages today, Hegel's arguments on marriage, gender relations, and inheritance seem to us either quaint, if one takes a charitable view, or outrageously conservative.

I wish to argue, however, that there is another narrative in which Hegel's eloquence on the subject of love will not seem so outmoded. This is the narrative not of the bourgeois family but of community. Think of the rhetoric in which, even in this age of the triumph of individualism, all movements that appeal to the "natural" solidarity of community speak. They claim precisely the right against externality and secession, they seek determinate existence precisely in "property" and "representation" through collectively recognized heads, they speak in the language of love and of self-recognition through the free surrender of individual will to others in the community. One might object that this idea of "natural" affiliation to a community (or an indeterminate set of communities) does violence to the freedom of choice inherent in the subjective will. It is this objection that becomes the basis for the identification in European sociological theory—fed, let us remember, on large doses of Orientalist literature and colonial anthropology—of all precapitalist gemeinschaften as the domain of ascription, and hence unfreedom, and of modern associations as the field where freedom and choice can blossom. Hegel's arguments on the family remind us, it seems to me, of the irreducible immediacy in which human beings are born in society: not as pure unattached individuals free to choose their social affiliations (whether gender, ethnicity, or class) but as already ascribed members of society. Liberal individualism seeks to erase this level of immediacy where people are not free to choose the social locus of their birth. Indeed, liberalism seeks to forget that the question of choice here is itself fallacious, for human beings cannot exist as "individuals" before they are born, and when they are born, they are already ascribed as particular members of society. Liberal theory then can only deal with this phenomenon as accidents of "natural inequality," which social policies of welfare or equal opportunity must mitigate. It can, in other words, deal with it only in bad faith.

If I am allowed the conceit of reading Hegel against the grain, I will choose to read this subsection of "Ethical Life" as a narrative of community where subjective rights must be negotiated within the "ascribed" field of the ethical life of the community. I will also recall here that Hegel makes the family the site for that other great process by which "individual" subjectivities could be negotiated in society, namely, the education of children,[17] which site too he would not be able to defend against the relentless sway of the modern disciplinary regime of power constantly striving to produce the "normalized" individual. Against the grain of liberal sociology, I prefer to read Hegel as saying that education properly belongs to the field of the ethical life of the community, and not to the compulsory discipline of the school, the prison, the hospital, and the psychiatrist's clinic. I will not describe this field of community ethical life as one devoid of choice, nor will I give it a place at some early stage in the sequence of development of the bourgeois nuclear family. Rather, I will read this as a narrative that continues to unfold to this day *against the grain* of that other narrative of bourgeois individualism.

To return to Hegel and civil society: families, united within themselves against the externality constituted by other families and each represented by its head—the burgher, the bourgeois—comprise the domain of civil society. This is the domain of particular interests, based on particular needs and the mutual satisfaction of the needs of all through contractually mediated exchange of the products of labor. This is also the domain where the property of each family is mutually protected through the administration of justice. Civil society, in other words, is the well-known domain of the market economy and civil law.

Hegel, however, also includes within civil society a residual category, providing for "contingencies still lurking" in the system of needs and the administration of justice and for the "care of particular interests as a common interest." This residual category includes the police and the corporation. Curiously, in demarcating the limits of public surveillance organized by civil society (Hegel is clearly thinking here of the administrative functions of what was known in eighteenth-century Germany and Italy as "the police" and which had become the subject of an entire discipline called *Polizeiwissenschaft*),[18] Hegel admits that "no objective line can be drawn." In other words, at this interface between family and civil society, no objective line separates the private from the public. The separation can be made only contextually, taking into view specific contingencies. "These details," Hegel says, "are determined by custom, the spirit of the rest of the constitution, contemporary conditions, the crisis of the hour, and so forth."[19] How is one to read this lack of objective separation between the civil and the familial, the public and the private? What is it that produces this zone of contingency and indeterminacy where "everything is subjective"? Can one read this as one more instance where a suppressed narrative of community is seeping through the interstices of the objectively constructed, contractually regulated structure of civil society?

A final illustration, and I will stop this strenuous reading of Hegel. Still on the subject of civil society and its residual function of taking care of particular interests as a common interest, Hegel writes:

> In its character as a universal family, civil society has the right and duty of superintending and influencing education, inasmuch as education bears upon the child's capacity to become a member of society. Society's right here is paramount over the arbitrary and contingent preferences of parents. . . . Parents usually suppose that in the matter of education they have complete freedom and may arrange everything as they like. . . . None the less, society has a right . . . to compel parents to send their children to school, to have them vaccinated, and so forth. The disputes that have arisen in France between the advocates of state supervision and those who demand that education shall be free, i.e. at the option of the parents, are relevant here.[20]

Once again, I wish to suggest, that suppressed narrative is raising its irrepressible head. How else can Hegel suddenly slip in the idea of civil society as "a universal family"? How can civil society represent itself as a family that, according to Hegel himself, is born not out of contract but out of love, the free surrender of individual wills? By reducing family to the single determinate form of the bourgeois nuclear family, Hegel has narrowed and impoverished its scope. The gap has to be filled in by civil society arrogating the role of a "universal family." Ironically, by admitting this, Hegel immediately opens himself to appropriation by that powerful strand of thinking which claims that this role of the universal family can be properly played by the only legitimate community in modern society—the nation—a role that must then be enforced by the disciplinary mechanisms of the nation-state. Hegel becomes complicit in this act of appropriation, not innocently but as an inevitable consequence of his own construction of the system of Right: the contingent contractual domain of civil society must, after all, be unified at the higher, universal level of the absolute idea of Right, embodied in the state as *the* political community.

CAPITAL AND COMMUNITY

I am suggesting, therefore, that this suppression in modern European social theory of an independent narrative of community makes possible both the posing of the distinction between state and civil society and the erasure of that distinction. At one extreme, then, we have arguments proclaiming the sovereignty of the individual will, insisting that the state has no business to interfere in the domain of individual freedom of choice and contractual arrangements. At the other extreme are the arguments that would have the *one* political community, given the single, determinate, demographically enumerable form of the nation-state, assume the directing role in all regulatory functions of society, usurping the domain of civil society and family, and blurring the distinctions between the public and the private. It is to this range of arguments that people must refer when they say that the state-civil society relation in Western thought is not one of simple opposition. I will argue that the possibilities of opposition as well as encapsulation arise because the concepts of the individual and the nation-state both become embedded in a new grand narrative: the narrative of capital. This narrative of capital seeks to suppress that other narrative of community and produce in the course of its journey both the normalized individual and the modern regime of disciplinary power.

The historical specificity of European social thought cannot be described simply by Taylor's conditions (A) to (E). It would not be surprising at all if one finds in the premodern histories of other, non-European, countries similar features in state-society relations. It is also difficult to explain why, if European thought is indeed conditioned by these specifics, people from Poland to the Philippines to Nicaragua should appeal to these philosophers from Britain, France, or Germany to think out and justify what they do to their own societies and states. If there is one great moment that turns the provincial thought of Europe to universal philosophy, the parochial history of Europe to universal history, it is the moment of capital—capital that is global in its territorial reach and universal in its conceptual domain. It is the narrative of capital that can turn the violence of mercantilist trade, war, genocide, conquest and colonialism into a story of universal progress, development, modernization, and freedom.

For this narrative to take shape, the destruction of community is fundamental. Marx saw this clearly when he identified as the necessary condition for capitalist production the separation of the mass of laborers from their means of labor. This so-called primitive accumulation is nothing else but the destruction of precapitalist community, which, in various forms, had regulated the social unity of laborers with their means of production. Thus community, in the narrative of capital, becomes relegated to the latter's prehistory, a natural, prepolitical, primordial stage in social evolution that must be superseded for the journey of freedom and progress to begin. And since the story of capital is universal, community too becomes the universal prehistory of progress, identified with medievalism in Europe and the stagnant, backward, undeveloped present in the rest of the world.

It could not, however, be entirely suppressed. The domain of civil society, ruled by "liberty, equality, property and Bentham," could not produce an adequate justification for the lack of freedom and equality within the industrial labor process itself and the continued division of society into the opposed classes of capital and labor. What Marx did not see too well was the ability of capitalist society to ideologically reunite capital and labor at the level of the political community of the nation, borrowing from another narrative the rhetoric of love, duty, welfare, and the like. Notwithstanding its universalist scope, capital remained parasitic upon the reconstructed particularism of the nation. (It would be an interesting exercise to identify in Marx's *Capital* the places where this other narrative makes a surreptitious appearance: for instance, money, the universal equivalent, which nevertheless retains the form of a national currency assigned a particular exchange-value by the national state; or the value of labor-power, homogeneous and normalized, which is nevertheless determined by specific historical and cultural particularities.)

We must remember that the rise of a public sphere in Europe, which is said to be a space outside the supervision of political authority where "opinion could present itself as that of society," was also crucial in connecting a reconstructed cultural identity of the people with the legitimate jurisdiction of the state. It was principally in this public space where, through the medium of print-capitalism, the homogenized forms of a national culture were forged—through the standardization of language, aesthetic norms, and consumer tastes. The public sphere, then, was not only a domain that marked the distinction of state and civil society; by creating the cultural standards through which "public opinion" could claim to speak on behalf of the nation, it also united state and civil society. Civil society now became the space for the diverse life of individuals in the nation; the state became the nation's singular representative embodiment, the only legitimate form of community.

But community is not easily appropriated within the narrative of capital. Community, from the latter's standpoint, belongs to the domain of the natural, the primordial. Only in its sanitized, domesticated form can it become a shared subjective feeling that protects and nurtures (good nationalism). But it always carries with it the threatening possibility of becoming violent, divisive, fearsome, irrational (bad nationalism). It is not so much the state/civil society opposition but rather the capital/community opposition that seems to me to be the great unsurpassed contradiction in Western social philosophy. Both state and civil-social institutions have assigned places within the narrative of capital. Community, which ideally should have been banished from the kingdom of capital, continues to lead a subterranean, potentially subversive, life within it because it refuses to go away.

Recent attempts in social philosophy to produce arguments from a "communitarian" standpoint against the dominant orthodoxy of liberal or bureaucratic individualism have sought either to rediscover premodern forms of the political community, lost under the rubble left behind by the onward march of modernity, or to find them among suppressed groups or deviant cults surviving on the margins of normalized society. Alasdair MacIntyre, for instance, sets up his argument against the Enlightenment project of modernity, and by implication against the Nietzschean critique of modernity, by vindicating a classical Aristotelian concept of virtue.[21] In doing this, he has to conjure up the vision of the polis, a determinate political community institutionalizing the practices, goals, and tradition of a moral community. Recent theorists of anarchism have looked for support in the ethnographic evidence on stateless tribal communities or in the practices of marginal utopian communities. And Michel Foucault, seeking in the last years of his life to find the ground for resistance to the all-conquering sway of disciplinary power, located it in the possibility of "an insurrection of subjugated knowledges," a localized but autonomous and noncentralized kind of theoretical production "whose validity is not dependent on the approval of the established régimes of thought."[22]

I am pointing out a different possibility. Looking at the relatively untheorized idea of "the nation" in Western social philosophy, one notices an inelegant braiding of an idea of community with the concept of capital. This is not an archaic idea buried in the recesses of history, nor is it part of a marginal subculture, nor can it be dismissed as a premodern remnant that an absentminded Enlightenment has somehow forgotten to erase. It is very much a part of the here-and-now of modernity, and yet it is an idea that remains impoverished and limited to the singular form of the nation-state because it is denied a legitimate life in the world of the modern knowledges of human society. This denial, in turn, is related to the fact that by its very nature, the idea of the community marks a limit to the realm of disciplinary power. My hypothesis, then, is that an investigation into the idea of the nation, by uncovering a necessary contradiction between capital and community, is likely to lead us to a fundamental critique of modernity from within itself.

But beyond the intellectual history of Europe, our inquiry into the colonial and postcolonial histories of other parts of the world is more likely to enable us to make this critique.[23] The contradictions between the two narratives of capital and community can be seen quite clearly in the histories of anticolonial nationalist movements. The forms of the modern state were imported into these countries through the agency of colonial rule. The institutions of civil society, in the forms in which they had arisen in Europe, also made their appearance in the colonies precisely to create a public domain for the legitimation of colonial rule. This process was, however, fundamentally limited by the fact that the colonial state could confer only subjecthood on the colonized; it could not grant them citizenship. The crucial break in the history of anticolonial nationalism comes when the colonized refuse to accept membership of this civil society of subjects. They construct their national identities within a different narrative, that of the community. They do not have the option of doing this within the domain of bourgeois civil-social institutions. They create, consequently, a very different domain—a cultural domain—marked by the distinctions of the material and the spiritual, the outer and the inner. This inner domain of culture is declared the sovereign territory of the nation, where the colonial state is not allowed entry, even as the outer domain remains surrendered to the colonial power. The rhetoric here (Gandhi is a particularly good example)[24] is of love, kinship, austerity, sacrifice. The rhetoric is in fact antimodernist, antiindividualist, even anticapitalist. The attempt is, if I may stay with Gandhi for a while, to find, against the grand narrative of history itself, the cultural resources to negotiate the terms through which people, living in different, contextually defined, communities, can coexist peacefully, productively, and creatively within large political units.

The irony is, of course, that this other narrative is again violently interrupted once the postcolonial national state attempts to resume its journey along the trajectory of world-historical development. The modern state, embedded as it is within the universal narrative of capital, cannot recognize within its jurisdiction any form of community except the single, determinate, demographically enumerable form of the nation. It must therefore subjugate, if necessary by the use of state violence, all such aspirations of community identity. These other aspirations, in turn, can give to themselves a historically valid justification only by claiming an alternative nationhood with rights to an alternative state.

One can see how a conception of the state-society relation, born within the parochial history of Western Europe but made universal by the global sway of capital, dogs the contemporary history of the world. I do not think that the invocation of the state/civil society opposition in the struggle against socialist-bureaucratic regimes in Eastern Europe or in the former Soviet republics or, for that matter, in China, will produce anything other than strategies seeking to replicate the history of Western Europe. The result has been demonstrated a hundred times. The provincialism of the European experience will be taken as the universal history of progress; by comparison, the history of the rest of the world will appear as the history of lack, of inadequacy—an inferior history. Appeals will be made all over again to philosophies produced in Britain, France, and Germany. The fact that these doctrines were produced in complete ignorance of the histories of other parts of the world will not matter: they will be found useful and enlightening.[25] It would indeed be a supreme irony of history if socialist industrialization gets written into the narrative of capital as the phase when socialist-bureaucratic regimes had to step in to undertake "primitive accumulation" and clear the way for the journey of capital to be resumed along its "normal" course.

In the meantime, the struggle between community and capital, irreconcilable within this grand narrative, will continue. The forms of the modern state will be forced into the grid of determinate national identities. This will mean a substantialization of cultural differences, necessarily excluding as "minorities" those who would not conform to the chosen marks of nationality. The struggle between "good" and "bad" nationalism will be played out all over again.

What, then, are the true categories of universal history? State and civil society? public and private? social regulation and individual rights?—all made significant within the grand narrative of capital as the history of freedom, modernity and progress? Or the narrative of community—

untheorized, relegated to the primordial zone of the natural, denied any subjectivity that is not domesticated to the requirements of the modern state, and yet persistent in its invocation of the rhetoric of love and kinship against the homogenizing sway of the normalized individual?

It is this unresolved struggle between the narratives of capital and community within the discursive space of the modern state that is reflected in our embarrassment at the many uses of *jāti*. Kamalakanta, if he is still around, is now, I suspect, laughing at us.

Notes

The following abbreviations have been used in the notes:

BI Tarinicharan Chattopadhyay. *Bhāratbarṣer itihās*. Vol. 1. 1858. Reprint. Calcutta, 1878.

BMRI Abdul Karim. *Bhāratbarṣe musalmān rājatver itibṛtta*. Vol 1. Calcutta: Sanskrit Press Depository, 1898.

BR Bankimchandra Chattopadhyay. *Baṅkim racanābalī*. Edited by Jogeshchandra Bagal. Vol. 2. Calcutta: Sahitya Samsad, 1965.

G [Mahendranath Gupta]. *The Gospel of Sri Ramakrishna*. Translated by Swami Nikhilananda. New York: Ramakrishna-Vivekananda Center, 1942.

GM Swami Saradananda. *Sri Ramakrishna the Great Master*. Translated by Swami Jagadananda. Madras: Sri Ramakrishna Math, 1952.

K Ma [Mahendranath Gupta]. *Śrīśrīrāmkṛṣṇa kathāmṛta*. 1902–32. Reprint. Calcutta: Ananda, 1983.

L Swami Saradananda. *Śrīśrīrāmakṛṣṇalīlāprasaṅga*. 2 vols. Calcutta: Udbodhan, 1965.

PK Prasannamayi Debi. *Pūrbba kathā*. 1917. Reprint. Calcutta: Subarnarekha, 1982.

R Mrityunjay Vidyalankar. *Rājābali*. Serampore: Baptist Mission Press, 1808.

Chapter One
Whose Imagined Community?

1. Benedict Anderson, *Imagined Communities: Reflections on the Origin and Spread of Nationalism* (London: Verso, 1983).

2. This is a central argument of my book *Nationalist Thought and the Colonial World: A Derivative Discourse?* (London: Zed Books, 1986).

3. Anderson, *Imagined Communities*, pp. 17–49.

4. Ibid., pp. 28–40.

5. The history of this artistic movement has been recently studied in detail by Tapati Guha-Thakurta, *The Making of a New "Indian" Art: Artists, Aesthetics and Nationalism in Bengal, 1850–1920* (Cambridge: Cambridge University Press, 1992).

6. See Anilchandra Banerjee, "Years of Consolidation: 1883–1904"; Tripurari Chakravarti, "The University and the Government: 1904–24"; and Pramathanath Banerjee, "Reform and Reorganization: 1904–24," in Niharranjan Ray and Pratulchandra Gupta, eds., *Hundred Years of the University of Calcutta* (Calcutta: University of Calcutta, 1957), pp. 129–78, 179–210, and 211–318.

7. Bipinchandra Pal, *Memories of My Life and Times* (1932; reprint, Calcutta: Bipinchandra Pal Institute, 1973), pp. 157–60.

8. Represented by the various essays in Ranajit Guha, ed., *Subaltern Studies*, vols. 1–6 (Delhi: Oxford University Press, 1982–90). The programatic statement of this approach is in Ranajit Guha, "On Some Aspects of the Historiography of Colonial India," in Guha, ed., *Subaltern Studies I* (Delhi: Oxford University Press, 1982), pp. 1–8.

Chapter Two
The Colonial State

1. Arthur Berriedale Keith, *A Constitutional History of India, 1600–1935* (1937; reprint, New York: Barnes and Noble, 1969), p. vii.
2. Edward Thompson and G. T. Garratt, *Rise and Fulfilment of British Rule in India* (1934; reprint, Allahabad: Central Book Depot, 1962), p. 654.
3. M. V. Pylee, *Constitutional History of India, 1600–1950* (Bombay: Asia, 1967), p. v. Emphasis mine. It is also not a coincidence that the title of Pylee's book replicates that of Keith's; it only extends the time period by fifteen years.
4. B. B. Misra, *The Bureaucracy in India: An Historical Analysis of Development up to 1947* (Delhi: Oxford University Press, 1977), pp. x, 157.
5. Vincent A. Smith, *Indian Constitutional Reform Viewed in the Light of History* (London: Humphrey Milford, 1919), p. 78. Emphasis in original.
6. Ibid., pp. 21, 22.
7. Ibid., p. 41.
8. Ibid., pp. 50–51.
9. T. R. Metcalf, *The Aftermath of Revolt* (Princeton: Princeton University Press, 1964), p. 96.
10. Stephen in *The Times*, 1 March 1883, cited in Metcalf, *The Aftermath of Revolt*, p. 318.
11. Kenneth Ballhatchet, *Race, Sex and Class under the Raj: Imperial Attitudes and Policies and Their Critics, 1793–1905* (London: Weidenfeld and Nicolson, 1980), p. 6.
12. See Misra, *Bureaucracy in India*, pp. 91–210.
13. C. E. Buckland, *Bengal under the Lieutenant Governors* (1901; reprint, New Delhi: Deep, 1976), 2:769.
14. S. Gopal, *British Policy in India, 1858–1905* (Cambridge: Cambridge University Press, 1965), p. 149; Anil Seal, *The Emergence of Indian Nationalism* (Cambridge: Cambridge University Press, 1971), p. 163.
15. Gopal, *British Policy*, p. 150.
16. Resolutions adopted at a public meeting of the European community at the Town Hall, Calcutta, 28 February 1883. Buckland, *Bengal* 2:775–76.
17. Seal, *Emergence*, p. 166.
18. Buckland, *Bengal* 2:787.
19. Cited in Gopal, *British Policy*, p. 151.
20. Seal, *Emergence*, pp. 170, 144.
21. For a brief account of this history, see H. E. A. Cotton, *Calcutta Old and New* (1909; reprint, Calcutta: General Printers, 1980), pp. 163–70.
22. Grant's minute, 19 June 1861, in Buckland, *Bengal* 1:198.
23. W. H. Seton-Karr's letter to the government of Bengal, 29 July 1861, ibid., p. 200.

24. Cotton, *Calcutta*, pp. 175–76.

25. Ibid, p. 176.

26. Note of Arthur Hobhouse, cited in Gopal, *British Policy*, p. 118.

27. Buckland, *Bengal* 2:716–17.

28. Letter by Lytton, 15 March 1878, cited in Gopal, *British Policy*, p. 118.

29. Buckland, *Bengal* 2:719. For an account of the making of the Vernacular Press Act and its impact, see Uma Dasgupta, *Rise of an Indian Public: Impact of Official Policy, 1870–1880* (Calcutta: Ṛddhi India, 1977), pp. 269–300.

30. For a review of some of these debates on recent Indian historiography, see Gyan Prakash, "Writing Post-Orientalist Histories of the Third World: Perspectives from Indian Historiography," *Comparative Studies in Society and History* 32, no. 2 (April 1990): 383–408; Dipesh Chakrabarty, "Postcoloniality and the Artifice of History: Who Speaks for 'Indian' Pasts?" *Representations* 37 (Winter 1992): 1–26.

31. Some of the methodological problems of autonomy and subjectivity involved in this project are discussed in Gayatri Chakravorty Spivak, "Can the Subaltern Speak?" in Cary Nelson and Lawrence Grossberg, eds., *Marxism and the Interpretation of Culture* (Urbana: University of Illinois Press, 1988); and Spivak, "Subaltern Studies: Deconstructing Historiography," in Ranajit Guha, ed., *Subaltern Studies IV* (Delhi: Oxford University Press, 1985), pp. 330–63.

32. Burton Stein, "State Formation and Economy Reconsidered," *Modern Asian Studies* 19, no. 3 (1985): 387–413.

33. Frank Perlin, "Of White Whale and Countrymen in the Eighteenth-Century Maratha Deccan," *Journal of Peasant Studies* 5, no. 2 (January 1978): 172–237; "Proto-Industrialization and Pre-Colonial South Asia," *Past and Present* 98 (February 1983): 30–95.

34. Frank Perlin, "State Formation Reconsidered," *Modern Asian Studies* 19, no. 3 (1985): 415–80.

35. C. A. Bayly, *Indian Society and the Making of the British Empire*, The New Cambridge History of India, pt. 2, vol. 1 (Cambridge: Cambridge University Press, 1988).

36. The last point is argued in C. A. Bayly, "The Pre-History of 'Communalism'? Religious Conflict in India, 1700–1860," *Modern Asian Studies* 19, no. 2 (1985): 177–203.

37. D. A. Washbrook, "Progress and Problems: South Asian Economic and Social History, c. 1720–1860," *Modern Asian Studies* 22, no. 1 (1988): 57–96.

38. Ibid., pp. 68, 76.

39. For a remarkable analysis of the general rhetorical patterns involved in what I have called the rule of colonial difference, see François Hartog, *The Mirror of Herodotus: The Representation of the Other in the Writing of History*, trans. Janet Lloyd (Berkeley and Los Angeles: University of California Press, 1988).

Chapter Three
The Nationalist Elite

1. To mention only a few of the more notable works: J. H. Broomfield, *Elite Conflict in a Plural Society: Twentieth-Century Bengal* (Berkeley: University of California Press, 1968); Anil Seal, *Emergence of Indian Nationalism* (Cambridge:

Cambridge University Press, 1971); Pradip Sinha, *Calcutta in Urban History* (Calcutta: Firma KLM, 1978); Sumit Sarkar, *The Swadeshi Movement in Bengal* (New Delhi: People's Publishing House, 1973); Rajat K. Ray, *Social Conflict and Political Unrest in Bengal, 1875–1914* (Delhi: Oxford University Press, 1984).

2. A recent work that raises this question is Tapan Raychaudhuri, *Europe Reconsidered: Perceptions of the West in Nineteenth-Century Bengal* (Delhi: Oxford University Press, 1988).

3. Ma [Mahendranath Gupta], *Śrīśrīrāmkṛṣṇa kathāmṛta*, 5 vols. (Calcutta: 1902–1932). For this study, I have used the single-volume complete edition (Calcutta: Ananda, 1983) (hereafter references are cited parenthetically in text as *K*).

4. Sumit Sarkar, "'Kaliyuga,' 'Chakri' and 'Bhakti': Ramkrishna and His Times," *Economic and Political Weekly* 27, 29 (18 July 1992): 1543–66.

5. Dipesh Chakrabarty, *Rethinking Working-Class History: Bengal, 1890–1940* (Princeton: Princeton University Press, 1989), pp. 15–32.

6. Sivanath Sastri, *History of the Brahmo Samaj* (1911–12; reprint, Calcutta: Sadharan Brahmo Samaj, 1974), p. 171.

7. *Punch*, 16 March 1870, cited in Meredith Borthwick, *Keshub Chunder Sen: A Search for Cultural Synthesis* (Calcutta: Minerva Associates, 1977), p. 108.

8. "Farewell Soirèe," address in London, 12 September 1870, in *Keshub Chunder Sen in England: Diaries, Sermons, Addresses and Epistles* (1871; reprint, Calcutta: Writers Workshop, 1980), p. 450.

9. "Jesus Christ: Europe and Asia," lecture in Calcutta, 5 May 1866, in David C. Scott, ed., *Keshub Chunder Sen* (Madras: Christian Literature Society, 1979), pp. 62–63.

10. *Keshub Chunder Sen in England*, pp. 454–55.

11. Borthwick, *Keshub Chunder Sen*, pp. 148–49.

12. Sastri, *History of the Brahmo Samaj*, pp. 160, 170–71, 172.

13. In 1931, there were a total of 1,554 Brahmos in Calcutta, nearly two-thirds of them concentrated in the single municipal ward of Sukea's Street. *Census of India, 1931*, vol. 6 (Calcutta), pts. 1 and 2 (Calcutta: Central Publication Branch, 1933), imperial table 13, pp. 169–71.

14. "Philosophy and Madness in Religion," lecture delivered in Calcutta, 3 March 1877, in T. E. Slater, *Keshab Chandra Sen and the Brahma Samàj* (Madras: Society for Promoting Christian Knowledge, 1884), app., pp. 85–86.

15. Ibid., pp. 86–87.

16. *Keshub Chunder Sen in England*, p. 271.

17. "India Asks—Who is Christ?" lecture delivered in Calcutta, 9 April 1879, in Slater, *Keshab and the Brahma Samàj*, app., pp. 91–92, 92–93, 93, 102.

18. Rajnarayan Basu, *Ātmacarit* (1909), in Nareschandra Jana, Manu Jana, and Kamalkumar Sanyal, eds., *Ātmakathā* (Calcutta: Ananya, 1981), 1:72.

19. "Great Men," lecture in Calcutta, 28 September 1866, in Scott, *Keshub Chunder Sen*, pp. 99–100.

20. Keshab's mother recounts this incident in talking about Ramakrishna and her son. Saradasundari Debi, *Keśabjananī debī sāradāsundarīr ātmakathā*, ed. Jogendralal Khastagir (Dhaka, 1913); reprint, *Ekṣaṇ* (Autumn 1983): 1–52.

21. P. C. Mozoomdar, *The Life and Teachings of Keshub Chunder Sen* (1887; reprint, Calcutta: Nababidhan Trust, 1931), p. 227.

22. Swami Saradananda, *Śrīśrīrāmakṛṣṇalīlāprasaṅga* (1908–20; reprint, Cal-

cutta: Udbodhan, 1965), 2:398–99 (hereafter references will be cited parenthetically in text as *L*).

23. Mozoomdar, *Life and Teachings*, p. 227.

24. *Life of Ramakrishna Compiled from Various Authentic Sources* (1924; reprint, Calcutta: Advaita Ashrama, 1964), pp. 269–70.

25. Ibid., p. 270.

26. Borthwick, *Keshub Chunder Sen*, pp. 140–41. Anil Seal, quoting Grierson, gives much lower figures: in 1882–83 there were, according to this government source, only two Bengali papers, the *Bañgabāsī* and *Sulabh samācār*, with circulations of four thousand. Seal, *Emergence*, p. 366.

27. Nanda Mookerjee, ed., *Sri Ramakrishna in the Eyes of Brahma and Christian Admirers* (Calcutta: Firma KLM, 1976), p. 2.

28. Swami Saradananda, *Sri Ramakrishna the Great Master*, trans. Swami Jagadananda (Madras: Sri Ramakrishna Math, 1952), p. 710 (hereafter references will be cited parenthetically in text as *GM*); Christopher Isherwood, *Ramakrishna and His Disciples* (New York: Simon and Schuster, 1965), pp. 168–72.

29. Isherwood, *Disciples*, pp. 172–74.

30. Ibid., p. 240.

31. Ibid., p. 248.

32. The closest devotees all arrived between 1879 and 1884. *GM*, p. 811. A recent study of Ramakrishna's disciples is Swami Chetanananda, *They Lived with God: Life Stories of Some Devotees of Sri Ramakrishna* (St. Louis, Mo.: Vedanta Society of St. Louis, 1989).

33. Prosanto Kumar Sen, *Keshub Chunder Sen* (Calcutta: Keshub Sen Birth Centenary Committee, 1938), p. 119.

34. Saratchandra Chakrabarti (1865–1927), who with the founding of the monastic order after Ramakrishna's death adopted the name Swami Saradananda, was the secretary of the Ramakrishna Math and Mission from 1898 to his death. Between 1908 and 1920 he wrote the series of articles that were later compiled to form the *Līlāprasañga*, the authorized account of the Master's life, of which *GM* is a translation.

35. See Partha Chatterjee, *Nationalist Thought and the Colonial World: A Derivative Discourse?* (London: Zed Books, 1986), pp. 58–60.

36. Sarkar, "'Kaliyuga,' 'Chakri' and 'Bhakti.'"

37. I have in mind the researches of Sisirkumar Das, Tarapada Mukhopadhyay, Anisuzzaman, Pradyumna Bhattacharya, Debes Ray, and Prabal Dasgupta. For a recent survey of the questions surrounding the development of the new Bengali prose, see Pradyumna Bhattacharya, "Rāmmohan rāy ebaṃ bāṅlā gadya," *Bāromās* 11, no. 2 (April 1990): 1–22.

38. Ernest Gellner, *Nations and Nationalism* (Oxford: Basil Blackwell, 1983); Benedict Anderson, *Imagined Communities: Reflections on the Origin and Spread of Nationalism* (London: Verso, 1983).

39. There have been many attempts in the last hundred years to place Ramakrishna in the tradition of classical Indian philosophy. One of the most erudite of these is Satis Chandra Chatterjee, *Classical Indian Philosophies: Their Synthesis in the Philosophy of Sri Ramakrishna* (Calcutta: University of Calcutta, 1963).

40. Sudipta Kaviraj, "Bankimchandra and the Making of Nationalist Consciousness. IV: Imaginary History," manuscript.

41. Girishchandra Ghosh, *Giriś racanābalī*, vol. 1, ed. Rathindranath Ray and Debipada Bhattacharya (Calcutta: Sahitya Samsad, 1969), pp. 113–28.

42. *K*, pp. 41–42; [Mahendranath Gupta], *The Gospel of Sri Ramakrishna*, trans. Swami Nikhilananda (New York: Ramakrishna-Vivekananda Center, 1942), pp. 142–43 (references hereafter cited parenthetically in text as *G*). Unless otherwise specified, I will quote from this translation of the *Kathāmṛta*. I must, however, point out that there is a quite deliberate attempt in the *Gospel* to "Christianize" Ramakrishna's language: the translation into English provides the opportunity to put yet another gloss on the language of the *Kathāmṛta*.

43. My translation: the *Gospel* here glosses over the words and phrases that appear in the English in the original.

44. I have changed the translation somewhat.

45. A useful account of these religious ideas will be found in Sashibhusan Das Gupta, *Obscure Religious Cults* (Calcutta: Firma KLM, 1969).

46. Ashis Nandy, *The Intimate Enemy: Loss and Recovery of Self under Colonialism* (Delhi: Oxford University Press, 1983).

47. See Sudipta Kaviraj, "Bankimchandra and the Making of Nationalist Consciousness: I. Signs of Madness; II. The Self-Ironical Tradition; III. A Critique of Colonial Reason," Occasional Papers 108, 109 and 110 (Calcutta: Centre for Studies in Social Sciences, 1989).

48. "Anukaraṇ," in Bankimchandra Chattopadhyay, *Baṅkim racanābalī* (Calcutta: Sahitya Samsad, 1965), 2:200–201 (hereafter cited parenthetically in text as *BR*). I have in the main followed Sudipta Kaviraj's translation in "Bankimchandra and the Making of Nationalist Consciousness."

49. The classic analysis of this process in Western Europe is in Jürgen Habermas, *The Structural Transformation of the Public Sphere: An Inquiry into a Category of Bourgeois Society*, trans. Thomas Burger (Cambridge: MIT Press, 1991).

50. Homi Bhabha points out an interesting distinction in nationalist narratives between the people as "a pedagogical object" and the people "constructed in the performance of the narrative." The former produces a self-generating tradition for the nation, while the latter "intervenes in the sovereignty of the nation's *self-generation* by casting a shadow between the people as 'image' and its signification as a differential sign of Self, distinct from the Other or the Outside." "DissemiNation: Time, Narrative, and the Margins of the Modern Nation," in Bhabha, ed., *Nation and Narration* (London: Routledge, 1990), pp. 291–322. I am trying to explore a similar disjunctive process in anticolonial nationalist encounters with the narrative of modernity.

51. I have attempted to trace the course of anticolonial nationalist politics in India in these terms in *Nationalist Thought and the Colonial World*.

Chapter Four
The Nation and Its Pasts

1. Ranajit Guha, *An Indian Historiography of India: A Nineteenth-Century Agenda and Its Implications* (Calcutta: K. P. Bagchi, 1988).

2. Although Bankim himself wrote very little that could be designated as his-

tory, his essays on historiography are widely regarded as a landmark in the growth of modern historical research and writing in Bengal. Prabodhchandra Sen makes them the canonical texts for Bengali historiography: *Bāṅgālār itihās sādhanā* (Calcutta: Visvabharati, 1953). A. R. Mallick calls them "the great force" that transformed history writing in Bengal: "Modern Historical Writing in Bengali," in C. H. Philips, ed., *Historians of India, Pakistan and Ceylon* (London: Oxford University Press, 1961), pp. 446–60. It is worth pointing out that although only six of the thirty-five essays in this volume edited by Philips deal with modern Indian historians, one of them is devoted exclusively to Bankimchandra: "The Role of Bankimchandra in the Development of Nationalism." For brief surveys of history writing in nineteenth-century Bengal, see Shyamali Sur, "Bāṅgālir itihāscarcār kayekṭi dik, 1835–1874," *Aitihāsik* 1 (1976): 17–35; and Subodh Kumar Mukhopadhyay, "Evolution of Historiography in Bengali (1800–1947): A Study of the Pattern of Growth," in Tarasankar Banerjee, ed., *Historiography in Modern Indian Languages, 1800–1947* (Calcutta: Naya Prokash, 1987), pp. 29–42.

3. These were included in vol. 2 of his "Bibidha prabandha" and are now published in *BR*.

4. There is some ambiguity in Bankim's writings about the status of the independent sultans of Bengal; I will discuss this point in the last section of chapter 5.

5. I have used in this section quotations from two of Bankim's essays: "Bāṅgālār itihās," in *BR*, pp. 330–33; and "Bāṅgālār itihās sambandhe kayekṭi kathā," in *BR*, pp. 336–40.

6. I have discussed these sources in my essay "Itihāser uttarādhikār," *Bāromās* 12, no. 2 (April 1991): 1–24.

7. Mṛtyuñjaya Śarmaṇah, *Rājābali* (Serampore: Baptist Mission Press, 1808) (hereafter references will be cited parenthetically in text as *R*).

8. R. C. Majumdar has discussed some of the dynastic lists in circulation among prominent landed families in eighteenth-century Bengal in Rameschandra Majumdar, "Saṃskṛta rājābalī grantha," *Sāhitya pariṣat patrikā* 46, no. 4 (1953): 232–39. I am grateful to Gautam Bhadra for this reference.

9. I cannot agree with Ranajit Guha that there is an "irresolvable contradiction" in Mrityunjay's introduction of "clockwork into the mythic time of the Kalpas" or of the authorial present into aeonic space. Guha, *An Indian Historiography*, pp. 35–36. The "traditional" form of recounting genealogical lists of ruling dynasties had no problems in combining "mythic matter" with the historical present. Indeed, the distinction between Puranic and historical time is not one that belongs to Mrityunjay's discourse; it has to be made outside that discourse for his text to be read as one informed by "a sense of the past still partially bound to tradition."

10. Munshi Alimaddin, *Dīllir rājādir nām* (Barisal, 1875).

11. Iswarchandra Vidyasagar, *Bāṅgālār itihās, dvitīya bhāg, sirāj uddaulār siṃhāsanārohaṇ abadhi lārḍ uiliām benṭiker adhikār paryyanta* (Calcutta, 1858).

12. Ramgati Nyayaratna, *Bāṅgālār itihās, pratham bhāg, hindu rājādiger caramābasthā abadhi nabāb ālībarddi khāṇr adhikār kāl paryyanta* (1859; revised and reprinted, Hooghly, 1867).

13. Ibid., pp. 179–80.

14. Ramsaday Bhattacharya, *Bāṅgālā itihāser praśnottar* (Calcutta, 1869), pp. 110–11, 126–27.

15. Kshetranath Bandyopadhyay, *Śiśupāṭh bāṅgālār itihās, bargīr hāṅgām haite lārḍ narthbruker āgaman paryyanta* (Calcutta, 1872), pp. 22, 27, 31.

16. Ibid., pp. 34–35.

17. Ibid., p. 41.

18. Ibid., pp. 39, 59, 98, 100.

19. Krishnachandra Ray, *Bhāratbarṣer itihās, iṃrejdiger adhikārkāl* (1859; reprint, Calcutta: J. C. Chatterjee, 1870), pp. 43–44, 70, 38, 40.

20. Ibid., pp. 214, 238.

21. Kshirodchandra Raychaudhuri, *Samagra bhārater saṃkṣipta itihās* (Calcutta, 1876), preface, and pp. 115, 211.

22. Tarakrishna Haldar, *Camatkār svapnadarśan* (Calcutta, 1868), pp. 134–36.

23. Bholanath Chakravarti, *Sei ek din ār ei ek din, arthāt bañger pūrbba o barttamān abasthā* (Calcutta: Adi Brahmo Samaj, 1876), p. 10.

24. Ibid., pp. 11–12.

25. Tarinicharan Chattopadhyay, *Bhāratbarṣer itihās*, vol. 1 (1858; reprint, Calcutta, 1878) (hereafter references will be cited parenthetically in text as *BI*).

Chapter Five
Histories and Nations

1. Ronald Inden has recently made this point with much force. *Imagining India* (Oxford: Basil Blackwell, 1990), pp. 45–46.

2. For a discussion of Mill's comparative treatment of the Hindu and Muslim periods in Indian history, see J. S. Grewal, *Muslim Rule in India: The Assessments of British Historians* (Calcutta: Oxford University Press, 1970), pp. 64–97.

3. Romila Thapar has argued that Mill's *History* nevertheless remained influential for Indian writers because "it laid the foundation for a communal interpretation of Indian history and thus provided the historical justification for the two-nation theory." His severe condemnations "led to a section of the Orientalists and later to Indian historians having to defend 'Hindu civilisation' even if it meant overglorifying the ancient past." "Communalism and the Writing of Ancient Indian History," in Romila Thapar, Harbans Mukhia, and Bipan Chandra, *Communalism and the Writing of Indian History* (Delhi: People's Publishing House, 1969), p. 4.

4. "Advertisement to the Fifth Edition," in Mountstuart Elphinstone, *The History of India: The Hindu and Mahometan Periods*, 9th ed. (London: John Murray, 1905), p. vii.

5. H. M. Elliot, *The History of India as Told by Its Own Historians: The Muhammadan Period*, ed. John Dowson, 8 vols. (London: Trübner, 1867–77).

6. The most detailed criticism was in Shahpurshah Hormasji Hodivala, *Studies in Indo-Muslim History: A Critical Commentary on Elliot and Dowson's "History of India as Told by Its Own Historians,"* 2 vols. (1939; reprint, Lahore: Islamic Book Service, 1979). But far more trenchant and politically significant is the criticism made in 1931 by Muhammad Habib: "An Introduction to the Study

of Medieval India (A.D. 1000–1400)," in K. A. Nizami, ed., *Politics and Society during the Early Medieval Period: Collected Works of Professor Muhammad Habib* (New Delhi: People's Publishing House, 1974), pp. 3–32. In it, Habib makes the following comment on the effects of this form of historical memory: "The Hindu feels it his duty to dislike those whom he has been taught to consider the enemies of his religion and his ancestors; the Mussalman, lured into the false belief that he was once a member of a ruling race, feels insufferably wronged by being relegated to the status of a minority community. Fools both! Even if the Mussalman eight centuries ago were as bad as they were painted, would there be any sense in holding the present generation responsible for their deeds? It is but an imaginative tie that joins the modern Hindu with Harshavardhana or Asoka, or the modern Mussalman with Shihabuddin or Mahmud" (p. 12).

7. "Sir Henry Elliot's Original Preface," in Elliot and Dowson, *Own Historians*, 1:xv–xxvii.

8. The point is discussed in Inden, *Imagining India*, pp. 117–22.

9. On this, see Grewal, *Muslim Rule*.

10. The same description occurs in Elphinstone, *History*, pp. 300–301, minus the last comment.

11. These details also appear in Elphinstone, *History*, p. 301, where the source mentioned is Tod's *Rajasthan*. James Tod, *Annals and Antiquities of Rajasthan, or the Central and Western Rajput States of India*, ed. William Crooke (1829–32; reprint, London: Oxford University Press, 1920). What is a story from Rajput folklore in Tod, having entered modern historiography in Elphinstone as the slaughter of a "Rájpút tribe by the Mahometans," becomes in Tarinicharan an episode in the history of the resistance by "Indians" to Muslim conquest.

12. The story occurs in Elphinstone, *History*, pp. 303–4, which is undoubtedly the source for Tarinicharan. There is a much more detailed account in an extract from "Chach-náma, or Taríkh-i Hind wa Sind," in Elliot and Dowson, *Own Historians* 1: 209–11, in which in the end the princess rebukes the Khalifa for passing such peremptory orders against an innocent man.

13. *BI*, pp. 43–44. All of these details, once again, are in Elphinstone, *History*, pp. 320–21, where the authority cited is David Price, *Chronological Retrospect, or Memoirs of the Principal Events of Mahommedan History*, vol. 2 (London, 1821).

14. These stories appear in Elphinstone, *History*, pp. 409–10.

15. I have seen one book that is little more than an abridged edition of Tarinicharan; entire paragraphs are plagiarized. Jibankrishna Chattopadhyay, *Bhāratbarṣer purābṛtta*, 5th ed. (Calcutta, 1875).

16. Saiyad Abdul Rahim, *Bhāratbarṣer itihāser praśnottar* (Dhaka, 1870), p. 2.

17. Ibid., pp. 16, 78.

18. Ibid., pp. 100–101.

19. Sheikh Abdar Rahim, *Hajrat mahammader jīban carit o dharmmanīti* (Calcutta, 1886), pp. 173, preface, 178.

20. Abdul Karim, *Bhāratbarṣe musalmān rājatver itibṛtta*, vol. 1 (Calcutta: Sanskrit Press Depository, 1898) (references hereafter cited parenthetically in text as *BMRI*).

21. For a discussion of these literary trends, see Rafiuddin Ahmed, *The Bengal*

Muslims, 1871–1906: A Quest for Identity (Delhi: Oxford University Press, 1981), pp. 93–97.

22. Ranajit Guha, *An Indian Historiography of India: A Nineteenth-Century Agenda and Its Implications* (Calcutta: K. P. Bagchi, 1988), pp. 55–67.

23. Ibid., p. 63.

24. As Guha does: ibid., pp. 66–67.

25. Bhudeb Mukhopadhyay, "Svapnalabdha bhāratbarṣer itihās," in *Bhūdeb racanā sambhār*, ed. Pramathanath Bisi (Calcutta: Mitra and Ghosh, 1969), pp. 341–74.

26. Rabindranath Thakur, "Grantha-samālocanā," in *Rabīndra racanābalī* (Calcutta: Government of West Bengal, 1961), 13:484–87.

27. Ibid., p. 487.

28. I quote here from the following essays in *Bibidha prabandha*: "Bañge brāhmaṇādhikār"; "Bāñgālār itihās"; "Bāñgālār itihās sambandhe kayekṭi kathā"; "Bāñgālīr utpatti." *BR* 2:319–27, 330–33, 336–40, 344–63.

29. The word *renaissance* is in the original.

30. Rajkrishna Mukhopadhyay, *Pratham śikṣā bāñgālār itihās* (Calcutta, 1875), pp. 61–62.

31. Krishnachandra Ray, *Bhāratbarṣer itihās, iṃrājdiger adhikārkāl*, 14th ed. (Calcutta: Sanskrit Press Depository, 1875), p. 245.

Chapter Six
The Nation and Its Women

1. Ghulam Murshid, *Reluctant Debutante: Response of Bengali Women to Modernization, 1849–1905* (Rajshahi: Rajshahi University Press, 1983).

2. Sumit Sarkar, *A Critique of Colonial Reason* (Calcutta: Papyrus, 1985), pp. 71–76.

3. J. W. Massie, *Continental India* (London: Thomas Ward, 1839), 2:153–54.

4. Lata Mani, "The Production of an Official Discourse on *Sati* in Early Nineteenth-Century Bengal," *Economic and Political Weekly: Review of Women's Studies* 21 (April 1986): WS 32–40; "Contentious Traditions: The Debate on *Sati* in Colonial India," in Kumkum Sangari and Sudesh Vaid, eds., *Recasting Women: Essays in Colonial History* (New Delhi: Kali for Women, 1989), pp. 88–126.

5. Amarendranath Datta, *Majā* (Calcutta, 1900), pp. 7–8.

6. *Meye manṣṭār miṭiṃ* (Calcutta: Girish Vidyaratna, 1874), pp. 28–31.

7. Tarasankar Sharma, *Strīgaṇer bidyā śikṣā* (Calcutta, 1851).

8. Sibchandra Jana, *Pātibratya-dharma-śikṣa* (Calcutta: Gupta Press, 1870).

9. Bhudeb Mukhopadhyay, "Gṛhakāryer byabasthā," in *Bhūdeb racanāsambhār*, ed. Pramathanath Bisi (Calcutta: Mitra and Ghosh, 1969), p. 480.

10. "Lajjāśīlatā," ibid., pp. 445–48.

11. Ibid., pp. 446, 447.

12. See the survey of these debates in Murshid, *Reluctant Debutante*, pp. 19–62; Meredith Borthwick, *The Changing Role of Women in Bengal, 1849–1905* (Princeton: Princeton University Press, 1984), pp. 60–108; and Malavika Kar-

lekar, "Kadambini and the Bhadralok: Early Debates over Women's Education in Bengal," *Economic and Political Weekly: Review of Women's Studies* 21 (April 1986): WS25–31.

13. M. A. Laird, *Missionaries and Education in Bengal, 1793–1837* (Oxford: Clarendon Press, 1972).

14. Murshid, *Reluctant Debutante*, p. 43.

15. The autobiographies of the early generation of educated middle-class women are infused with this spirit of achievement. For a recent study, see Malavika Karlekar, *Voices from Within: Early Personal Narratives of Bengali Women* (Delhi: Oxford University Press, 1991).

16. Cited in Murshid, *Reluctant Debutante*, p. 60.

17. Cited in Borthwick, *Changing Role of Women*, p. 105.

18. See ibid., pp. 245–56.

19. See Murshid, *Reluctant Debutante*.

Chapter Seven
Women and the Nation

1. "Prācīnā ebaṃ nabīnā," in *BR*, pp. 249–56.

2. "Tin rakam," in *BR*, pp. 254–56.

3. Sudipta Kaviraj has analyzed the use of self-irony in Bankim's writings. "Bankimchandra: I. Signs of Madness; II. The Self-Ironical Tradition," Occasional Papers 108 and 109 (Calcutta: Centre for Studies in Social Sciences, 1989).

4. That every such critique and its subsequent appropriation also sows the seeds of instability in the field of discourse goes without saying. Bankim, for instance, as Sibaji Bandyopadhyaya has reminded me, has to cover the risk of his statement about universal male dominance by asserting the ethical truth, independent of male actions, of the virtue of wifely devotion. The contradiction is only barely concealed.

5. "This generally signifies an addition of women into the framework of conventional history. . . . In this sense, with a few exceptions, the women worked within boundaries laid down by men. The history uncovered in this way is a 'contributive' history." Kumari Jayawardena, *Feminism and Nationalism in the Third World* (London: Zed Books, 1986), pp. 260–61.

6. This is the central argument of the most systematic study of the biographical genre in Bengali literature: Debipada Bhattacharya, *Bāṃlā carit sāhitya* (Calcutta: Dey's, 1982).

7. Sibnath Sastri, *Rāmtanu lāhiḍī o tatkālīn baṅgasamāj* (1904), in *Śibnāth racanāsaṃgraha* (Calcutta: Saksharata Prakashan, 1979).

8. Surendranath Banerjea, *A Nation in Making: Being the Reminiscences of Fifty Years of Public Life* (1925; reprint, Bombay: Oxford University Press, 1966).

9. This is how Mary Mason identifies the difference between women's autobiographies and those of men. Mary G. Mason, "The Other Voice: Autobiographies of Women Writers," in James Olney, ed., *Autobiography: Essays Theoretical and Critical* (Princeton: Princeton University Press, 1980), pp. 207–35.

10. The point is made—famously—in Georges Gusdorf, "Conditions and

Limits of Autobiography," trans. James Olney, in Olney, *Autobiography*, pp. 28–48. Also, more recently, Philippe Lejeune, *On Autobiography*, trans. Katherine Leary (Minneapolis: University of Minnesota Press, 1989).

11. I should qualify this statement a bit. There are no women's autobiographies that are called *ātmacarit*, but I have seen two nineteenth-century biographies of women that are called *carit*. Of these, *Kumudinī-carit* (1868) is the life of a Brahmo woman presented as a devout and exemplary, almost saintly, figure. The other, *Lakṣīmaṇīcarit* (1877), is an account by a husband of his deceased wife.

12. Chitra Deb, *Antahpurer ātmakathā* (Calcutta: Ananda, 1984); Srabashi Ghosh, " 'Birds in a Cage': Changes in Bengali Social Life as Recorded in Autobiographies by Women," *Economic and Political Weekly: Review of Women's Studies* 21 (October 1986): WS88–96; Meenakshi Mukherjee, "The Unperceived Self: A Study of Five Nineteenth-Century Autobiographies," in Karuna Chanana, ed., *Socialisation, Education and Women: Explorations in Gender Identity* (New Delhi: Orient Longman, 1988).

13. Karlekar, *Voices from Within*. The publication of this recent work makes it unnecessary for me to talk at length about the social-historical location of these autobiographical texts.

14. Rabindranath Thakur, "Naṣṭanīḍ," in *Rabīndra racanābalī* (Calcutta: Government of West Bengal, 1962), 7:433–74.

15. Shanta Nag, *Pūrbasmṛti* (1970; reprint, Calcutta: Papyrus, 1983), p. 16.

16. Rassundari Dasi, *Āmār jīban* (1876; reprint, Calcutta: De Book Store, 1987), pp. 5–6.

17. See Ghulam Murshid, *Reluctant Debutante: Response of Bengali Women to Modernization, 1849–1905* (Rajshahi: Rajshahi University Press, 1983); and Meredith Borthwick, *The Changing Role of Women in Bengal, 1849–1905* (Princeton: Princeton University Press, 1984).

18. Rassundari, *Amār jīban*, p. 14.

19. Ibid., pp. 38–39.

20. Ibid., pp. 32, 41.

21. Ibid., p. 41.

22. Ibid., p. 56.

23. Ibid., pp. 57–58.

24. Ibid., pp. 63–66.

25. Ibid., pp. 97, 109.

26. Jyotirindranath Thakur, "Bhūmikā," ibid., p. v.

27. Dineshchandra Sen, "Grantha paricay," ibid., pp. vii-xiii.

28. Conventional history has it that Bengali women in general were illiterate before the period of social reform in the middle of the nineteenth century. We have some evidence, however, that this was not necessarily the case. See, for instance, Paramesh Acharya, *Bāṃlār deśaja śikṣādhārā*, vol. 1 (Calcutta: Anushtup, 1989). Even upper-caste women, for whom the prohibitions on reading and writing were likely to have been the most stringent, sometimes managed to escape them. Prasannamayi Debi, whose autobiography I discuss later in this chapter, mentions that several women from an earlier generation in her village were literate and one even ran a school, where she taught both male and female children.

Prasannamayi Debi, *Pūrbba kathā*, ed. Nirmalya Acharya (1917; reprint, Calcutta: Subarnarekha, 1982) (references hereafter cited parenthetically in text as *PK*).

29. Saradasundari Debi, *Keśabjananī debī sāradāsundarīr ātmakathā*, ed. Jogendralal Khastagir (Dhaka, 1913); reprint, *Ekṣaṇ* 17 (Autumn 1983): 4.

30. Being an "as-told-to" account, this is not, strictly speaking, an autobiography, although that is how it is titled. It is clearly directed toward satisfying the curiosity of Keshab Sen's followers and admirers. Saradasundari herself seems quite conscious of the role she is expected to play, but she also resists it. I am grateful to Kamala Visweswaran for alerting me to the need to point this out.

31. Saradasundari, *Sāradāsundarīr ātmakathā*, pp. 17, 33–34.

32. Kailasbasini Debi, *Janaikā gṛhabadhūr ḍāyerī* (1952); reprint, *Ekṣaṇ* 15, nos. 3–4 (Autumn 1981): 7–48. Page references are to reprint.

33. Ibid., pp. 11, 44.

34. Ibid., pp. 42–43.

35. Ibid., p. 21.

36. Ibid., p. 32.

37. Ibid., p. 45.

38. This Kailasbasini is not to be confused with the Kailasbasini Debi (Gupta) who wrote the well-known early tracts on women's education, *Hindu mahilādiger hīnābasthā* (1863) and *Hindu abalākuler bidyābhyās o tāhār samunnati* (1865).

39. Nirmalya Acharya, "Grantha-pariciti," in *PK*, pp. 99–104.

40. As described for Western Europe by Jürgen Habermas, *Structural Transformation of the Public Sphere: An Inquiry into a Category of Bourgeois Society*, trans. Thomas Burger (Cambridge: MIT Press, 1991), pp. 43–51.

41. For instance, the annual pilgrimage for a bath in the Ganga, which often led to numerous deaths in boat disasters. *PK*, p. 34.

42. Binodini Dasi, *Āmār kathā o anyānya racanā*, ed. Soumitra Chattopadhyay and Nirmalya Acharya (1912; reprint, Calcutta: Subarnarekha, 1987).

43. Ibid., pp. 17–18.

44. Ibid., pp. 16, 78.

45. Ibid., pp. 38–45.

46. Ibid., p. 13.

47. Ibid., p. 62.

48. Ibid., p. 64.

49. Girishchandra Ghosh, "Bañga-rañgālaye Śrīmatī binodinī," ibid., pp. 135–44.

50. Binodini Dasi, *Āmār kathā*, p. 8.

51. Ibid., p. 3.

52. Edward W. Said, "Identity, Negation and Violence," *NLR* 171 (1988): 46–60.

53. Partha Chatterjee, *Nationalist Thought and the Colonial World: A Derivative Discourse?* (London: Zed Books, 1986), pp. 1–35.

54. Edward W. Said, "Third World Intellectuals and Metropolitan Culture," *Raritan Quarterly* 9, no. 3 (Winter 1990): 27–50. For the same reason, I am not persuaded by Habermas's invitation to an "unconstrained consensus formation in

a communication community standing under cooperative constraints." See, especially, Jürgen Habermas, *The Philosophical Discourse of Modernity*, trans. Frederick Lawrence (Cambridge: MIT Press, 1987).

55. Sarajubala Debi, letter to the editor, *Ānandabājār patrikā*, 6 April 1991.

Chapter Eight
The Nation and Its Peasants

1. A well-known account of this process is Eugen Weber, *Peasants into Frenchmen: The Modernization of Rural France, 1870–1914* (London: Chatto and Windus, 1979).

2. G. W. F. Hegel, *Philosophy of Right*, trans. T. M. Knox (1952; reprint, London: Oxford University Press, 1967), par. 203 and additions 128–29, pp. 131–32 and 270–74.

3. For instance, David Hardiman, *Peasant Nationalists of Gujarat* (Delhi: Oxford University Press, 1984); Gyanendra Pandey, *The Ascendancy of the Congress in Uttar Pradesh, 1926–1934* (Delhi: Oxford University Press, 1978); Majid Hayat Siddiqi, *Agrarian Unrest in North India: The United Provinces, 1918–1922* (New Delhi: Vikas, 1978); Arvind Narayan Das, *Agrarian Unrest and Socio-economic Change, 1900–1980* (Delhi: Manohar, 1983); Atlury Murali, "Civil Disobedience Movement in Andhra, 1920–1922: The Nature of Peasant Protest and the Methods of Congress Political Mobilization," in Kapil Kumar, ed., *Congress and Classes: Nationalism, Workers and Peasants* (New Delhi: Manohar, 1988), pp. 152–216.

4. A telling example of this can be found in Shahid Amin, "Gandhi as Mahatma: Gorakhpur District, Eastern UP, 1921–1922," in Ranajit Guha, ed., *Subaltern Studies III* (Delhi: Oxford University Press, 1984), pp. 1–61.

5. Ranajit Guha, *Elementary Aspects of Peasant Insurgency in Colonial India* (Delhi: Oxford University Press, 1983).

6. Gyanendra Pandey, "Encounters and Calamities: The History of a North Indian *Qasba* in the Nineteenth Century," in Guha, *Subaltern Studies III*, pp. 231–70; David Hardiman, "The Bhils and Shahukars in Eastern Gujarat," in Ranajit Guha, ed., *Subaltern Studies V* (Delhi: Oxford University Press, 1987), pp. 1–54; Tanika Sarkar, "Jitu Santal's Movement in Malda, 1924–1932: A Study in Tribal Protest," in Ranajit Guha, ed., *Subaltern Studies IV* (Delhi: Oxford University Press, 1985), pp. 136–64; Partha Chatterjee, *Bengal 1920–1947: The Land Question* (Calcutta: K. P. Bagchi, 1984).

7. Argued most powerfully by Louis Dumont, *Homo Hierarchicus*, trans. Mark Sainsbury (London: Paladin, 1970).

8. For two recent surveys of these debates, see Rosalind O'Hanlon, "Recovering the Subject: *Subaltern Studies* and Histories of Resistance in Colonial South Asia," *Modern Asian Studies* 22, no. 1 (1988): 189–224; and Mridula Mukherjee, "Peasant Resistance and Peasant Consciousness in Colonial India: 'Subaltern' and Beyond," *Economic and Political Weekly* 23, nos. 41 and 42 (8 and 15 October 1988): 2109–20 and 2174–85.

9. A point made by Irfan Habib, "The Peasant in Indian History," *Social Scientist* 11, no. 3 (March 1983): 21–64.

10. James Scott, *Weapons of the Weak: Everyday Forms of Peasant Resistance* (New Haven, Conn.: Yale University Press, 1985).

Chapter Nine
The Nation and Its Outcasts

1. "Caste and Class in India," in A. J. Syed, ed., *D. D. Kosambi on History and Society: Problems of Interpretation* (Bombay: University of Bombay, 1985), p. 132.

2. M. K. Gandhi, "Dr. Ambedkar's Indictment II," in *Collected Works* (New Delhi: Publications Division, 1976), 63:153.

3. S. Radhakrishnan, *Eastern Religions and Western Thought* (1939; reprint, New York: Oxford University Press, 1959).

4. Some of the most distinguished examples being Nirmal Kumar Bose, *Hindu samājer gaḍan* (Calcutta: Visvabharati, 1949), later translated into English by André Beteille as *The Structure of Hindu Society* (New Delhi: Orient Longman, 1975); G. S. Ghurye, *Caste and Class in India* (Bombay: Popular Prakashan, 1957); Irawati Karve, *Hindu Society: An Interpretation* (Poona: Deccan College, 1961); M. N. Srinivas, *Caste in Modern India and Other Essays* (Bombay: Asia, 1962); and *Social Change in Modern India* (Bombay: Allied, 1966).

5. The reader will notice that this "dialectical" exercise closely follows the form laid out in Hegel's "Little Logic." G. W. F. Hegel, *Encyclopaedia of the Philosophical Sciences*, pt. 1, trans. William Wallace (Oxford: Clarendon Press, 1975).

6. Louis Dumont, *Homo Hierarchicus*, trans. Mark Sainsbury (London: Paladin, 1970).

7. Louis Dumont, *Homo Hierarchicus*, rev. English ed. (Delhi: Oxford University Press, 1988), p. xxx.

8. Ibid., pp. 242–43.

9. Dipankar Gupta, "Continuous Hierarchies and Discrete Castes," *Economic and Political Weekly* 19, nos. 46–48 (17 and 24 November and 1 December 1984): 1955–58, 2003–5, 2049–53.

10. P. V. Kane, *History of Dharmasastra*, vol. 2, pt. 1 (Poona: Bhandarkar Oriental Research Institute, 1974), p. 52. It is thus that when the exception to endogamy is allowed, it is only in the case of *anuloma*, which literally means "with the hair," that is, in the natural order, and never in the case of *pratiloma*, which would be against the natural order.

11. A recent work which argues that the domain of power, specifically represented by the institution of kingship, may actually influence the ideology and practice of caste is Nicholas B. Dirks, *The Hollow Crown: Ethnohistory of an Indian Kingdom* (Cambridge: Cambridge University Press, 1987). Dirks, however, retains the scheme of separation between the domains of ideology and power; in criticizing Dumont, he reverses the relation between the two domains.

12. In empirical terms, this is now well recognized in recent ethnographic literature. See, for example, Pauline Mahar Kolenda, "Religious Anxiety and Hindu Fate," *Journal of Asian Studies* 23 (1964): 71–82; Owen Lynch, *The Politics of Untouchability: Social Mobility and Social Change in a City of India* (New York: Columbia University Press, 1969); Mark Juergensmeyer, *Religion as Social Vi-*

sion: The Movement against Untouchability in Twentieth-Century Punjab (Berkeley and Los Angeles: University of California Press, 1982); R. S. Khare, *The Untouchable as Himself: Ideology and Pragmatism among the Lucknow Chamars* (Cambridge: Cambridge University Press, 1983); Rosalind O'Hanlon, *Caste, Conflict and Ideology: Mahatma Jotirao Phule and Low Caste Protest in Nineteenth-Century Western India* (Cambridge: Cambridge University Press, 1985).

13. Louis Dumont, "World Renunciation in Indian Religions," in *Homo Hierarchicus*, rev. English ed., app. B, pp. 267–86.

14. Ramakanta Chakrabarty, *Vaiṣṇavism in Bengal* (Calcutta: Sanskrit Pustak Bhandar, 1985), p. 349.

15. Ibid., p. 321.

16. Five of this celebrated circle of six *gosvāmīs* were Brahmans. The intellectual leaders of the circle—the brothers Rūpa and Sanātana and their nephew Jīva—were Karnataka Brahmans settled in Bengal and came from a family of senior ministers to the Bengal Sultan. They are said to have considered themselves somewhat impure because of their close contact with the Muslim ruling elite, but were all highly learned in the philosophical and literary disciplines. Gopāla Bhaṭṭa is also said to have been a Karnataka Brahman. Raghunātha Bhaṭṭa was a Brahman settled in Varanasi and may have been of Bengali origin, while Raghunātha Dāsa was from a Kayastha landlord family of Hooghly. The last two, however, made virtually no significant contribution to the doctrinal development of Gauḍīya Vaiṣṇavism. See Sushil Kumar De, *Early History of the Vaisnava Faith and Movement in Bengal* (Calcutta: Firma KLM, 1961), pp. 111–65.

17. Hitesranjan Sanyal, "Trends of Change in the Bhakti Movement in Bengal," Occasional Paper 76 (Calcutta: Centre for Studies in Social Sciences, 1985).

18. The slurs on the sexual reputation of the women followers of Vaiṣṇava sects are legion. A popular saying has a Vaiṣṇava woman declaring: "I was a prostitute first, a maid-servant later, and a procuress in between; now at last I am a Vaiṣṇavī." ("Āge beśye, pare dāsye, madhye madhye kuṭnī, sarba karma parityājya ekhan boṣṭamī.") Sushilkumar De, *Bāṃlā prabād* (1946; reprint, Calcutta: A. Mukherjee, 1986), p. 9.

19. For an account of these processes in the period of Caitanya and after, see Hitesranjan Sanyal, *Social Mobility in Bengal* (Calcutta: Papyrus, 1981), pp. 33–64.

20. Chakrabarty, *Vaiṣṇavism in Bengal*, p. 324.

21. Ibid., p. 342.

22. Sashibhusan Das Gupta, *Obscure Religious Cults* (Calcutta: Firma KLM, 1969), pp. 113–46.

23. The activity of "remembrance" of the *līlā* was ritually formalized in the eighteenth century. See Chakrabarty, *Vaiṣṇavism in Bengal*, pp. 309–18.

24. Antonio Gramsci comments on this phenomenon with great insight, especially in the context of Catholicism ("in reality a multiplicity of distinct and often contradictory religions"). See especially *Selections from the Prison Notebooks*, trans. Quintin Hoare and Geoffrey Nowell Smith (New York: International Publishers, 1971), pp. 325–43. I have discussed Gramsci's ideas on popular religion,

and particularly what he calls "common sense," in my essay "Caste and Subaltern Consciousness," in Ranajit Guha, ed., *Subaltern Studies VI* (Delhi: Oxford University Press, 1989), pp. 169–209.

25. On the Bāul, see Upendranath Bhattacharya, *Bāṃlār bāul o bāul gān* (Calcutta: Orient Book Company, 1957). On the relationship between the Bāul and the Sufi doctrines, also see Muhammad Enamul Haq, *A History of Sufi-ism in Bengal* (Dhaka: Asiatic Society of Bangladesh, 1975), pp. 260–367.

26. On the Sāhebdhanī, see Sudhir Chakrabarti, *Sāhebdhanī sampradāy: Tāder gān* (Calcutta: Pustak Bipani, 1988); on the Kartābhajā, see the brief account in Chakrabarty, *Vaiṣṇavism in Bengal*, pp. 346–84.

27. Computed from imperial table 18, *Census of India, 1931*, vol. 5 (Bengal and Sikkim), pt. 2, pp. 226–42. The Hāḍi is in fact more numerous in the western districts of Bengal such as Burdwan, Birbhum, and Midnapore.

28. "Hāḍittun ḍom kulīn, ḍomattun hāḍi kulīn." Mohammad Hanif Pathan, ed., *Bāṃlā prabād pariciti*, vol. 2, pt. 1 (Dhaka: Bangla Academy, 1982), p. 86.

29. H. H. Risley, *The Tribes and Castes of Bengal* (1891; reprint, Calcutta: Firma KLM, 1981), 1:314–16.

30. James Wise, *Notices on the Races, Castes and Tribes of Eastern Bengal* (London, 1883), cited in Risley, *Tribes and Castes* 1:314–16.

31. Meherpur is now an *upajilā* (subdistrict) in Bangladesh.

32. This account is based on the biographical details collected by Sudhir Chakrabarti, *Balāhāḍi sampradāy ār tāder gān* (Calcutta: Pustak Bipani, 1986). Unless otherwise indicated, all information on the sect and its songs are also from the same source. Dr Chakrabarti, of course, is not to be blamed for my interpretation of his material.

33. Akshaykumar Datta, *Bhāratbarṣīya upāsak-sampradāy*, ed. Benoy Ghosh (1870; reprint, Calcutta: Pathabhavan, 1969), pp. 137–39. Balaram's argument here resembles a much older form of *nāstika* argumentation found in the so-called Cārvāka philosophy. "If those living in heaven can be nourished by the offerings of those living on earth, then why should not those living on the upper floor of a building be nourished by the offerings made on the lower floor?" See Sāyaṇamādhava, *Cārvāka-darśanam*, trans. (from Sanskrit to Bengali) Panchanan Sastri (Agarpara: Samyabrata Chakravarti, 1987), p. 87.

34. J. N. Bhattacharya, *Hindu Castes and Sects* (1896; reprint, Calcutta: Editions Indian, 1973), pp. 388–89.

35. Chakrabarti, *Balāhāḍi sampradāy*, pp. 27–28.

36. Sudhir Chakrabarti thinks the latter is more probable, and that version is certainly accepted by the sectarians. Ibid., p. 20.

37. This, according to Sudhir Chakrabarti, is confirmed by the land records at Meherpur, where a gift of 0.35 acres of land from the landlord Jiban Mukherjee to Balaram Hāḍi is recorded. Ibid., p. 31.

38. The meeting of this English-educated Brahman scholar with Brahmamātā was not without a touch of irony. "I met her in the year 1872. Her first question to me was about my caste. I knew well about the hatred of the sect towards Brahmans, and instead of mentioning that I was a Brahman, I used a pun to say that I was a human being. She was very much pleased, and after offering me a seat

she went on propounding the tenets of her sect. The greater part of her utterances was meaningless jargon, but she talked fluently and with the dignity of a person accustomed to command. Though a Hari by caste, she did not hesitate to offer me her hospitality. I declined it as politely as I could but considering the courtesy that she showed to me, I could not but feel some regret that the barrier of caste rendered it quite impossible for me to comply with her request." Bhattacharya, *Hindu Castes and Sects*, p. 389.

39. Chakrabarti, *Balāhāḍi sampradāy*, pp. 44–45.

40. See Das Gupta, *Obscure Religious Cults*, pp. 311–37.

41. Ibid., pp. 211–55, 367–98. For a detailed account of the religion of the Nāth sect, see Kalyani Mallik, *Nāth-sampradāyer itihās, darśan o sādhan praṇālī* (Calcutta: University of Calcutta, 1950).

42. This is undoubtedly the source of the story picked up by James Wise about the origin of the Bhuiṅmālī.

43. Here again is an element of commonality with the *Śūnyapurāṇa* cosmogony, for there too it is Śiva alone of the three sons of Ādyāśakti who is able to recognize the supreme lord in disguise.

44. *Ghām* = sweat. In the *Śūnyapurāṇa* myths, the first female Ādyāśakti is born from the sweat of the lord, but the relation here has been transposed to the progeny of Brahmā.

45. Actually, the classification of jātis in Hābel's line is elaborated still further and includes divisions such as Shia and Sunni among the Mughals, or Sur, Surani, Lodi, and Lohani among Pathans. Hābel's line seems to comprise groups that claim an aristocratic Muslim lineage, while Kābel's is definitely of inferior social status, although the inclusion of Rajputs in the latter line remains a complete mystery.

46. This may be a good reason why it does not claim any allegiance to the religion of the Nāth siddhas. However, the stories about Balarām's own miraculous powers of transportation indicate a claim of considerable facility in haṭhayoga skills.

47. "Hāḍir lakṣmī śuṅḍir ghare yāy." Sushilkumar De, *Bāṃlā prabād*, p. 224.

48. Once a month, before sunrise on the fourth day after the end of the wife's menstrual cycle. It will also be evident that the attempt to claim proprietorship over one's own body is an exclusively male enterprise. Woman is in fact the embodiment of external pravṛtti, which tempts, subjugates, and destroys the male body. This raises a crucial question about the relationship of subaltern consciousness to gender, a matter that is only beginning to receive serious attention.

49. For an account of the legal muddle on this question, see Marc Galanter, *Competing Equalities: Law and the Backward Classes in India* (Delhi: Oxford University Press, 1984).

50. Numerous studies have shown this. See, for example, John Harriss, *Capitalism and Peasant Farming: Agrarian Structure and Ideology in Northern Tamil Nadu* (Delhi: Oxford University Press, 1982).

51. Antonio Gramsci: "A philosophy of praxis . . . must be a criticism of 'common sense', basing itself initially, however, on common sense in order to demonstrate that 'everyone' is a philosopher and that it is not a question of introducing

from scratch a scientific form of thought into everyone's individual life, but of renovating and making 'critical' an already existing activity." *Prison Notebooks*, pp. 330–31.

Chapter Ten
The National State

1. This section is largely based on Raghabendra Chattopadhyay, "The Idea of Planning in India, 1930–1951" (Ph.D. diss., Australian National University, Canberra, 1985).

2. Jawaharlal Nehru, *The Discovery of India* (New York: John Day, 1946), p. 405.

3. M. K. Gandhi, *Collected Works of Mahatma Gandhi*, 90 vols. (New Delhi: Publications Division, 1978), 70:56.

4. Jawaharlal Nehru, *Jawaharlal Nehru's Speeches* (New Delhi: Publications Division, 1954), 2: 93.

5. Sukhamoy Chakravarty, *Development Planning: The Indian Experience* (Oxford: Clarendon Press, 1987).

6. Ibid., pp. 40–42.

7. Ibid., p. 7.

8. Ibid., pp. 2–3. Emphases mine.

9. Karl Marx, *Capital*, vol. 1, trans. Samuel Moore and Edward Aveling (Moscow: Progress Publishers, 1971), pp. 667–70.

10. See T. H. Aston and C. H. E. Philpin, eds., *The Brenner Debate: Agrarian Class Structure and Economic Development in Pre-Industrial Europe* (Cambridge: Cambridge University Press, 1987).

11. Chakravarty, *Development Planning*, p. 14.

12. Ibid., p. 21.

13. Antonio Gramsci, *Selections from the Prison Notebooks*, trans. Quintin Hoare and Geoffrey Nowell Smith (New York: International Publishers, 1971), pp. 44–120.

14. Asok Sen, "The Frontiers of the *Prison Notebooks*," *Economic and Political Weekly: Review of Political Economy* 23, no. 5 (1988): PE31–36.

15. On this point, see the discussion in Ajit Chaudhuri, "From Hegemony to Counter-hegemony," and Partha Chatterjee, "On Gramsci's 'Fundamental Mistake,'" *Economic and Political Weekly: Review of Political Economy*, 23, no. 5 (1988): PE19–23 and 24–26.

16. I am grateful to Kalyan Sanyal for suggesting this point.

17. Chakravarty, *Development Planning*, p. 21.

18. For instance, in Pranab Bardhan, *The Political Economy of Development in India* (Oxford: Basil Blackwell, 1984); or Lloyd H. Rudolph and Susanne Hoeber Rudolph, *In Search of Lakshmi: The Political Economy of the Indian State* (Chicago: University of Chicago Press, 1987).

19. For instance, once again, Bardhan, *Political Economy*; and Rudolph and Rudolph, *In Search of Lakshmi*.

20. See Arun Patnaik, "Gramsci's Concept of Hegemony: The Case of Devel-

opment Administration in India," *Economic and Political Weekly: Review of Political Economy* 23, no. 5 (1988): PE12–18; Atul Kohli, *The State and Poverty in India: The Politics of Reform* (Cambridge: Cambridge University Press, 1987).

Chapter Eleven
Communities and the Nation

1. "Kamalākānter jobānbandī," in *BR*, pp. 101–8.
2. For an analysis of the Kamalakanta writings, see Sudipta Kaviraj, "Signs of Madness: The Figure of Kamalakanta in the Work of Bankimchandra Chattopadhyay," *Journal of Arts and Ideas* 17–18 (June 1989): 9–32.
3. Jnanendramohan Das, *Bāṅgālā bhāṣār abhidhān*, 2d ed. (1937; reprint, Calcutta: Sahitya Samsad, 1988), 1:848–49.
4. Haricharan Bandyopadhyay, *Baṅgīya śabdakoṣ* (New Delhi: Sahitya Akademi, 1966), 1:936.
5. Govindagopal Mukhopadhyay and Gopikamohan Bhattacharya, *A Tri-lingual Dictionary*, Calcutta Sanskrit College Research Series 47, lexicon no. 1 (Calcutta: Sanskrit College, 1966).
6. Bhudeb Mukhopadhyay, "Svapnalabdha bhāratbarṣer itihās," in *Bhūdeb racanāsambhār*, pp. 341–74.
7. Sudipta Kaviraj, "The Imaginary Institution of India," in Partha Chatterjee and Gyanendra Pandey, eds., *Subaltern Studies VII* (Delhi: Oxford University Press, 1992), pp. 1–39.
8. Bernard S. Cohn, "The Census, Social Structure and Objectification in South Asia," in Cohn, *An Anthropologist among the Historians and Other Essays* (Delhi: Oxford University Press, 1987), pp. 224–54.
9. Ranajit Guha, "Discipline and Mobilize," in Chatterjee and Pandey, *Subaltern Studies VII*, pp. 69–120.
10. Hitesranjan Sanyal, "Abhayer kathā," *Bāromās* 7, no. 2 (Autumn 1984): 97–128.
11. Sujit Sen, ed., *Jātpāter rājnīti* (Calcutta: Pustak Bipani, 1989).
12. Hindi dictionaries list the word *jātpāṇt* under the entry for *jāt*, the corrupt form of *jāti*, and give as its meaning *birādarī*, "the collective 'brotherhood' of a subcaste." There is also a listing for *jātipāṇtī*, once again a non-Sanskritic Hindi word, which could mean *varṇa*, "caste" or "tribe." Kalika Prasad, Rajballabh Sahay, and Mukundilal Srivastava, *Bṛhat hindī koś* (Banaras: Gyanmandal, 1970).
13. While I do not wish to reduce the importance of the immensely suggestive writings of Ashis Nandy, it nevertheless seems to me that they often lend themselves to this kind of interpretation.
14. Charles Taylor, "Modes of Civil Society," *Public Culture* 3, no. 1 (Fall 1990): 102–19.
15. G. W. F. Hegel, *Philosophy of Right*, trans. T. M. Knox (London: Oxford University Press, 1967), par. 158, p. 110.
16. Ibid., addition 101, pp. 261–62; addition 102, p. 262.
17. Ibid., par. 175, pp. 117–18.
18. Foucault, of course, makes much of these "police functions" of the early

modern state. See, in particular, his Tanner Lectures at Stanford University, reprinted as "Politics and Reason," in Michel Foucault, *Politics, Philosophy, Culture: Interviews and Other Writings, 1977–1984*, trans. Alan Sheridan et al. (New York: Routledge, 1988), pp. 58–85.

19. Hegel, *Philosophy of Right*, par. 234, p. 146.

20. Ibid., par. 239, p. 148, and addition 147, p. 277.

21. Alasdaire MacIntyre, *After Virtue: A Study in Moral Theory* (London: Duckworth, 1981).

22. Michel Foucault, *Power/Knowledge: Selected Interviews and Other Writings, 1972–1977*, ed. Colin Gordon (New York: Pantheon, 1980), pp. 78–92.

23. Foucault was well aware of the fact that contemporary non-Western cultures contained powerful resources for resisting disciplinary power. This was shown quite dramatically, if rather embarrassingly for many of Foucault's admirers, in his enthusiasm for the Iranian revolt against the shah. Those events, he wrote, "did not represent a withdrawal of the most outmoded groups before a modernization that is too brutal. It was, rather, the rejection by an entire culture, an entire people, of a modernization that is an archaism in itself." In their will for an "Islamic government," he added, the Iranian people were seeking, "even at the price of their own lives, something that we have forgotten, even as a possibility, since the Renaissance and the great crises of Christianity: a political spirituality. I can already hear the French laughing. But I know they are wrong." See Didier Eribon, *Michel Foucault*, trans. Betsy Wing (Cambridge: Harvard University Press, 1991), pp. 281–91; Foucault, "Iran: The Spirit of a World without Spirit," in *Politics, Philosophy, Culture*, pp. 211–24. Foucault's so-called Iran mistake tells us a great deal about both the possibilities as well as the difficulties of an "antistrategic" theoretical practice: "be respectful when singularity rises up, and intransigent when power infringes on the universal."

24. I have discussed this aspect of Gandhi in *Nationalist Thought*, pp. 85–130.

25. I am grateful to Dipesh Chakrabarty for pointing out to me the implications of this formulation. Chakrabarty has argued this point in his *Rethinking Working-Class History* and in "Postcoloniality and the Artifice of History."

Bibliography

Bengali Sources

Abdar Rahim, Sheikh. *Hajrat mahammader jīban carit o dharmmanīti*. Calcutta, 1886.

Abdul Karim. *Bhāratbarṣe musalmān rājatver itibṛtta*. Vol. 1. Calcutta: Sanskrit Press Depository, 1898.

Abdul Rahim, Saiyad. *Bhāratbarṣer itihāser praśnottar*. Dhaka, 1870.

Akshaykumar Datta. *Bhāratbarṣīya upāsak-sampradāy*. Edited by Benoy Ghosh. 1870. Reprint. Calcutta: Pathabhavan, 1969.

Alimaddin, Munshi. *Dīllir rājādir nām*. Barisal, 1875.

Amarendranath Datta. *Majā*. Calcutta, 1900.

Bankimchandra Chattopadhyay. *Baṅkim racanābalī*. Edited by Jogeshchandra Bagal. Vol. 2. Calcutta: Sahitya Samsad, 1965.

Binodini Dasi. *Āmār kathā o anyānya racanā*. 1912. Edited by Soumitra Chattopadhyay and Nirmalya Acharya. Reprint. Calcutta: Subarnarekha, 1987.

Bholanath Chakravarti. *Sei ek din ār ei ek din, arthāt bañger pūrbba o barttamān abasthā*. Calcutta: Adi Brahmo Samaj, 1876.

Bhudeb Mukhopadhyay. *Bhūdeb racanāsambhār*. Edited by Pramathanath Bisi. Calcutta: Mitra and Ghosh, 1969.

Chitra Deb. *Antahpurer ātmakathā*. Calcutta: Ananda, 1984.

Debipada Bhattacharya. *Bāṃlā carit sāhitya*. Calcutta: Dey's, 1982.

Girishchandra Ghosh. *Giriś racanābalī*. Edited by Rathindranath Ray and Debipada Bhattacharya. Vol. 1, Calcutta: Sahitya Samsad, 1969.

Haricharan Bandyopadhyay. *Bañgīya śabdakoṣ*. Vol. 1. New Delhi: Sahitya Akademi, 1966.

Hitesranjan Sanyal. "Abhayer kathā." *Bāromās* 7, no. 2 (Autumn 1984): 97–128.

Iswarchandra Vidyasagar. *Bāñgālār itihās, dvitīya bhāg, sirāj uddaulār siṃhāsanārohaṇ abadhi lārḍ uiliām benṭiker adhikār paryyanta*. Calcutta, 1858.

Jibankrishna Chattopadhyay. *Bhāratbarṣer purābṛtta*. 5th ed. Calcutta, 1875.

Jnanendramohan Das. *Bāñgālā bhāṣār abhidhān*. Vol. 1. 1937. Reprint. Calcutta: Sahitya Samsad, 1988.

Kailasbasini Debi. *Janaikā gṛhabadhur ḍāyerī*. 1952. Reprint. *Ekṣaṇ* 15, nos. 3 and 4 (Autumn 1981): 7–48.

Kalyani Mallik. *Nāth-sampradāyer itihās, darśan o sādhan praṇālī*. Calcutta: University of Calcutta, 1950.

Krishnachandra Ray. *Bhāratbarṣer itihās, iṃrejdiger adhikārkāl*. 9th ed. Calcutta: J. C. Chatterjee, 1870; 14th ed. Calcutta: Sanskrit Press Depository, 1875.

Kshetranath Bandyopadhyay. *Śiśupāṭh bāñgālār itihās, bargīr hāñgām haite lārḍ narthbruker āgaman paryyanta*. Calcutta, 1872.

Kshirodchandra Raychaudhuri. *Samagra bhārater saṃkṣipta itihās*. Calcutta, 1876.

Ma [Mahendranath Gupta]. *Śrīśrīrāmkṛṣṇa kathāmṛta*. 1902–32. Reprint. Calcutta: Ananda, 1983.
Meye manṣṭār miṭiṃ. Calcutta: Girish Vidyaratna, 1874.
Mohammad Hanif Pathan, ed. *Bāṃlā prabād pariciti*. Vol. 2. Pt. 1. Dhaka: Bangla Academy, 1982.
Mrityunjay Vidyalankar. *Rājābali*. Serampore: Baptist Mission Press, 1808.
Nirmalkumar Basu. *Hindu samājer gaḍan*. Calcutta: Visvabharati, 1949.
Paramesh Acharya. *Bāṃlār deśaja śikṣādhārā*. Vol. 1. Calcutta: Anushtup, 1989.
Partha Chattopadhyay. "Itihāser uttarādhikār." *Bāromās* 12, no. 2 (April 1991): 1–24.
Prabodhchandra Sen. *Bāṅgālār itihās sādhanā*. Calcutta: Visvabharati, 1953.
Pradyumna Bhattacharya. "Rāmmohan rāy ebaṃ bāṅlā gadya." *Bāromās* 11, no. 2 (April 1990): 1–22.
Prasannamayi Debi. *Pūrbba kathā*. Edited by Nirmalya Acharya. 1917. Reprint. Calcutta: Subarnarekha, 1982.
Rabindranath Thakur. "Naṣṭanīḍ." In *Rabīndra racanābalī*, 7: 433–74. Calcutta: Government of West Bengal, 1961.
———. "Grantha-samālocanā." In *Rabīndra racanābalī*, 13:484–87. Calcutta: Government of West Bengal, 1961.
Rajkrishna Mukhopadhyay. *Pratham śikṣā bāṅgālār itihās*. Calcutta, 1875.
Rajnarayan Basu. *Ātmacarit* (1909). In Nareschandra Jana, Manu Jana, and Kamalkumar Sanyal, eds., *Ātmakathā*, vol. 1. Calcutta: Ananya, 1981.
Rameschandra Majumdar. "Saṃskṛta rājābalī grantha." *Sāhitya pariṣat patrikā* 46, no. 4 (1953): 232–39.
Ramgati Nyayaratna. *Bāṅgālār itihās, pratham bhāg, hindu rājādiger caramābasthā abadhi nabāb ālībarddi khāṇr adhikār kāl paryyanta*. 1859. Revised and reprinted. Hooghly, 1867.
Ramsaday Bhattacharya. *Bāṅgālā itihāser praśnottar*. Calcutta, 1869.
Rassundari Dasi. *Āmār jīban*. 1876. Reprint. Calcutta: De Book Store, 1987.
Saradananda, Swami. *Śrīśrīrāmakṛṣṇalīlāprasaṅga*. Vol. 2. Reprint. Calcutta: Udbodhan, 1965.
Saradasundari Debi. *Keśabjananī debī sāradāsundarīr ātmakathā*. Edited by Jogendralal Khastagir. Dhaka, 1913. Reprint. *Ekṣaṇ* 17 (Autumn 1983): 1–52.
Sāyaṇamādhava. *Cārvāka-darśanam*. In *Sarvadarśana-saṃgraha*. Translated from Sanskrit to Bengali by Panchanan Shastri. (Agarpara: Samyabrata Chakravarti, 1987).
Shanta Nag. *Pūrbasmṛti*. 1970. Reprint. Calcutta: Papyrus, 1983.
Shyamali Sur. "Bāṅgālir itihāscarcār kayekṭi dik, 1835–1874," *Aitihāsik* 1 (1976): 17–35.
Sibchandra Jana. *Pātibratya-dharma-śikṣa*. Calcutta: Gupta Press, 1870.
Sibnath Sastri. *Rāmtanu lāhiḍī o tatkālīn baṅgasamāj*. 1904. In *Śibnāth racanāsaṃgraha*. Calcutta: Saksharata Prakashan, 1979.
Sudhir Chakrabarti. *Balāhāḍi sampradāy ār tāder gān*. Calcutta: Pustak Bipani, 1986.
———. *Sāhebdhanī sampradāy: Tāder gān*. Calcutta: Pustak Bipani, 1988.

Sujit Sen, ed. *Jātpāter rājnīti*. Calcutta: Pustak Bipani. 1989.
Sushilkumar De. *Bāṃlā prabād*. 1946. Reprint. Calcutta: A. Mukherjee, 1986.
Tarakrishna Haldar. *Camatkār svapnadarśan*. Calcutta, 1868.
Tarasankar Sharma. *Strīgaṇer bidyā śikṣā*. Calcutta, 1851.
Tarinicharan Chattopadhyay. *Bhāratbarṣer itihās*. Vol. 1. 1858. Reprint. Calcutta, 1878.
Upendranath Bhattacharya. *Bāṃlār bāul o bāul gān*. Calcutta: Orient Book Company, 1957.

Hindi Source

Kalika Prasad, Rajballabh Sahay, and Mukundilal Srivastava. *Bṛhat hindī koś*. Banaras: Gyanmandal, 1970.

European-Language Sources

Ahmed, Rafiuddin. *The Bengal Muslims, 1871–1906: A Quest for Identity*. Delhi: Oxford University Press, 1981.
Amin, Shahid. "Gandhi as Mahatma: Gorakhpur District, Eastern UP, 1921–1922." In Ranajit Guha, ed., *Subaltern Studies III*, pp. 1–61. Delhi: Oxford University Press, 1984.
Anderson, Benedict. *Imagined Communities: Reflections on the Origin and Spread of Nationalism*. London: Verso, 1983.
Aston, T. H., and C. H. E. Philpin, eds. *The Brenner Debate: Agrarian Class Structure and Economic Development in Pre-Industrial Europe*. Cambridge: Cambridge University Press, 1987.
Ballhatchet, Kenneth. *Race, Sex and Class under the Raj: Imperial Attitudes and Policies and Their Critics, 1793–1905*. London: Weidenfeld and Nicolson, 1980.
Banerjea, Surendranath. *A Nation in Making: Being the Reminiscences of Fifty Years of Public Life*. 1925. Reprint. Bombay: Oxford University Press, 1966.
Banerjee, Anilchandra. "Years of Consolidation: 1883–1904." In Niharranjan Ray and Pratulchandra Gupta, eds., *Hundred Years of the University of Calcutta*, pp. 129–78. Calcutta: University of Calcutta, 1957.
Banerjee, Pramathanath. "Reform and Reorganization: 1904–24." In Niharranjan Ray and Pratulchandra Gupta, eds., *Hundred Years of the University of Calcutta*, pp. 211–318. Calcutta: University of Calcutta, 1957.
Bardhan, Pranab. *The Political Economy of Development in India*. Oxford: Basil Blackwell, 1984.
Bayly, C. A. "The Pre-History of 'Communalism'? Religious Conflict in India, 1700–1860." *Modern Asian Studies* 19, no. 2 (1985): 177–203.
———. *Indian Society and the Making of the British Empire*. The New Cambridge History of India, Part 2, vol. 1. Cambridge: Cambridge University Press, 1988.
Bhabha, Homi. "DissemiNation: Time, Narrative, and the Margins of the Modern Nation." In Bhabha, ed., *Nation and Narration*, pp. 291–322. London: Routledge, 1990.

Bhattacharya, J. N. *Hindu Castes and Sects*. 1896. Reprint. Calcutta: Editions Indian, 1973.

Borthwick, Meredith. *Keshub Chunder Sen: A Search for Cultural Synthesis*. Calcutta: Minerva Associates, 1977.

———. *The Changing Role of Women in Bengal, 1849–1905*. Princeton: Princeton University Press, 1984.

Bose, Nirmal Kumar. *The Structure of Hindu Society*. Translated by André Beteille. New Delhi: Orient Longman, 1975.

Broomfield, J. H. *Elite Conflict in a Plural Society: Twentieth-Century Bengal*. Berkeley and Los Angeles: University of California Press, 1968.

Buckland, C. E. *Bengal under the Lieutenant Governors*. 2 vols. 1901. Reprint. New Delhi: Deep, 1976.

Chakrabarty, Dipesh. *Rethinking Working-Class History: Bengal, 1890–1940*. Princeton: Princeton University Press, 1989.

———. "Postcoloniality and the Artifice of History: Who Speaks for 'Indian' Pasts?" *Representations* 37 (Winter 1992): 1–26.

Chakrabarty, Ramakanta. *Vaiṣṇavism in Bengal*. Calcutta: Sanskrit Pustak Bhandar, 1985.

Chakravarti, Tripurari. "The University and the Government: 1904–24." In Niharranjan Ray and Pratulchandra Gupta, eds., *Hundred Years of the University of Calcutta*, pp. 179–210. Calcutta: University of Calcutta, 1957.

Chakravarty, Sukhamoy. *Development Planning: The Indian Experience*. Oxford: Clarendon Press, 1987.

Chatterjee, Partha. *Bengal 1920–1947: The Land Question*. Calcutta: K. P. Bagchi, 1984.

———. *Nationalist Thought and the Colonial World: A Derivative Discourse?* London: Zed Books, 1986.

———. "On Gramsci's 'Fundamental Mistake.'" *Economic and Political Weekly: Review of Political Economy* 23, no. 5 (1988): PE19–23 and 24–26.

———. "Caste and Subaltern Consciousness." In Ranajit Guha, ed., *Subaltern Studies VI*, pp. 169–209. Delhi: Oxford University Press, 1989.

Chatterjee, Partha, and Gyanendra Pandey, eds. *Subaltern Studies VII*. Delhi: Oxford University Press, 1992.

Chatterjee, Satis Chandra. *Classical Indian Philosophies: Their Synthesis in the Philosophy of Sri Ramakrishna*. Calcutta: University of Calcutta, 1963.

Chattopadhyay, Raghabendra. "The Idea of Planning in India, 1930–1951." Ph.D. diss., Australian National University, Canberra, 1985.

Chaudhuri, Ajit. "From Hegemony to Counter-hegemony." *Economic and Political Weekly: Review of Political Economy* 23, no. 5 (1988): PE19–23.

Chetanananda, Swami. *They Lived with God: Life Stories of Some Devotees of Sri Ramakrishna*. St. Louis, Mo.: Vedanta Society of St. Louis, 1989.

Cohn, Bernard S. "The Census, Social Structure and Objectification in South Asia." In Cohn, *An Anthropologist among the Historians and Other Essays*, pp. 224–54. Delhi: Oxford University Press, 1987.

Cotton, H. E. A. *Calcutta Old and New*. 1909. Reprint. Calcutta: General Printers, 1980.

Das, Arvind Narayan. *Agrarian Unrest and Socio-economic Change, 1900–1980*. Delhi: Manohar, 1983.

Das Gupta, Sashibhusan. *Obscure Religious Cults*. Calcutta: Firma KLM, 1969.

Dasgupta, Uma. *Rise of an Indian Public: Impact of Official Policy, 1870–1880*. Calcutta: Ṛddhi India, 1977.

De, Sushil Kumar. *Early History of the Vaisnava Faith and Movement in Bengal*. Calcutta: Firma KLM, 1961.

Dirks, Nicholas B. *The Hollow Crown: Ethnohistory of an Indian Kingdom*. Cambridge: Cambridge University Press, 1987.

Dumont, Louis. *Homo Hierarchicus*. Translated by Mark Sainsbury. London: Paladin, 1970.

Elliot, H. M. *The History of India as Told by Its Own Historians: The Muhammadan Period*. Edited by John Dowson. 8 vols. London: Trübner, 1867–77.

Elphinstone, Mountstuart. *The History of India: The Hindu and Mahometan Periods*. 9th ed. London: John Murray, 1905.

Eribon, Didier. *Michel Foucault*. Translated by Betsy Wing. Cambridge: Harvard University Press, 1991.

Foucault, Michel. *Power/Knowledge: Selected Interviews and Other Writings, 1972–1977*. Edited by Colin Gordon. New York: Pantheon, 1980.

———. *Politics, Philosophy, Culture: Interviews and Other Writings, 1977–1984*. Translated by Alan Sheridan et al. New York: Routledge, 1988.

Galanter, Marc. *Competing Equalities: Law and the Backward Classes in India*. Delhi: Oxford University Press, 1984.

Gandhi, M. K. *The Collected Works of Mahatma Gandhi*. 90 vols. New Delhi: Publications Division, 1958–.

Gellner, Ernest. *Nations and Nationalism*. Oxford: Basil Blackwell, 1983.

Ghosh, Srabashi. "'Birds in a Cage': Changes in Bengali Social Life as Recorded in Autobiographies by Women." *Economic and Political Weekly: Review of Women's Studies* 21 (October 1986): WS88–96.

Ghurye, G. S. *Caste and Class in India*. Bombay: Popular Prakashan, 1957.

Gopal, S. *British Policy in India, 1858–1905*. Cambridge: Cambridge University Press, 1965.

Gramsci, Antonio. *Selections from the Prison Notebooks*. Translated by Quintin Hoare and Geoffrey Nowell Smith. New York: International Publishers, 1971.

Grewal, J. S. *Muslim Rule in India: The Assessments of British Historians*. Calcutta: Oxford University Press, 1970.

Guha, Ranajit. "On Some Aspects of the Historiography of Colonial India." In Ranajit Guha, ed., *Subaltern Studies I*, pp. 1–8. Delhi: Oxford University Press, 1982.

———. *Elementary Aspects of Peasant Insurgency in Colonial India*. Delhi: Oxford University Press, 1983.

———. *An Indian Historiography of India: A Nineteenth-Century Agenda and Its Implications*. Calcutta: K. P. Bagchi, 1988.

———. "Discipline and Mobilize." In Partha Chatterjee and Gyanendra Pandey, eds., *Subaltern Studies VII* pp. 69–120. Delhi: Oxford University Press, 1992.

Guha, Ranajit, ed. *Subaltern Studies I–VI*. Delhi: Oxford University Press, 1982–90.

Guha-Thakurta, Tapati. *The Making of a New "Indian" Art: Artists, Aesthetics and Nationalism in Bengal, 1850–1920*. Cambridge: Cambridge University Press, 1992.

Gupta, Dipankar. "Continuous Hierarchies and Discrete Castes." *Economic and Political Weekly* 19, nos. 46–48 (17 and 24 November and 1 December 1984): 1955–58, 2003–5, 2049–53.

[Gupta, Mahendranath.] *The Gospel of Sri Ramakrishna*. Translated by Swami Nikhilananda. New York: Ramakrishna-Vivekananda Center, 1942.

Gusdorf, Georges. "Conditions and Limits of Autobiography." Translated by James Olney. In James Olney, ed. *Autobiography: Essays Theoretical and Critical*, pp. 28–48. Princeton: Princeton University Press, 1980.

Habermas, Jürgen. *The Philosophical Discourse of Modernity*. Translated by Frederick Lawrence. Cambridge: MIT Press, 1987.

———. *The Structural Transformation of the Public Sphere: An Inquiry into a Category of Bourgeois Society*. Translated by Thomas Burger. Cambridge: MIT Press, 1991.

Habib, Irfan. "The Peasant in Indian History." *Social Scientist* 11, no. 3 (March 1983): 21–64.

Habib, Muhammad. "An Introduction to the Study of Medieval India (A.D. 1000–1400)." In K. A. Nizami, ed., *Politics and Society during the Early Medieval Period: Collected Works of Professor Muhammad Habib*, pp. 3–32. New Delhi: People's Publishing House, 1974.

Haq, Muhammad Enamul. *A History of Sufi-ism in Bengal*. Dhaka: Asiatic Society of Bangladesh, 1975.

Hardiman, David. *Peasant Nationalists of Gujarat*. Delhi: Oxford University Press, 1984.

———. "The Bhils and Shahukars in Eastern Gujarat." In Ranajit Guha, ed., *Subaltern Studies V*, pp. 1–54. Delhi: Oxford University Press, 1987.

Harriss, John. *Capitalism and Peasant Farming: Agrarian Structure and Ideology in Northern Tamil Nadu*. Delhi: Oxford University Press, 1982.

Hartog, François. *The Mirror of Herodotus: The Representation of the Other in the Writing of History*. Translated by Janet Lloyd. Berkeley and Los Angeles: University of California Press, 1988.

Hegel, G. W. F. *Philosophy of Right*. Translated by T. M. Knox. 1952. Reprint. London: Oxford University Press, 1967.

———. *Encyclopaedia of the Philosophical Sciences*. Pt. 1. Translated by William Wallace. Oxford: Clarendon Press, 1975.

Hodivala, Shahpurshah Hormasji. *Studies in Indo-Muslim History: A Critical Commentary on Elliot and Dowson's "History of India as Told by Its Own Historians."* 2 vols. 1939. Reprint. Lahore: Islamic Book Service, 1979.

Inden, Ronald. *Imagining India*. Oxford: Basil Blackwell, 1990.

Isherwood, Christopher. *Ramakrishna and His Disciples*. New York: Simon and Schuster, 1965.

Jayawardena, Kumari. *Feminism and Nationalism in the Third World*. London: Zed Books, 1986.

Juergensmeyer, Mark. *Religion as Social Vision: The Movement against Untouchability in Twentieth-Century Punjab*. Berkeley and Los Angeles: University of California Press, 1982.

Kane, P. V. *History of Dharmasastra*. Vol. 2. Pt. 1. Poona: Bhandarkar Oriental Research Institute, 1974.

Karlekar, Malavika. "Kadambini and the Bhadralok: Early Debates over

Women's Education in Bengal." *Economic and Political Weekly: Review of Women's Studies* 21 (April 1986): WS25–31.

———. *Voices from Within: Early Personal Narratives of Bengali Women.* Delhi: Oxford University Press, 1991.

Karve, Irawati. *Hindu Society: An Interpretation.* Poona: Deccan College, 1961.

Kaviraj, Sudipta. "Bankimchandra and the Making of Nationalist Consciousness: I. Signs of Madness; II. The Self-Ironical Tradition; III. A Critique of Colonial Reason." Occasional Papers 108, 109, and 110. Calcutta: Centre for Studies in Social Sciences, 1989; "IV. Imaginary History." Manuscript.

———. "Signs of Madness: The Figure of Kamalakanta in the Work of Bankimchandra Chattopadhyay," *Journal of Arts and Ideas* 17–18 (June 1989): 9–32.

———. "The Imaginary Institution of India." In Partha Chatterjee and Gyanendra Pandey, eds., *Subaltern Studies VII*, pp. 1–39. Delhi: Oxford University Press, 1992.

Keith, Arthur Berriedale. *A Constitutional History of India, 1600–1935.* 1937. Reprint. New York: Barnes and Noble, 1969.

Khare, R. S. *The Untouchable as Himself: Ideology and Pragmatism among the Lucknow Chamars.* Cambridge: Cambridge University Press, 1983.

Kohli, Atul. *The State and Poverty in India: The Politics of Reform.* Cambridge: Cambridge University Press, 1987.

Kolenda, Pauline Mahar. "Religious Anxiety and Hindu Fate." *Journal of Asian Studies* 23 (1964): 71–82.

Kosambi, D. D. "Caste and Class in India." In A. J. Syed, ed., *D. D. Kosambi on History and Society: Problems of Interpretation*, pp. 127–32. Bombay: University of Bombay, 1985.

Laird, M. A. *Missionaries and Education in Bengal, 1793–1837.* Oxford : Clarendon Press, 1972.

Lejeune, Philippe. *On Autobiography.* Translated by Katherine Leary. Minneapolis: University of Minnesota Press, 1989.

Life of Ramakrishna Compiled from Various Authentic Sources. 1924. Reprint. Calcutta: Advaita Ashrama, 1964.

Lynch, Owen. *The Politics of Untouchability: Social Mobility and Social Change in a City of India.* New York: Columbia University Press, 1969.

MacIntyre, Alasdair. *After Virtue: A Study in Moral Theory.* London: Duckworth, 1981.

Mallick, A. R. "Modern Historical Writing in Bengali." In C. H. Philips, ed., *Historians of India, Pakistan and Ceylon*, pp. 446–60. London: Oxford University Press, 1961.

Mani, Lata. "The Production of an Official Discourse on *Sati* in Early Nineteenth-Century Bengal." *Economic and Political Weekly: Review of Women's Studies* 21 (April 1986): WS32–40.

———. "Contentious Traditions: The Debate on *Sati* in Colonial India." In Kumkum Sangari and Sudesh Vaid, eds., *Recasting Women: Essays in Colonial History*, pp. 88–126. New Delhi: Kali for Women, 1989.

Marx, Karl. *Capital.* Vol. 1. Translated by Samuel Moore and Edward Aveling. Moscow: Progress Publishers, 1971.

Mason, Mary G. "The Other Voice: Autobiographies of Women Writers." In

James Olney, ed., *Autobiography: Essays Theoretical and Critical*, pp. 207–35. Princeton: Princeton University Press, 1980.

Massie, J. W. *Continental India*. Vol. 2. London: Thomas Ward, 1839.

Metcalf, T. R. *The Aftermath of Revolt*. Princeton: Princeton University Press, 1964.

Misra, B. B. *The Bureaucracy in India: An Historical Analysis of Development up to 1947*. Delhi: Oxford University Press, 1977.

Mookerjee, Nanda, ed. *Sri Ramakrishna in the Eyes of Brahma and Christian Admirers*. Calcutta: Firma KLM, 1976.

Mozoomdar, P. C. *The Life and Teachings of Keshub Chunder Sen*. 1887. Reprint. Calcutta: Nababidhan Trust, 1931.

Mukherjee, Meenakshi. "The Unperceived Self: A Study of Five Nineteenth-Century Autobiographies." In Karuna Chanana, ed., *Socialisation, Education and Women: Explorations in Gender Identity*. New Delhi: Orient Longman, 1988.

Mukherjee, Mridula. "Peasant Resistance and Peasant Consciousness in Colonial India: 'Subaltern' and Beyond." *Economic and Political Weekly* 23, nos. 41, and 42 (8 and 15 October 1988): 2109–20 and 2174–85.

Mukhopadhyay, Govindagopal, and Gopikamohan Bhattacharya. *A Tri-lingual Dictionary*. Calcutta Sanskrit College Research Series 47, lexicon no. 1. Calcutta: Sanskrit College, 1966.

Mukhopadhyay, Subodh Kumar. "Evolution of Historiography in Bengali (1800–1947): A Study of the Pattern of Growth." In Tarasankar Banerjee, ed., *Historiography in Modern Indian Languages, 1800–1947*, pp. 29–42. Calcutta: Naya Prokash, 1987.

Murali, Atlury. "Civil Disobedience Movement in Andhra, 1920–1922: The Nature of Peasant Protest and the Methods of Congress Political Mobilization." In Kapil Kumar, ed., *Congress and Classes: Nationalism, Workers and Peasants*, pp. 152–216. New Delhi: Manohar, 1988.

Murshid, Ghulam. *Reluctant Debutante: Response of Bengali Women to Modernization, 1849–1905*. Rajshahi: Rajshahi University Press, 1983.

Nandy, Ashis. *The Intimate Enemy: Loss and Recovery of Self under Colonialism*. Delhi: Oxford University Press, 1983.

Nehru, Jawaharlal. *The Discovery of India*. New York: John Day, 1946.

———. *Jawaharlal Nehru's Speeches*. Vol 2. New Delhi: Publications Division, 1954.

O'Hanlon, Rosalind. *Caste, Conflict and Ideology: Mahatma Jotirao Phule and Low Caste Protest in Nineteenth-Century Western India*. Cambridge: Cambridge University Press, 1985.

———. "Recovering the Subject: *Subaltern Studies* and Histories of Resistance in Colonial South Asia." *Modern Asian Studies* 22, no. 1 (1988): 189–224.

Pal, Bipinchandra. *Memories of My Life and Times*. 1932. Reprint. Calcutta: Bipinchandra Pal Institute, 1973.

Pandey, Gyanendra. *The Ascendancy of the Congress in Uttar Pradesh, 1926–1934*. Delhi: Oxford University Press, 1978.

———. "Encounters and Calamities: The History of a North Indian *Qasba* in the Nineteenth Century." In Ranajit Guha, ed., *Subaltern Studies III*, pp. 231–70. Delhi: Oxford University Press, 1984.

Patnaik, Arun. "Gramsci's Concept of Hegemony: The Case of Development Administration in India." *Economic and Political Weekly: Review of Political Economy* 23, no. 5 (1988): PE 12–18.

Perlin, Frank. "Of White Whale and Countrymen in the Eighteenth-Century Maratha Deccan." *Journal of Peasant Studies* 5, no. 2 (January 1978): 172–237.

———. "Proto-Industrialization and Pre-Colonial South Asia." *Past and Present* 98 (February 1983): 30–95.

———. "State Formation Reconsidered." *Modern Asian Studies* 19, no. 3 (1985): 415–80.

Prakash, Gyan. "Writing Post-Orientalist Histories of the Third World: Perspectives from Indian Historiography." *Comparative Studies in Society and History* 32, no. 2 (April 1990): 383–408.

Pylee, M. V. *Constitutional History of India, 1600–1950*. Bombay: Asia, 1967.

Radhakrishnan, S. *Eastern Religions and Western Thought*. 1939. Reprint. New York: Oxford University Press, 1959.

Ray, Rajat K. *Social Conflict and Political Unrest in Bengal, 1875–1914*. Delhi: Oxford University Press, 1984.

Raychaudhuri, Tapan. *Europe Reconsidered: Perceptions of the West in Nineteenth-Century Bengal*. Delhi: Oxford University Press, 1988.

Risley, H. H. *The Tribes and Castes of Bengal*. Vol. 1. 1891. Reprint. Calcutta: Firma KLM, 1981.

Rudolph, Lloyd H., and Susanne Hoeber Rudolph. *In Search of Lakshmi: The Political Economy of the Indian State*. Chicago: University of Chicago Press, 1987.

Said, Edward W. "Identity, Negation and Violence." *New Left Review* 171 (1988): 46–60.

———. "Third World Intellectuals and Metropolitan Culture." *Raritan Quarterly* 9, no. 3 (Winter 1990): 27–50.

Sanyal, Hitesranjan. *Social Mobility in Bengal*. Calcutta: Papyrus, 1981.

———. "Trends of Change in the Bhakti Movement in Bengal." Occasional Paper 76 (July 1985). Calcutta: Centre for Studies in Social Sciences.

Saradananda, Swami. *Sri Ramakrishna the Great Master*. Translated by Swami Jagadananda. Madras: Sri Ramakrishna Math, 1952.

Sarkar, Sumit. *The Swadeshi Movement in Bengal*. New Delhi: People's Publishing House, 1973.

———. *A Critique of Colonial Reason*. Calcutta: Papyrus, 1985.

———. "'Kaliyuga,' 'Chakri' and 'Bhakti': Ramakrishna and His Times." *Economic and Political Weekly* 27, 29 (18 July 1992): 1543–66.

Sarkar, Tanika. "Jitu Santal's Movement in Malda, 1924–1932: A Study in Tribal Protest." In Ranajit Guha, ed., *Subaltern Studies IV*, pp. 136–64. Delhi: Oxford University Press, 1985.

Sastri, Sivanath. *History of the Brahmo Samaj*. 1911–12. Reprint. Calcutta: Sadharan Brahmo Samaj, 1974.

Scott, David C., ed., *Keshub Chunder Sen*. Madras: Christian Literature Society, 1979.

Scott, James. *Weapons of the Weak: Everyday Forms of Peasant Resistance*. New Haven, Conn.: Yale University Press, 1985.

Seal, Anil. *The Emergence of Indian Nationalism.* Cambridge: Cambridge University Press, 1971.

Sen, Asok. "The Frontiers of the *Prison Notebooks.*" *Economic and Political Weekly: Review of Political Economy* 23, no. 5 (1988): PE31–36.

[Sen, Keshabchandra.] *Keshub Chunder Sen in England: Diaries, Sermons, Addresses and Epistles.* 1871. Reprint. Calcutta: Writers Workshop, 1980.

Sen, Prosanto Kumar. *Keshub Chunder Sen.* Calcutta: Keshub Sen Birth Centenary Committee, 1938.

Siddiqi, Majid Hayat. *Agrarian Unrest in North India: The United Provinces, 1918–1922.* New Delhi: Vikas, 1978.

Sinha, Pradip. *Calcutta in Urban History.* Calcutta: Firma KLM, 1978.

Slater, T. E. *Keshab Chandra Sen and the Brahma Samàj.* Madras: Society for Promoting Christian Knowledge, 1884.

Smith, Vincent A. *Indian Constitutional Reform Viewed in the Light of History.* London: Humphrey Milford, 1919.

Spivak, Gayatri Chakravorty. "Subaltern Studies: Deconstructing Historiography." In Ranajit Guha, ed., *Subaltern Studies IV*, pp. 338–63. Delhi: Oxford University Press, 1985,

———. "Can the Subaltern Speak?" In Cary Nelson and Lawrence Grossberg, eds., *Marxism and the Interpretation of Culture.* Urbana: University of Illinois Press, 1988.

Srinivas, M. N. *Caste in Modern India and Other Essays.* Bombay: Asia, 1962.

———. *Social Change in Modern India.* Bombay: Allied, 1966.

Stein, Burton. "State Formation and Economy Reconsidered." *Modern Asian Studies*, 19, no. 3 (1985): 387–413.

Taylor, Charles. "Modes of Civil Society." *Public Culture* 3, no. 1 (Fall 1990): 102–19.

Thapar, Romila. "Communalism and the Writing of Ancient Indian History." In Romila Thapar, Harbans Mukhia, and Bipan Chandra, *Communalism and the Writing of Indian History.* Delhi: People's Publishing House, 1969.

Thompson, Edward, and G. T. Garratt. *Rise and Fulfilment of British Rule in India.* 1934. Reprint. Allahabad: Central Book Depot, 1962.

Tod, James. *Annals and Antiquities of Rajasthan, or the Central and Western Rajput States of India.* Edited by William Crooke. 1829–32. Reprint. London: Oxford University Press, 1920.

Washbrook, D. A. "Progress and Problems: South Asian Economic and Social History, c. 1720–1860." *Modern Asian Studies* 22, no. 1 (1988): 57–96.

Weber, Eugen. *Peasants into Frenchmen: The Modernization of Rural France, 1870–1914.* London: Chatto and Windus, 1979.

Index